MW01626830

NUDE:THEORY

L U S T R U M

ALL RIGHTS RESERVED UNDER INTERNATIONAL AND
PAN-AMERICAN COPYRIGHT CONVENTIONS
PUBLISHED IN THE UNITED STATES OF AMERICA
BY LUSTRUM PRESS, INC., BOX 450, CANAL STREET
STATION, NEW YORK CITY, N.Y. 10013
COPYRIGHT © 1979 LUSTRUM PRESS, INC.
JOHN FLATTAU, RALPH GIBSON AND ARNE LEWIS
DESIGNED BY ARNE LEWIS AND DEBORAH BLOWERS
TYPOGRAPHY BY THE STUART FINE CORPORATION, N.Y.
PRINTED BY RAPOPORT PRINTING CORPORATION, N.Y.
BOUND BY SENDOR BINDERY, INC., N.Y.
DISTRIBUTED IN GREAT BRITAIN BY TRAVELLING
LIGHT PHOTOGRAPHY LIMITED
MANUFACTURED IN THE UNITED STATES OF AMERICA
LIBRARY OF CONGRESS CATALOG CARD NUMBER: 79-2427
ISBN: 0-912810-24-6
FOR MAXIMUM SHADOW DETAIL, OVEREXPOSE
AND DON'T DEVELOP

EDITED BY JAIN KELLY

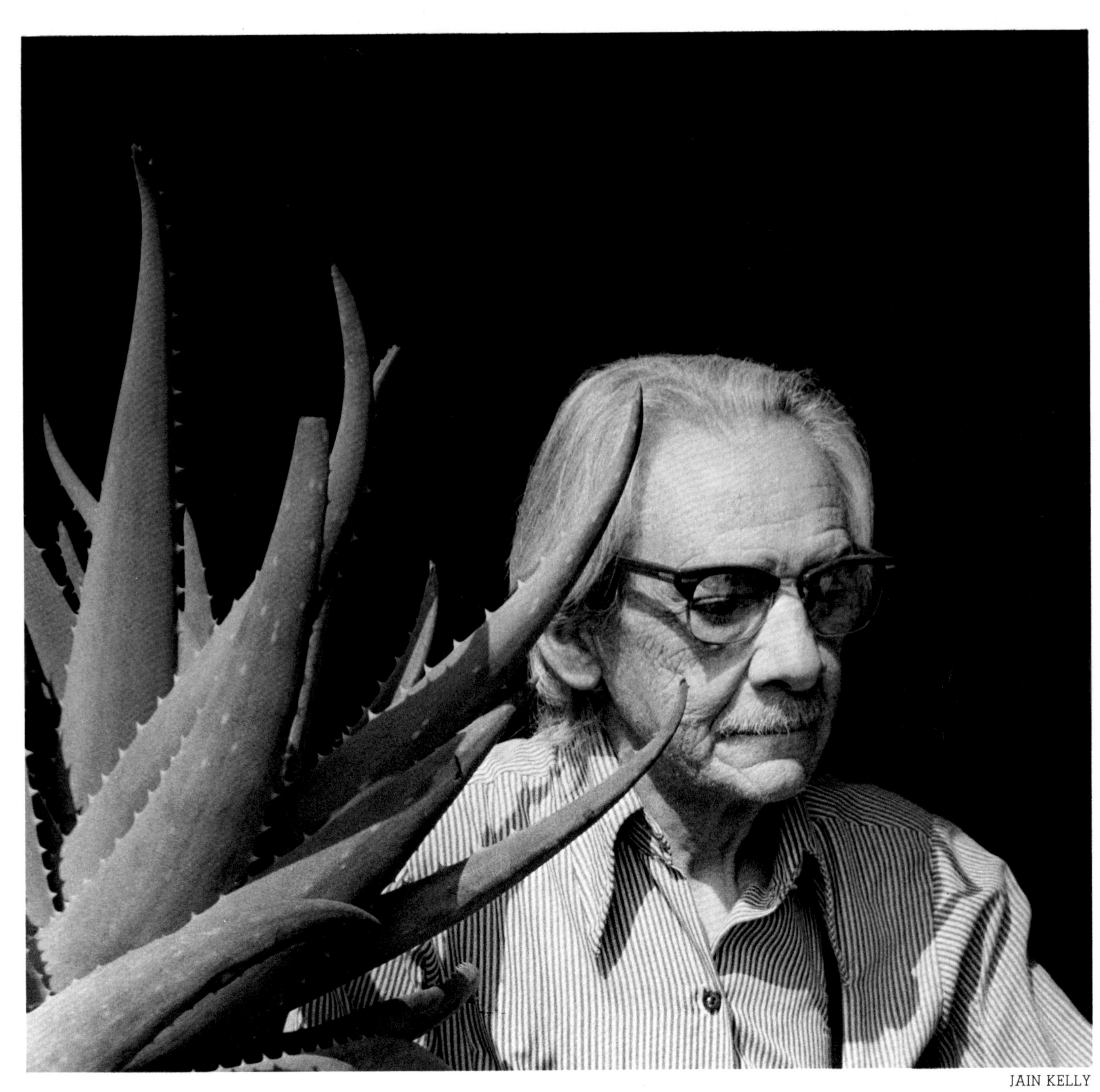

JAIN KELLY

MANUEL ALVAREZ BRAVO: "ACEPTO LO QUE SE VE." ("I ACCEPT THAT WHICH IS SEEN.")

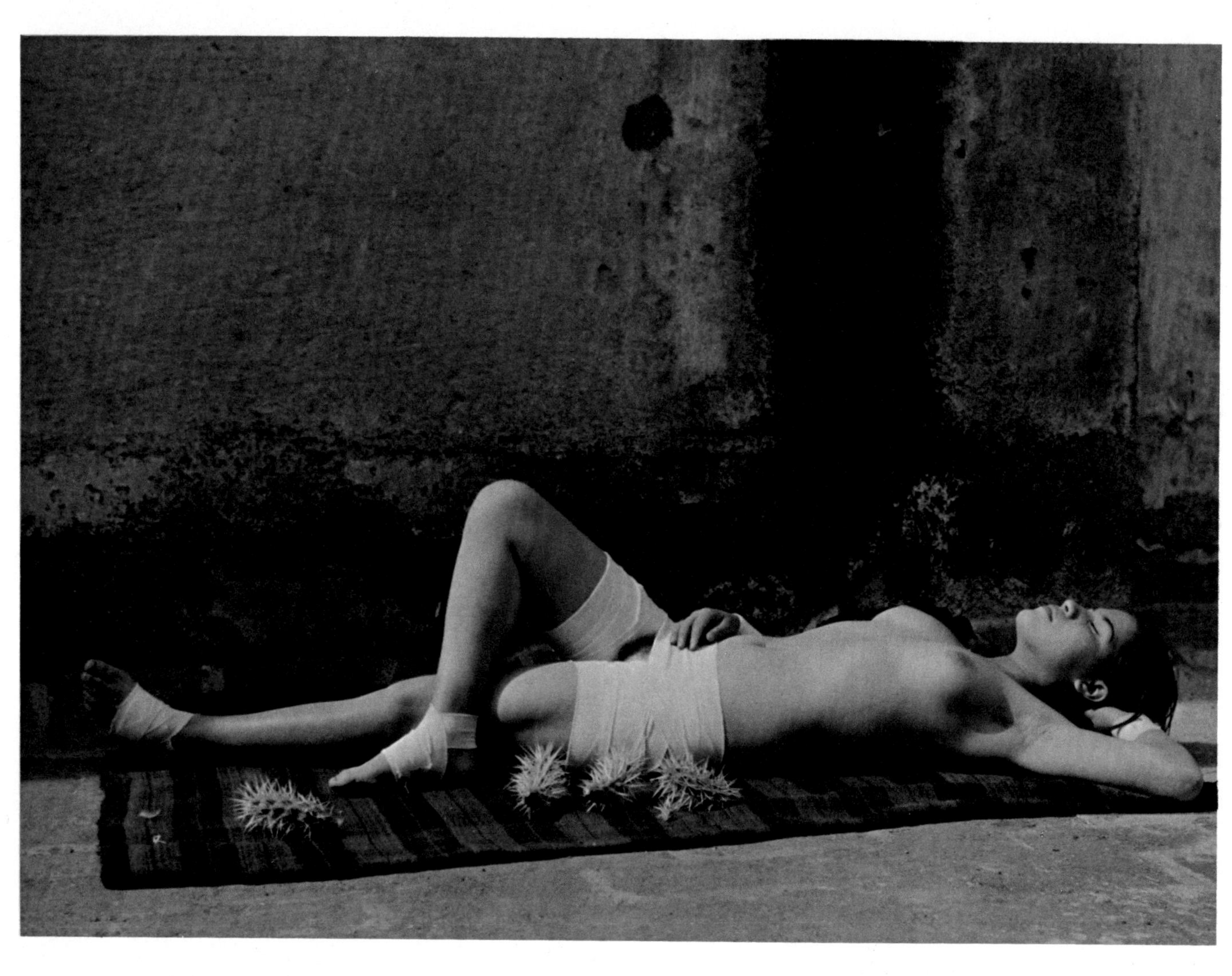

FIGURE 1: LA BUENA FAMA DURMIENDO, 1938 (GOOD REPUTATION SLEEPING, 1938)

People are very curious. They always ask the artist why he made something and what it means. They should hold discourse with the work of art itself, and perhaps it would say something different to them than its author would indicate. This would signify that the work has a richness and can express itself by itself. It is not necessary that it be explained; its only necessity is to exist.

When one looks at a work of art, one recreates it. The work demands the same creativity of the viewer that it gives him. And yet, always, always, at whatever exhibition or conference I attend, I am asked, "Why this?" and "Why the other?"

"Why the bandages and cactus thorns in LA BUENA FAMA DURMIENDO?" "Why is PARÁBOLA ÓPTICA printed in reverse?" In the latter case, a lithographer reproduced the image backward. When I saw it in the proofs, I liked it, and I told him to do it that way. But he corrected the proofs because he did not want people to think he had made a mistake. After that, I continued to use the image in reverse. When I am asked about it, I say, "Well, because I liked it." I liked it this way, nothing more. But the "why" remains.

Perhaps the importance of these questions is that the author, the creator of the work of art, may come to realize himself what he wanted to do. He may find another meaning in his own work.

A constant inquiry, especially in the United States, is: "What is your philosophy?" For me it would be difficult to define a philosophy, because the circumstances in which we live are in a state of flux. The artist's mind, like a weathervane, is subject to the essential changes of the times. The diverse experiences of personal life, as well as the natural changes of temperament during the course of life itself, also force one to redefine one's concepts continually. I would say the artist's manner of thinking is very much implicit in the work. When the work of art is being made, the artist is not completely conscious of his philosophy because he is not a philosopher.

While I am speaking of art and the artist, there is another aspect to consider. This is the question: "Is photography art?" I believe that it is absurd to think that photography and painting and sculpture are, of themselves, arts. The medium is not the essential thing; art is produced by the individual. I believe art exists when it has arrived at its resolution. If the individual has a capacity, a level of experience, an inner motivation, then at some point he will come into existence as an artist, whatever his medium.

Now, in respect to the work with the nude: I believe that the nude is a genre like any other, like landscape, street photography, portraiture or still life. These are all themes subject to the expression of the individual. In my case, the nude is photographed in the same manner as, for example, the landscape. On the spur of the moment, an opportunity presents itself. One is chatting with a friend and suddenly it occurs to the two that Sunday might be a good day to take a drive in the country. We are going to take a drive; if there are results, they probably depend on the state of the spirit and not on the state of nature. There is absolutely no reason for having a predetermined theme in mind. One must open the eyes to find whether there is, or is not, an interaction of the individual with reality at the moment. The results are determined by the baggage of human experiences of the artist.

It was in the year 1938 that I made the photograph called LA BUENA FAMA DURMIENDO (GOOD REPUTATION SLEEPING) (Figure 1). At the time I was a teacher at the Academy of San Carlos in Mexico City. André Breton was in town making arrangements for an exhibition of surrealism at the Gallery of Mexican Art. One day I was standing in line to collect my salary and I received a telephone call from someone who spoke in the name of Breton, who did not speak Spanish. This person indicated that Breton wished me to do a photograph for the title page of the exhibition catalogue.

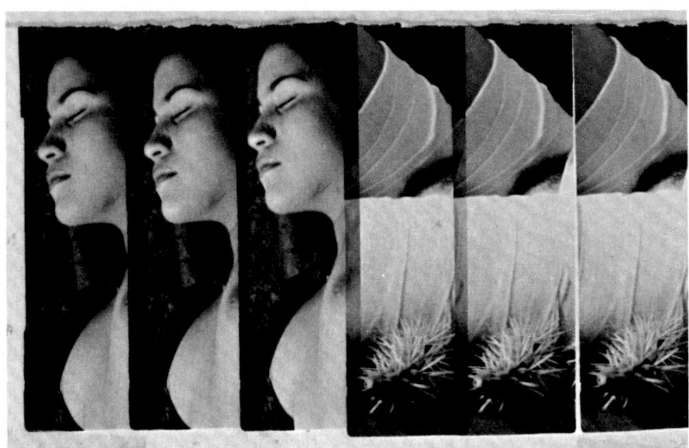

PRUEBAS DE "LA BUENA FAMA DURMIENDO, 1938"
(PROOFS OF "GOOD REPUTATION SLEEPING, 1938")

It happened that in the group waiting for salary was a model named Alicia who had posed in the nude in my photography class. I asked her if she would go up to the rooftop of the school to make a photograph. Then, on the same telephone on which I had received Breton's call, I spoke to a friend of mine, Dr. Francisco Marín, to ask if he would come to the school to bandage a model. The doctor thought this must be some urgent case, and he arrived with great rapidity in his car, with the bandages.

Meanwhile, I had sent the school watchman to the nearby marketplace, "La Merced," to buy some "abrojos." These are very strong thorns produced by a type of cactus that grows in rocky ground. In Spanish, "abrojos" means "abre ojos" or open eyes. The thorns are called "abrojos" to remind one to keep on the lookout, because they are very sharp and can penetrate the skin through the shoes. Then I asked the watchman to lend me the blanket he used at night.

The doctor arrived. He bandaged the woman (Figure 2) and I took the photograph. I worked very suddenly and very rapidly, obeying a sense of surrealistic automatism.

People ask me, "Why the bandages? Why the 'abrojos?'" I have also thought, "Why the bandages and 'abrojos?'"

I believe that very often there is a slight exaggeration of psychology in the interpretation of art. Sometimes one sees or discovers something that has interesting possibilities in the plastic arts as form, as composition. It can be that a visual experience may or may not have a relationship to the psychology of the person, but I don't think this necessarily indicates a complex. In this case there is the circumstance of the

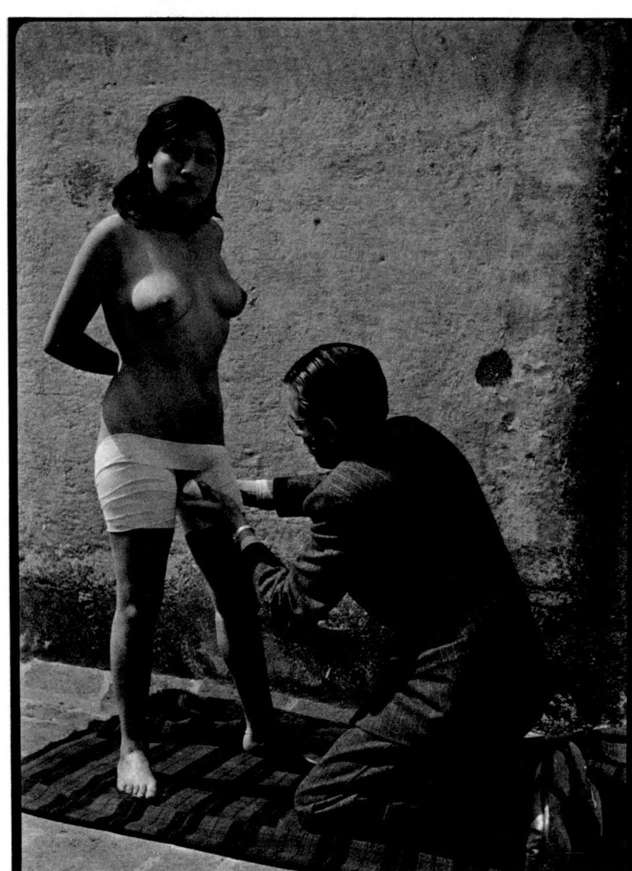

DR. FRANCISCO MARÍN VENDANDO Á ALICIA, 1938
(DR. FRANCISCO MARÍN BANDAGING ALICIA, 1938)
FIGURE 2

continuation of the use of bandages in my photographs. The theme pursues the individual; the individual does not pursue the theme.

I saw bandages used for the first time when Anna Sokolow's dance troupe came to Mexico, brought by a photographer and engraver, Emilio Amero. Since he was a friend of mine, he introduced me to Anna Sokolow and the group. I had the opportunity to make photographs, and the thing that especially interested me was photographing the rehearsals.

I had seen dance rehearsals in Chicago when I lived there in a guest house in a room obtained for me by Emily Edwards, a painter who had been disciple to Diego Rivera for a while. Another tenant was a ballerina named Anne Heisy. She had taken me to a dance rehearsal in which Martha Graham played a tambourine and the women danced. That was my first contact with rehearsals and the source of my great interest in them, because for me, all that is art is in them.

In the course of time, I was casually looking for some other negative one day, and I found one of two dancers in Anna Sokolow's group (Figure 3). When I was taking photographs of them in rehearsal, their feet were strongly bandaged for the exercises. Since this happened in 1937, not long before the making of BUENA FAMA, there undoubtedly remained with me, in the archive of my visual memories, the question of the use of the bandaged body for purposes other than those of surgery. Therefore the possibility existed of utilizing bandages as elements of visual interest.

There is another aspect: In surrealism there are elements of the dream, and in this connection one can think about the reactions that may have stimulated this photograph. It is possible that the person lying down, Alicia, can be thinking of herself in relation to danger, produced by the idea of the thorns. I believe it is possible that this idea of unconscious danger while sleeping can be related to the influence of the painting SLEEPING GYPSY (LA BOHÉMIENNE ENDORMIE) by Henri Rousseau. I have on various occasions been influenced by paintings, although the influence has not been sought out. In that epoch I knew SLEEPING GYPSY only in reproduction, but it gave me great pleasure and caused me great emotion. It seems to me that an idea from the painting could have returned in LA BUENA FAMA DURMIENDO. In Rousseau's work, the person is sleeping, and nearby danger is signified by the lion, as it is signified in BUENA FAMA by the thorns.

This interpretation has been a long time in unfolding; it is only about two years ago that it came to me completely. I repeat it now with the motive of answering the many questions that have been put to me, and I believe that it is all I have to say in respect to LA BUENA FAMA DURMIENDO.

I have been discussing BUENA FAMA in relation to surrealism. Many times my work, taken as a

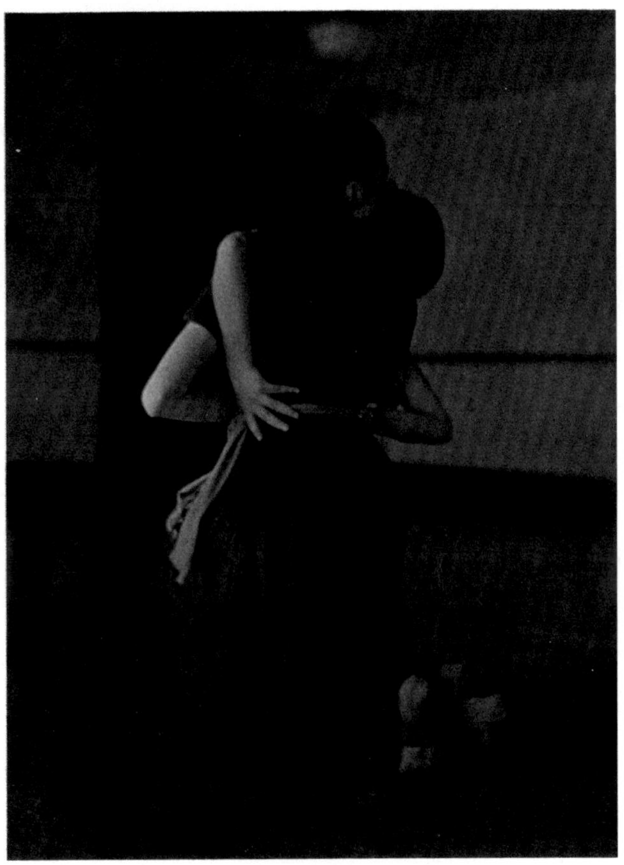

ENSAYO DE DANZA, CA. 1937
(DANCE REHEARSAL, CA. 1937)
FIGURE 3

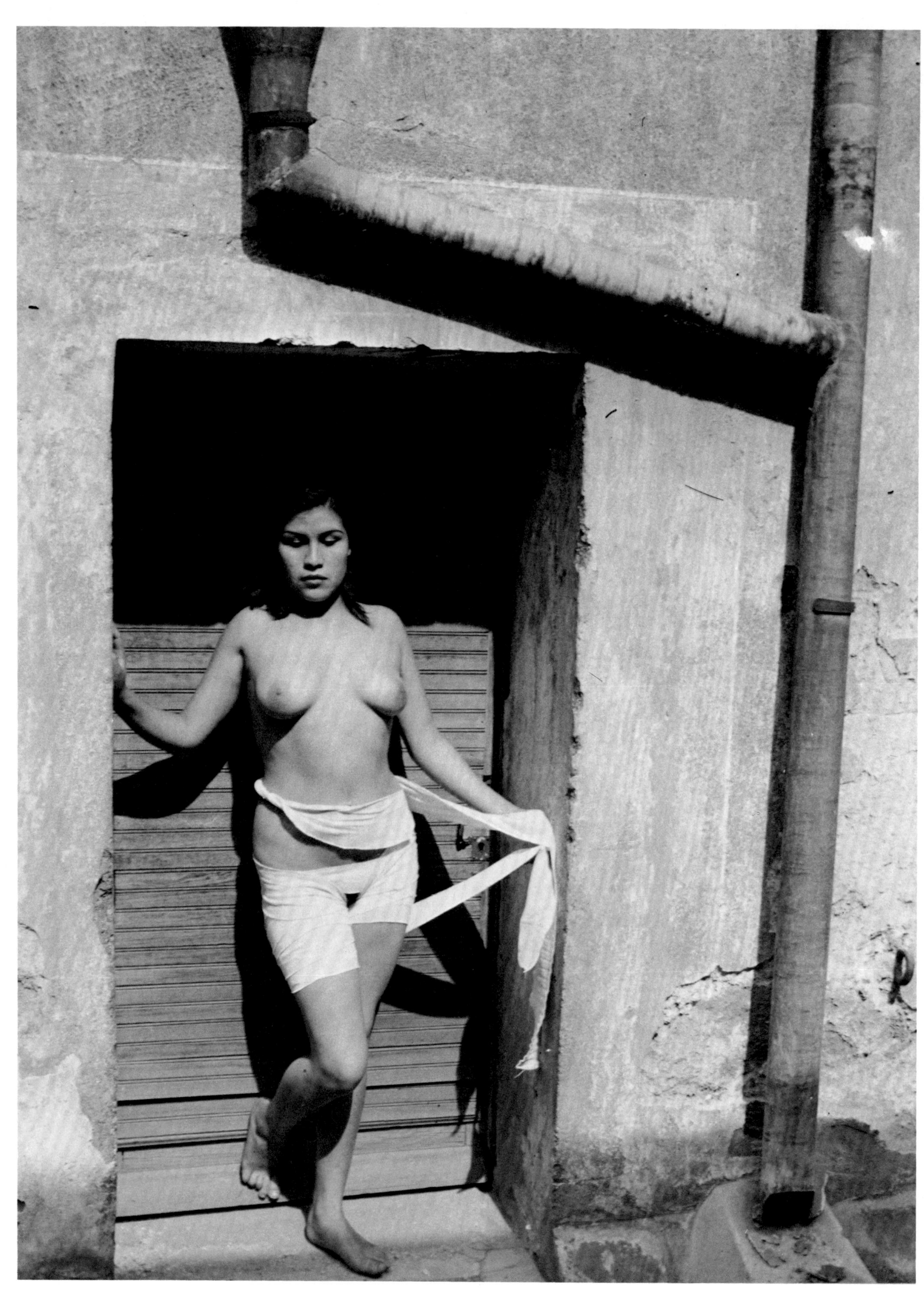

FIGURE 4: LA DESVENDADA, 1938 (THE UNBANDAGING, 1938)

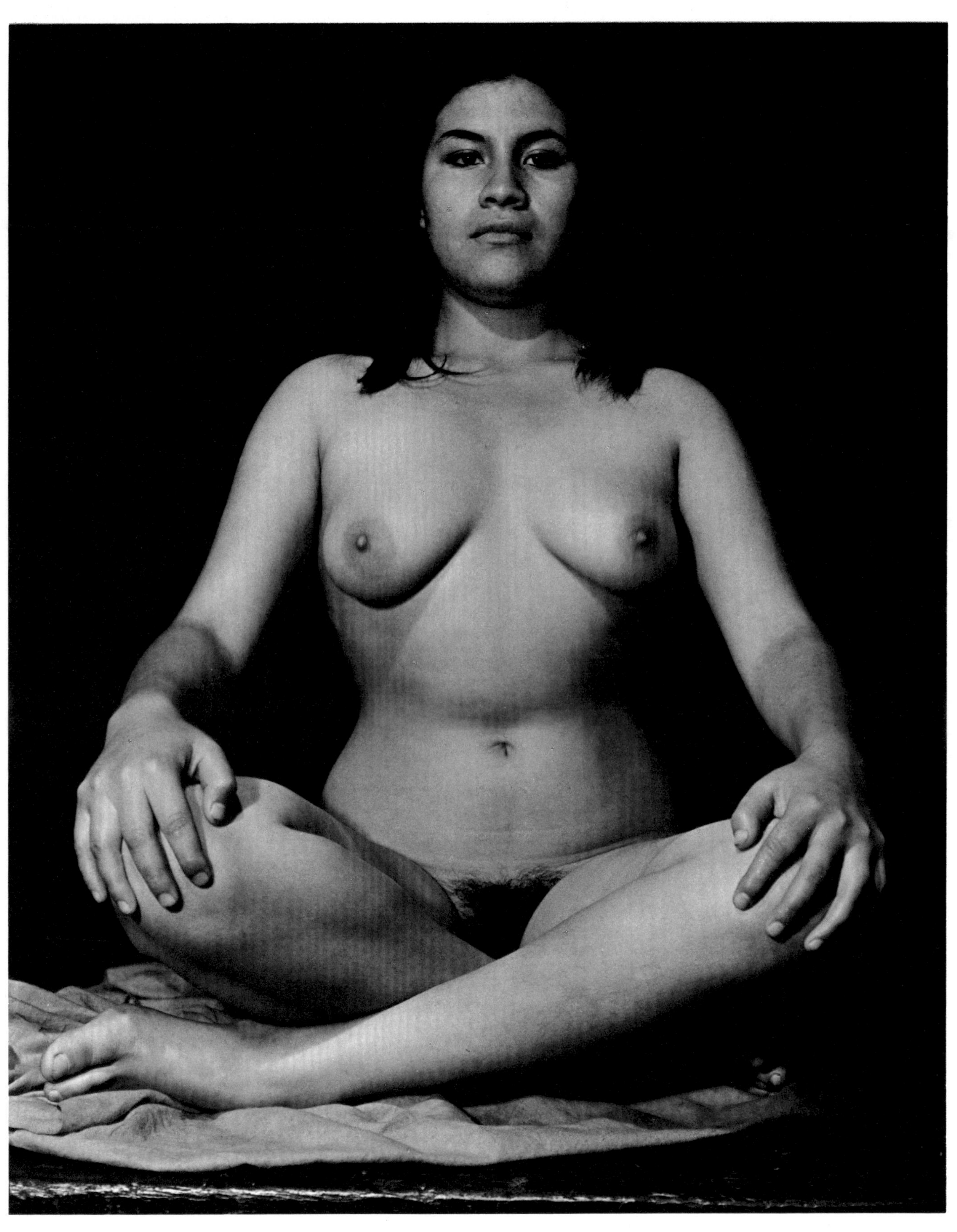

FIGURE 5: ALICIA, DESNUDO ACADÉMICO, CA. 1937 (ALICIA, ACADEMIC NUDE, CA. 1937)

whole, has been related to surrealism. I believe that this is an equivocation. I believe that when a person is attentive to reality he finds all that is fantastic. People don't realize the fantasy that life itself contains. There was a French writer, Renan, who said that here on earth are symbol and mystery. He lived before surrealism as a school existed; he was speaking of symbol and mystery in daily life. When people look for it, they find a contact with that enormous surprise: reality.

On the same day as BUENA FAMA, I made LA DESVENDADA (THE UNBANDAGED ONE or THE UNBANDAGING) (Figure 4). I like this photograph, but, of course, it seems to me that the impetus behind the first photograph was of greater importance. For me, the second was taken in order to make good use of the opportunity, just as one does when photographing the landscape. Taking one picture of the landscape does not mean the photographer has exhausted the subject; the eye continues seeing. Meanwhile, the photographer is walking in the countryside and looking around for the possibility of doing diverse things. This is what happened with THE UNBANDAGING. It was made as an afterthought.

I have no idea what happened to Alicia, if she is alive; I remember her with nostalgia. One or two years before BUENA FAMA, I made the ACADEMIC NUDE of her (Figure 5). I've never published this photograph. It was almost abandoned. I made it when I was a teacher, as an exercise in class for the young people. Many times pretexts are needed in the school, and the professor naturally looks for those pretexts in the history of art. In the ACADEMIC NUDE Alicia was posing as a pre-Hispanic sculpture from the "Culture of the Occident."

One can see the relationship of the photographic approach to the underlying motive for making a picture. Motive does not necessarily rise out of philosophy; it can be an instantaneous interpretation of an assignment in response to immediate necessity.

There have been long periods in which I have left off photographing completely, and during other periods I have made negative after negative. They accumulate; time passes; groups of negatives are forgotten. And then another period comes in which I return to work and must go about making a choice of theme and of negatives to print for exhibition, or other purposes. It has always happened with me that I have made a bad group of photographs and then, suddenly, another group that is really good.

During the periods in which I have worked well, different circumstances have implied the necessity of different ways of seeing, different kinds of thought as a form of seeing in the photograph. From the beginning of my work, there have been apparently ironic aspects, dramatic aspects, completely serious aspects, and so on, according to the circumstances, according to the reality that is in front of one, and according to the temperament that is subject to varying reactions. Although there is a unity that produces the individual, there are different aspects of the individual, and the responses of a person vary. There is drama, there is melancholy, there is death, there is life. There are all the things that the human temperament is subject to, not just my temperament.

When I began work as a still photographer in the film industry of Mexico in 1943, I left the Academy of San Carlos, but I began to teach classes at the Institute of Cinematography. The demands of professional work left me with the capacity to do almost no personal work, although during some slow periods I attempted landscape photography. After leaving the film industry in 1959, I entered the Editorial Foundation of the Mexican Plastic Arts (Fondo Editorial de la Plástica Mexicana).

It is possible to say that only by chance did my old friend, the photographer Antonio Reynoso, invite me to his garden to make photographs of the nude. He had been my assistant at the Academy of San Carlos, and our friendship has continued uninterrupted. The point is, I produced some work when he invited me over to his house two or three times. I did not pursue the idea of photographing nudes. There are things that suddenly become of interest or necessity, one does not know which. When I produced what could be called a "series," it was not thought out, but something casually arrived at.

A series done in 1970 was called LAS TENTACIONES EN LA CASA DE ANTONIO (TEMPTATIONS IN THE HOUSE OF ANTHONY). The photograph that both I and other people have liked the most is the one in which the sheet covers the face of the nude (Figure 6). I mention this idea of the covered face to show how certain themes go back almost to the beginning of my work. I remember a photograph I made about 1931 called LA TRILLA (THE THRESHER). In the photograph, the thresher is behind a horse, so that his face is covered. I made the photograph on a trip to Michoacan and other places with the painter Rufino Tamayo. The theme returns later as, for example in LOS AGACHADOS (THE CROUCHED ONES), done in 1934. The heads of the men in the photograph appear to be cut off. The theme recurs in LAS TENTACIONES EN LA CASA DE ANTONIO, and, as we shall see, it returns in the series of nudes done recently titled XIPETOTEC (Figures 23 and 24). In the new series, the face of the model disappears completely into nature, and there is an integration of the nude with the earth and plants.

There is another circumstance that I believe is interesting in relation to TENTACIONES. At the same time that one has in front of himself a

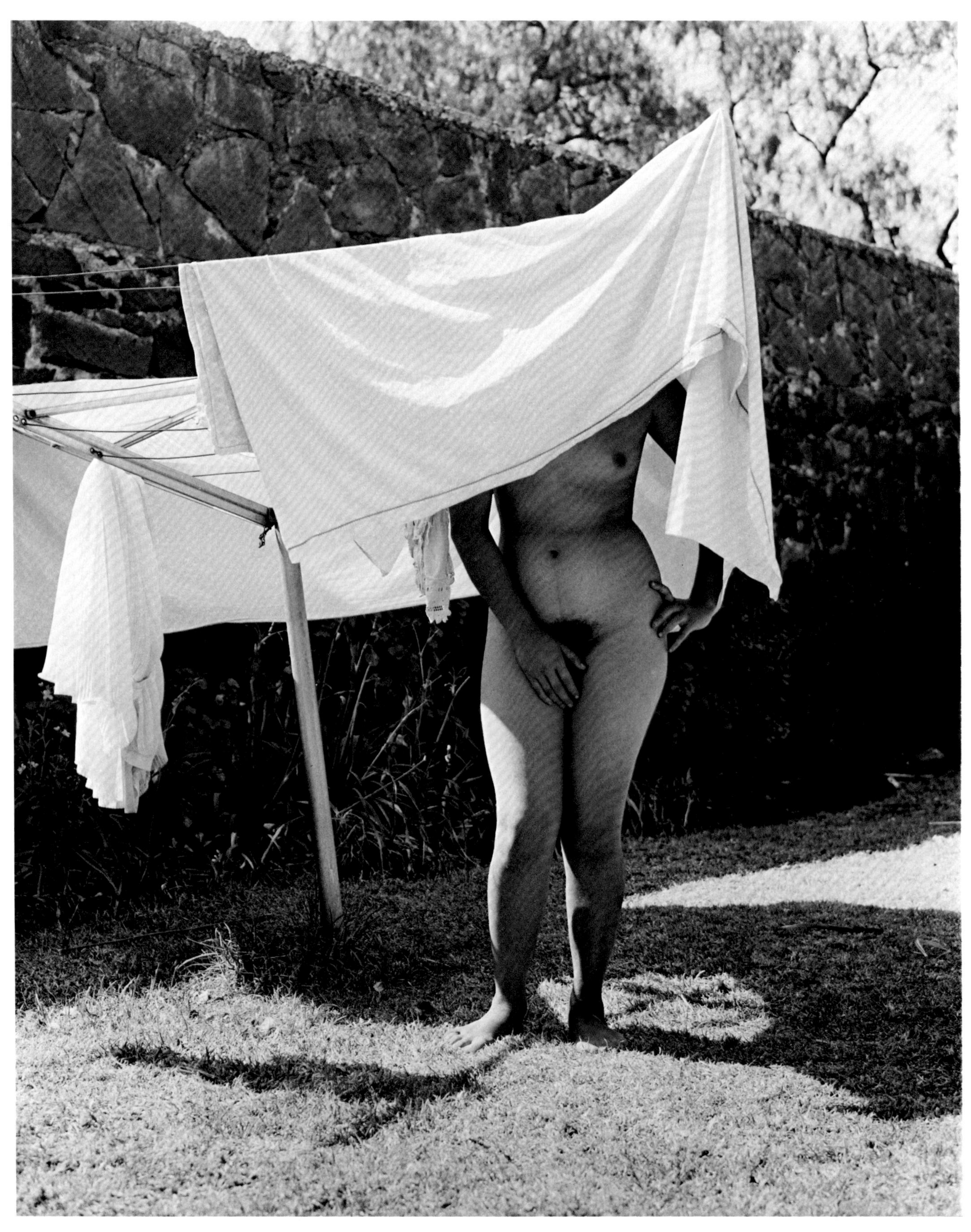

FIGURE 6: LAS TENTACIONES EN LA CASA DE ANTONIO, 1970 (TEMPTATIONS IN THE HOUSE OF ANTHONY, 1970)

theme, a subject matter, something to be dealt with aesthetically, there are also technical problems implied. It seems to me that the same thing happens with technical problems as with aesthetic themes. They are not pursued consciously, but they are presented to one. For a long time I have been interested in white; the transformation of white is the basis of photography. An area of white existed, for example, in the photograph of laundry stretched out to dry, LAS LAVANDERAS SOBREENTENDIDAS, 1932 (THE WASHERWOMEN IMPLIED). In TENTACIONES a white sheet was put on a line not by Antonio or me, but it was put there, who knows by whom or why. The pleasure of the white produced the motivation for the photograph. I never know what I am going to do until the problem is in front of me, and then comes the resolution.

Finally, the woman in TENTACIONES is not entirely covered by the sheet and the hand. The concept of modesty contains an ironic aspect. In the woman's apparent intention to cover herself, she has revealed herself completely. The photograph, then, has to do with this contradiction: to cover = to uncover.

I have found that artists in other media can greatly help the photographer, and in my case these lessons extend to composition. I photographed the murals of Diego Rivera, José Clemente Orozco, David Alfaro Siqueiros, and Rufino Tamayo. First, this work afforded me a living. Then, I had the opportunity to work with the details of the paintings. Photographing details of a large work of art involves choice and, therefore, the making of a personal composition. Since the works of the painters are so varied, the murals taught me how to observe the diverse possibilities of composition. Inevitably, when a detail of a composition is to be photographed, something must be cut out: the head, arms or feet of a person's body might be omitted from the photograph. There is the moment of choice, and that choice has an influence on one's personal work. There are early examples of my work which involve only parts of the body, like UN POCO ALEGRE Y GRACIOSA, 1942 (SOMEWHAT GAY AND GRACEFUL). But the early examples of my nudes reproduce the complete figure, like BUENA FAMA. The majority of my recent nudes are like details of a reality. At the moment of beginning to work, I had not had a consciousness of what I was going to do, but many photographs in the new series have dealt with details of the body.

The new series of nudes began in 1977, and has extended over a period of approximately a year and a half. I don't look for anything specific in a model. I accept that which is seen. The woman in BUENA FAMA was extraordinary; she understood with half a word what one wanted. In all of the new models there was a great understanding.

The photographs were made in several locations in my house and yard: in the rooms, on the steps of the glass doors leading to the garden, inside the glass doors, on the balcony, or in the garden itself with the plants and "pirú" trees.

The theme of nature is of great importance in the history of photography. The first self-portrait that was exhibited was done in a garden, by Hippolyte Bayard. Here nature was not represented by a backdrop, but by his own garden. The primitive portraitists had such a nostalgia for the countryside, and felt such a necessity to relate the person to nature, that they put painted landscapes in their studios. Academic painters in France constructed a kind of greenhouse in which plants constituted a personal landscape. There were early professional workshops, called "galleries," that utilized painted backgrounds. On top of one of my workdesks, I have propped a small cabinet card made in the last century, a portrait by some early photographer, Montes de Oca. It represents a man of the epoch standing in a portrait studio by a piece of furniture. But in the background is a painted landscape. A painted backdrop is still used in Mexico in some kinds of photographic "folk art."

My interest was in leaving the formal studio with its controlled light. I didn't always want to make portraits in an interior and so I began to make them in the streets, with the walls, with the plants, with the landscape in the background. About five years ago, I made a series of portraits of painters. In one portrait I had the opportunity of photographing a person visiting Mexico for only a short time, and so it was an important thing. When he came to my house, I thought, well, we'll go someplace in the garden. The use of the garden integrates another feeling into the photograph: the activity of one working in the garden, or photographing in the garden. There is always the interrelation of circumstances that offers the artist a pretext for a photograph.

The first time I utilized the garden for the nude was in 1977 in the photograph called FRUTA PROHIBIDA (FORBIDDEN FRUIT) (Figure 7). A young woman was visiting the house and we were speaking of the problems of photographing the nude. I asked her to pose for me and she accepted. When she returned, she was prepared for the sitting with a simple dress. I had the camera set up in the garden, and at the moment she was disrobing, I asked her to pause. It is the moment in which she is making herself nude.

Then, upon looking at the contact sheets, I encountered this picture with the breast, as it is seen with the branches of the plant. It could have been the idea of a fruit. That immediately relates to the classic idea of forbidden fruit. If it is true that photographs have historic antecedents, the antecedent in this case (the idea of forbidden fruit) leads one to Paradise!

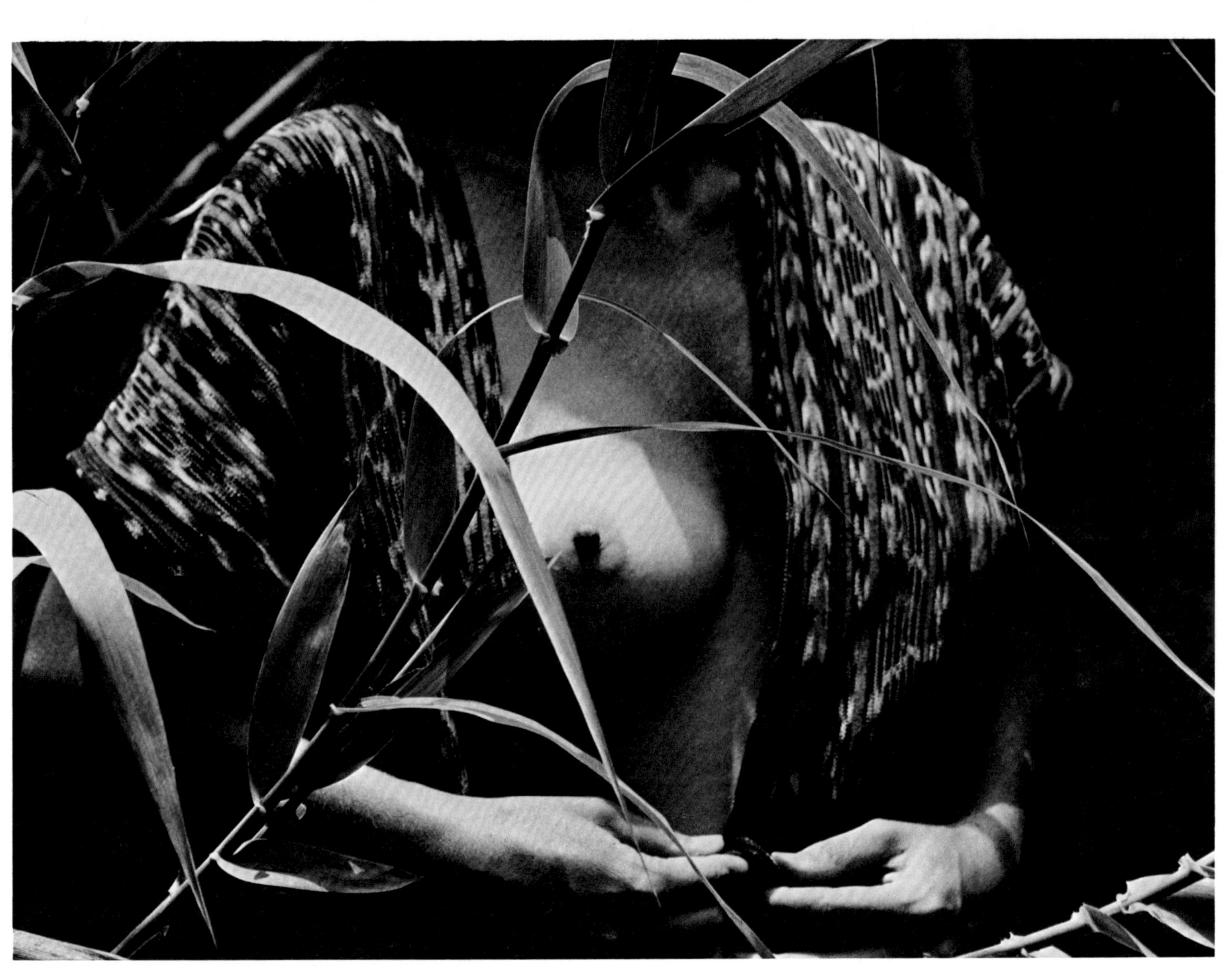

FIGURE 7: FRUTA PROHIBIDA, 1977 (FORBIDDEN FRUIT, 1977)

One of my models was a young woman named Jan, a very sensitive and intelligent person. She saw one of my recent nudes called TÍTULO: SIN TÍTULO (TITLE: WITHOUT TITLE), a photograph soon to be published. Jan told me that I had returned to utilizing the idea of bandages, but in TÍTULO: SIN TÍTULO the bandages were formed by bands of shadow on a woman's body. This is a lovely interpretation. Jan, upon seeing the picture, recreated the memory of my other photographs and defined the image in that context. In this book Jan appears in the photograph LA DEL PIRÚ (SHE OF THE PIRÚ TREE) (Figure 25), and in this case the bandages are formed by the boughs and the shade of the "pirú" tree.

The photographs of XIPETOTEC (Figures 23 and 24) also return to certain themes. There are the plants, the model and her clothing in her hands. The clothing is equal in this case to something that belongs to her, something she is parting with. It is like a "sobrepiel," an overskin, a skin that she is taking off. This is a reference to the pre-Hispanic era, to Xipetotec, who was the god of springtime. In the spring, the earth changes its skin. The skin that has been taken off returns to nature. This is the moment of the taking off of the skin.

Xipetotec took off skin, that is, clothing, and became nude. But it is possible to say that there is another kind of nude. Death is the ultimate nude. Death removes flesh; it removes everything; nothing is left but Death, the Great One. Nothing is left but the Great Nude, the bones.

I believe that in the contact sheet, one can see the type of process that I follow regularly whether I am photographing the countryside or architecture, or the nude, or making a portrait. That is, my attitude is to deal with what is in front of me, what is present. In the moment that the work begins, I don't know what I am going to do. Here, at the beginning of the contact sheet, one sees, more or less, a timidity. Catalina, the model, has not finished disrobing. She is still wearing her slacks. After the beginning, there comes a moment of doubt. Then the doubt is dissipating, it regresses. Finally she removes the skin that is her clothing. She has the clothing in her hand, and this particular theme is exhausted. In the last three photographs the theme of unity with nature is explored, as her head and arms disappear into the plants. Now Xipe is dressed with nature, with the herbs, with the grasses.

When I make a title for a photograph, the same process takes place as with the themes in my work. In the moment of taking a picture, I have no idea of a title. It would be absurd to have a title in mind inasmuch as I am not pursuing an idea while photographing, but an image. I believe that what I have said defines well enough the form in which I, personally, confront problems during the making of a photograph. The titles are suggested by the image, as the image is suggested by the person being photographed.

People have always asked me about my titles, sometimes attacking them, sometimes accepting them. I had to make titles because I was asked for them when exhibitions or catalogues were done. The first titles I gave were descriptions, for example, PORTRAIT OF X or EL POPOCATÉPETL (the volcano). I didn't like doing this, but in reaction to this bother of making titles, I began to give any title whatsoever. I remember that the first of these was LAS LAVANDERAS SOBREENTENDIDAS, 1932 (THE WASHERWOMEN IMPLIED). This is a photograph of bedsheets over maguey plants, and, although they are not seen, the presence of the washerwomen is implied.

I have been to see some exhibitions in which there is a card by each photograph with the word "Untitled." All the same. I have asked myself, if I were interested in buying a photograph later, how could I request it? It is good to give a unique title, because there is not another photograph that is named LA BUENA FAMA DURMIENDO; no other photograph called LAS LAVANDERAS SOBREENTENDIDAS, etc. The titles are essential to distinguish the pictures. I think that "Untitled" is a false title, but I have utilized the word with a different intention in the previously mentioned picture TITLE: UNTITLED, 1977. Now "Untitled" has become a title.

I will mention one more incident in connection with my work with the nude. I have made a photograph titled CASA DE MUÑECAS (HOUSE OF DOLLS) (Figure 26). When I had terminated the sitting with the model, Jan, I was arranging my camera, taking out the roll of film, and so on. She was heading toward the bathroom to dress. Suddenly her image was reflected in the mirror in such a way that it looked as if my daughter's doll were holding the woman suspended in midair. If I had had the fixed idea of doing such-and-such a thing, then this photograph would never have come into existence. What the artist has to do is to see, to leave off so much philosophy about the work, and to see. It was the great musician Telemann who instructed his music students that they should always be whistling something. I would say that the photographer should always be seeing something.

There are those photographers who search for the perfect technique, the perfect camera, the perfect lens and the perfect developer. To me, all of these questions are relative. Many times when the photographer spends too much time investigating technique, the work gets weaker. This is a decadent thing, but quite common. It is, of course, important to have a general knowledge, to have a technique, and one can utilize advances. But their importance must not be exaggerated. One can look at Eugène Atget. Atget used a rapid rectilinear lens that is now very outmoded; and his work was in the tradition of masters like David Octavius Hill and the French Primitives, who made negatives on paper and used inferior lenses.

It seems to me that Ansel Adams is a person who has had a great importance in the development of technical knowledge. Even those who have not understood the basis of his work have received partial lessons from him. He has been useful, very useful to the present-day epoch of photography. As for the other part, he is a great artist who has produced masterpieces. There are those who follow blindly the technical contributions he has made; they have made a mechanical utilization of his teachings.

I have used many cameras, lenses, papers and developers throughout my career. BUENA FAMA was made with a 6 x 9cm Plaubel camera and an Anticomar *f*/4.2 lens. I remember because it was a camera I used a lot. A great part of the work that satisfied me the most was made with the Plaubel. It is possible that I used Adox film and developer for BUENA FAMA, and during that era I was printing most of my work on Leonar Grandamo paper. The manufacturer Leonar no longer exists, but Agfa-Gevaert manufactures Grandamo today, and I still use it sometimes. TENTACIONES was made with a Linhof, but I don't recall the lens.

Today I normally use a Hasselblad 2¼ x 1 5/8 (16 magazine) with a variety of lenses. For years, I used Kodak Plus-X film and Microdol-X developer. Presently, I use Kodak Tri-X and develop in HC-110 (Solution B) or D-76. My tendency has always been to overexpose and underdevelop. A typical outdoor exposure in bright sunlight might be *f*/16 or *f*/22 at 1/125th or 1/250th of a second with Tri-X. For glossy paper, I like Agfa Brovira and Agfa Portriga. For matte paper, I sometimes use Kodak Ektalure.

My first platinum prints were made around 1928. It was at this time that the photographer Tina Modotti left off making this kind of print due to changes in her aesthetic and technical concepts. She gave me the remainder of her commercially manufactured platinum paper.

She also gave me her formula for developing platinum prints, written on a small piece of paper.

TINA MODOTTI'S DEVELOPER
FOR PLATINUM PRINTS
Water, 43 oz.
Sodium citrate, 10 oz.
Citric acid, 1 oz.
FIXING BATH
Water, 150 oz.
Sodium citrate, 5 oz.
Citric acid, 2 oz.

In the margin of the piece of paper, Tina wrote the temperature: 45 to 60 F.

The developer is very strange, very different from what we use now, and I have not tried it lately. On the back of the card, Tina wrote the price of a roll of platinum paper in Mexico at that time, $24. It was sent over from England, and probably was sufficient for about 12 8 x 10 prints.

Time passed. When I wanted to make more platinum prints, the paper Tina had given me had spoiled because it was very sensitive to humidity. I could not buy more because it was no longer manufactured. My interest in the process remained, but due to various circumstances I could not pursue it for many years. I had obtained an old copy of THE PHOTO MINIATURE MAGAZINE, VOL. 1, NO. 7, Oct. 1899; Platinotype Process by Tennant and Ward, 289 Fourth Ave., New York; in London, Dawbarn and Ward, Ltd. This magazine gave instructions on how to make platinum paper, but my general impression was that the process was difficult for the novice and that it was hard to obtain materials.

The matter remained hanging until some two years ago when I was entrusted with a group of Tina Modotti's negatives. I could have made silver prints from the negatives, but I wanted to make platinum or palladium prints. My difficulties were smoothed over by John Szarkowski of The Museum of Modern Art in New York, who obtained for me a booklet by Richard Benson of typewritten instructions on the process.

One of my personal modifications is the use of the mercury light BTC Ascor 24 x 28 Vacuum Printer, instead of using the sun or a sunlamp. Around 1959 I was in Holland working on a book about Mexican mural painting. There I saw a technique for utilizing ultraviolet light to print sheets of a low threshold of sensitivity. When I returned to Mexico, I took advantage of this ultraviolet light for collotype, a printing procedure I had studied since the 30s. With the Dutch ultraviolet light, the exposures were very long, perhaps 20 or 30 minutes. Sometimes I worked with the sun. Because of my relationship to Mexican print shops, I saw the new procedures they were using for making plates out of metal of low sensitivity. I got to know the ultraviolet mercury light apparatus. I understood that the apparatus would facilitate my work. Instead of 125 watts of the Dutch light, it operates at 2000 watts. Therefore it is 16 times more rapid.

The exposure dial can be set up to 240 units, which do not necessarily correspond to watch time. The machine has the advantage of an integrator, so that if the current fluctuates, it will give more or less time to compensate. Most of the time I use about 45 or 60 units to expose a palladium print. The dial can also be set to manual, and seconds counted on a watch.

Besides the speed and control of exposure, the apparatus has another advantage. Because it operates on a vacuum principle, the contact of the negative with the paper is perfect. Also, the apparatus has a Wratten filter that cuts down on the danger of the rays (Figure 8).

I don't know if this machine can be recommended for general use because of the great cost, but I believe that one could, with ingenuity, make the same kind of machine. The commercially manufactured apparatus has the advantage of maximum safety and repeatability.

To make platinum or palladium prints, it is necessary to have a negative the same size as the desired print. I have 8 x 10 negatives from the 30s, but the nudes that interest me now are made with a smaller camera, the Hasselblad 2¼ x 1 5/8 (16 magazine), and so there is the necessity of making large negatives. There are procedures to make duplicates. One is making an 8 x 10 enlargement on silver paper, and then re-photographing it on an 8 x 10 sheet of film. The procedure I prefer is to make a small positive enlargement on film, and, directly from the film, to make a negative 8 x 10 or larger in size. Sometimes it is necessary to make corrections, and for me it is preferable to make the corrections in the enlarged negative so that dodging is not needed in each print. The film I use is the same one employed in the graphic arts industry to make masks for color separations. It is called "Kodak Pan Masking Film;" it is very thin and dries quickly. It is developed with the recommended developers, HC-110 or DK-50.

For safety and ease of handling, I tape the four outside edges of the 8 x 10 negative onto a larger sheet of clear acetate. I use red Scotch tape for this purpose (Figure 9). Often I tape four strips of cut, developed and fixed film around the edges of the negative, so that the outer edges of the sensitized paper are not accidentally exposed.

According to what I have seen, different photographers are experimenting with various papers for platinum and palladium prints. There are some papers that give one more difficulties than others. One's choice is a question of technical considerations and personal circumstances. The same thing happens with papers sensitized by hand as with silver papers which have been sensitized previously: one must make a choice between the different qualities produced by the papers. For example, for silver papers there are matte surfaces, brilliant surfaces, different degrees of contrast, etc.

For platinum and palladium printing, there are papers like Rives BFK that are porous and absorbent, and so the image is more what one might call "tactile." This is a sensation that is defined by a phrase from a poem by the Mexican poetess Sor Juana Inés De La Cruz, "Tengo en los ojos los dedos, y lo que miro, tiento." ("I have fingers in the eyes, and what I look at, I touch.") Arches Perigeaux and Schoeller are harder, less absorbent and the surfaces are smoother.
These surfaces still conserve the feeling of paper (as compared with the smooth gelatin surface of

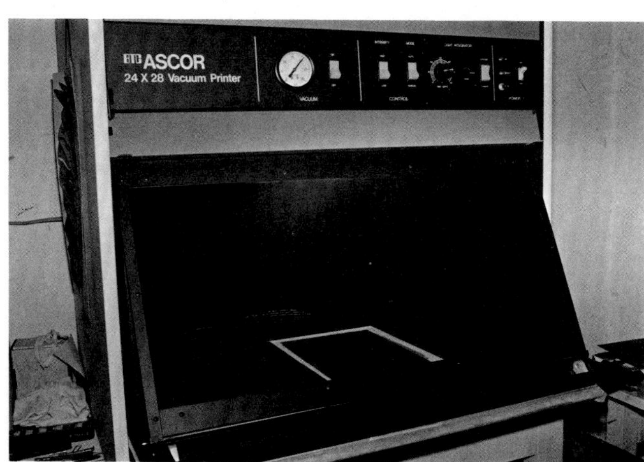

FIGURE 8

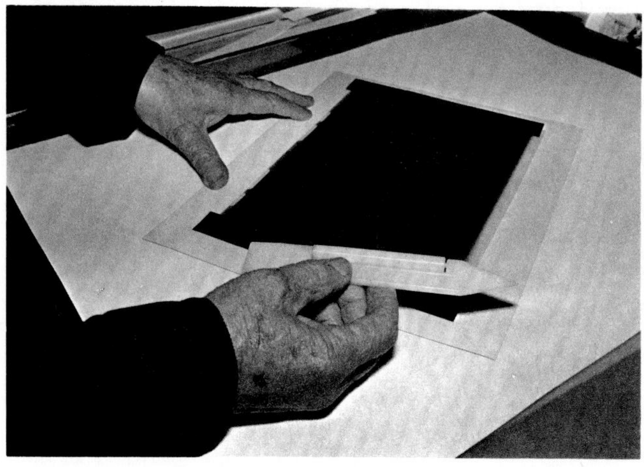

FIGURE 9

silver paper), but to a lesser degree than Rives BFK. The hardest of the three is Schoeller. I got it in Mexico without knowing exactly its source, but I understand it is a German paper. Its color is warmer, more yellowish, but the results I have obtained are very interesting. It has given me the sensation of sun on the skin. For the nudes, this feeling of sun seems to me of importance.

There is another observation to be made in respect to the choice of papers. Not all images work well in platinum and palladium; I don't believe in the supremacy of any one method of printing. I believe that with the diverse papers, it is possible to get the different results that the photograph wants. There is, nevertheless, the difficulty of achieving a sense of unity if different papers are utilized within a portfolio of palladium or platinum prints. One print in the portfolio might be colder, the next, warmer in tonality. It does not affect me personally to see different papers and tonalities within the same portfolio of prints, if the textures and tonalities of the papers correspond well to the image. But there are some people who are bothered by it.

Finally, there is one other consideration in the choice of papers. This is the reproduction of the body's skin. I think that the chlorobromide glossy papers like Agfa Portriga reproduce the sensation of the skin itself better than the papers for platinum and palladium. It is difficult for me to define, but I believe that the brilliance of the gelatin probably reproduces the brilliance of the skin better. With palladium and platinum, especially with the most porous papers, the sensation could perhaps better define itself as more pictorial. The problem, then, is to select the proper paper according to the intention.

Various formulae for palladium printing can be encountered in many publications, and they don't differ much from the old ones. I use Richard Benson's formula.

RICHARD BENSON'S PALLADIUM SENSITIZER FORMULA

SOLUTION A

20% ferric oxalate solution
(every 50cc of distilled water contains 1 gram of oxalic acid)

SOLUTION B

1% solution potassium chlorate
(this bottle should be replaced every two weeks)

SOLUTION C

Sodium chloropalladite
(which consists of 10 grams palladium chloride ($PdCl_2$); 7 grams common salt; and 80cc distilled water)

When I am preparing the paper to receive the chemicals, I don't insert pushpins into the four corners of the sheet to hold it down on a piece of wood. This is one of the differences in my personal darkroom procedure. I prefer to fasten the paper with masking tape onto a piece of glass larger than the piece of paper (Figure 10). Three

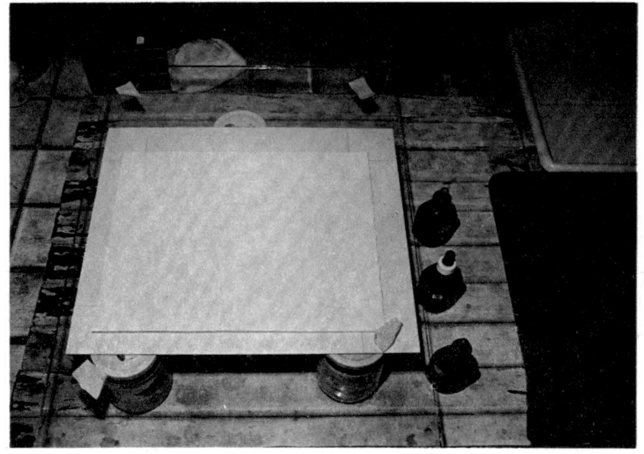

FIGURE 10

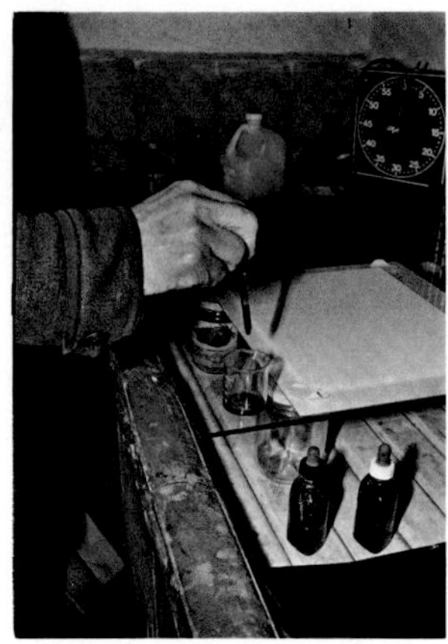

FIGURE 11

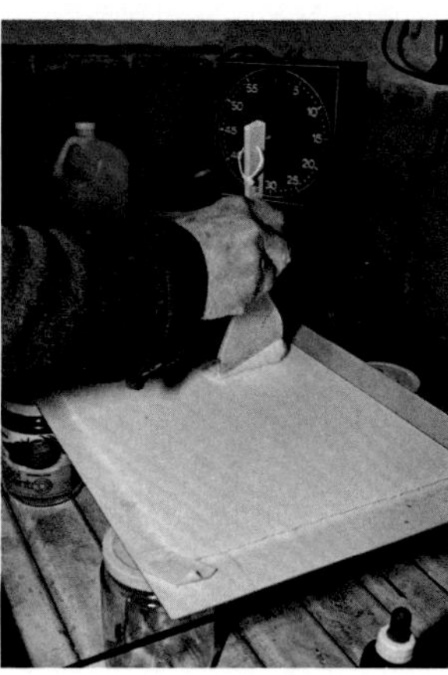

FIGURE 12

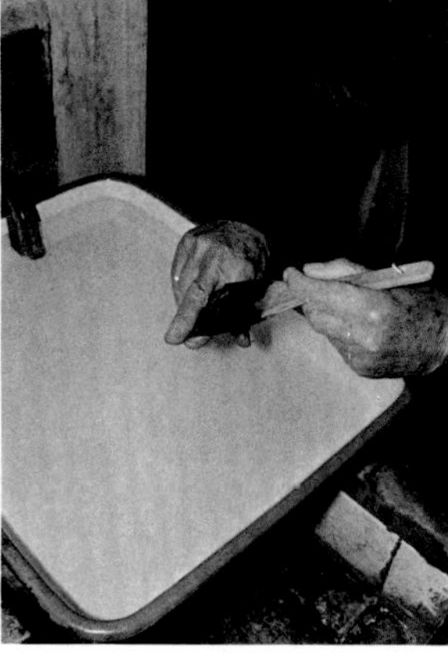

FIGURE 13

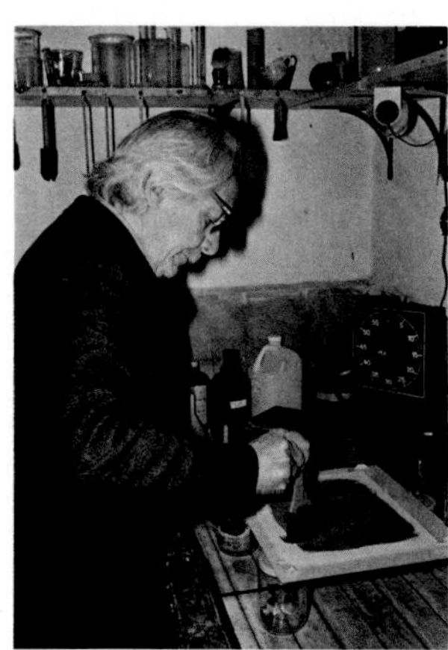

FIGURE 14

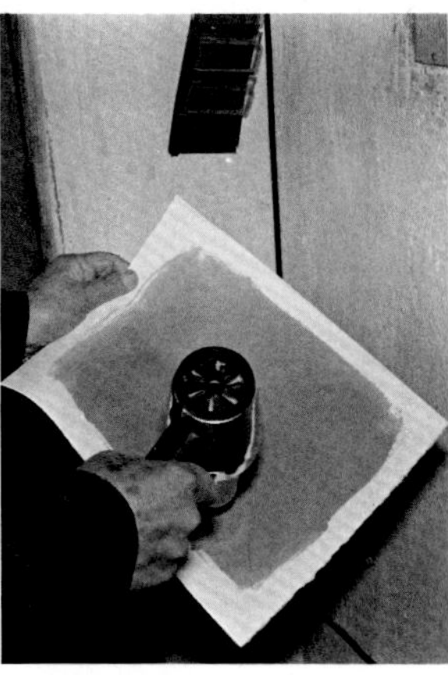

FIGURE 15

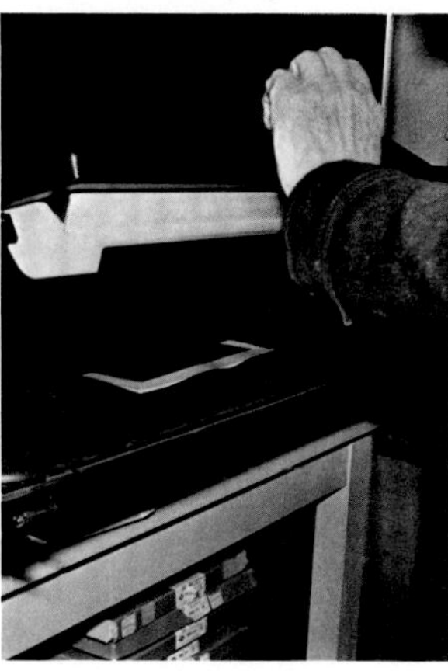

FIGURE 16

ordinary food bottles hold up the piece of glass. I also put a board underneath the glass, marked in the proportions of the image. The object is to have a guideline while using the brush, so I don't exceed the limits of the image. Many times, when the brush marks go outside the image, the resulting stains are very pretty and agreeable. They have a feeling of an abstraction outside the image itself. But since it is a thing so different from the image, at this time I prefer to leave the margins completely clean. This also has the advantage of leaving room for the signature under the image, on the same side of the sheet.

With the eyedroppers from the bottles of solution, generally I put 14 drops of Solution A, 8 drops of B, and 24 drops of C into a small beaker (Figure 11). I sometimes change the proportions of A and B to control the contrast. Solution B augments the contrast.

Before spreading the sensitizer on paper, I clean the surface of the sheet with a smooth, dry brush. At times contact with the fingers or some other circumstance prevents the uniform entrance of the chemicals into the paper. Sometimes portions of the image that look streaked at first can smooth over upon drying. The first time that I used more absorbent paper and saw irregular streaks, I was at the point of throwing it away. But I thought it would be good to use the paper to make a proof, so that the sheet would be made good use of. The final result was perfect.

After cleaning the surface of the paper with the dry brush (Figure 12), I dip another brush momentarily into distilled water and flick off the excess (Figure 13). This is the brush I will use for spreading the chemicals. I pour the small beaker of sensitizer rapidly over the paper, and brush the solution on as uniformly as possible (Figure 14).

Next, I use a hairdryer to dry the damp paper. First I apply cold air to the sensitized side of the sheet (Figure 15); and then warm air to the reverse side. When the paper is completely dry, I place it in the Ascor Vacuum Printer (Figure 16). For this print, on Rives BFK, I set the dial at 60 units.

The exposed paper is put into the developer tray (Figure 17), usually for about 2 minutes, with continuous agitation. The developer consists of 1 lb. of potassium oxalate in 48 oz. of water. On a certain occasion it occurred to me to utilize an ordinary paper developer on a palladium print. I had some Dektol prepared and I used it, and the image came out. I believe it would be possible, by playing a little, to get different interesting results with diverse developers, like Amidol, etc.

The rest, the clearing agent and the wash, are presently popular, very simple and very ordinary. The clearing agent consists of hydrochloric acid diluted in water to a proportion of 1:60. I use three separate baths of clearing agent, and I give about 6 or 8 minutes in each of the three baths (Figure 18). As the print rests in each of the first two trays, I agitate occasionally; but continuously in the third bath.

After the three clearing baths, the paper is usually given the normal wash of 20 or perhaps 30 minutes in a tray with a Kodak siphon (Figure 19). A Paterson print washer has the great advantage of using less water, and the results are very good. The Paterson tank is used for 20 minutes.

Afterward, as much water as possible is removed by using a heavy roller on the image while it is on a piece of glass (Figure 20). Once no more water comes out, I gently wipe the other side with a very lightly dampened sponge, removing the moisture that might have remained on the image.

Then I stretch a string across the glass doors and suspend the palladium prints with Paterson clips that are very convenient (Figure 21). The sun and air dry the prints very rapidly.

When the palladium prints are dry, they are placed directly into a well-heated Seal mounting press (Figure 22). If it is late, I leave them until the next day in the press, after I have turned off the heat. If there is a little more urgency, I remove them from the press after a while and put them under a heavy glass that keeps them flattened and very easy to place into overmattes right away.

When Schoeller paper is used, the very hard paper, there is the possibility of producing wrinkles. To prevent them, I pull the paper downward gently over the edge of a desk. Once stretched a little, it goes into the mounting press.

For touching up palladium prints, I use Conté drawing pencils in two colors: sepia and black.

For overmattes, I prefer Crestwood 100% pure rag acid-free mount board, which I have used in "natural white" (actually a "bone" color) for my portfolios in palladium.

I have left off drymounting platinum and palladium prints. Presently I use "palomitas" to insert the prints into overmattes. They are really little corners cut out of acid-free paper. My daughter Genoveva helps me cut them, and she gave them the name "palomitas," or "little doves." The "palomitas" are fastened to the bottom board of the overmatte with acid-free Talas tape, or, more regularly, with Filmoplast P, a thinner tape.

As I mentioned before, if the image is left with margins on the same sheet, it is possible to sign in pencil directly underneath the picture. This brings back a remembrance of many years ago. At the very beginning of my work in photography, I bought an Italian book of instructions which touched on many little points. After the discussion of mounting the print, the book ended with a sentence that is both funny and appropriate: "The moment has arrived in which the artist, satisfied with his work, signs it."

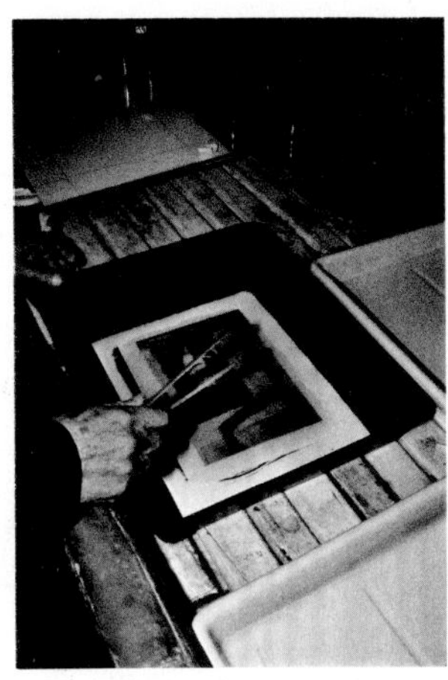

FIGURE 17

FIGURE 18

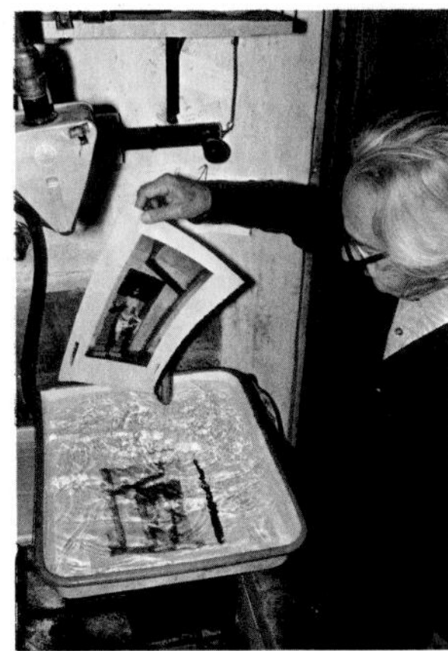

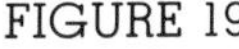

FIGURE 19

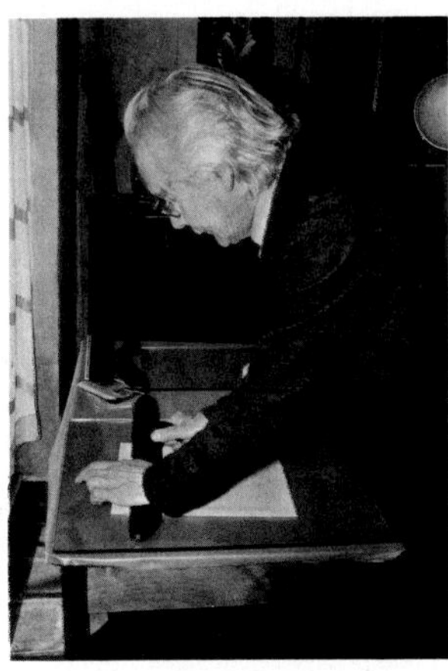

FIGURE 20

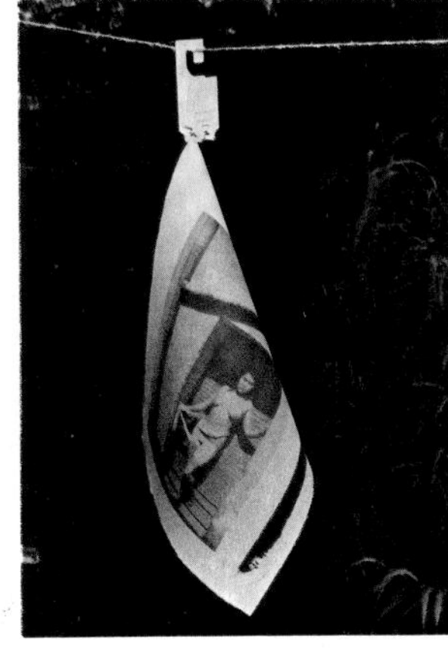

FIGURE 21

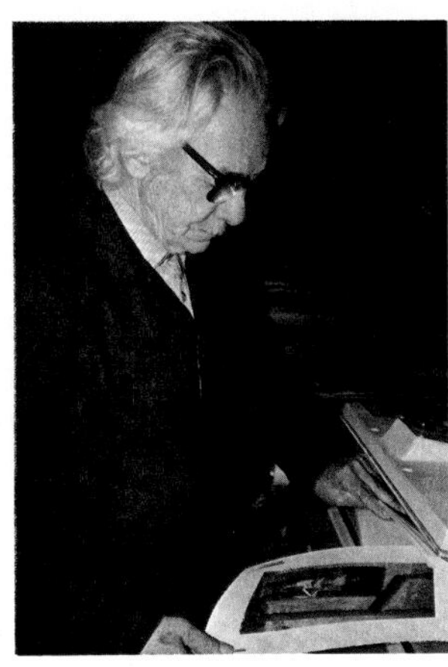

FIGURE 22

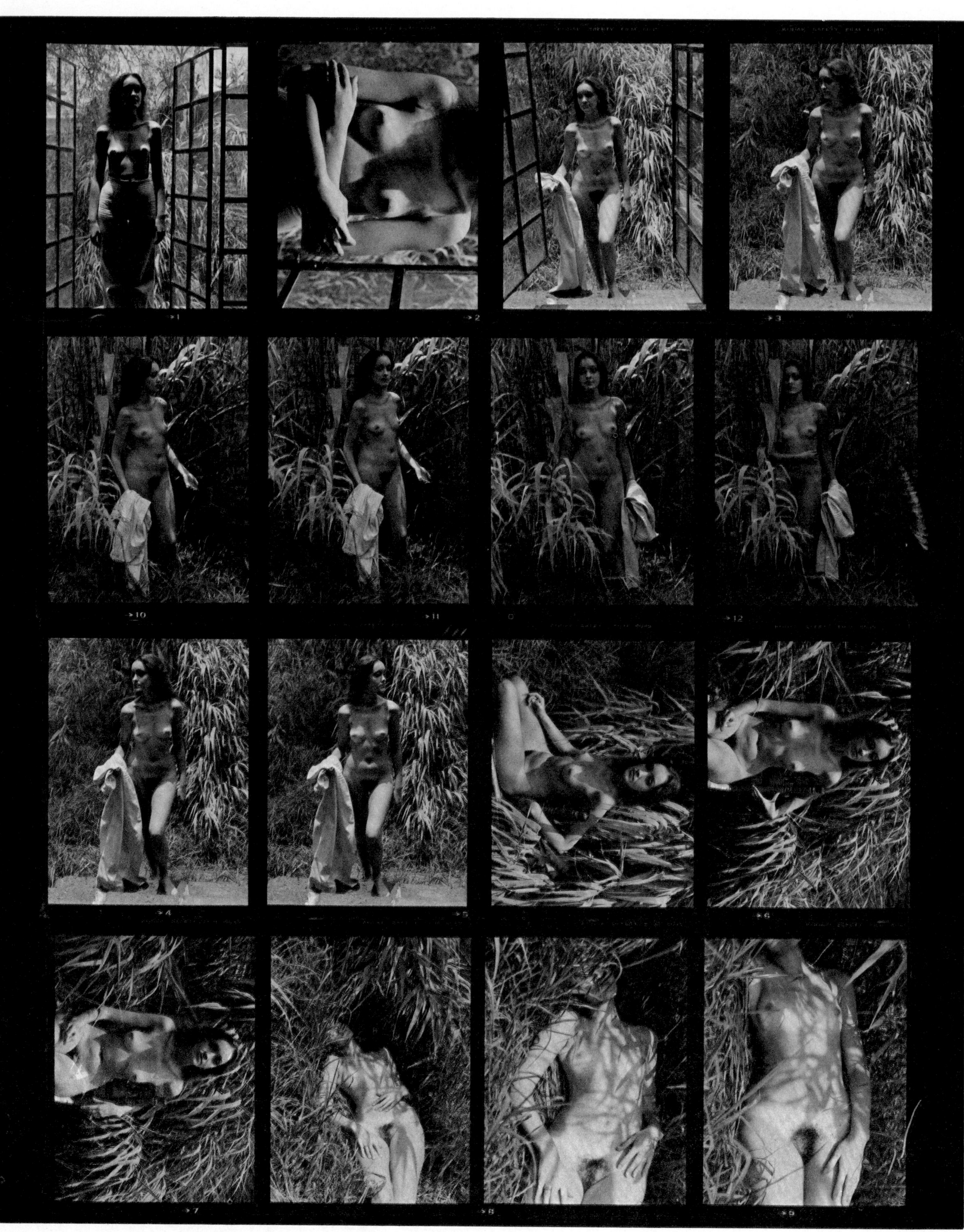

FIGURE 23: PRUEBAS EN PAPEL SOLIO DE "XIPETOTEC, 1978" (PROOFS ON P.O.P. OF "XIPETOTEC, 1978")

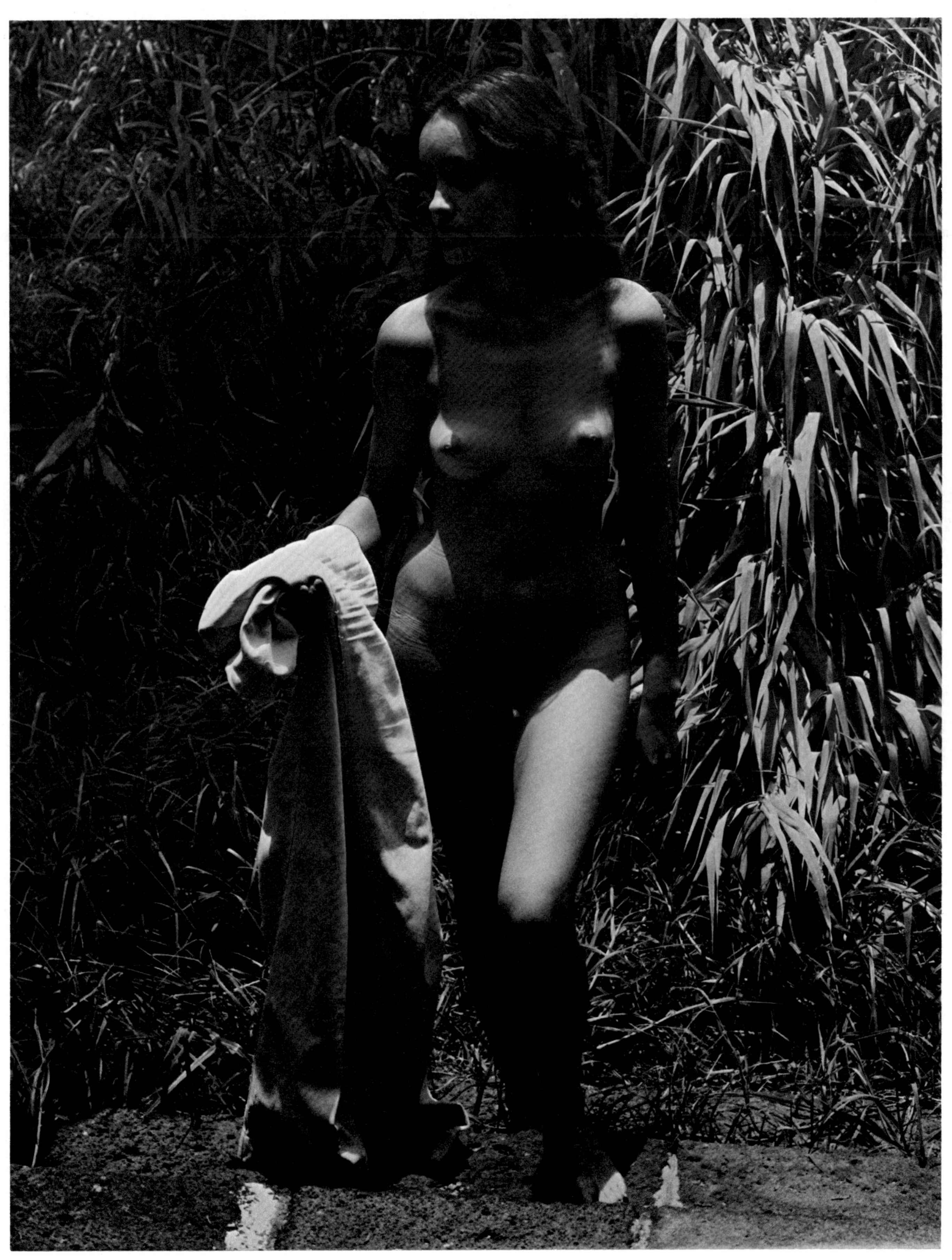

FIGURE 24: XIPETOTEC, 1978

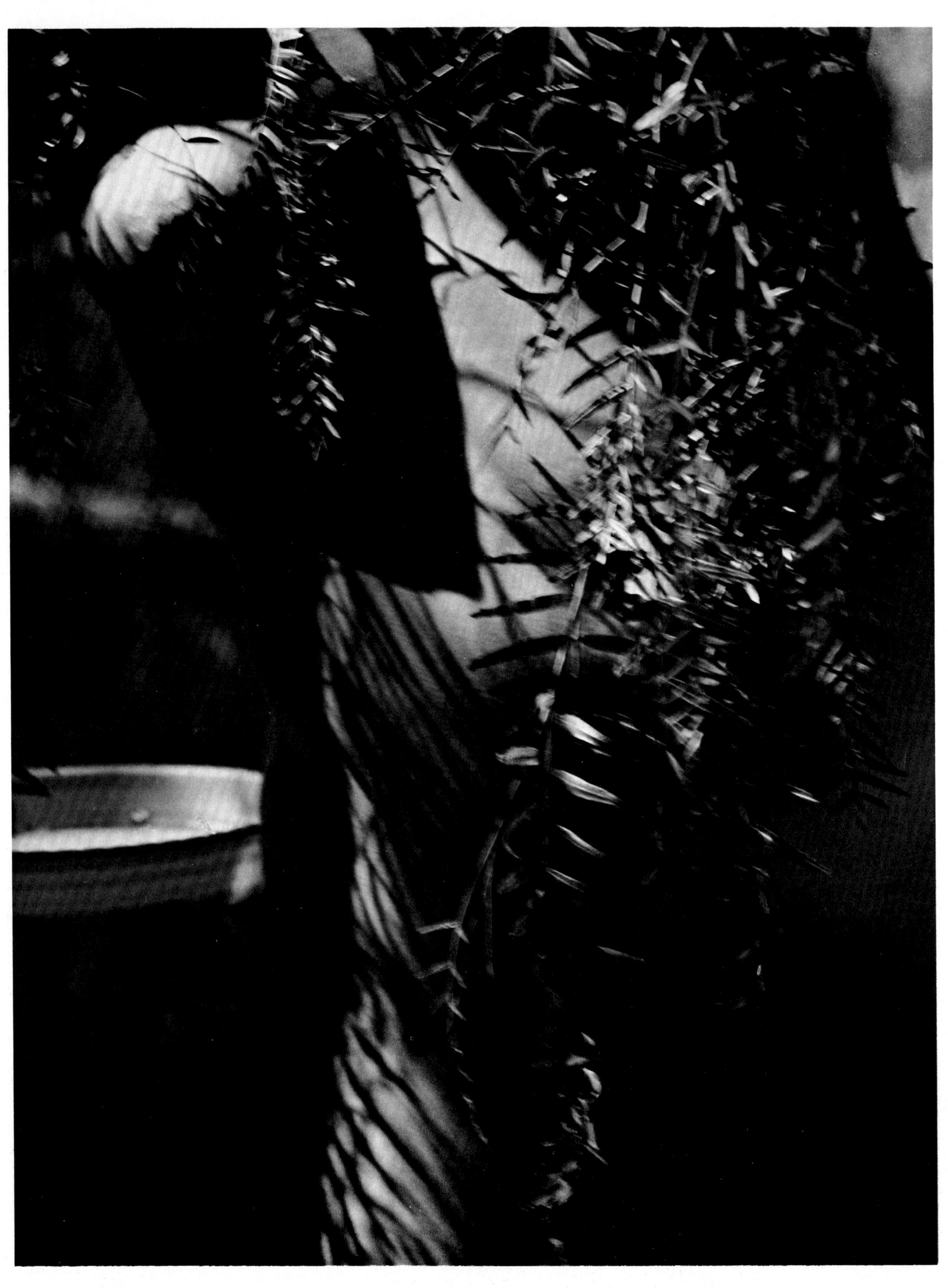

FIGURE 25: LA DEL PIRÚ, 1978 (SHE OF THE PIRÚ TREE, 1978)

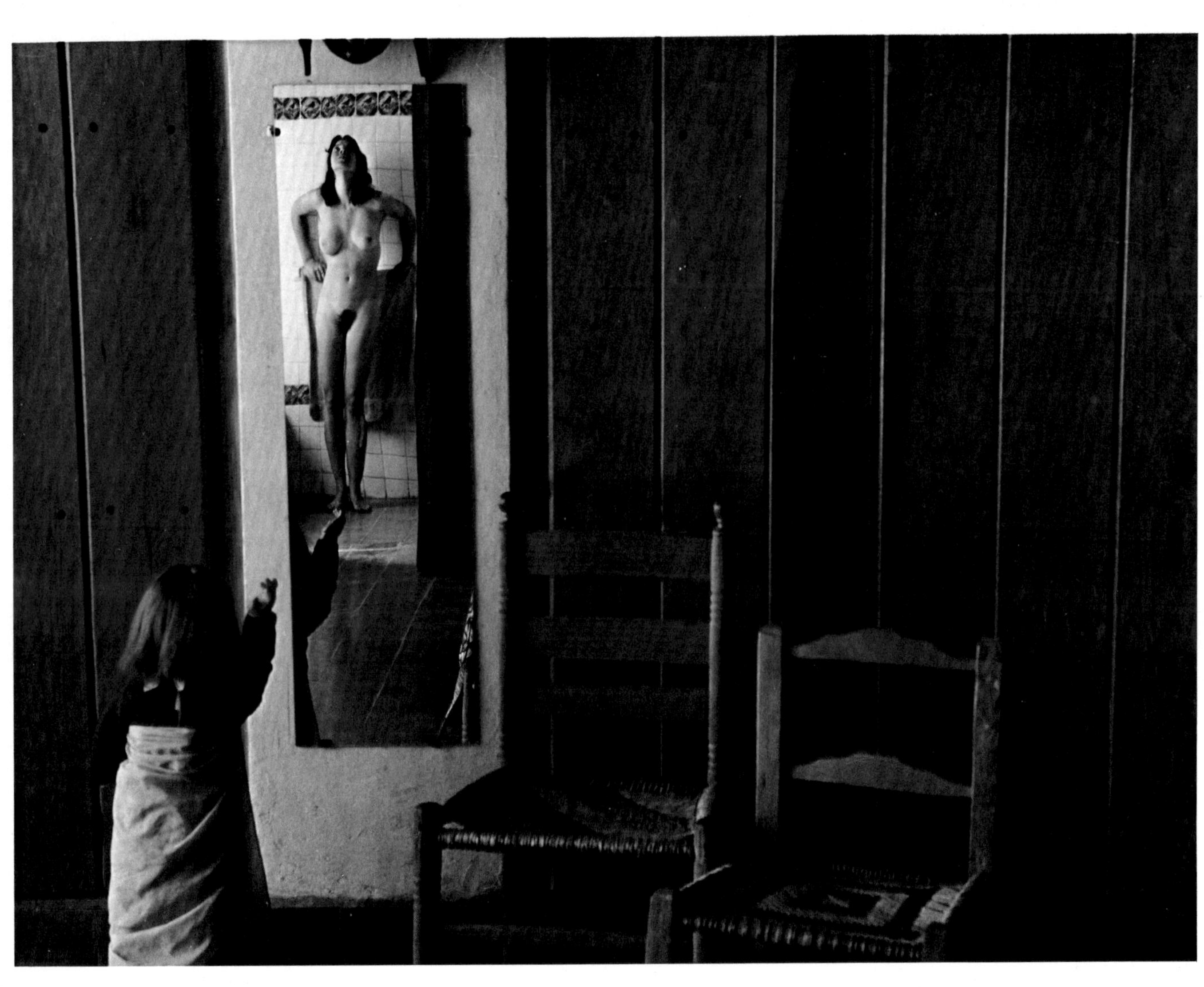

FIGURE 26: CASA DE MUÑECAS, 1978 (HOUSE OF DOLLS, 1978)

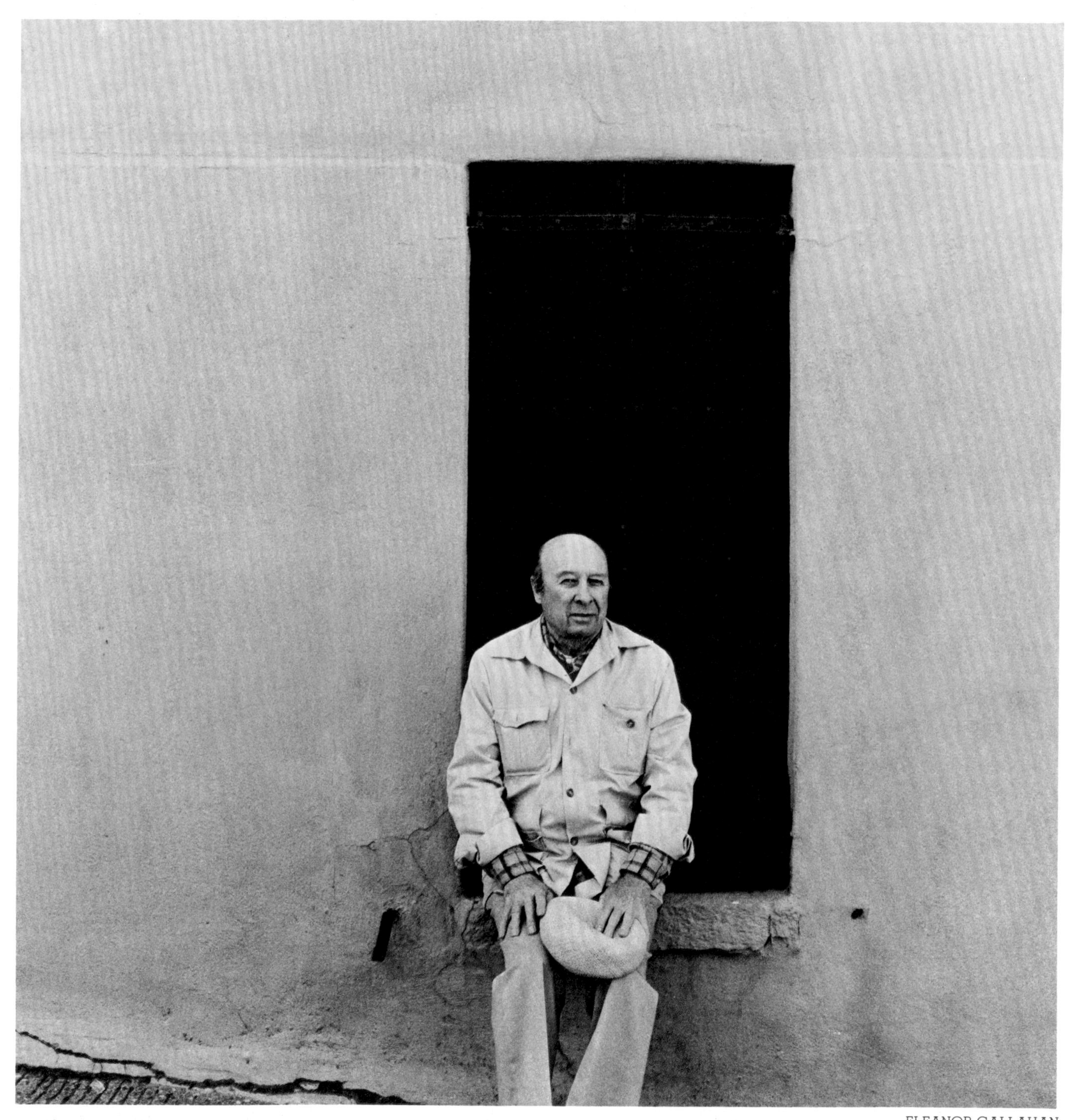

ELEANOR CALLAHAN

HARRY CALLAHAN: "LIFE AND ART HAVE TO GO TOGETHER IF ART IS TO BE TRULY MEANINGFUL."

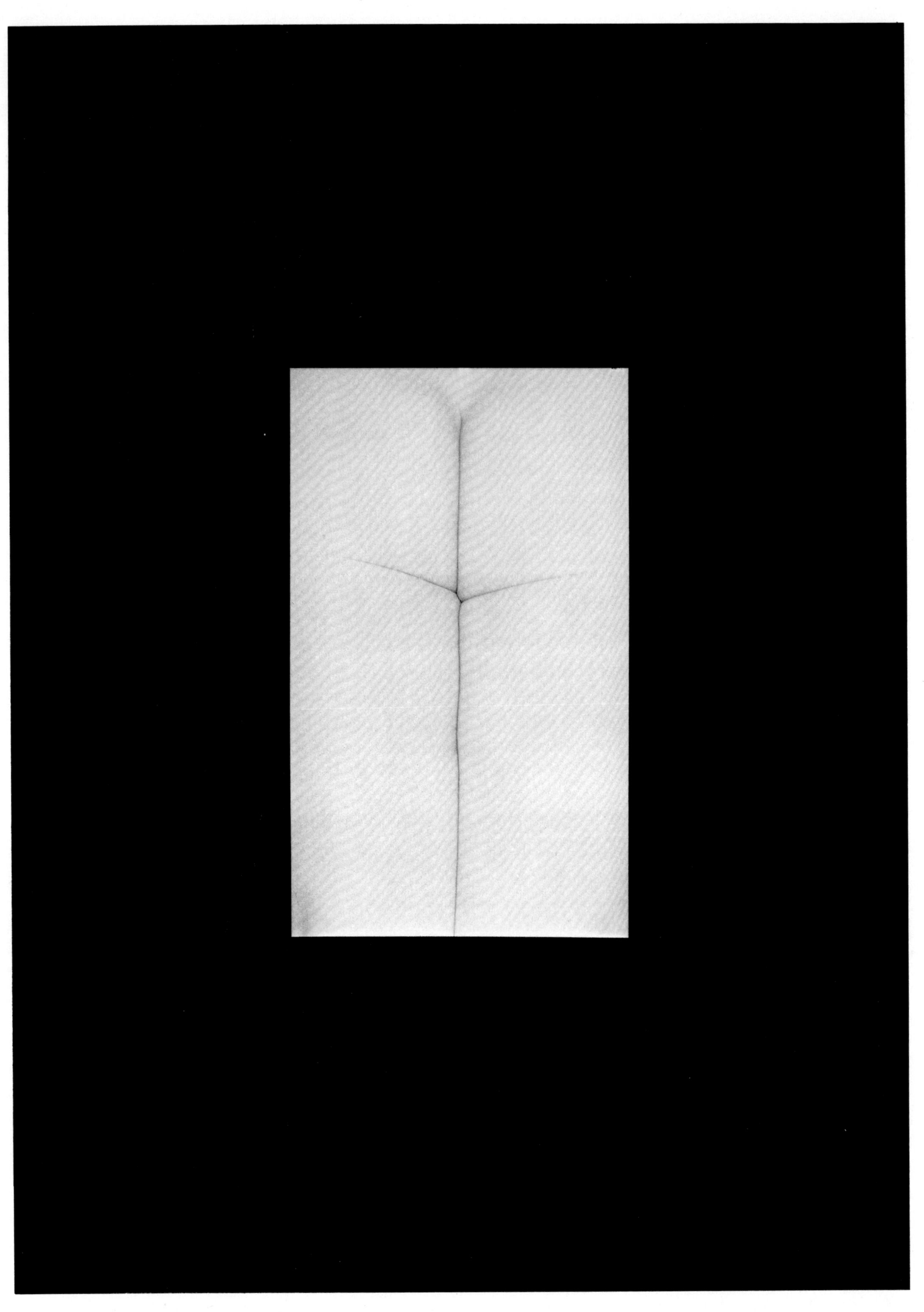

FIGURE 1: ELEANOR, 1947

Life and art have to go together if art is to be truly meaningful. I've watched a lot of people who are good at photographing something like windows. But then they just let go, as if to say, "I'm a good window photographer." They don't want to grow and do other things. They have found a style and they're not presenting much beyond that to other people. They end up with ten beautiful pictures; art is more than that. I think that when you look at a work of art you should feel something about the person, not just that he's a good window photographer. It's not that I'm anti-beautiful window or anti-beautiful photograph. I'm just anti-people staying in the same place, anti-becoming a window photographer without reaching full growth.

I can talk only about myself. I change all the time. My work is really a result of the changes happening in my life. A photographer doesn't grow until he understands himself. When I've been in the throes of growing I haven't made good pictures because I was too complicated. Maybe for somebody else the reverse is true: he makes his best pictures when he is getting complicated. My whole feeling about producing anything is to know your own life, to know what has happened to you, to continue growing, and to be lucky enough to have a medium with which to express it all. I don't think the medium is going to be any good if the life doesn't work right.

If I hadn't had photography, I wouldn't have had any way of expressing myself. When I started, I knew that this was about the only thing I did know.

My mother was rather religious, and I grew up believing in Christian humanity. I thought I should help mankind in some way. I had a friend, an Italian count, who had grown up in Paris and who was somewhat sophisticated. He talked me out of religion, and I wanted something to fill that space. When I look back I realize that I benefited from him somehow. When photography came along, I thought I would benefit from it, too. This is the way your life receives direction, through this kind of search to fulfill need. If I hadn't found photography, then I would have had a lot of problems. Maybe I have problems anyway, but I don't feel bad about the ones I have.

There's something about photography that is different from the other arts. I think it's because it's new. I suppose you could say all the arts are new. Painting has a long way to go yet and sculpture has a long way to go, too. But it does seem that photography was born just a little while ago and it's got to catch up awfully fast. I think that has something to do with my approach. I wanted to do as many things as I could in relation to the medium, and as fast as I could. But each thing I tried had to mean something to me.

Take the multiple image. I wouldn't want to do what Jerry Uelsmann does, and that's not because I'm anti-Jerry Uelsmann. It just wouldn't mean anything to me to work the way he does. He takes one negative and puts it together with another negative to make a print. I want all my exposures on one negative. I think of the negative in terms of a musical score. I want it to be complete.

My relationship to the negative and the multiple image probably has something to do with the fact that in the early days I couldn't figure out how to earn a living. It occurred to me that maybe I could make money printing for some really good photographer. I had dreams of being a great photographer and I thought that in the future someone might want to print from my negatives, too. That person should be able to concentrate on making a decent print, not on figuring out how to put everything together. All these thoughts affect the photographer.

Photography means so much to me that I don't have many distractions. It's not that I'm intellectually clear on the reasons behind everything I do. It's just that I know the answer to the question, "What am I going to be doing tomorrow?" I'm going to be doing photography.

I have found the things in photography that are most important to me. I don't judge anybody else on the basis of what they "should" be doing in their work; I don't want anybody else to judge me. I just feel that a person finds the way he functions best. This way he is contributing something to the world. If I tried to make myself do some other kind of photography, like photography as a kind of social concern, then I'd be wasting what I have to work with and I'd be a mediocre social documentarian.

I knew that I wanted to photograph and the nude was one of the subjects that I wanted to work with, like the beaches and the city. It's hard to say exactly why the nude seemed so important. The female figure was strong to me and I wanted to photograph it inside a house, in silhouette, and in the landscape. I would not have been very interested in taking a rock or something like that and placing it in a landscape. There was another aspect, too: I wanted to see how many different kinds of pictures I could put together using variations on an idea.

I had photographed a nude model once or twice at the Detroit Camera Club in the early 1940s, but it didn't mean anything to me. It seemed as if you had to think, "What can I do that's different from what everybody else is doing?" That didn't make much sense to me. Also, I wanted to photograph the person for whom I had feeling. It wasn't enough just photograph a nude.

My wife, Eleanor, was willing to pose for me because she felt it was part of what I was doing, although it probably wasn't any fun for her. At the time she didn't seem to express anything one way or the other. My daughter, Barbara, got tired of being photographed, and, being a child, she expressed that it was not always fun. Eleanor didn't make suggestions about locations. She didn't pay any attention to it. She did it only because I asked her, so she had no desire to make herself do more than she had to. She was just super-cooperative.

When I started photographing Eleanor, I didn't know about Alfred Stieglitz' work. It wasn't until later that I saw one or two of his pictures of Georgia O'Keeffe. It clarified something for me that Stieglitz had photographed O'Keeffe. That isn't what started me making pictures of the nude, but it did make me more aware of what I was doing. What influenced me even more about Stieglitz was the mystery of the way he talked. He created all kinds of strange dreams someplace inside me. It's not that I ever had what you would call extended conversations with him. I did visit him in New York, however, and I sat in while people came to call on him, and an assistant showed his pictures. When Ansel Adams had visited Detroit in 1941, he had spoken very reverently about Stieglitz, as if he were a god. Ansel's work and attitudes attracted me so strongly that seeing Stieglitz became something to look forward to, as if it were part of a formula for learning about photography. The experience affected me for a long time, until finally I started feeling it was rather ridiculous. Of course, Stieglitz wasn't really a god. Actually, he was kind of a cranky old fellow. But it was something I had to go through and get over.

It was Ansel Adams who helped me a great deal with technical matters. For years I used ABC Pyro film developer, Isopan film and Amidol print developer, all on Ansel's recommendations. It was a big thing later on for me to break away from the way in which Ansel helped me. I thought it was a sin not to get texture in your picture. It was a sin to print on No. 3 paper instead of No. 2, because he said he almost always printed on No. 2. That's how powerful an influence he was on me.

Ansel had made a big issue out of texture and the camera's ability to record fine detail. When I began to eliminate tone and show only lines in my landscape pictures, it was the breaking of tradition for me. At that time it was anti-photography to me.

ELEANOR, 1947 (Figure 1) was done during the same period that I was photographing things like weeds in the snow, black lines against white. In this picture of Eleanor, the tone in the skin is very delicate. It's just a little tone here and there that you can hardly see, and the line is also very, very delicate. The picture was done with a 9 x 12cm Linhof camera. It's one of the few pictures I've cropped. The only reason I don't crop is that

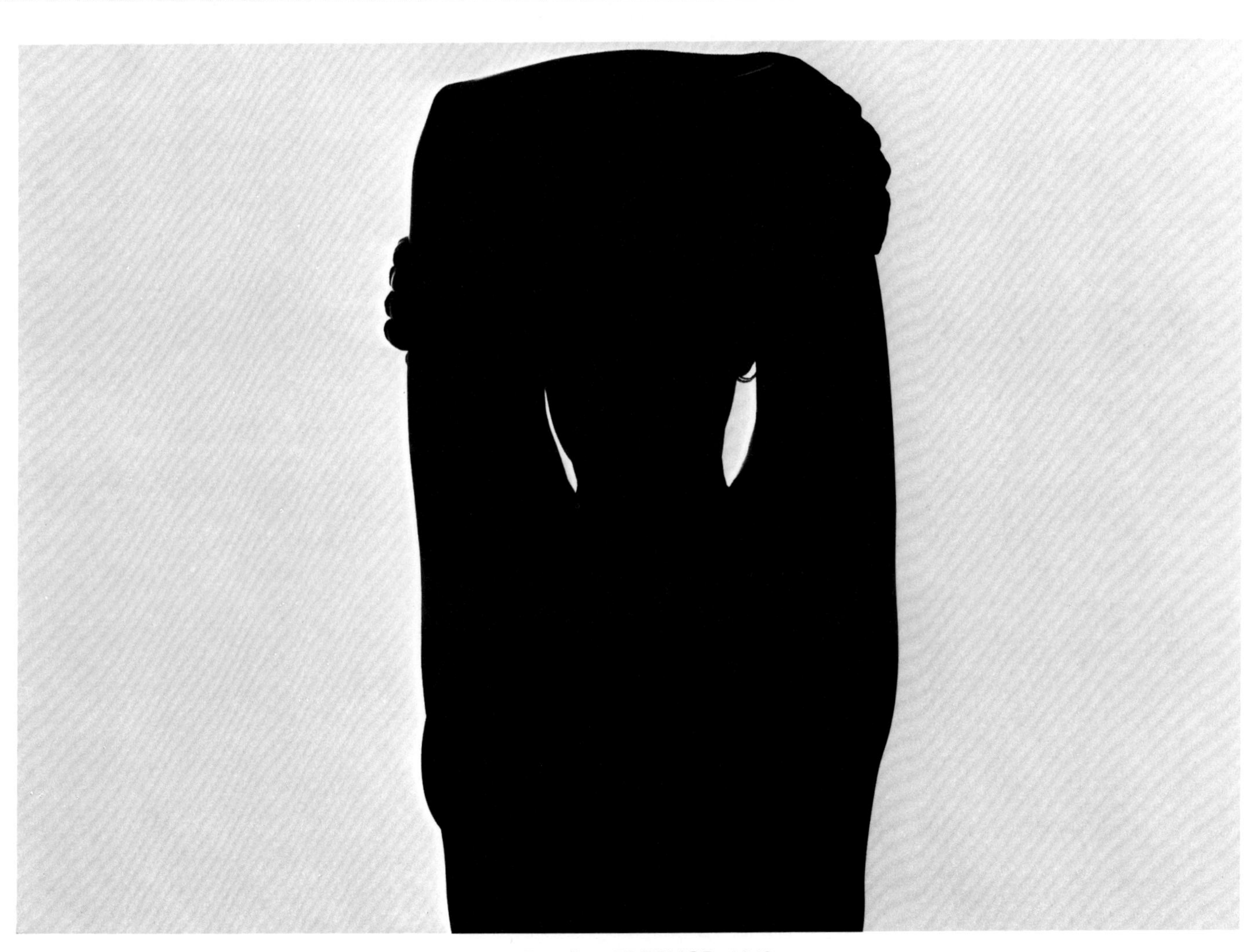

FIGURE 2: ELEANOR, 1948

it seems to make everything more complicated. This negative of Eleanor is cut, just to settle things once and for all. It's easier to print this way. I just lay it down to make a contact print.

ELEANOR, 1948 (Figure 2) is a strong black against white with just an edge of detail on the hand and breast. I don't really know why I chose this particular pose for Eleanor. It may have been something she did from time to time, and then I just continued with it. I think I have an old-fashioned, conventional attitude, that I don't want her to look awkward. As far as poses go, I think I photographed her so much that she just did the same thing all the time, really.

When I placed Eleanor by the window (Figure 3), it was because I was curious about shooting straight into the light. Also, I wanted to make the picture with an 8 x 10 camera. It was a very long exposure, 20 seconds, and Eleanor had to sit still all that time. She did move a little, but that's all right. This picture is another example of my desire to photograph her in an endless number of ways. Every time I could get an idea, I'd do something else. In this case, I wanted to shoot into the light with her as a kind of accent.

The window was in a ballroom that we were living in right after World War II. The landlord of a big old mansion with a lake view had rented out the rooms. Other people got the master bedrooms and so on, and we happened to get the ballroom. It was 55 feet long and about 45 feet wide. So I had a lot of room to photograph in, and I took a lot of pictures of Eleanor there.

One day our friend Hugo Weber was visiting us in the ballroom. He asked Eleanor if he could put some drawings on our wall with a paint that dries very fast (Figure 4). The paint had just come out, and Hugo was having a lot of fun with it. Eleanor didn't know what he was talking about, or I don't think she would have let him. He made those drawings on the wall and I was very happy about it, and they never went away.

During this session I took very few photographs. This was with my 8 x 10 Deardorff and the light was an open flashbulb, which gave the most even light. The light source was right by the camera, as close as I could get to the lens. I didn't care for the shadows. It's not that I'm anti-shadow; it simply would not have been right for the photograph.

The very tiny figure of Eleanor was also done in the ballroom (Figure 5). I had a real urge to work with the figure very small. I put a 90mm lens on my 8 x 10. I directed one flood light in a reflector on her. The light is actually in the picture itself, but it can't be seen because the back of the reflector is facing the camera.

To photograph ELEANOR, 1953 (Figure 6), I used a 4 x 5 Linhof. This is a triple exposure on one negative. It's of an egg with light from behind; a silhouette of Eleanor done with a flood light in a reflector; and a landscape. I wanted to form her body out of the branches, so I had to have a silhouette. I made each shot on the sheet of film at the same exposure. It would have made a difference if I had given full exposure to one shot and half exposure to another. I might have lost something in the half-exposure. But when each thing is given full exposure, nothing comes out too dim.

I loaded up a whole batch of holders and did an entire series like this using the same method. I shot all sorts of things on a sheet of glass: paper cutouts, leaves, and so on (Figures 7 through 9). Then I did silhouettes of Eleanor and added things that I thought would go together.

With ELEANOR, PORT HURON, 1960 (Figure 10) I was consciously trying to produce a shape using a wide-angle lens. I "grew up" with a wide-angle lens, but in the beginning people used it just to get everything into the photograph, not to distort. Things are different now, and photographers often use the distortion on purpose. This picture was made with a 20mm lens. I took a lot of these with a 35mm Contax camera, and this is the one that came out.

ELEANOR, PORT HURON, 1954 has been reproduced very widely (Figure 11). There is another version of it that I like very much on the top left side of the contact sheet (Figure 12). When I've shown these versions to other people they have chosen the one on the bottom right-hand side on the sheet, so that's the one that got to be known, and I just let the matter go. If somebody had chosen the other one, then things might have been different.

ELEANOR, AIX-EN-PROVENCE, 1958 (Figures 13 and 14) involves only two exposures on one sheet of 4 x 5 film. I photographed Eleanor against a dark background, in this case an Aix-en-Provence piece of fabric, and then I went out to take pictures of the landscape. I photographed on this idea for two or three weeks. I must have at least 100 4 x 5s like this.

When I did multiple exposures like this, I was not consciously pursuing a surrealistic feeling. I think that in the early days I loved the idea of Magritte and the surrealists. But then I forgot all about that sort of thing. I do think photography takes a lot from painting and probably from sculpture, but when I go out to take pictures, I don't think about movements in art.

I think I used different cameras a lot because it gets boring to see pictures that are all the same shape. Each camera is a different kind of experience. I've used a 2¼, a 4 x 5, a 9 x 12cm, an 8 x 10 and a 35mm. The one camera I've ever sold is my 8 x 10 Deardorff, and I'm sorry about it. For most of my work now I use a Rollei SL66 and a couple of Leicas and a Canon. I no longer have the kind of passion for cameras that I had in the old days. At that time I knew everything new

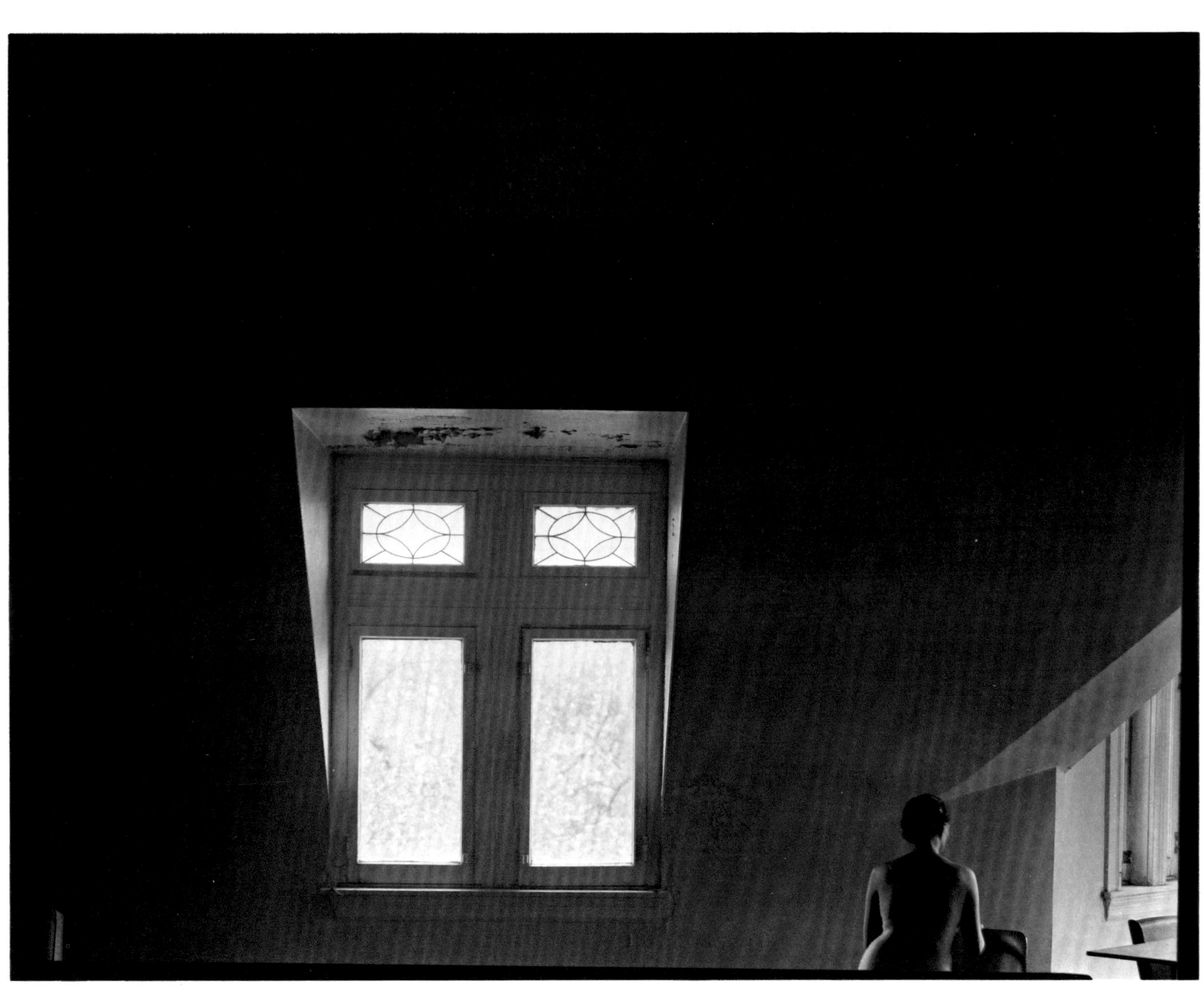

FIGURE 3: ELEANOR, 1948

that came out. Part of the reason had to do with my teaching. If a student asked you a question about a camera that you couldn't answer, he might not come back to you for help again. Now there are so many new cameras coming out that I've just about forgotten about equipment.

As far as black-and-white printing is concerned, I think you go through phases about films, developers and papers. I've tried various things, but after a while I always come back to old Kodak D-76 film developer, used normally, and Dektol print developer. My desire is to keep things simple, and, also, Kodak is pretty consistent. I like Kodak Plus-X film rated at 125 ASA and Tri-X at 400 ASA or 600.

For a long time I printed everything dark and for a long time I printed everything soft. I think that all those matters related to technique are vehicles that allow you to see. If you print contrasty then you begin to see differently; you begin to look at different things to photograph. Today I use Kodak Polycontrast paper almost entirely, except when I need Agfa Brovira in the higher grades.

As I am thinking about all these things, I realize that in the past I felt compelled to photograph all the time. Probably I didn't feel secure. Now it doesn't seem to bother me quite so much to wait. Even so, I am aware that I would like to go out and photograph at this very moment. I want to go along the East Coast and photograph the beach and the ocean and the skyscrapers and the foliage. I want to do these things in color now. I want to change. I want to grow. I've had a good year photographing the houses in Providence, Rhode Island. I've taken pictures of them on and off ever since we came here to live in the early 60s. But I've had enough of them for now. That's why I want the beach again. And when I'm tired of the beach, I'll find something else.

I worked on the nudes from the 1940s through the 60s. But then our lives changed and Eleanor went back to work, and that was that. When I look back on the nudes, I feel good about them. I have always felt that when I made a good picture, it was as good as anyone's. I'm not a very literary person, but maybe I can explain what I mean in terms of literature. I've always liked the idea of the way Walt Whitman wrote his LEAVES OF GRASS. He kept working on it all his life. Basically, he kept most of the same ideas, but he was always throwing out some parts and putting in some new things. I'm kind of like that. I just keep shooting, and the good pictures made at first are just as important to me as the good ones made at the last. Now, of course, I'm a different person and so I might bring something else to a picture if I attempted the same subject again, but that doesn't change the validity of the photographs made in the past.

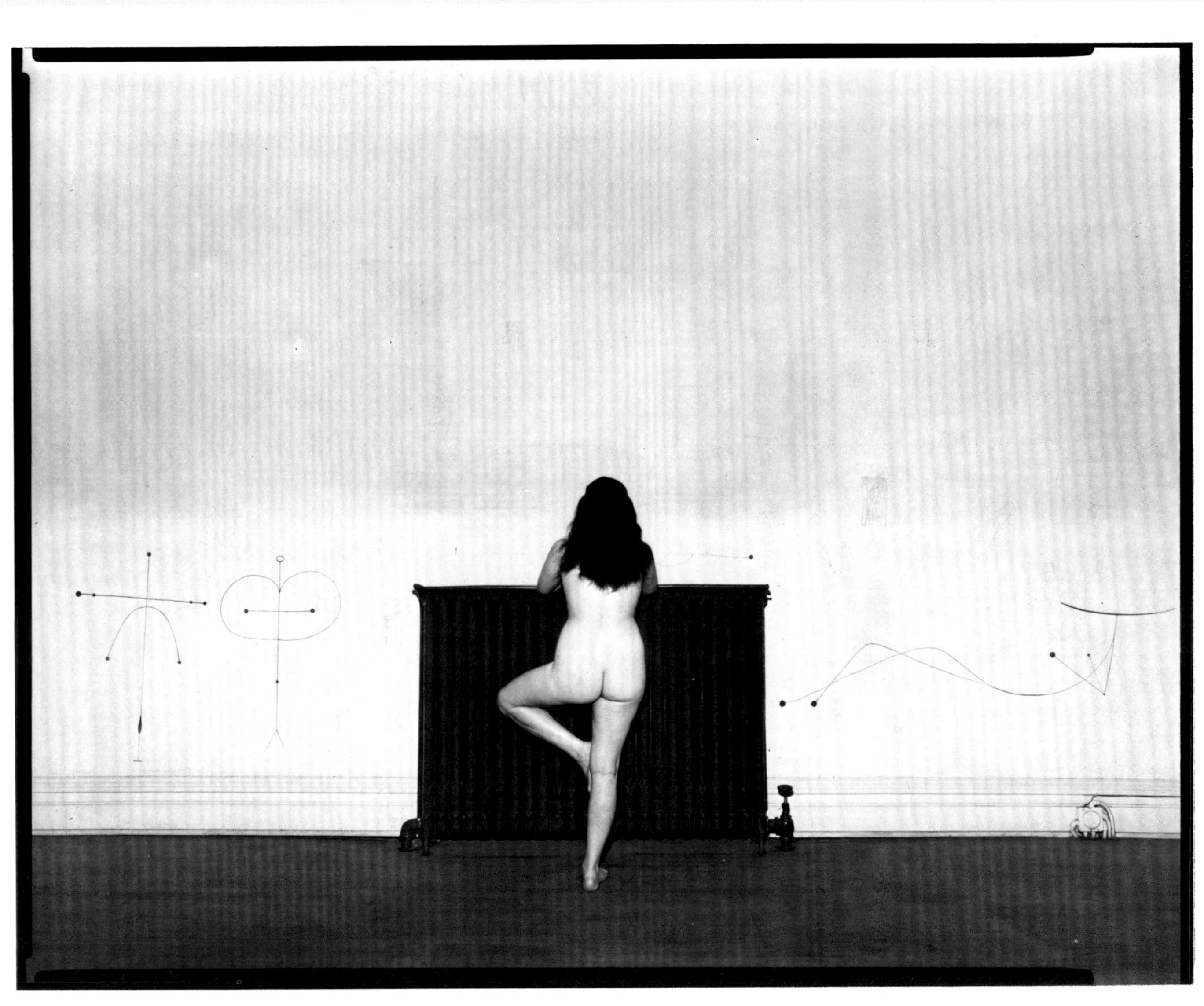

FIGURE 4: ELEANOR, CHICAGO, 1949

ELEANOR CALLAHAN

I knew that Harry wanted to photograph the nude very much, but, since we were just starting out, we didn't really have the money for professional models. It was not only a question of money, of course. It was simply not Harry's way to work with someone he had hired, and this is why he asked me to work with him. I wanted to help him in whatever way I could, and he took many photographs of me in the nude as well as in clothing.

At no time did I ever have the feeling that the photographs Harry took of me would be anything less than beautiful. It was part of our daily life for 25 years. We never had a schedule that said from 4 to 5 will be nude-photographing time. He took pictures wherever we happened to be. I might be cooking dinner and Harry would say, "Eleanor, the light is just beautiful right now. Come on, I'd like to take a picture of you." And we'd go make a photograph. Or we might be at our cottage and we'd go into the fields where it was isolated, and take pictures of the nude in nature.

Harry's work is on more of a regular schedule now. He goes out mornings and takes pictures and then prints and does other things in the afternoon. But in the early days he might be photographing any time of day, morning, noon, afternoon. And he didn't take pictures of only me. It was our daughter, Barbara, too, both of us. Now he has gone on to other areas of work.

When he first thought of photographing me in the nude, I felt very shy. I thought, "Oh, no, nice girls don't have their picture taken in the nude." I protested a couple of times, but I soon got over that. Harry assured me he would never do anything to embarrass me. I knew that his work was done with an eye to the beauty of the nude.

Before he started taking pictures, Harry would have me try out different poses. Not being a professional model, I couldn't invent poses. He had to tell me, "All right, put your hands over your head." Or, "Put this arm up and that arm down." The arrangement was all Harry's idea.

I would say he must have taken thousands of pictures of me. When we worked, he might shoot one roll, maybe two rolls. There are many, many nudes that I'm sure no one has ever seen.

When I look back on those photographs, I don't see them as myself. I see them as very beautiful pictures, but I don't think, "That's <u>me</u>." If I did, I might hold back. I might feel strange. As it is, they are something separate from me.

I can't really say I have a favorite among the nudes. I like the nature ones a great deal, especially the ones of me reclining in the field. But I like the others, too. I just think that regardless of who the model is, the nude is really a beautiful form. If you can capture that form, put it on a negative, then you're very lucky.

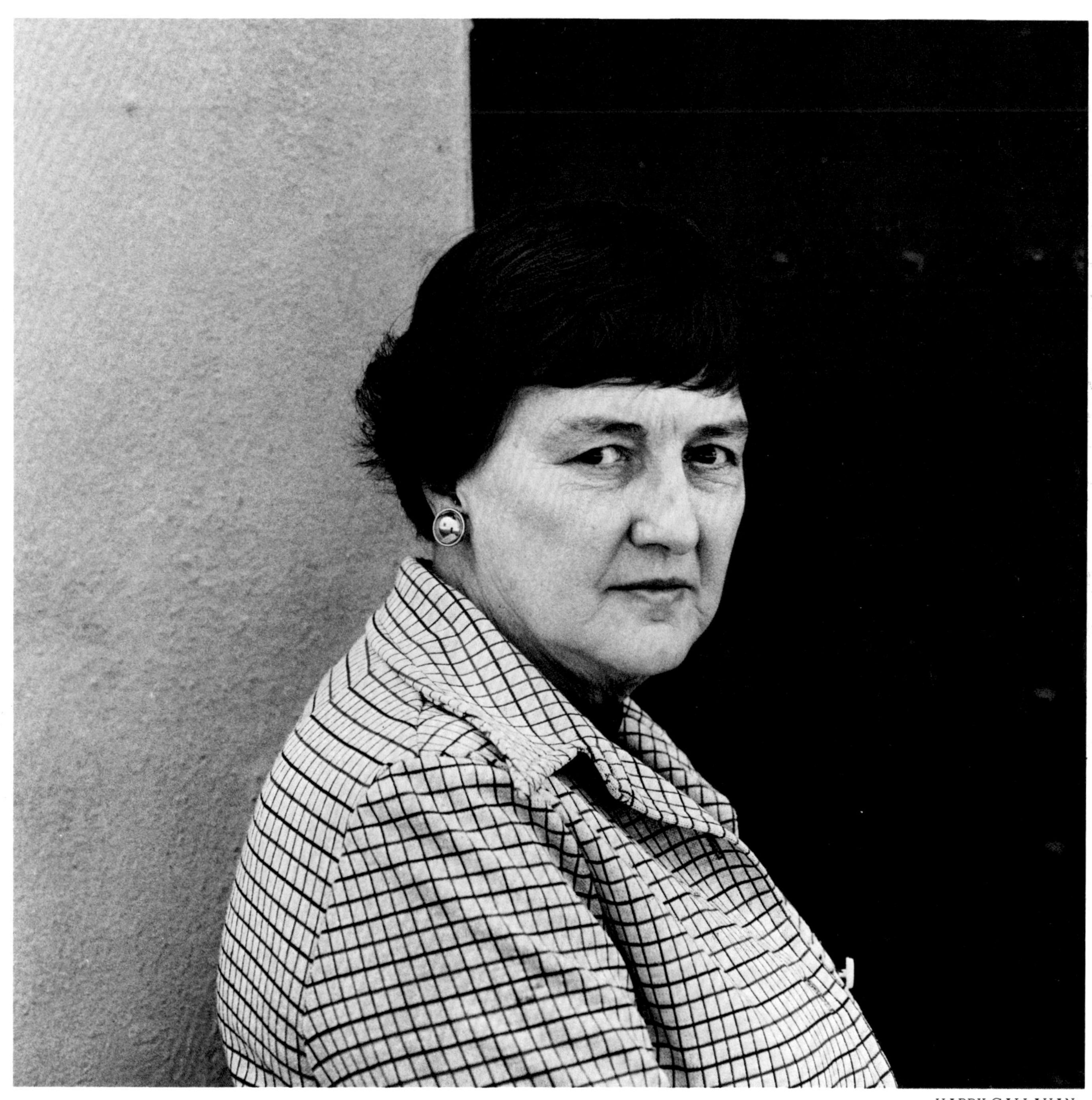

HARRY CALLAHAN

ELEANOR, 1979

FIGURE 5: ELEANOR, 1949

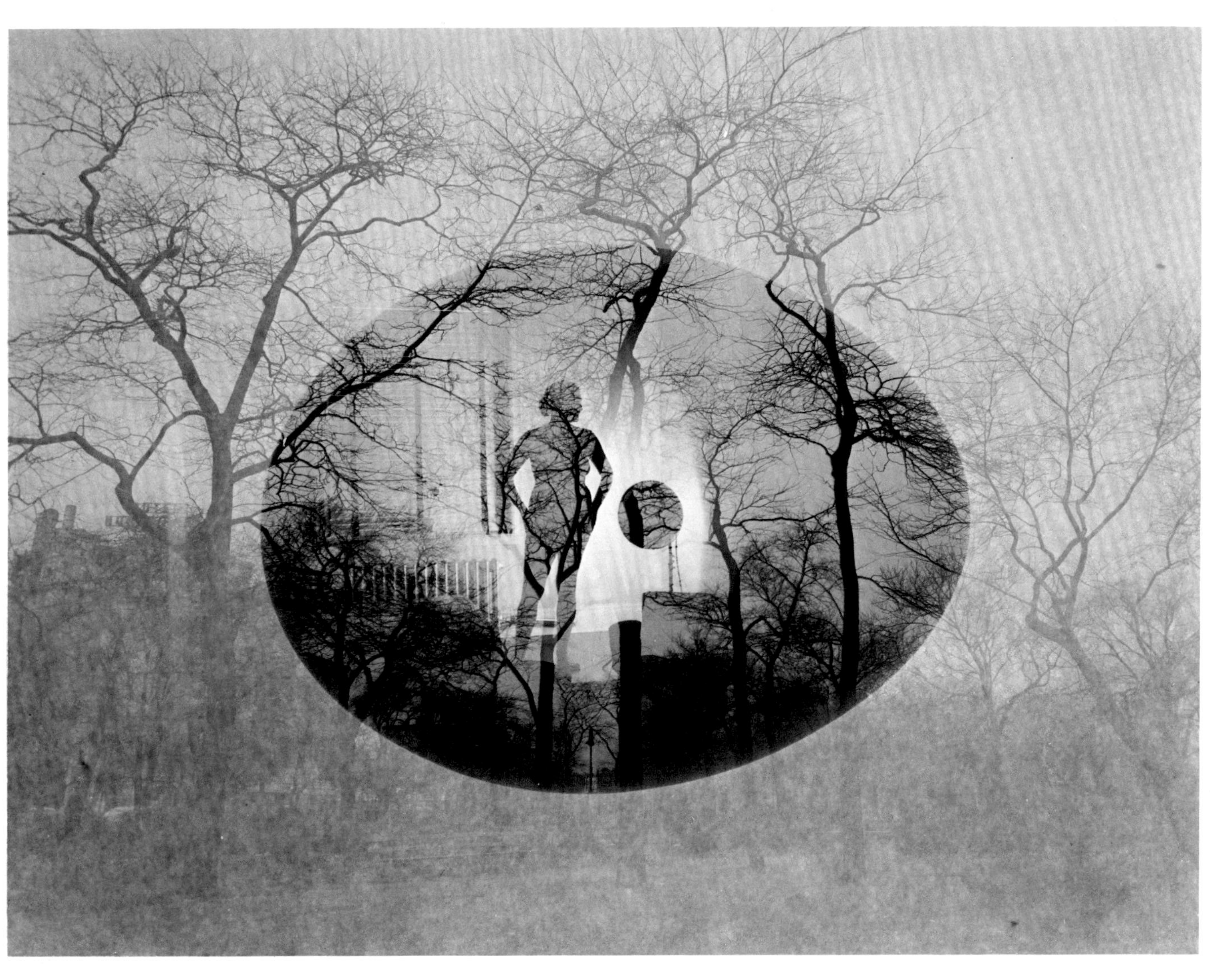

FIGURE 6: ELEANOR, CHICAGO, 1953

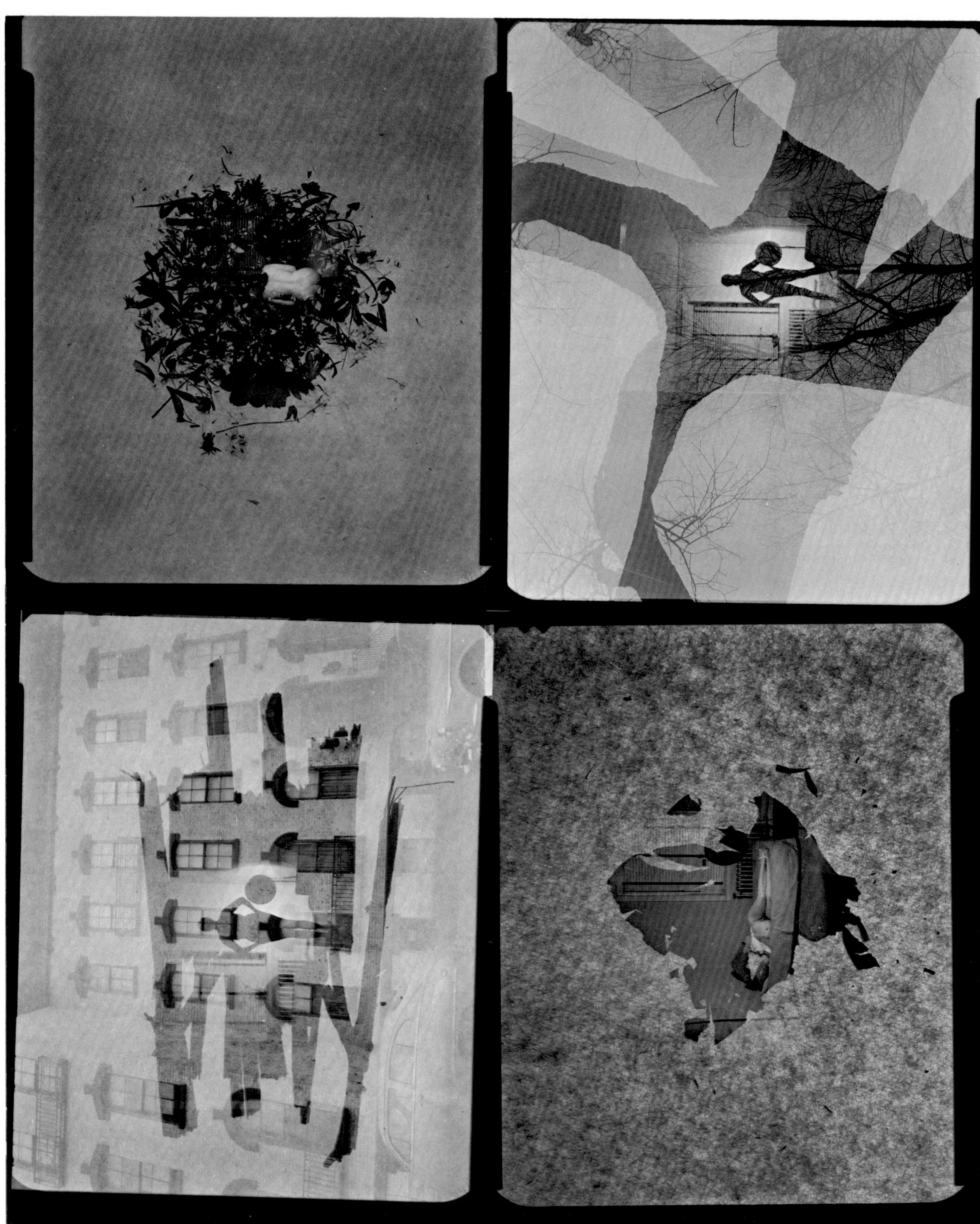

FIGURE 7

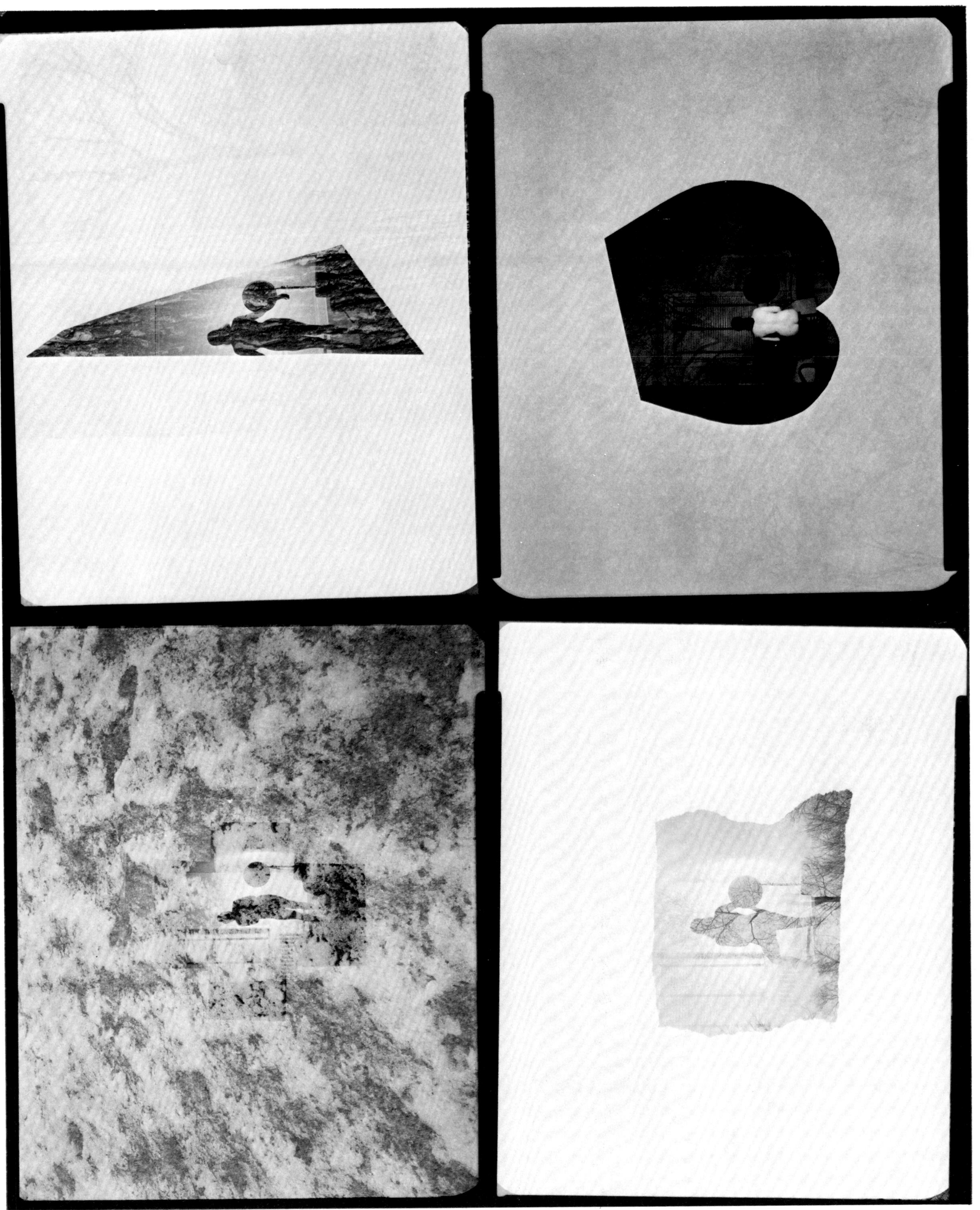

FIGURE 8

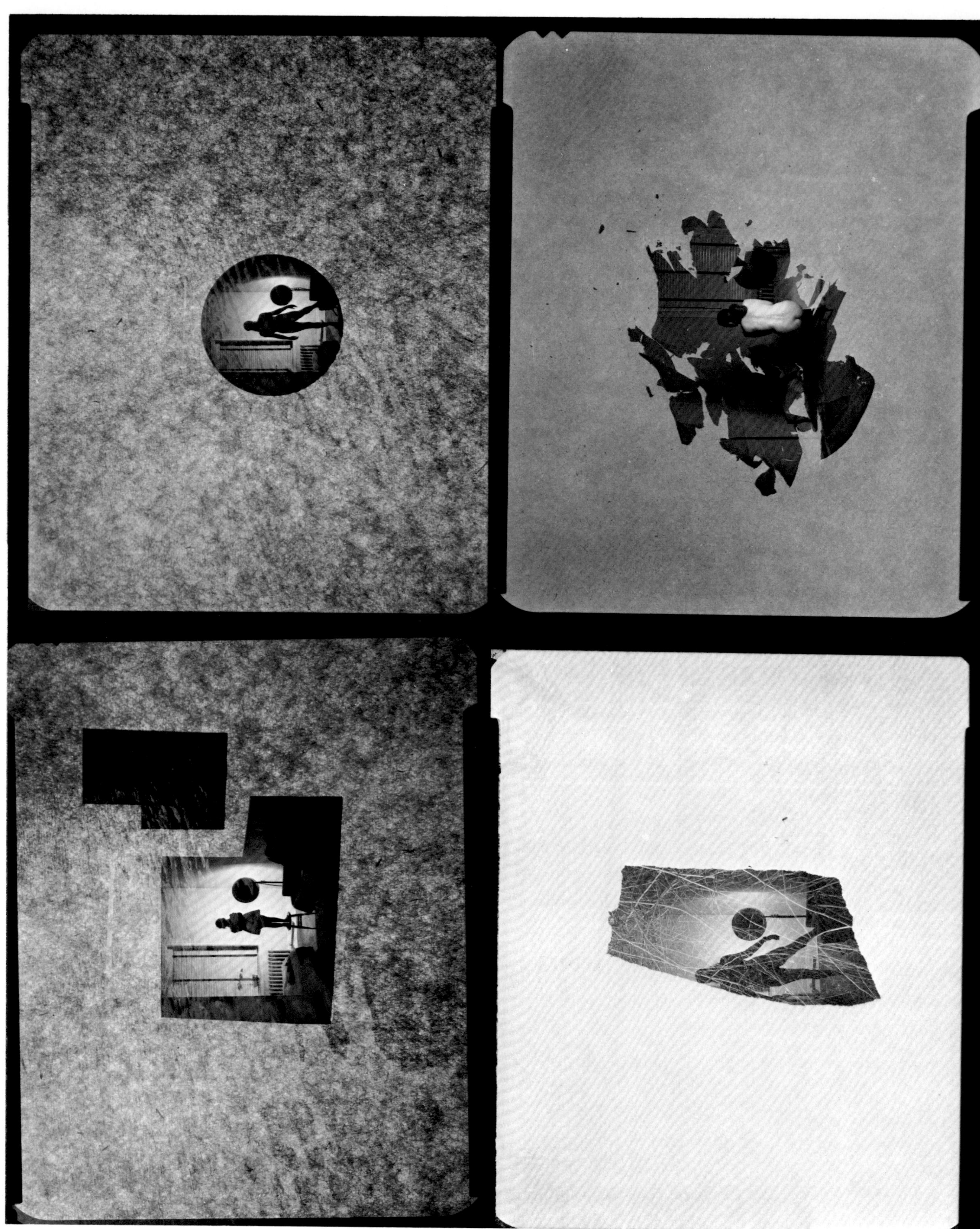

FIGURE 9

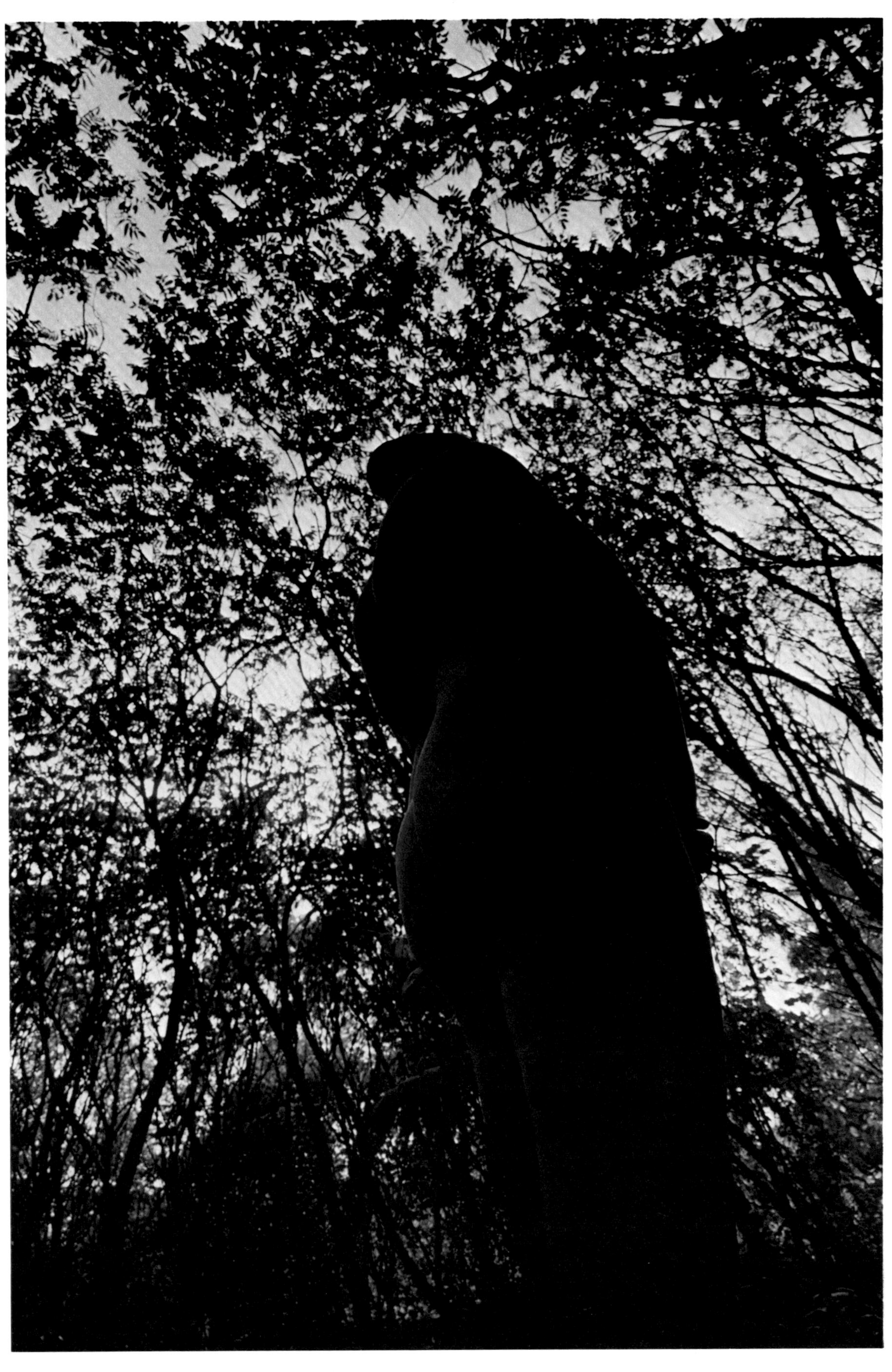

FIGURE 10: ELEANOR, PORT HURON, 1960

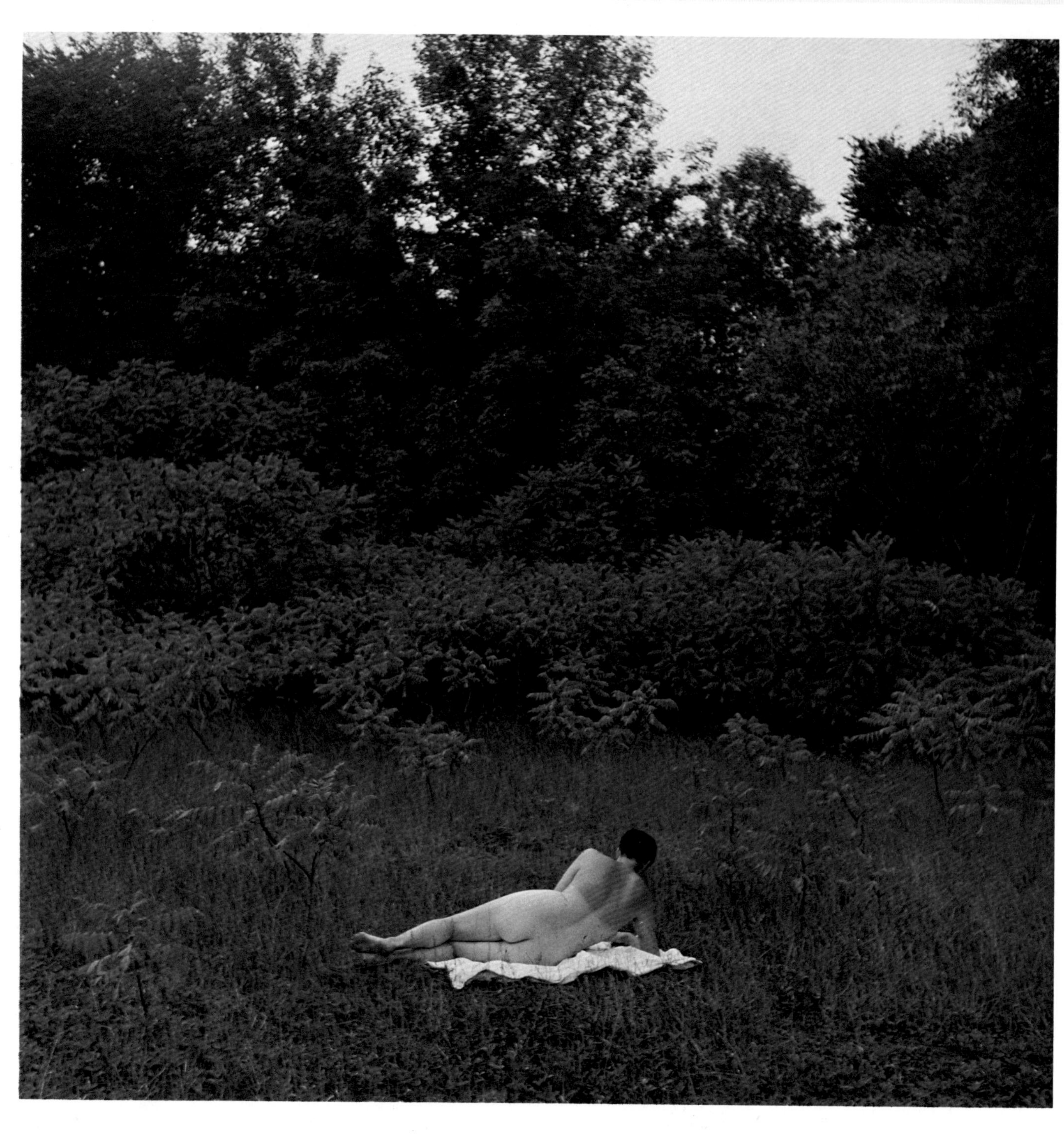

FIGURE 11: ELEANOR, PORT HURON, 1954

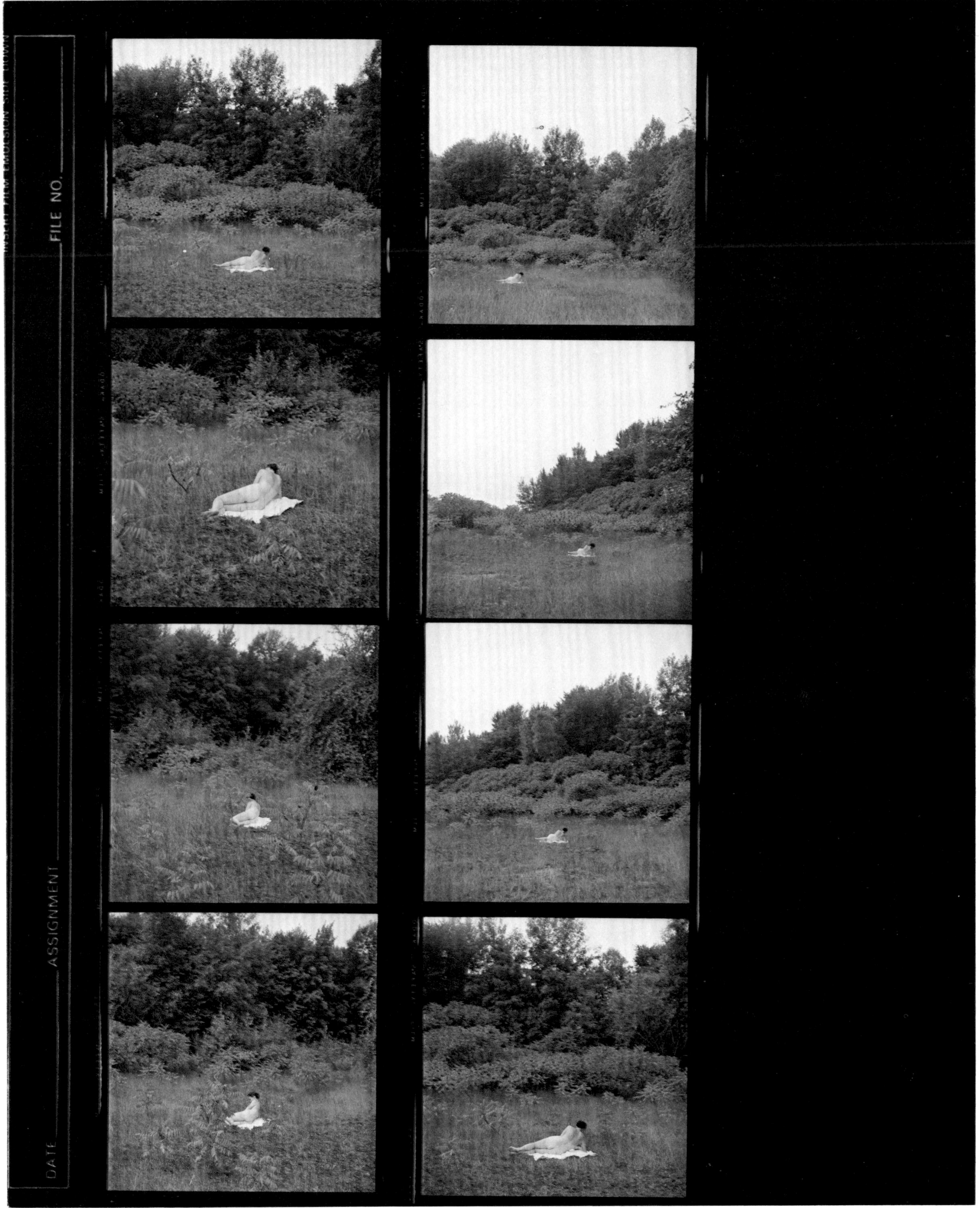

FIGURE 12

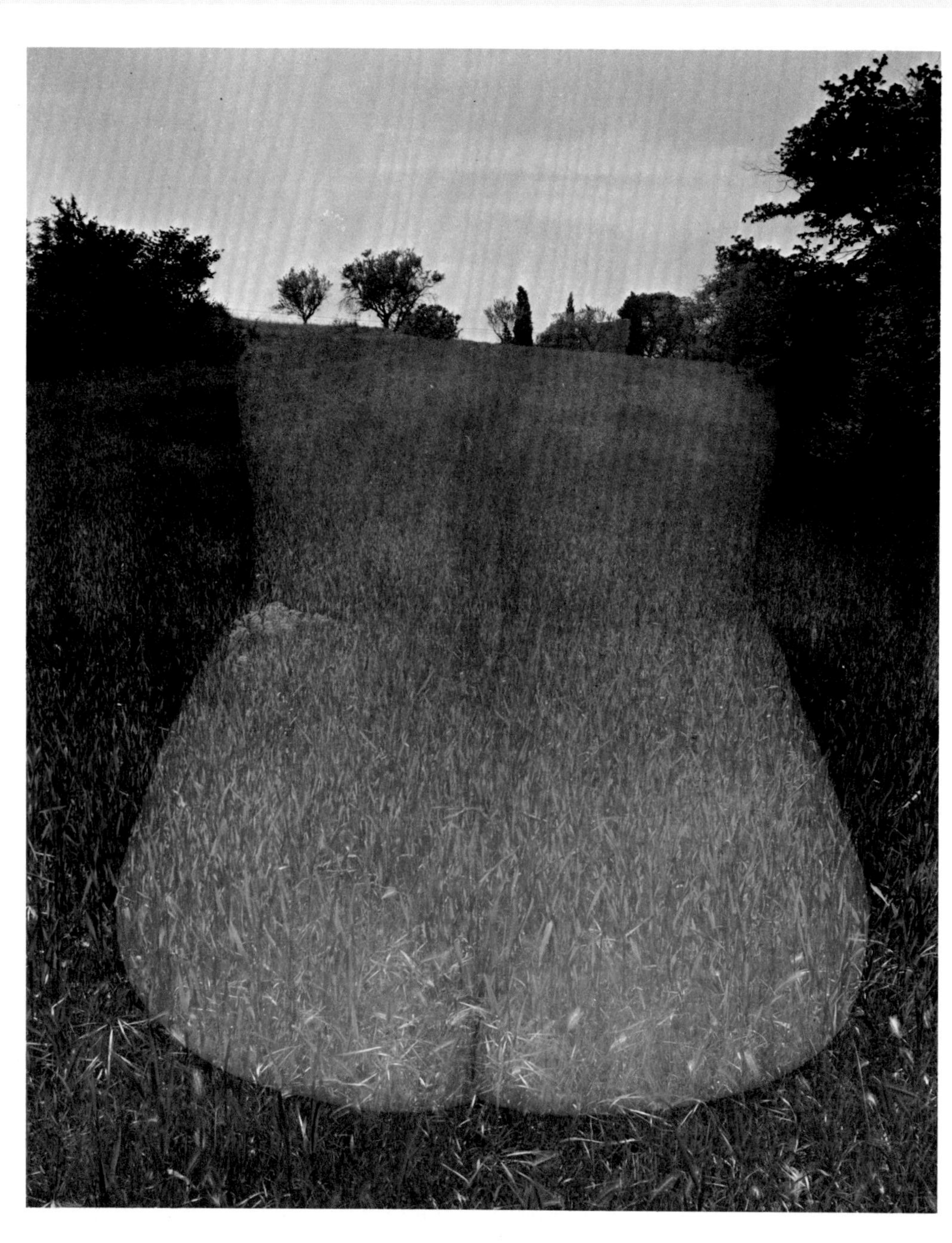

FIGURE 13: ELEANOR. AIX-EN-PROVENCE, 1958

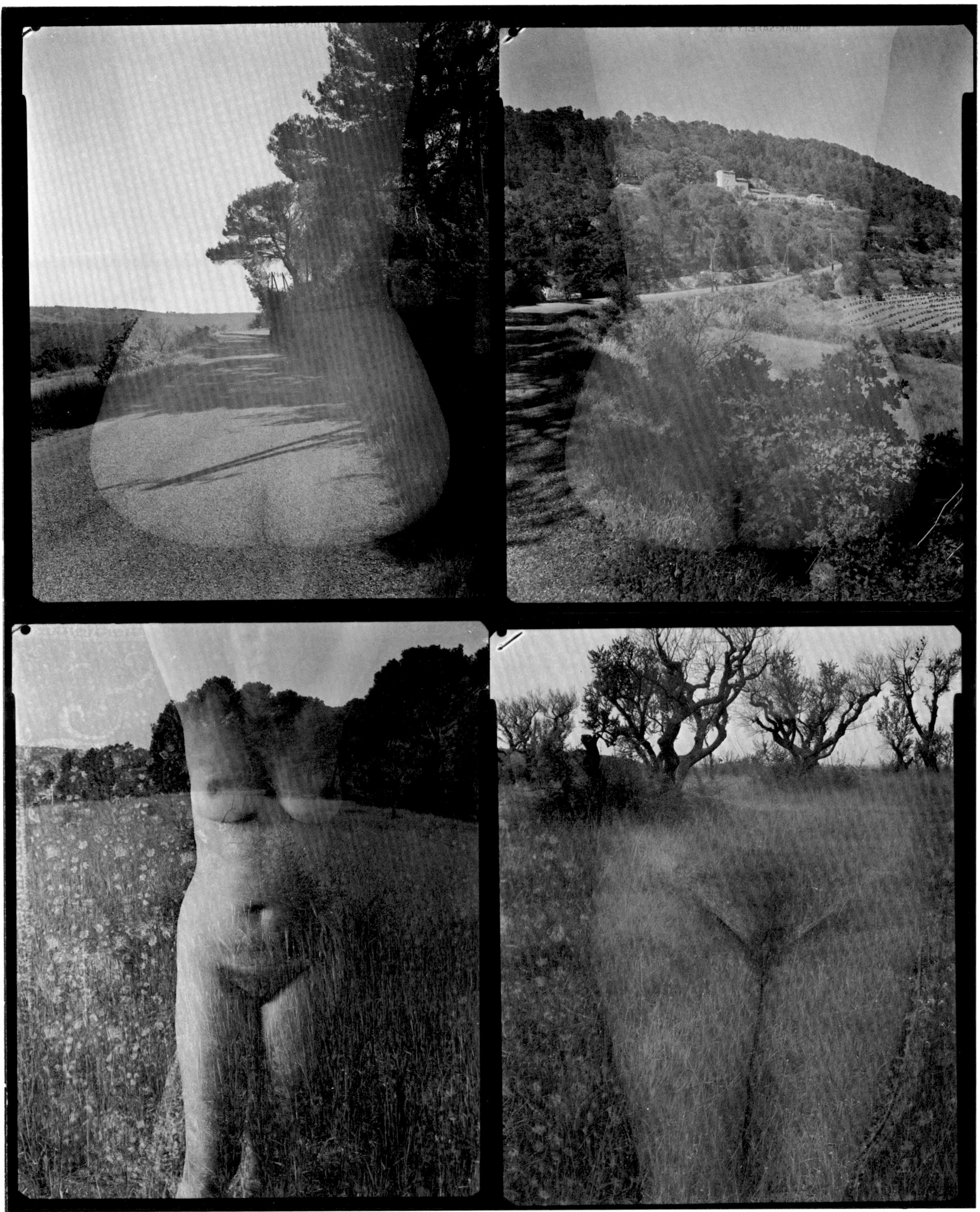

FIGURE 14

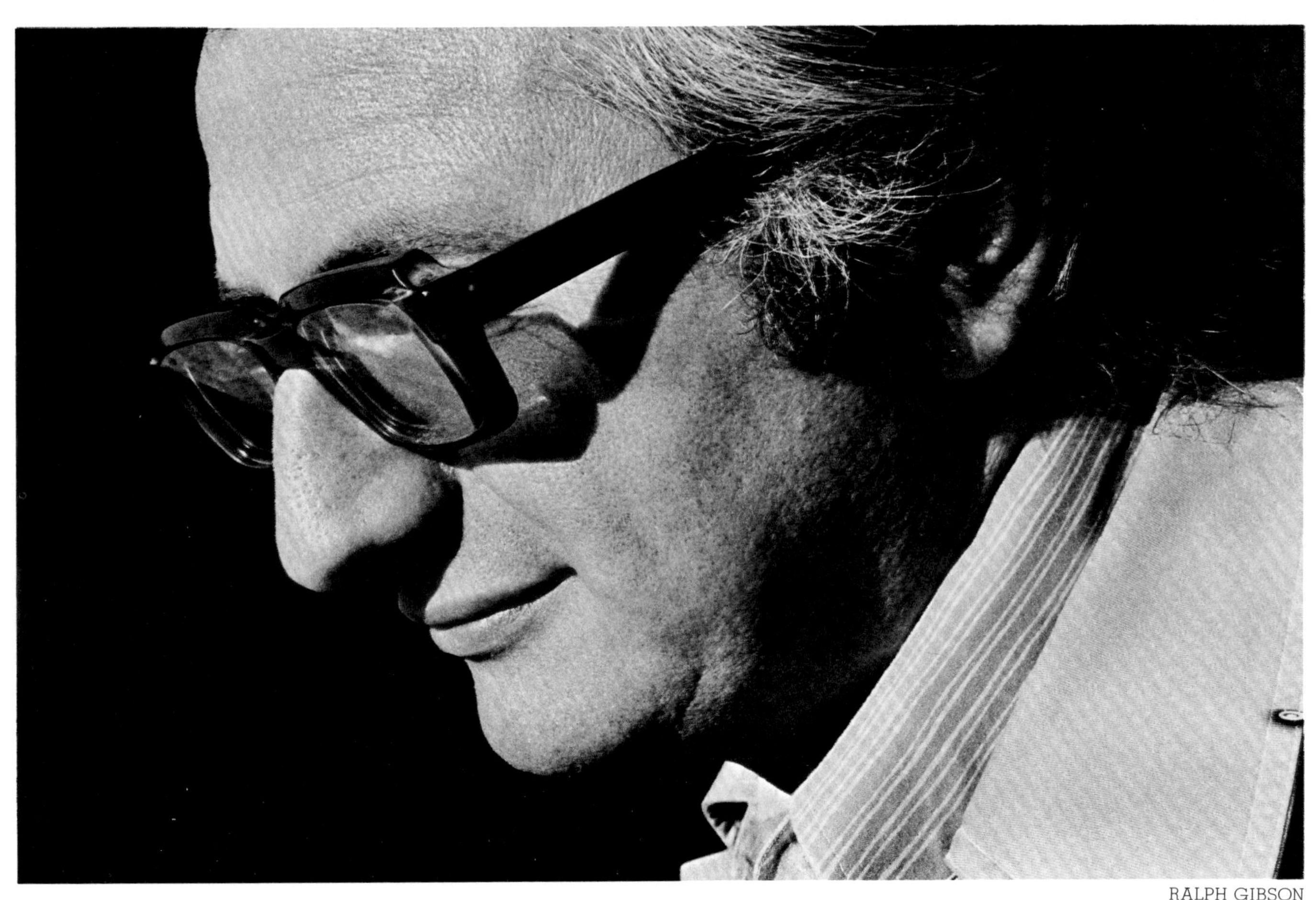

RALPH GIBSON

LUCIEN CLERGUE: "EACH PART OF THE BODY HAS ITS OWN LIFE; EACH WOMAN IS DIFFERENT."

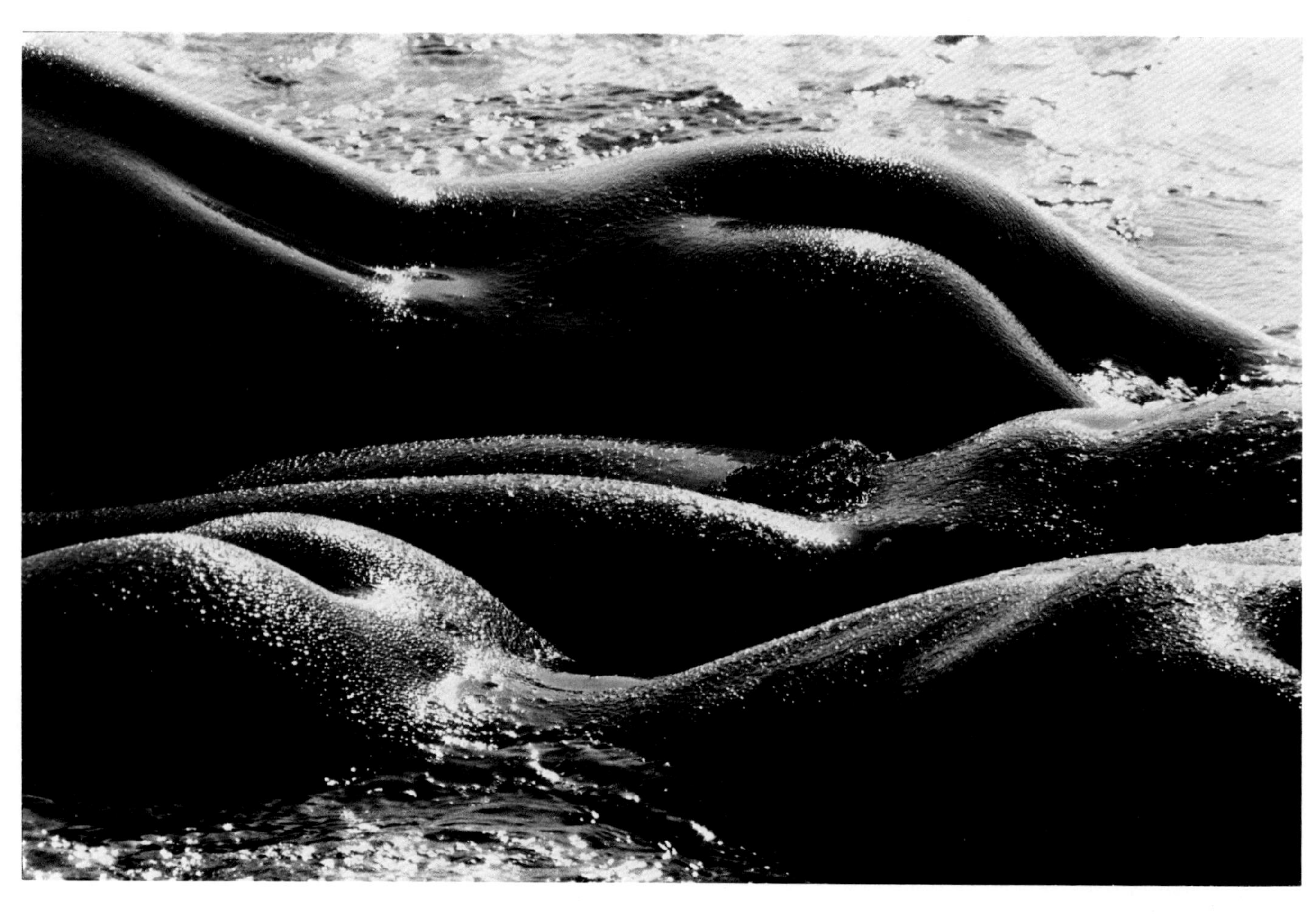

FIGURE 1: LES GÉANTES, 1977

To understand my interest in photographing the nude, you have to know something about my early life and my parents' relationship. Although my mother had been advised by her doctor not to have children, she gave birth to me by Caesarean section in 1934. Evidently, the operation was not well done, and as a child I was given to understand that afterward she and my father could no longer live together as man and wife. Now, my father was a man who liked women very much. To save the marriage and to prevent my father from having a mistress, my mother told him he should go to prostitutes. This is the kind of arrangement that a man does not necessarily like, and my parents were divorced when I was seven years old.

As I was growing up, I heard stories about all this from my mother's lips. You can understand how it was possible for me to feel guilty because I thought I was responsible for my parents' divorce and my mother's unhappiness.

My mother kept a grocery store in Arles, our town in France. When I was 10, the store was destroyed by German bombs. Another woman who had a similar store offered to share it with my mother, and the women in the neighborhood gave her clothing. This was really something, this generosity of the people to each other. The townspeople became a real family because everyone had been ruined in some respect.

As her contribution, my mother was able to give a room in our house to an old blind woman who needed a home. The old woman was very religious. She went to church morning and evening, and asked me to read the Bible to her every night. This religiosity made a deep impression on my mother because she knew that due to her divorce she could not have a funeral in the Roman Catholic Church. I was also upset because I could not believe that God and the Church would not receive my mother. The idea of death was close to us because my mother became extremely ill when I was 14.

She became weaker and weaker over the next few years. Often she fell down, and I had to run in terror to get the doctor or a friend, only to find upon my return that she had forced herself to her feet again to continue working. Eventually, things reached the point where I had to wash her emaciated body in the mornings, and the sight of her poor, thin breasts affected me deeply. It was really her body that formed my concept of a woman's body.

Death was part of my life; my mother spoke to me each night about what would happen to me tomorrow if she died before dawn. When she finally did die, I really lost two people: my mother and this invisible presence of death.

At the hospital, a priest from the Church offered a funeral service to my mother. He meant it as a kindness because he knew our family and was willing to overlook Church law. My mother had thought this would happen and she declined the offer. But two weeks after her death, the priests celebrated a special Mass for her, which only my aunt and I knew about and attended.

Not only did I feel responsible for my mother's divorce, but also for her illness and death. And, always, there had been the problem of the concept she had conveyed of the sexual relationship between men and women: for her it was something evil, something terrible, something which had ruined her life.

All this made me very nervous in my relationships with women. Much later, when I was married and my wife and I were expecting a baby, I was in a complete panic. I was quite sure my wife and baby would die. But the birth of our first child was so easy that I felt safe forever, because I saw that life was something that could come into existence without difficulty.

When my mother died, I was almost 19, and very, very poor. I had been working in a factory where my salary was $80 a month. I had become interested in photography, and on my lunch break I went out into the countryside to take pictures. After my job in the factory was finished for the day, I worked in the darkroom from 6 p.m. to midnight. Each morning I got up at 6 or 7 a.m. to work in the factory again. This schedule completely exhausted me.

I went to the river to watch and then photograph dead animals floating in the water. The first real work I had done in photography was of children in the shadow of an abandoned city. The children never stood in the sun. But one day I discovered the sun on the bodies of the animals. To me, the sun meant life and in this way death and life were brought together.

Even before my mother's death, I decided to open myself to life, to try photographing the nude. Frankly, this was just a pretext to see a woman naked. I asked prostitutes to model for me, but when you ask a prostitute if you can photograph her, she says, "What do you think I am?" This made a problem.

I asked my first girlfriend to pose for me. We tried to create a Mediterranean scene in my home with fishermen's nets. Of course, this was very artificial, and it didn't work. But I tried to understand about light and the human body. I didn't use flash or electricity. I tried candles, which create a light that is very beautiful because it is a moving light. We also tried photographs on the beach, but they didn't come out very well. These and other nudes were done around 1952.

It was not until 1956 that I did my first nude in the sea. When I made this photograph, I felt totally free and I understood the relationship between me and the past. I would say that my nudes in the sea represent an affirmation of life, a reaching out to beauty and health. I took the first of these photographs to my family doctor, to whom I had been going to talk about all the things that troubled me. He looked at it and said, "Now you are well. You don't need me anymore."

I had had the great good fortune to meet Pablo Picasso the year before, and to show him my work. I returned to him with this first nude in the sea. He was astonished and said, "You did this? I can hardly believe it. Someone could cut a piece from a Velázquez canvas and place it next to your photograph, and it would not be possible to say, 'This is Clergue, this is Velázquez.'"

This was a great compliment to someone only 22 and just starting out.

For over 20 years I have continued photographing the nude in the sea. When I think of these pictures I am reminded of the statue of the Venus of Arles; I saw it many times in my childhood. In my work I have sought to photograph the living Venus rising out of the water.

The photograph LES GÉANTES (Figure 1) was made in the summer of 1977. The idea was to group three nudes as closely together as possible in the water. The main secret of the sea in terms of the nude is to use the water to redesign the bodies of the women. With a very slender woman, the nudes don't work because the body is swallowed up by the water. This is why a woman with a full figure looks best in the sea. She has enough flesh to retain a little water on the surface and to be "restructured."

LES GÉANTES was photographed at 5 p.m. because I wanted strong backlighting. I wanted to place the women absolutely against the sun for maximum brilliance of lighting on the water. I planned to print on sensitized aluminum sheets, rather than conventional photo paper. Aluminum sheets can make an image look quite dark, so it was important to get this brilliance.

The camera I have used for many years is the 35mm Minolta. Earlier in my career I tried several different cameras, including the 2¼ x 2¼ Rolleiflex, but the Minolta has worked the best for me. I like using the 35mm with the nudes because it's so easy to move around with and the possibilities for lenses are fantastic. It is less intimidating to the models to see a smaller camera.

For the nudes in the sea, I need a long lens rather than a wide angle because the subjects are usually far away. For LES GÉANTES I used a 400mm lens mounted on a tripod on top of my car on the beach. There were unusual problems involved here: I had to move the car in relation to the women, and I had to call to them over the sound of the sea to give instructions. There was the additional problem of getting a good focus on all three women. I used a small aperture, *f*/32, at 1/125th or 1/60th of a second.

To determine film exposure, I always use the built-in light meter of my Minolta, which is very good. I can always decide on the basis of experience whether or not to open up or close down a stop or two.

My film is usually Ilford FP4 rated at an exposure index of 200. Only occasionally do I need Ilford HP5 rated at 400 ASA for use indoors. I like Ilford products in general and I am pleased with the fine grain of their film.

As you are looking at my photographs, you must bear in mind that I am steeped in mythology and that I have the mentality of what I call the Mediterranean man. The evolution of my work with the nude reflects this mentality. First, I placed the goddess Venus in the sea. In time she rose from the waves and went to the forest to become Eve. Finally, in my most recent work, this goddess/human being arrived in the city to oversee civilization.

I did not think this out consciously beforehand. I believe that it is like the movements of a sonata written in three parts. This rhythm of three is important in my life. It is something I cannot escape.

The idea for the series on the nude in the forest came to me in 1970. There was a fire in a forest where my family and I spent our vacations. I was not at our house that day. I was in Nice, where, coincidentally, there was also a fire. My wife and children were in the forest fire, but they managed to escape. It was a terrible day. All the roads were blocked and my family and I could not rejoin each other. I spoke with a friend on the phone who said, "Don't worry, your family is safe."

Then I talked by phone with my wife, who said, "We are in a hotel. We are protected."

The day after, I picked my family up and we went to see the ruins. Our house was all right, but the forest was destroyed and still smoking.

I wanted to show my daughters that life can begin again, even in the ruins. We decided to return in two days with models to take photographs.

There is a different set of problems to be considered in working with the nude in the forest. With the nude in the sea, the water itself redesigns the woman's body. In the forest the only thing that can act on the woman's body is light and shadow.

In the burnt forest there was a chance to work without the darkness caused by the leaves on the trees. This was a special opportunity, a mysterious gift. I had the idea that the woman would become the tree, as in the sea she became one with the water. And, of course, there is no doubt that the tree itself can be seen as a phallic symbol. This is the first introduction of this motif in my work (Figure 2).

For both the nudes in the forest and in the city I have preferred to use the 17mm lens because I want to work close to the figure most of the time. Occasionally I need the 28mm or the 50mm macro. (This particular image in the forest is done with the 50mm macro.) Only rarely do I use an 85mm lens to bring the background closer.

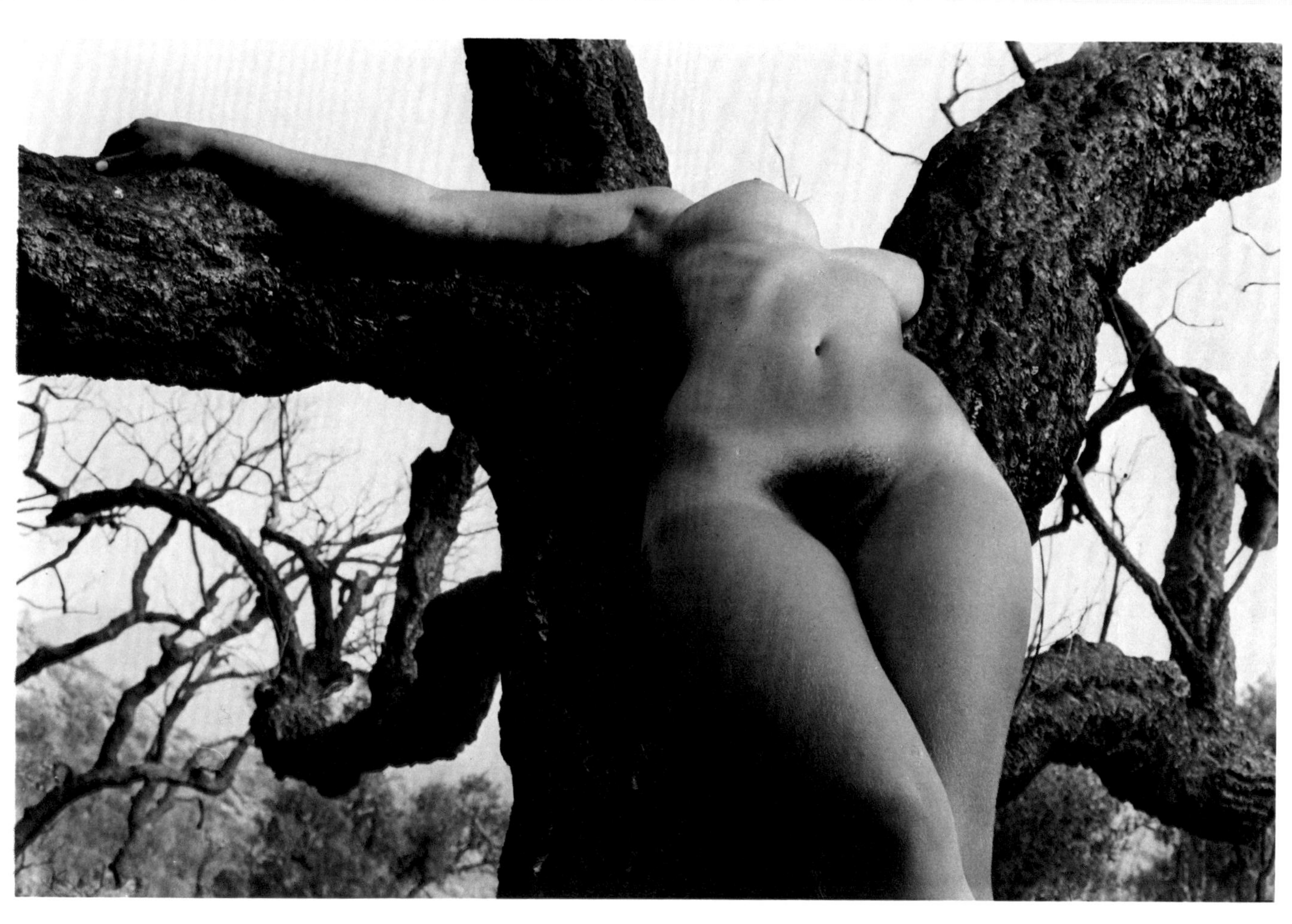

FIGURE 2: NU DE LA FORÊT, 1973

The woman in the burnt forest has a small body. I have found that a slender figure works best with the trees. I think it's interesting to comment on the proportions of a smaller woman. The relationship between the navel, the pubic area and the breasts is in better balance with the smaller woman. With a tall woman there is too much distance between these areas.

The female body is formed in triangles and circles. I became very aware of this in the 1950s when I discovered the nudes of Edward Weston. His nude seated in a doorway, NUDE, 1936, is one of the greatest works in the history of art. It is still as fresh and modern as it was in the 1930s.

I have found in working with the nude that the process of creation is something that cannot be predicted. Of course, you have to have discipline to organize the cameras, the locations, the models and the lighting. But, in the middle of all this, you have to be responsive to what the model brings you. The models are not objects. They are real people, who, with a single gesture, can convey a special feeling. These women become my friends and we cooperate in the making of the photographs. I don't like to work with professional models. It makes me nervous because I have to be watching the clock very carefully, and this interferes with my relationship with the women.

With the nude in the forest it is possible to point out some of the problems concerning skin tone. There are models who are sunburned; there are pale blondes; there are brunettes and redheads. In the making of the print, these variations must be dealt with. Even the volume of the breasts affects the way the light falls on the skin. Almost invariably you must mask certain areas and/or burn in other areas.

Occasionally I encounter that rare woman who brings her own light from the inside. This is something to celebrate. The inner light of the woman and the outer light of the sun mix together and make a brilliant glow on the skin.

There is one other aspect to consider about the skin. It is not possible to photograph a model who is cold. She gets goosebumps and this introduces another element into the picture. People look at the image and notice immediately what has happened.

In 1975 I began my series on the urban nude. I think of the sequence of the nudes at Les Baux as the first step in this body of work. I first saw the walls of Les Baux in 1959 when I took six weeks off from working in the factory to be a photographer's assistant on Jean Cocteau's movie, "Le Testament d'Orphée." Les Baux is a very strange and beautiful place with enormous white walls on which all sorts of words have been written and drawings made.

Almost 20 years later I took a group of models, both female and male, to this location and tried photographing them against the wall. It was very difficult to work here because I realized that everyone was standing on the same level, and the photographs were going to be too much like still lifes. At a certain point one of the models, Deborah, had the idea of starting to climb the stone. I applauded and said, "You have found a way. You've discovered something and now I know what to do." Then I began photographing with a 100mm lens (Figure 3).

For me, the stones represent the building blocks of the city. Perhaps even my own house was built from the stone of Les Baux. I felt that in photographing the nude here I was going back to the very origins of the concept of the city. I also wanted to place the people in the midst of the names on the wall. To me, it was as if these were the names of the people who were standing there, and this created a connection between the human figure and the written word.

In MONTPARNASSE, PARIS, 1975 (Figure 4) I used a mirror, which has reflective properties similar to those of water. Since I have been photographing in buildings I have experimented with both mirrors and glass. I think of reflections as elements of a dream state. I have photographed the reflections in the marshes of the Camargue; this is the dream of nature. The photographer can create a dream in another context. He can organize it himself or he can use what is happening before his eyes.

I used the 17mm Minolta lens here, as with all the nudes reproduced in this article. If you hold this lens parallel to your subject matter, you can avoid distortion and achieve fantastic depth of field. For my indoor work I prefer to set the lens at *f*/16 and then adjust the shutter speed accordingly. For this photograph I used a tripod, and the shutter speed was 1 second with HP5 film rated at 400 ASA. During printing I had to dodge the area of the mirror.

CAROLL IN CHICAGO, 1976 (Figure 5) was photographed in a very interesting old building. The windows overlooked a building that appeared to be a church or a convent. I was interested in putting the woman in an intimate space which in turn overlooked an enormous space. I also liked this idea of the coming together of the woman and the church. It was such a pleasure to use the 17mm lens here. In this space and at this angle it created a feeling of three dimensionality that I love.

DENISE ON THE LAKE, 1976 (Figure 6) was photographed from the 20th floor of a building just near the lake in Chicago. It is the idea of the woman as a goddess looking with serenity on our busy world. The civilization around her is not really important. A group of automobiles is below her in the street, but they are meaningless compared to her. She is truth; she is happiness; she is perfection.

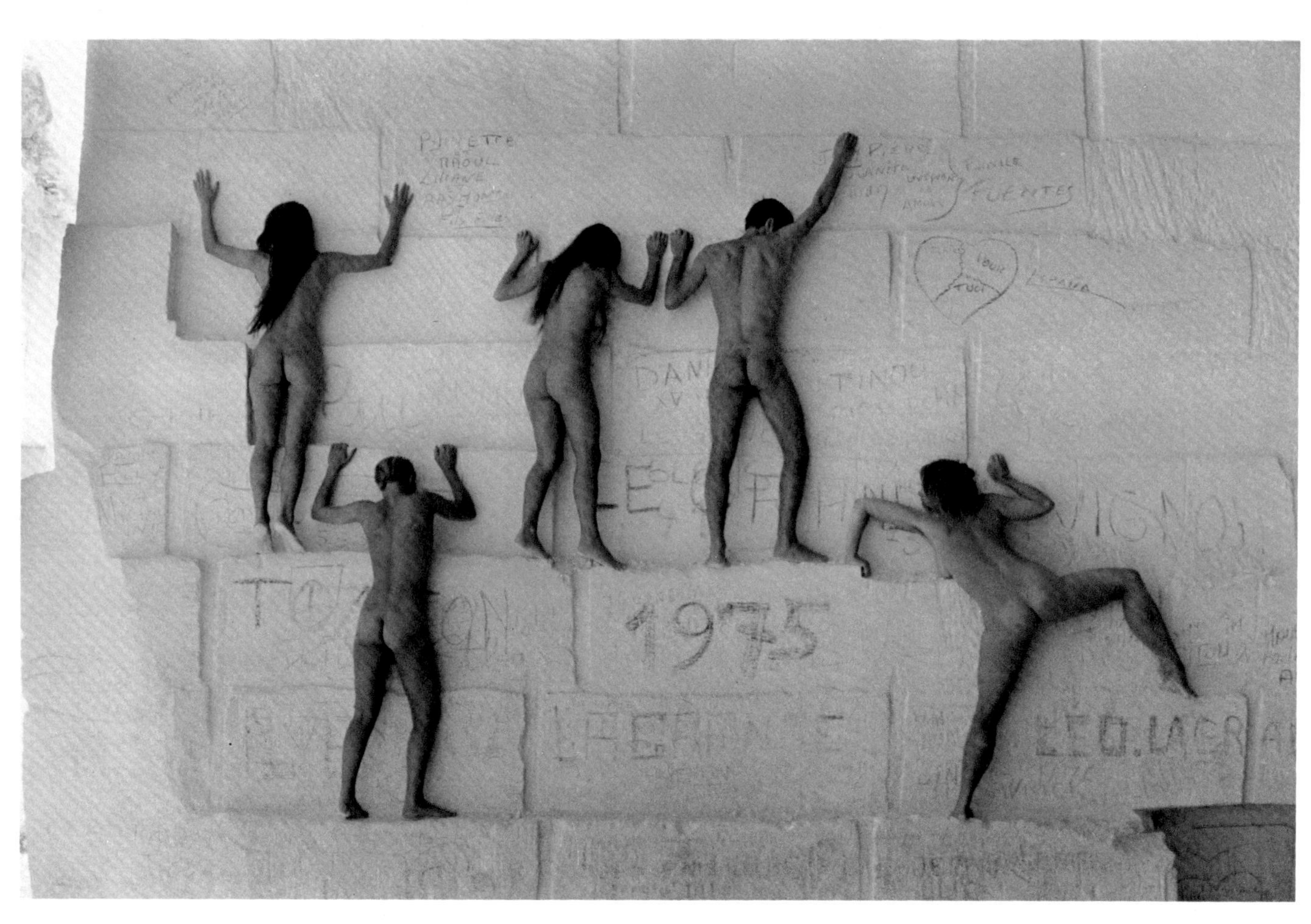

FIGURE 3: LES BAUX, 1975

When I made NIGHT IN NEW YORK, 1977 (Figure 7) I had just arrived in New York on a visit and was staying in the apartment of a friend of mine on 51st Street. As I was making phone calls to set up appointments, I looked up at the windows in the apartment and I realized that I wanted to make a photograph with a black model against the city buildings. One of the things I love in this picture is the difference in size between the three people at the stop light below in the street, and the fabulous woman the size of the city. The concept of the urban nude is to make the woman equivalent to the size of the city.

SELF-PORTRAIT IN TUCSON III, 1977 (Figure 8) was made in the desert of Arizona. I called a friend and asked him to find a model and we all worked in the bright sunlight. Because of the hard sun, my shadow was everywhere and I did a lot of self-portraits. In this photograph I introduced my leg into the frame. The image can be considered in two senses. Of course, it is a self-portrait, and, at the same time, it conveys the idea of the leg as a male sexual symbol.

I was quite fascinated by the male model in FRED AT LA DÉFENSE, PARIS, 1978 (Figure 9) because I had the feeling of him that he was androgynous. I decided to use him as a model because I knew he would help me break a personal taboo against photographing men. I remember that in 1956 or '57 I showed my work to Jean Cocteau and he said, "Why don't you try photographing the male nude? It would be as nice as photographing the female."

So I decided to try. I took a man to the beach, a fellow with a good physique, and we tried to work. But male genitals floating in the water are a disaster. We were collapsing with laughter and we couldn't continue the session.

Later I saw Picasso and I told him what Cocteau had suggested. Picasso thought it was absurd. "He said that? I hope you didn't do it."

I said, "Well, yes, I did. But you're right. It was impossible!"

In 1977 I told myself that this was a ridiculous taboo. A man has as interesting a body as a woman, and this can be seen in the ancient Greek and Roman sculptures. I photographed Fred's body in relation to a woman's body, and the result proved to be quite worthwhile.

When I develop my film, I use a product called Promicrol, manufactured by May and Baker in London. This developer has produced a very fine grain and a good skin tone for me. I develop by inspection under a green safelight.

For many years I used Lumière Élysée paper. Later, after Lumière was bought by Ilford, I worked with Ilfobrom. The paper size I preferred for a long time was 20 x 24. I felt this scale was right for my images. Also, I believed that if European art collectors were to become seriously interested in photography, the prints had to be the same size as large etchings and lithographs.

I used to ferrotype my prints by drying them emulsion side down on a mirror to get a brilliant glossy surface. But over the years the prints have become progressively more prone to damage when I remove them from the mirror. I don't know why this is. The problem of damage was a major consideration in my decision to stop ferrotyping.

Within the last year and a half I have started to use a new Ilford paper called Galerie, in 11 x 14. This paper is still not available in the United States, but it is scheduled to appear in 1979.

The story behind Ilford Galerie paper is quite interesting. Three years ago at the photographic workshop in Arles a group of photographers signed a petition to paper manufacturers. We stated that we were opposed to this terrible RC paper, and we wanted to be able to continue buying real paper. Jean Dieuzaide of Toulouse started to build a symposium around this problem. We invited Kodak, Ilford, Agfa and Guilleminot to join us for a real talk.

At one point during the manufacturers' discussion with the group of 150 photographers, the representative from Ilford said, "Look, we are ready to study a new paper. We would like to make inquiries through you about what kind of paper you want: weight, tonality, quantity of silver, etc." Ilford did exactly that. They made studies and last summer they sent us at Arles some samples of a new paper called Galerie. Now I am printing exclusively on this paper for my exhibitions.

Ilford Galerie comes in three grades: No. 1 is soft; No. 2 is normal; and No. 3 is hard.

Recently I had a conversation about this paper when I delivered some prints to a gallery for exhibition. I was talking with the young fellows who were overmatting my photographs, and I commented on the excellent quality of another photographer's prints.

"Oh," they said, "You are modest."

"What do you mean?"

"We have worked with the other photographer's prints and we can tell you that yours are better. Yours are richer, with more detail in the blacks."

I did not take this as a personal compliment. I knew that it was a remark on the quality of this new paper.

My paper developer is Ilford PQ Universal which comes in easy-to-mix liquid form. Previously I had used Kodak Dektol, but it was inconvenient for me to mix powdered chemicals. I am not really involved in chemicals and formulae. There is a balance between technical matters and creation, and the individual must find what works best for him.

My hypo is Ilford Hypam. Galerie paper is supposed to remain in the hypo only 30 seconds. The idea is to allow as little hypo as possible to

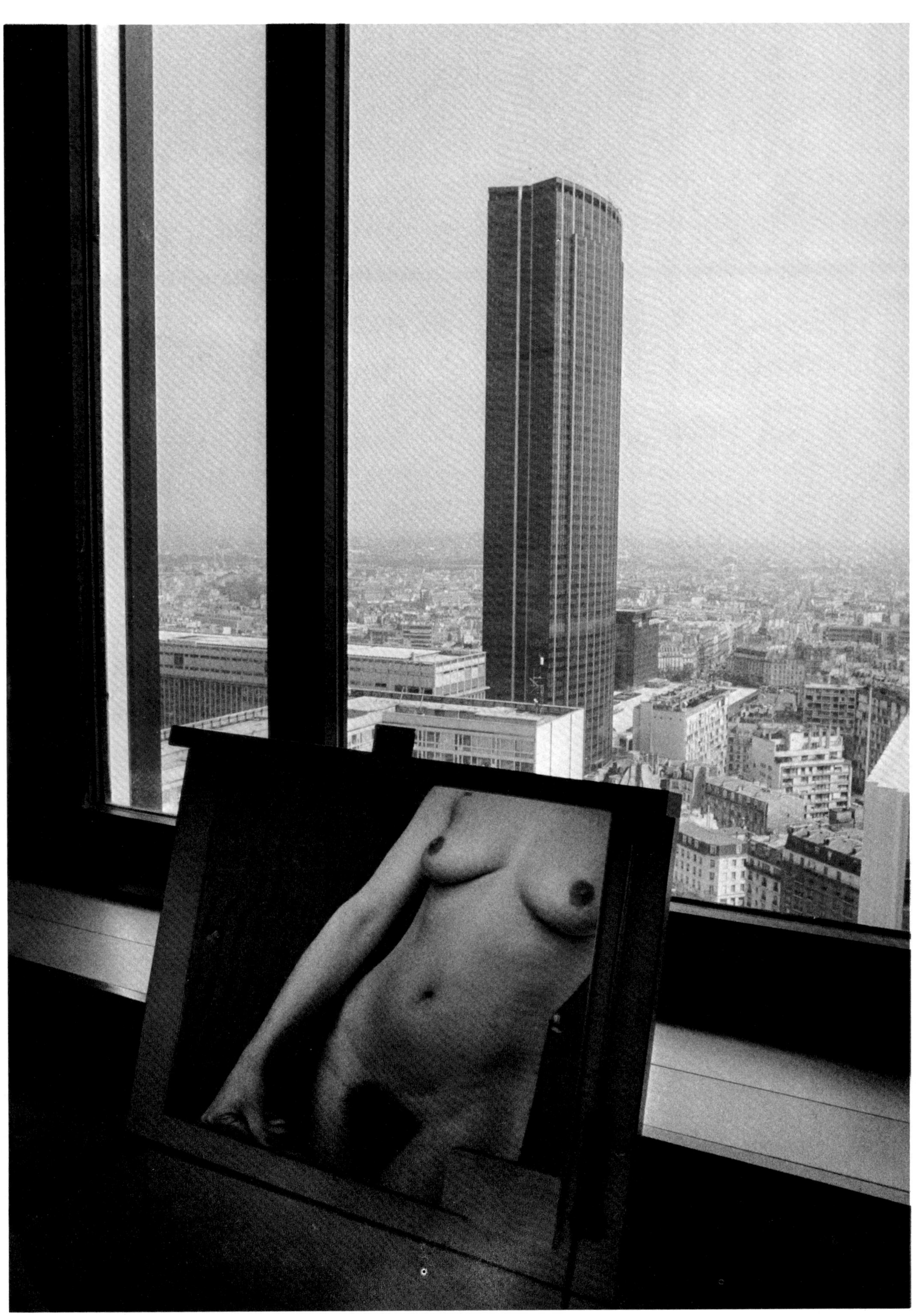

FIGURE 4: MONTPARNASSE, PARIS, 1975

soak into the fiber base of the paper. This is important to the archival permanence of the print. After the print is fixed, it goes into hypo eliminator. Ilford is preparing a new hypo eliminator for Galerie.

After the print is washed, I place it emulsion side up on a flat glass or mirror. Because I am very concerned about archival matters I have a unique system of drying my prints. I don't squeegee a print or wipe off the excess water with my hand because I prefer to handle the print as little as possible. Instead, I tape down the four sides of the photograph with a tape backed by gum. The next morning, after the print has dried, I remove the tape. The prints tend to curl a little when they are dried this way but it doesn't bother me. I don't drymount the prints and I never flatten them in a heated drymount press.

I would say that many of the changes in my technique have been brought about by contact with other photographers, particularly American photographers. I feel that I must be open to new ideas about technical matters, just as I must be open to new possibilities about how to photograph the nude.

In terms of my learning experiences about the nude, I would say that many of my most important lessons have been derived from sculpture. Laurens, Renoir, Maillol, Lipchitz and Rodin are among those whose sculptures have helped me. There is a reason why sculpture is so important to the photographer of the nude: it teaches you about the possibilities for restructuring the human body. You can draw your hand up the leg; you can place your hand on the hollow of the back. Suddenly you understand about balance. You touch the breast and the buttocks. And through this tactile relationship to the sculpture you come to a knowledge of volume. Why did the sculptor place the leg in a certain position? Why is the statue's hand outstretched in a certain gesture? These questions have had a great influence on me.

I love the idea of rebuilding the human body. I think my own conceptual approach to this problem has been to start with the center of the body, the navel, and to work outward in triangles and circles. Each part of the body has its own life; each woman is different.

Seeing how the human body works is a kind of happiness for me. When I am photographing the nude I am completely content. It is never work. Both the model and I may be exhausted at the end of a picture-taking session, but it's a good kind of exhaustion.

Each time I photograph the nude, I try to learn from mistakes made in the past. Sometimes when I look back at work, I think, "I missed something here." It is not until the photographer himself has more maturity that he can understand how to improve his work.

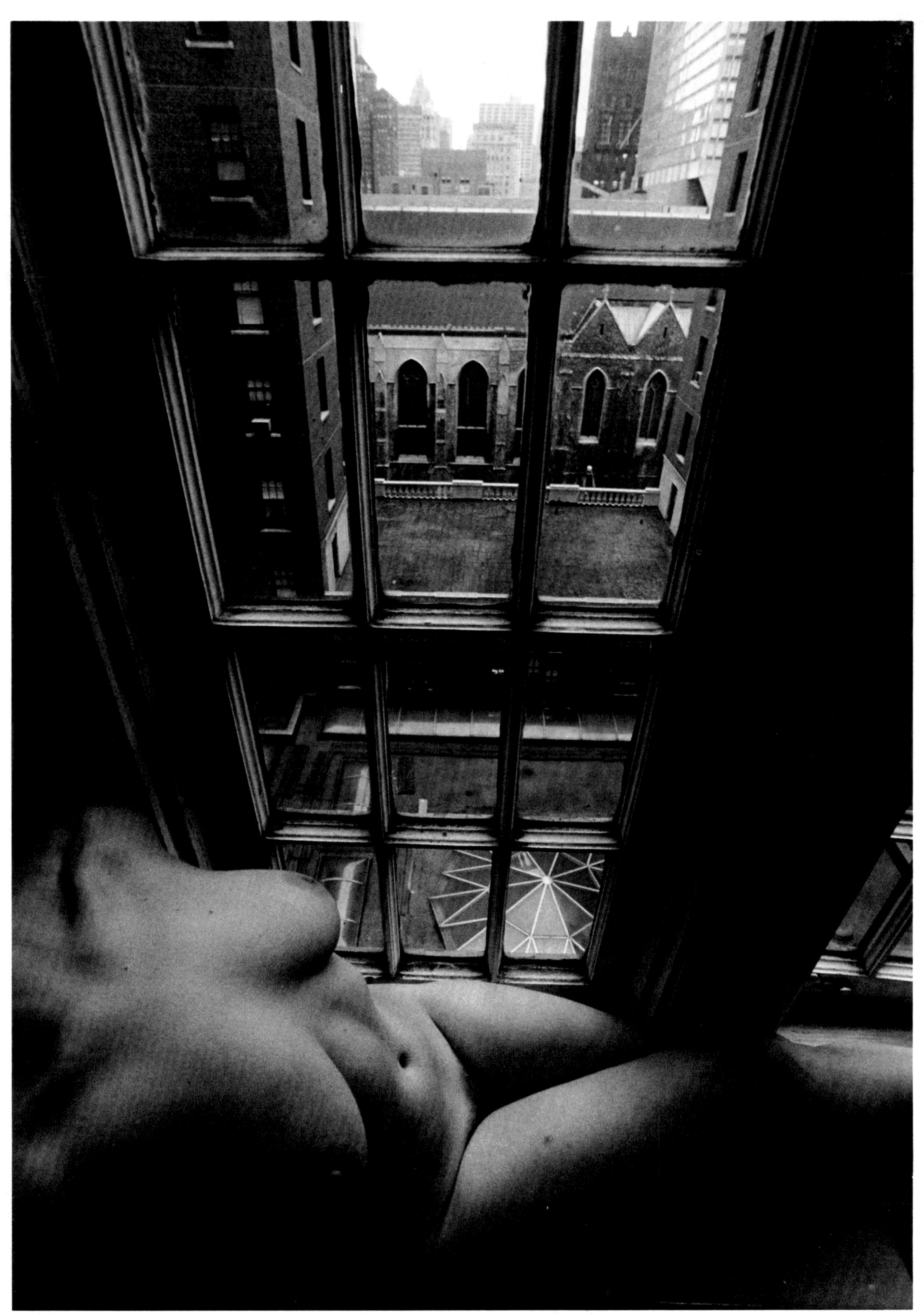

FIGURE 5: CAROLL IN CHICAGO, 1976

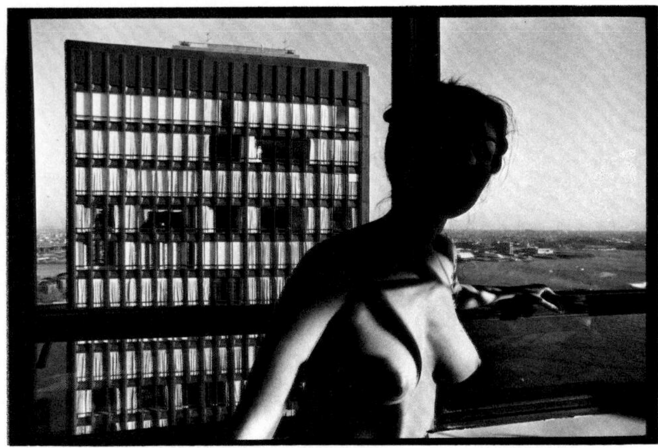

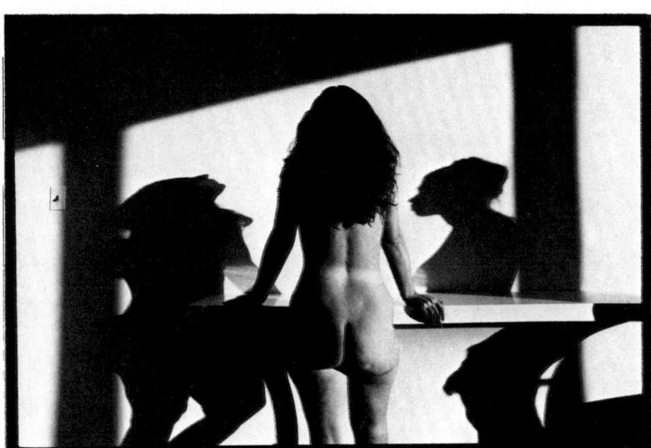

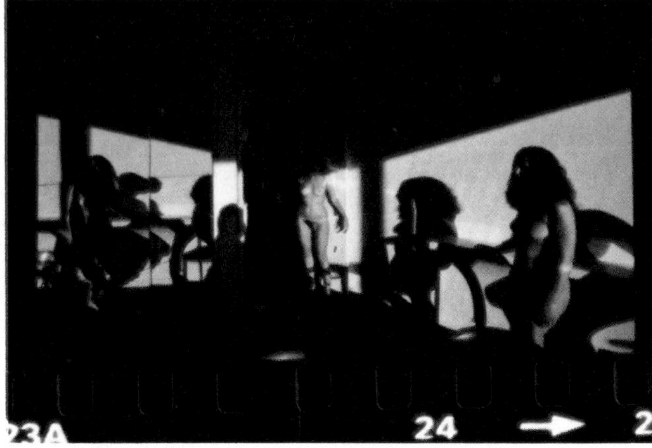

Contact Sheet No. 1

Frames No. 2 through 15 show the relationship of the woman to the building behind her. This sequence looks very interesting to me. We have the square of the building, the cross of the window dividers, and the circular shape of the woman's breasts. The shadows of the window dividers begin to form different patterns on the woman's body. The dividers are themselves straight, but they form curves on her breasts and stomach. Offhand, I would say that frames No. 4 and 5 work very well, but I will have to enlarge the negatives to find the one in which the face and eyes show up best. Frames No. 14 and 15 also interest me because of the very exaggerated distortion that you can get from the 17mm lens. I used the 17mm lens in all these sessions in New York because I wanted to include the woman, the apartment and the city in the photographs. Frame No. 14 appears to be the better exposure.

The next sequence runs from frames No. 16 to 27, and I think it will be fantastic because it is a visual redesign of the inside of the apartment. There were two mirrored doors and I opened them a little. There are two women in the photographs, and the shadow of a third shows although you cannot see her. I am beginning to work with the shadows of the women here. I haven't worked much with shadow in the urban nude series; I really began to discover it in this apartment. In the summer, shadows seem to pass more quickly than in wintertime. This set of photographs was done in winter, so I have a lot of time to experiment. It is possible that Nos. 19 and 24 have the most interesting shadows and the best exposure.

I think I will simply forget about Nos. 28 through 31. I made a mistake here in the positioning of the woman's body, and the relationships to the apartment and between the women don't work.

Of Nos. 32 through 38, I will probably use No. 36. In this one, the woman's body and the shadows of the other two models make a very good triple, and the shadows of the building are quite good.

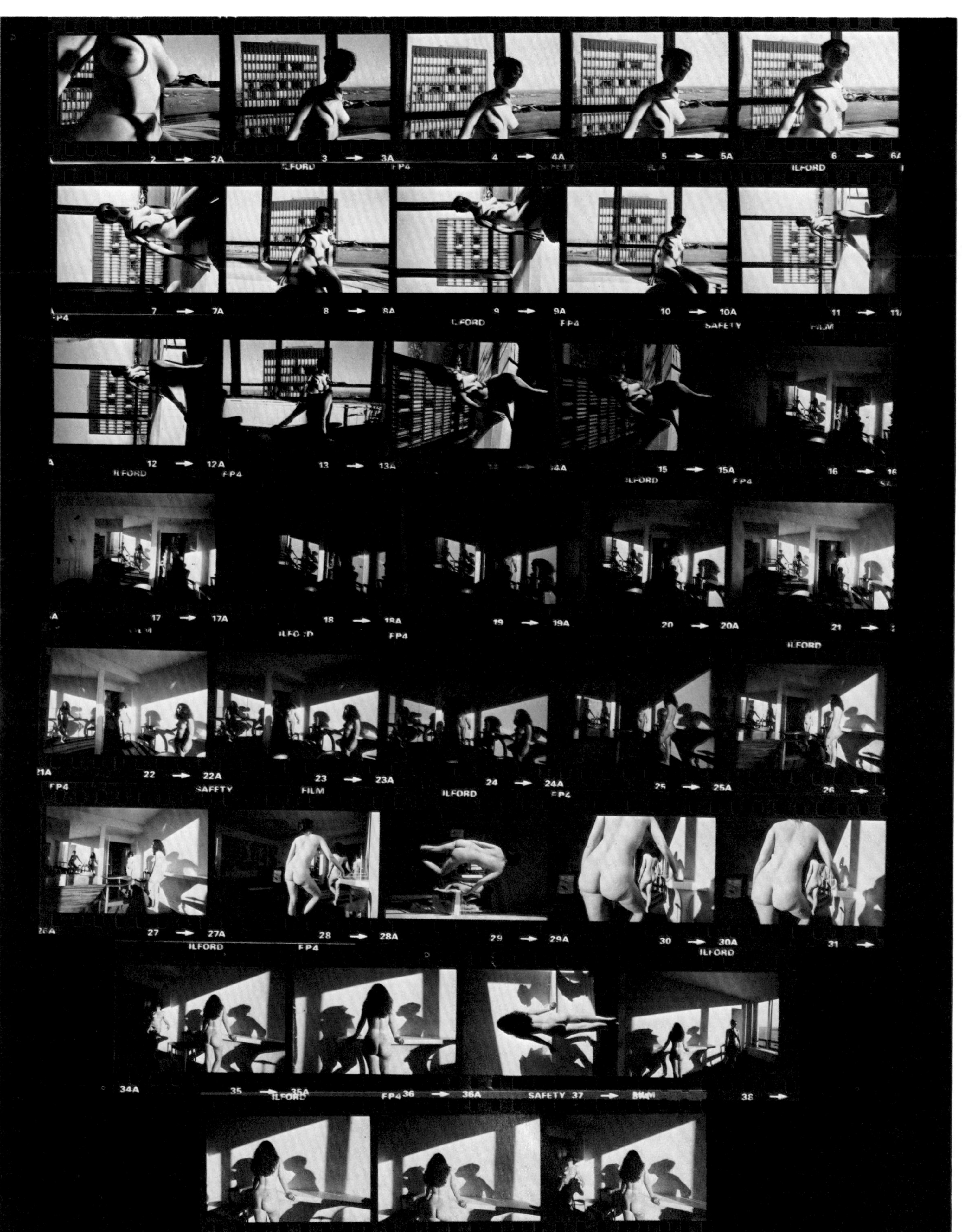

NUS DE LA VILLE, NEW YORK, 1979

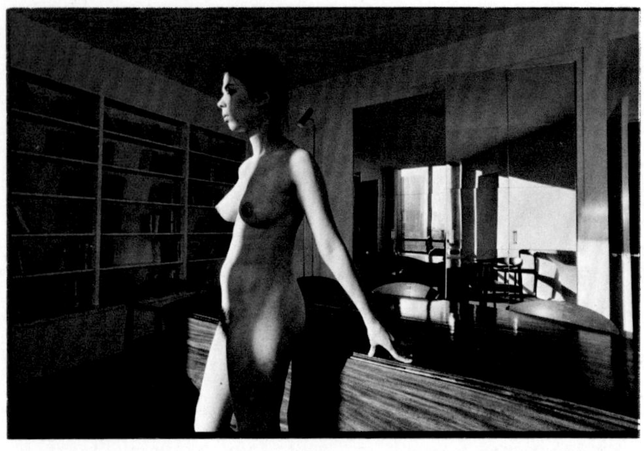

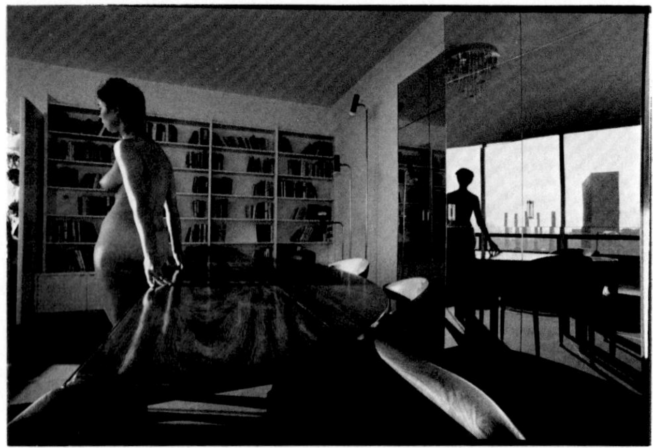

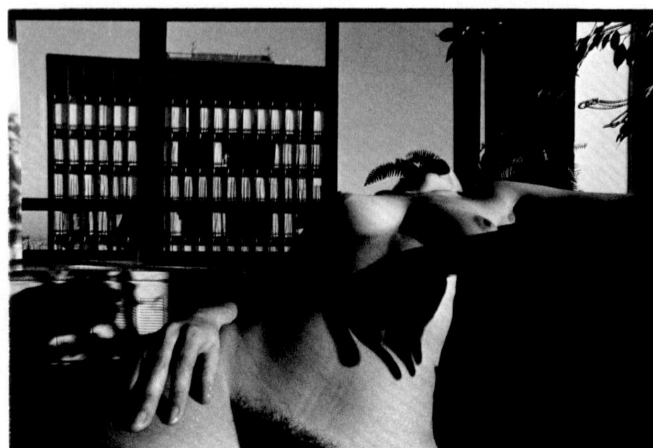

Contact Sheet No. 2

The object of frames No. 1 through 12 is to try to divide the body into two parts, placing one part in the shadow and one in the sun. I think that there is an element of cubism showing up here in my work. The extreme difference in lighting on the two sides of the body will make these frames difficult to print. Probably I should select No. 7 because I like the way the body and the light work together in it. Perhaps No. 12 will also be good. Here you have relationships among the building on the right, the reflections of the woman's back, and her profile on the left. It all seems to be coming together well.

I made an attempt on Nos. 14 through 16 to work with the strong reflection of the sun in the window. I can't tell yet whether or not there is anything here.

I think I will pass up the close-ups in Nos. 17 through 19. On Nos. 20 through 29 I will have to work with the prints to see how well the exposure worked for the buildings seen through the windows. This was a case of an extreme difference in exposure between the strong sunlight and the interior.

When I am establishing exposure, I try always to use *f*/16 on the 17mm lens for great depth of field. Usually in the daylight photographs of the urban nude the shutter speed works out to be between 1/125th and 1/500th of a second with FP4 film rated at EI 200.

You have also to consider that this was the first day I was working with this model in this apartment. Therefore the session was an introduction in how to perceive this woman in these surroundings.

The last group, Nos. 30 to 34, appears interesting because of the relationship between the woman's real hand and the shadow of the hand. It may be too extreme, too artificial. You never know until it's enlarged. The overall design of this photograph works well, with the square building in the background and the woman's body to the side of the building.

Most of the time in the city you find rectangular and square shapes in the buildings. Only rarely do you find a circle to work with. Of course, the city has many male symbols such as chimneys and skyscrapers.

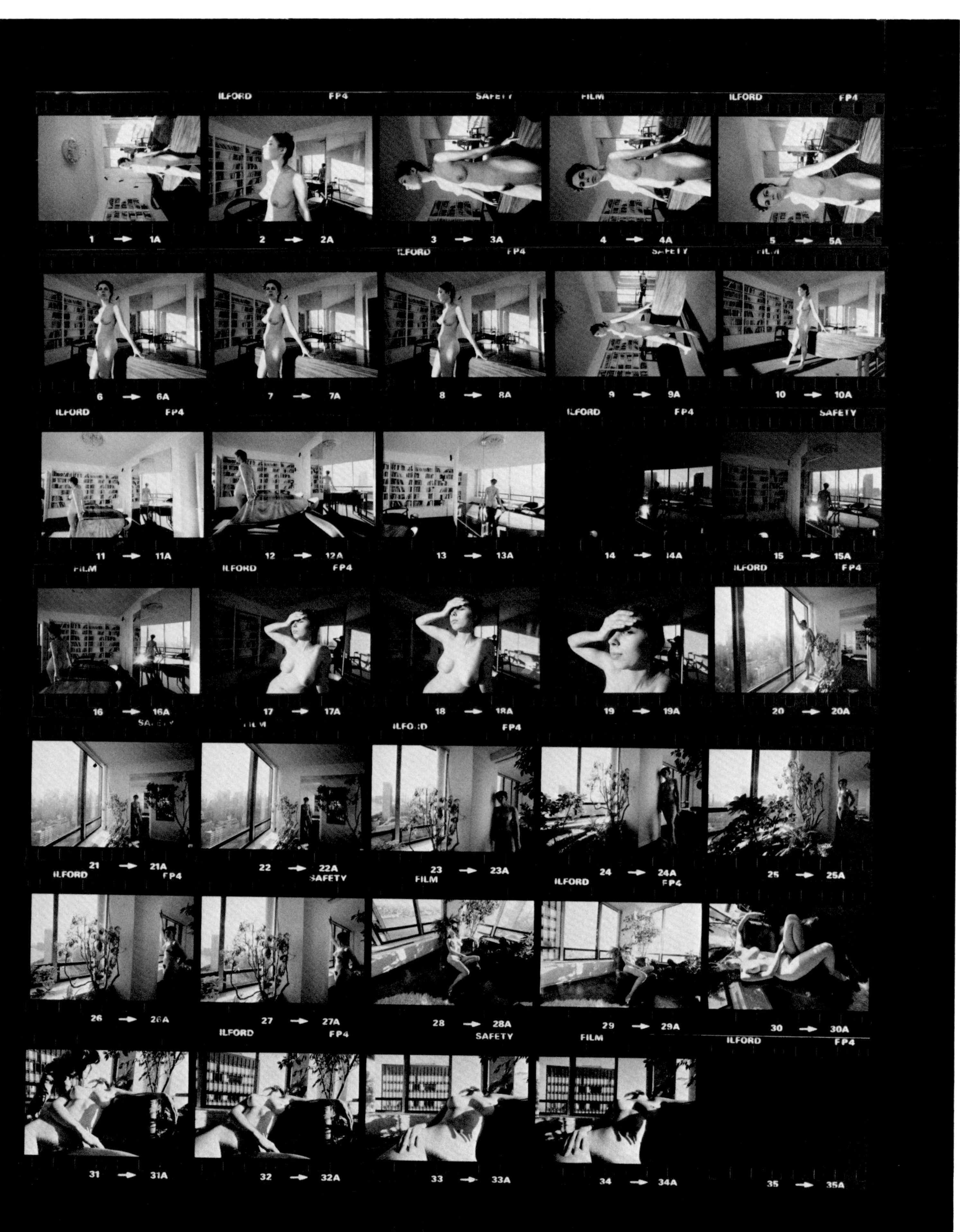

NUS DE LA VILLE, NEW YORK, 1979

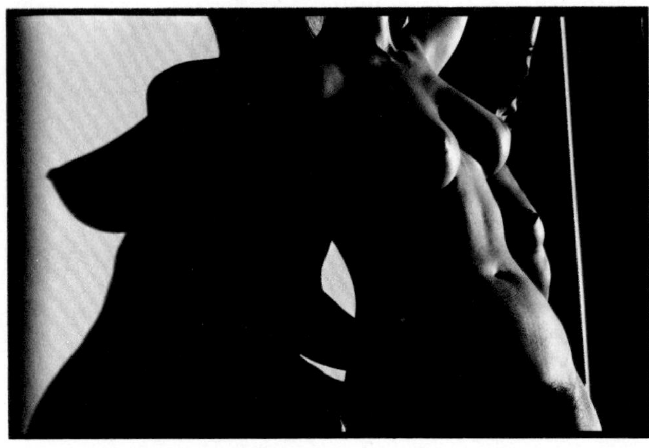

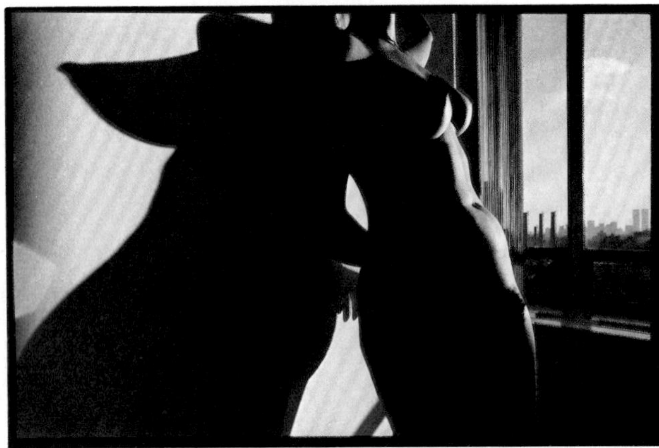

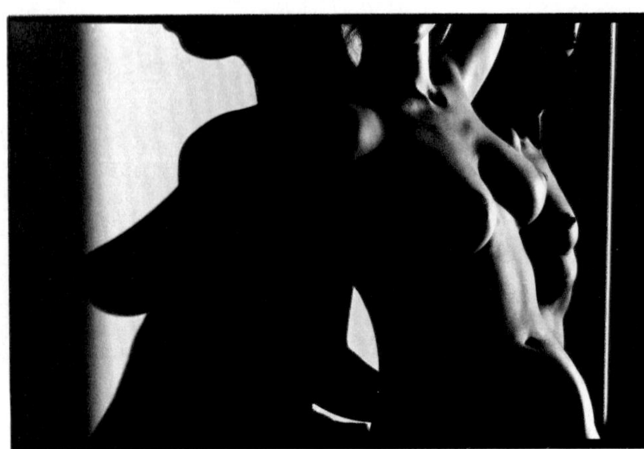

Contact Sheet No. 3

Frames No. 1 through 9 look very interesting on this contact sheet, but it is a little difficult to tell if they will work out because they are visually complicated. I think frame No. 7 looks very good. The shadows and the bodies of the three women work well together.

I like the idea behind Nos. 10 through 15 because of the visual ambiguity. It's hard to tell where the shadows are coming from. The woman's own shadow falls to the left; the shadow of another model is on the right. Probably No. 12 or 13 will work out best from this series. The woman's body fills the frame better and the vertical frames are preferable to the horizontal frames.

I won't use No. 16 because the other woman can be seen, and the sense of visual ambiguity of the shadows is lost. Frame No. 17 or 18 would work out better because the relationship between the woman and the city can be seen. There is some flare on the left-hand side which eliminates these two frames as possibilities. This problem crops up with the 17mm lens sometimes.

I don't particularly care for the relationships between the bodies and the shadows in Nos. 19 through 23. Frames No. 24 through 29 work because of the way the body and shadow fill the frame. In No. 25 I like the relationship between the breasts of the two women. But in Nos. 26 and 27 this relationship doesn't work. No. 28 might work out best because the other woman's body is not in the frame.

In Nos. 30 through 32 there is, again, the problem of flare.

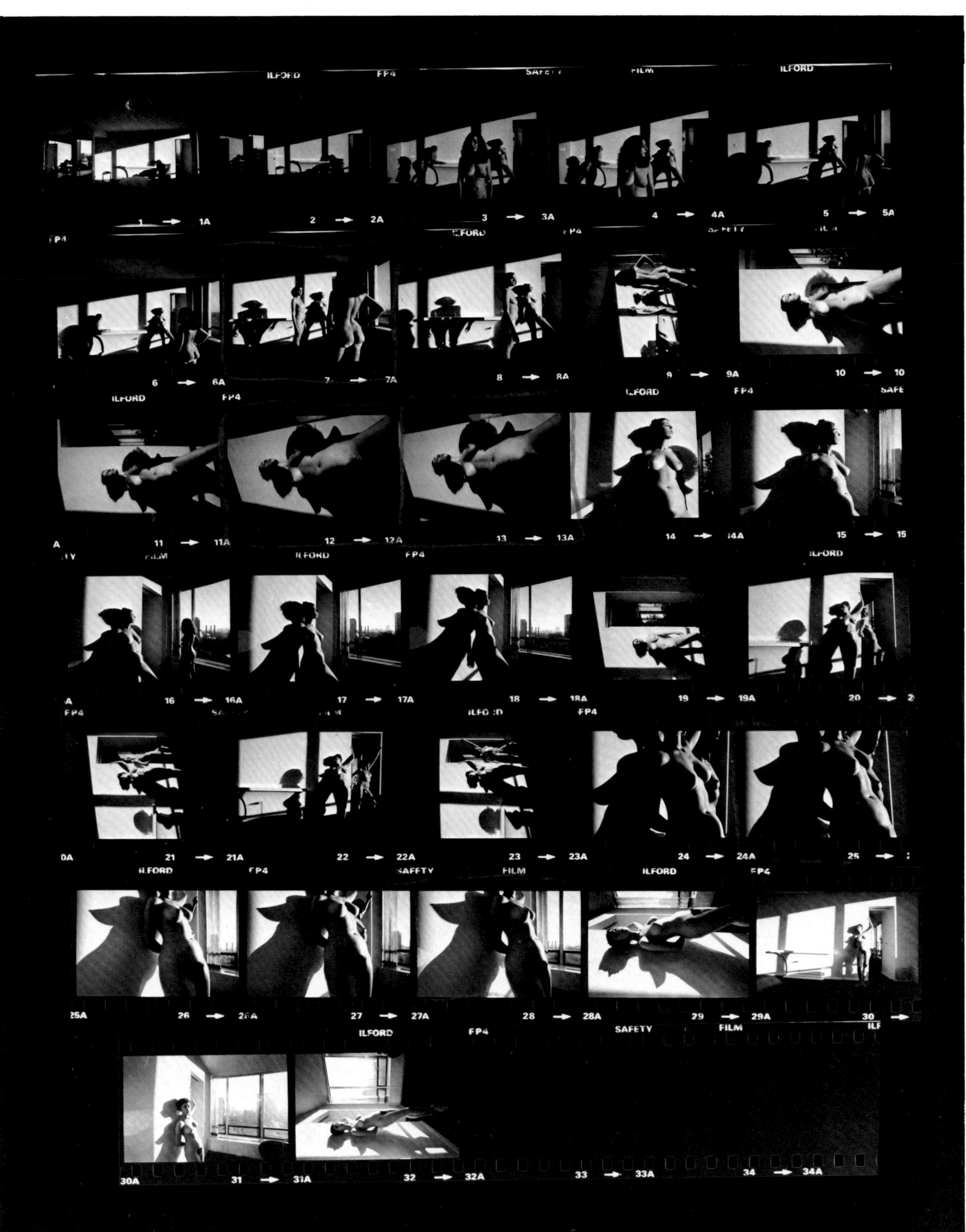

NUS DE LA VILLE, NEW YORK, 1979

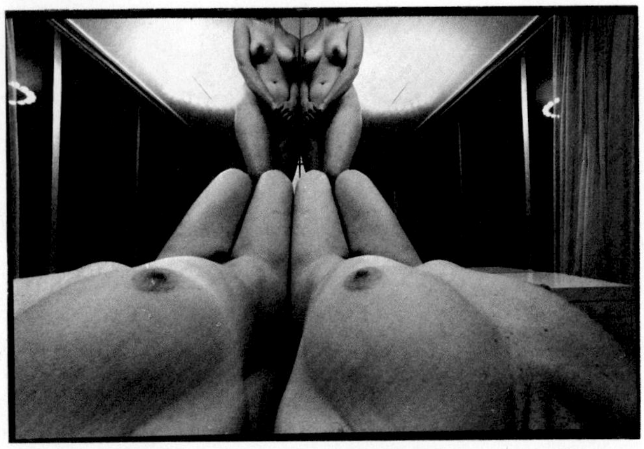

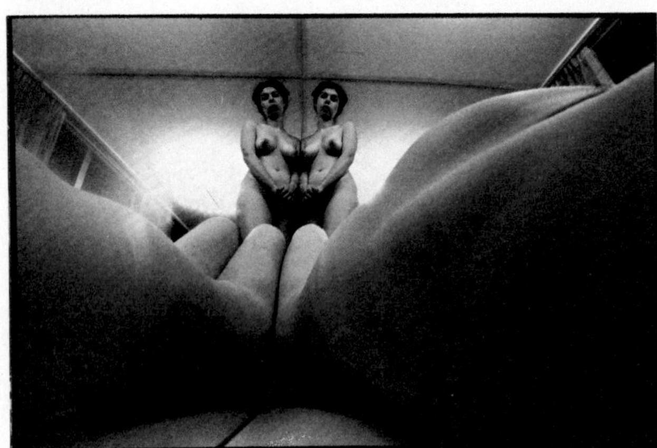

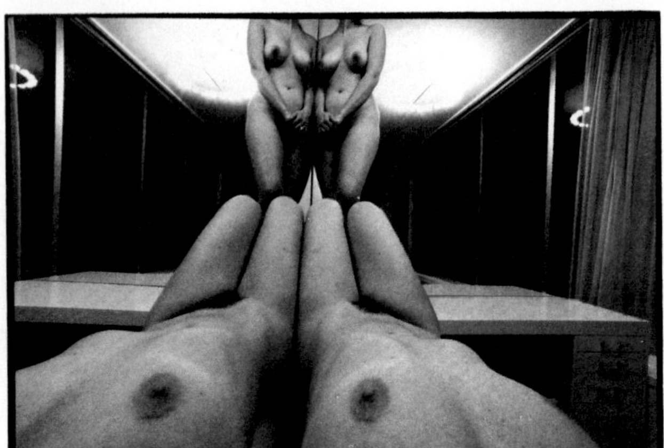

Contact Sheet No. 4

This is the first time I've ever played with this type of distortion with mirrors. To me it seems this series is something very exciting, and it makes me think a little bit of André Kertész' distorted nudes.

We did this series by night with the available light within the apartment. I used a tripod, with a setting of *f*/16 at 1 second, with HP5 film at 400 ASA.

In this session, the most difficult problem was to hide myself. The secret of most of this sequence was that I positioned myself at the middle of the mirror, and that I used the bodies of the women to hide my reflection.

The images that appeal to me most are frames No. 20, 29, 30, 32 and 34. I am very drawn to them because I like the effect of the extreme distortion in the foreground. This series is a real gamble. Sometimes I push myself to the extreme in my work, and this is done for a reason. It enables me to find and correct my errors more easily, for future reference.

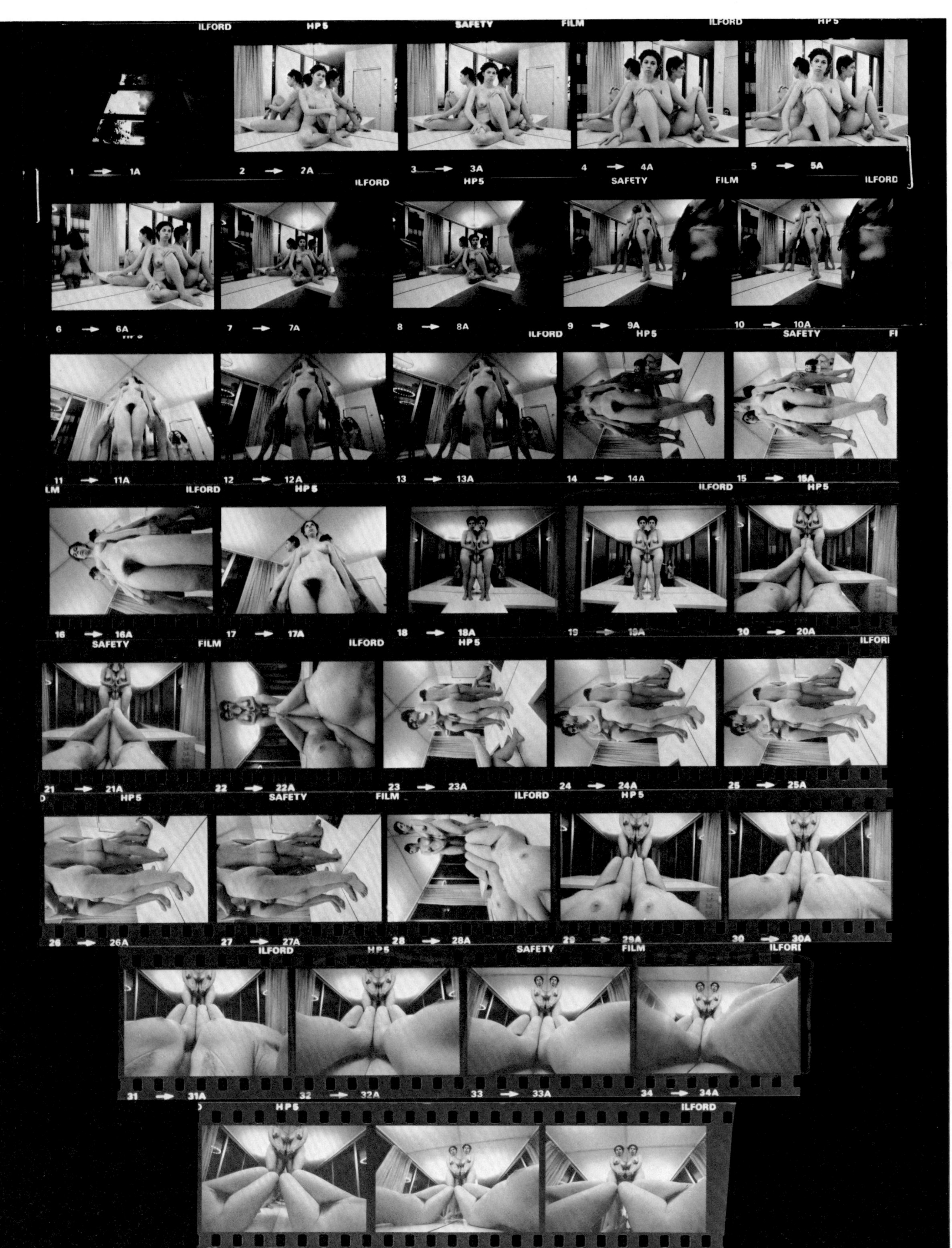

NUS DE LA VILLE, NEW YORK, 1979

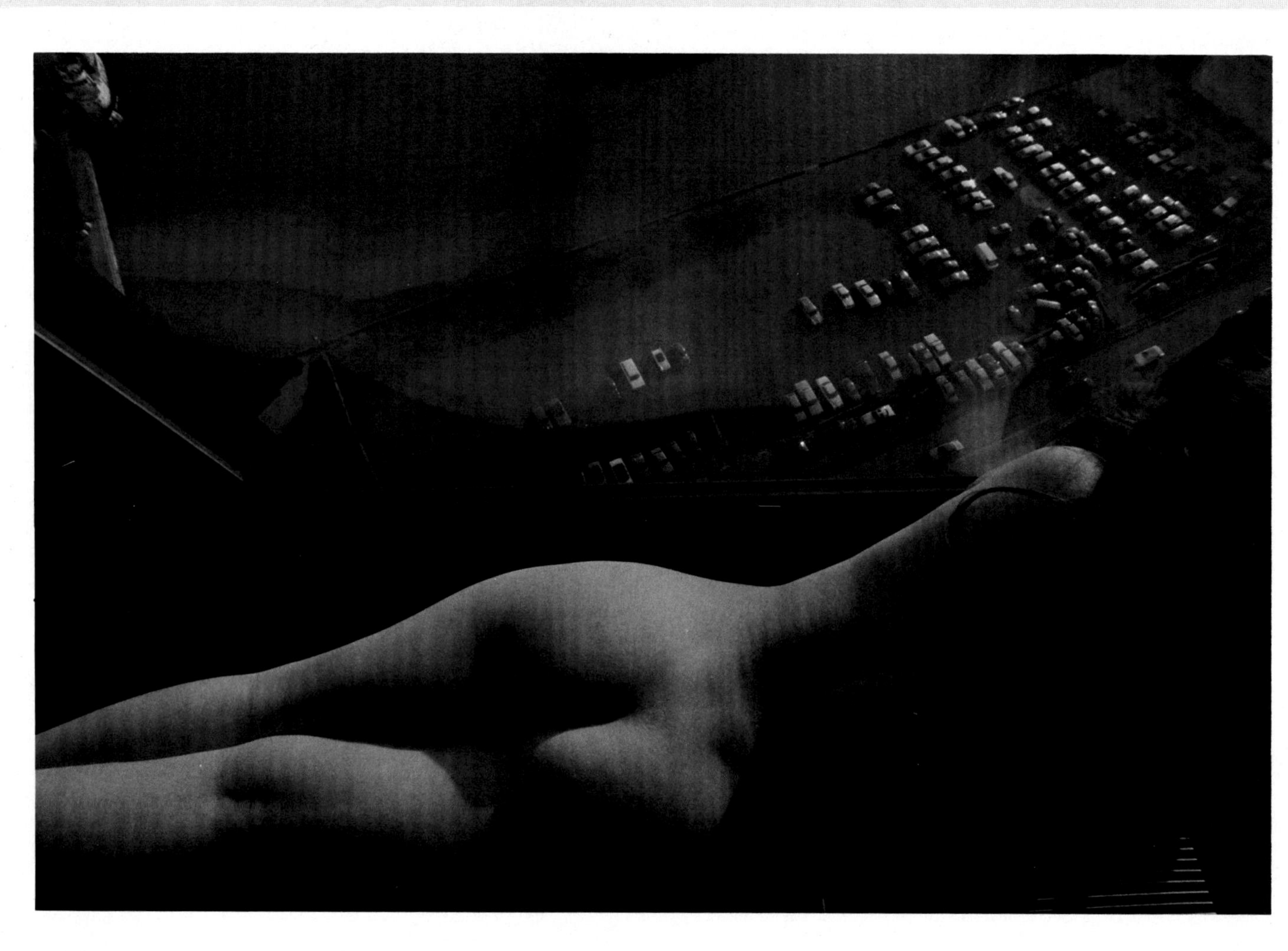

FIGURE 6: DENISE ON THE LAKE, 1976

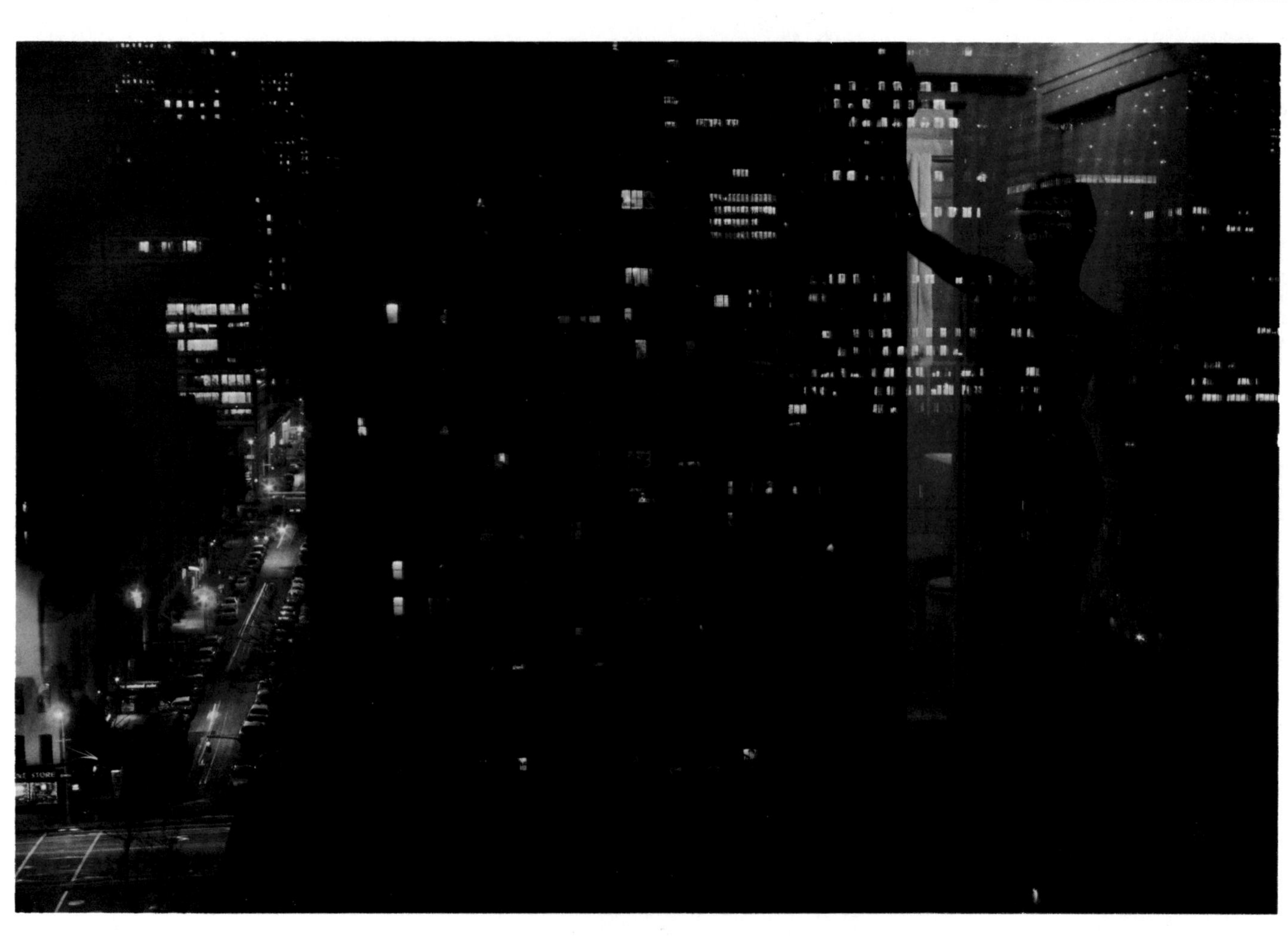

FIGURE 7: NIGHT IN NEW YORK, 1977

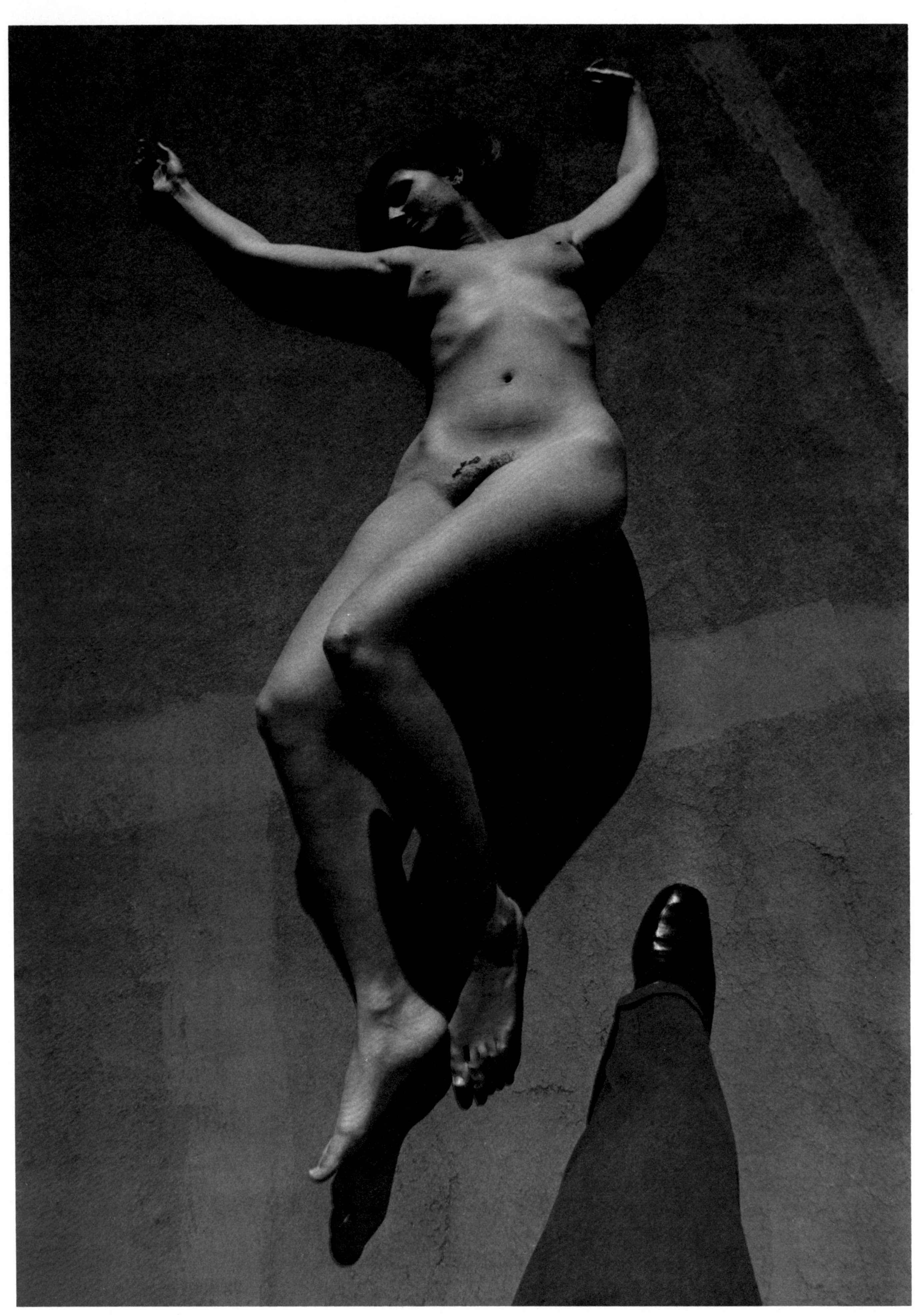

FIGURE 8: SELF-PORTRAIT IN TUCSON III, 1977

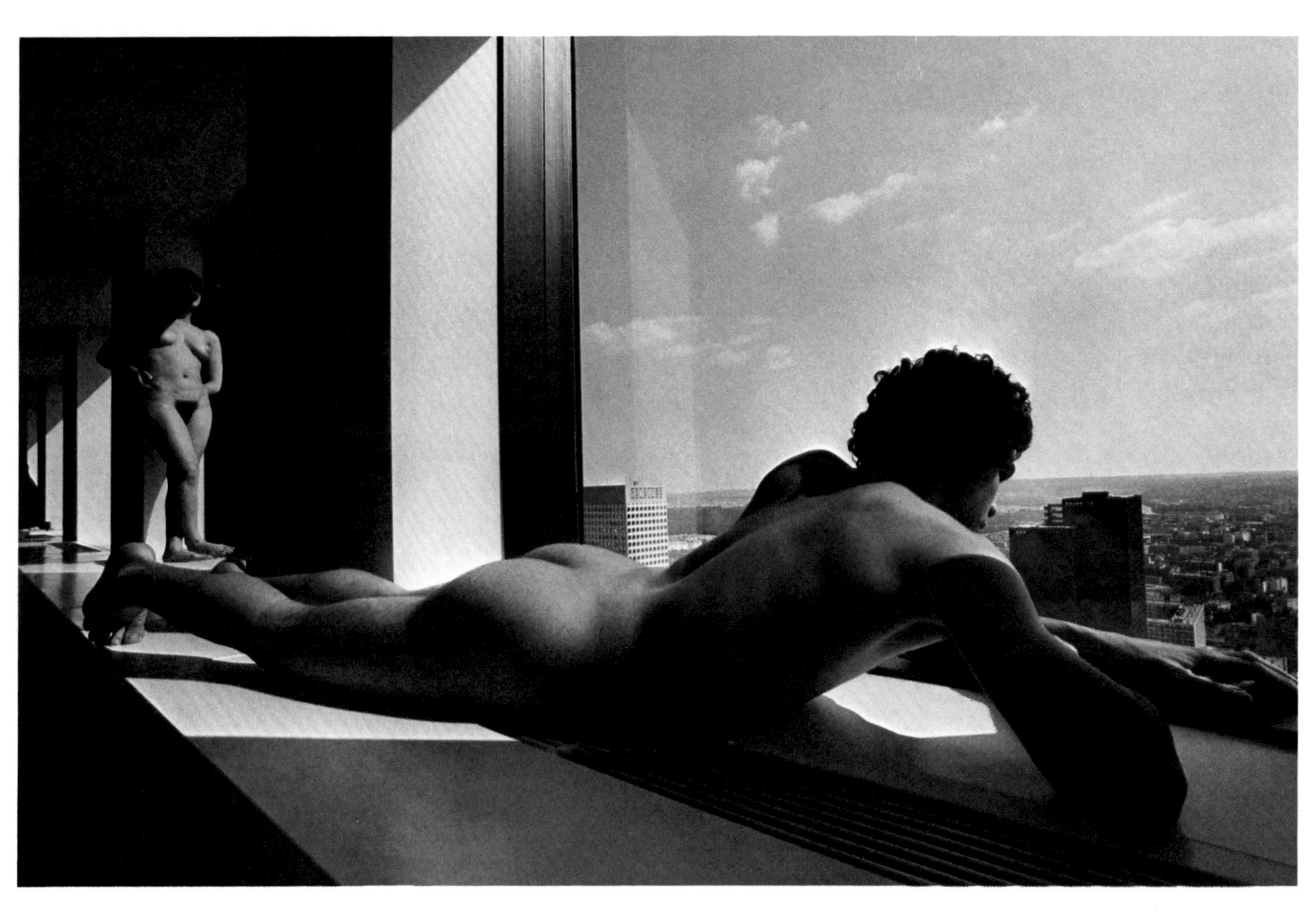

FIGURE 9: FRED AT LA DÉFENSE, PARIS, 1978

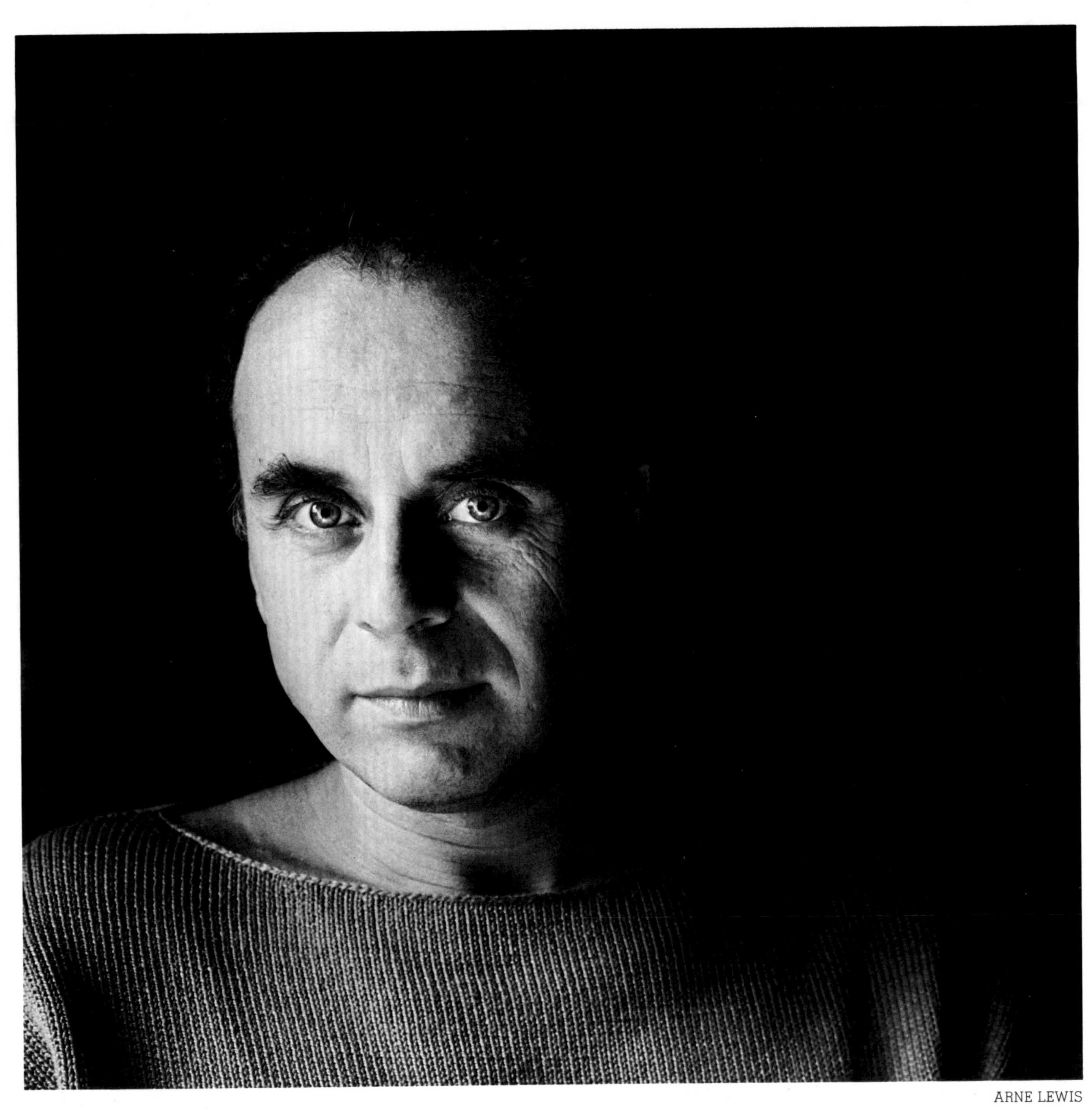

ARNE LEWIS

RALPH GIBSON: "WHAT IS PHOTOGRAPHIC TRUTH."

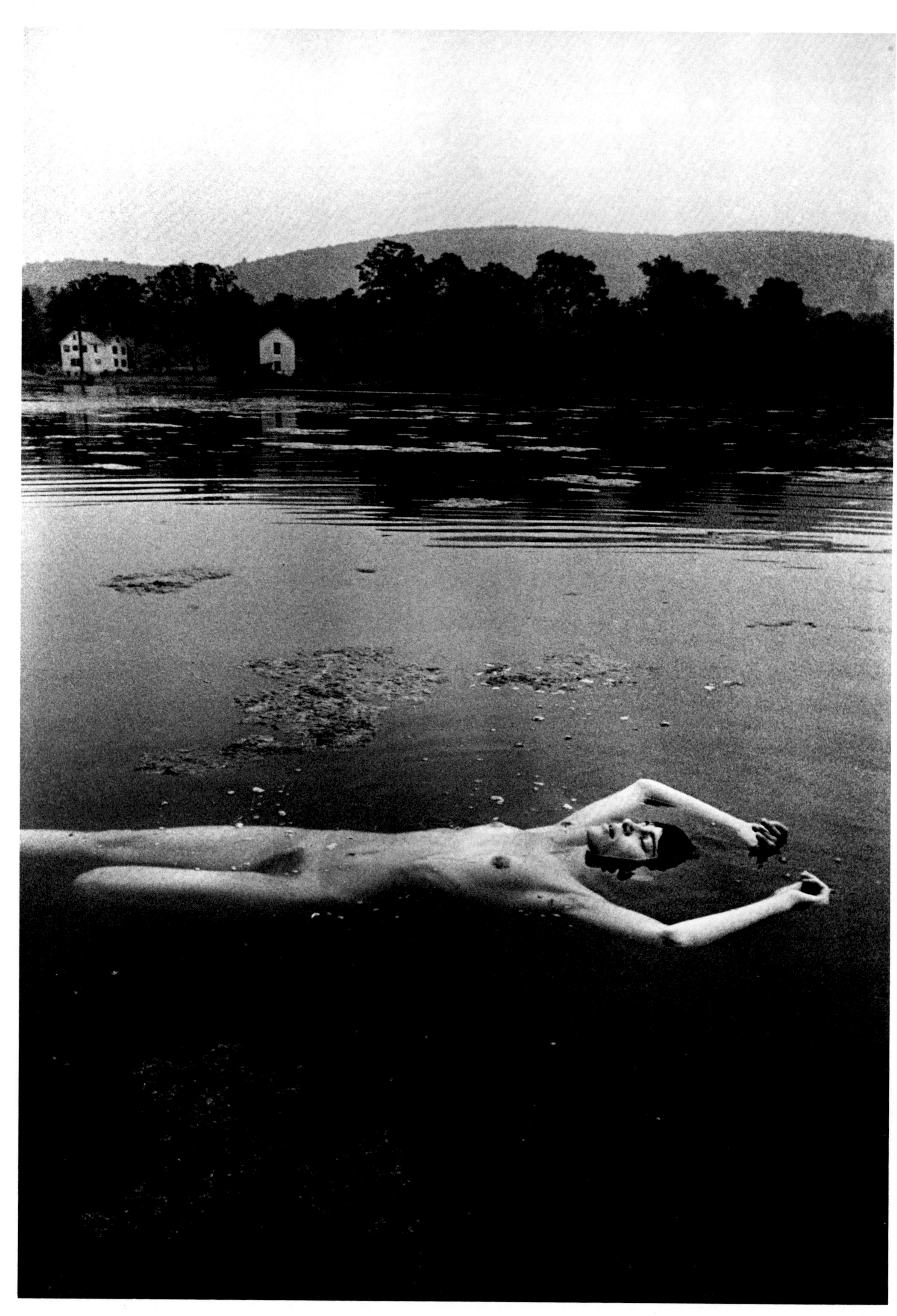

FIGURE 1: UNTITLED, 1967 (From THE SOMNAMBULIST)

When I photograph the nude, I'm interested in producing truncated shapes in proportion to the frame and composition, shapes that are preferably quite luminous. I'm not interested in the full figure; I want to abstract forms. I've understood this for years as my concerns have changed from allegorical surrealism, as in the floating nude (Figure 1), to a minimalistic flattening of the figure, as in my most recent nude, which utilizes the triangular shape created by a woman's thigh, arm and torso (Figure 4). The nude has always reflected the artistic concerns I was involved with at the time.

My work is always at its best when I'm at the curious stage, feeling very loose and just seeing what's going on. After I have been pursuing something for a while, perhaps I become a little more rigid. There are always the quantum leap shots that are unlike anything the photographer has done before. When I reach that stage, once I get an idea, I attempt to pursue it, expand on it, come up with more. Now I want to start working on shorter series, shorter projects, to achieve more distance between images.

I learned to photograph the body one part at a time. For a long time most of my best photographs of the figure were of a woman's buttocks. It's unusual that I would reproduce three or four pictures that include the breast. The hand is a theme that recurs throughout my work. I also photograph many faces and details of the body at different perspectives. More recently, I have become involved with photographing the substructure of the body.

During the period in which I did the floating nude, I was very much involved with how photography takes the three dimensional world of reality and reduces it to two dimensions. I was also influenced by the thought that it reduces the world in scale; it makes things smaller. The ocean could become a 5 x 7 picture window in space. I knew that the degree to which I could suggest a third dimension influenced my statement and how the pictures were perceived, and so I wanted to get a deep perspective.

When I saw the nude floating on the lake, I had my choice of a 28, 35 or 50mm lens. I chose the 28mm lens immediately, in order to include a deep foreground, middle ground and background. There are many recurring themes here: the curves of her body in relation to the mountain range, and the angles at the top of the roofs of the buildings and in the woman's bent elbows. For me, the success of a composition, whether a long shot or a close-up, depends on the harmony of the recurring forms.

I want to make photographs that resonate for a while. At the time I made this picture, I was interested in producing dream states, not necessarily surreal states. I know there's a strong overlap between dreams and surrealism, but, in my case, at the time I was simply making pictures to put in a dream book. I was interested in producing a kind of Ophelia in this image. The minute the woman started floating, I understood that the image was very pre-Raphaelite, very 19th-century romantic.

The floating nude is the most seemingly natural of all the photographs in this article. The question, of course, remains: What is photographic truth? Bill Brandt says it's the results that count; I think truth is the result that you are seeking. I'm not a newspaper photographer, and I'm not trying to do a rendition of a box of soap. I'm trying to produce a photograph that evokes feelings, and one's feelings and photographs change.

I never make a picture of a nude without adhering to certain self-imposed restrictions and criteria. I know what I like about a figure. I like a certain quality and luminosity of skin tone; I want a certain proportion; I want to be careful of the point where I cut off the figure. These are all questions of balance and rhythm. I like the weightlessness of this figure, the flotation. I include the image because it's one of the first serious works I made of the figure. It is also one in which I became aware of the responsibility one bears in photographing the nude.

I like the black silhouetted form of the standing nude (Figure 2), the way her knee intersects her left leg. There are more rectangular shapes than triangular shapes in this image. The tonality in this picture (the slight shadow on the right leg and thigh, the highlight area and the black line around the legs) was produced by a very long exposure. The photograph was made in a very dim room, with window light coming from a light well. The exposure was *f*/2 for perhaps a full second or even two, while the camera was set on bulb. In fact, this photograph is brighter than the room was at the time the picture was made. If the picture had duplicated the circumstances, it would be a much darker print.

In the reclining nude (Figure 3), we see one breast and the collarbone line. We know it's a human figure, but the photograph isn't producing anything akin to a figure. The nipple looks more like something else. It seems to resemble an eye.

I've always felt that regardless of how minimal my work becomes, whatever presence it retains is based on an idea that I discovered in surrealism: matter within the universe is sentient; that is, objects (both organic and inorganic) are aware of themselves. Perhaps it is possible that a gun knows it can kill.

I had made a picture that is an homage to Max Ernst, of knots in wood (Figure 6). The reclining nude seems to have some expressiveness similar to that photograph. All of the elements of the photograph are important; the cut forms; the truncation; the relationship between the breast and the shadow of the collarbone; and the relationship between the lower right-hand corner and the shadow under her figure in the middle left-hand side of the frame. The three shapes of the shadow of the collarbone, the lower right-hand corner, and the left-hand corner tend to triangulate and increase the surrealistic suspense. So there is an ambiguity: This is a figure lying on the beach. Does a figure lying on the beach think the way this picture looks? Probably not. This is where the photographer is in a position to change everything through context.

In the nude from the QUADRANTS SERIES (Figure 14), the negative shape is very important. There is more black shadow than flesh tone here. The picture is more about the angle of the shadow and the angle of the woman's far hip than anything else. When I made the photograph, there was a light streaming into a bathroom from an extremely small window, about 10″ square. I wanted to keep the detail of the arm coming out of the black on the left-hand side.

The QUADRANTS SERIES coincided with my studies of Kazimir Malevich and constructivism, and this picture is very much an example of a geometric concern. It was photographed with a 50mm lens with a close-up attachment (dual-range 50mm *f*/2 Summicron).

The photograph includes the hand, which is the leitmotif I've used for years. Without the hand, this would be an extremely abstract image, but the hand gives it humanity. I think my interest in the hand comes from the gestural aspect of street shooting. At one time I worked for Dorothea Lange and planned to be a documentary photographer. When one is a documentary photographer, one often spends time waiting until the subject makes a gesture.

In Figure 7 there are many sharp, fine black lines that are part of the creation of an area that looks like water but which is, in fact, just a shadow area on the lower abdomen. These lines are like razor-sharp paper cutouts. If I had felt compelled to adhere to a documentary notion of truth in photography, I would have allowed the darker print on the left to stand for the work. As it turns out, I'm more interested in the way the black razor-sharp lines stand out in the print on the right (Figure 8).

The two versions of this image illustrate how profoundly a picture can be changed in printing. Both prints are on No. 5 Agfa Brovira paper. The darker print on the left was exposed for 30 seconds and it is unmanipulated. The print on the right was also exposed for 30 seconds in total, but it is manipulated. On it, I gave a 15-second exposure overall, while dodging the inner thigh and calf. Then for another 15 seconds, I burned in just enough to hold detail at the edge of the image area. The two prints are from the same box of paper, and exposed at the same *f*/stop during the same printing session.

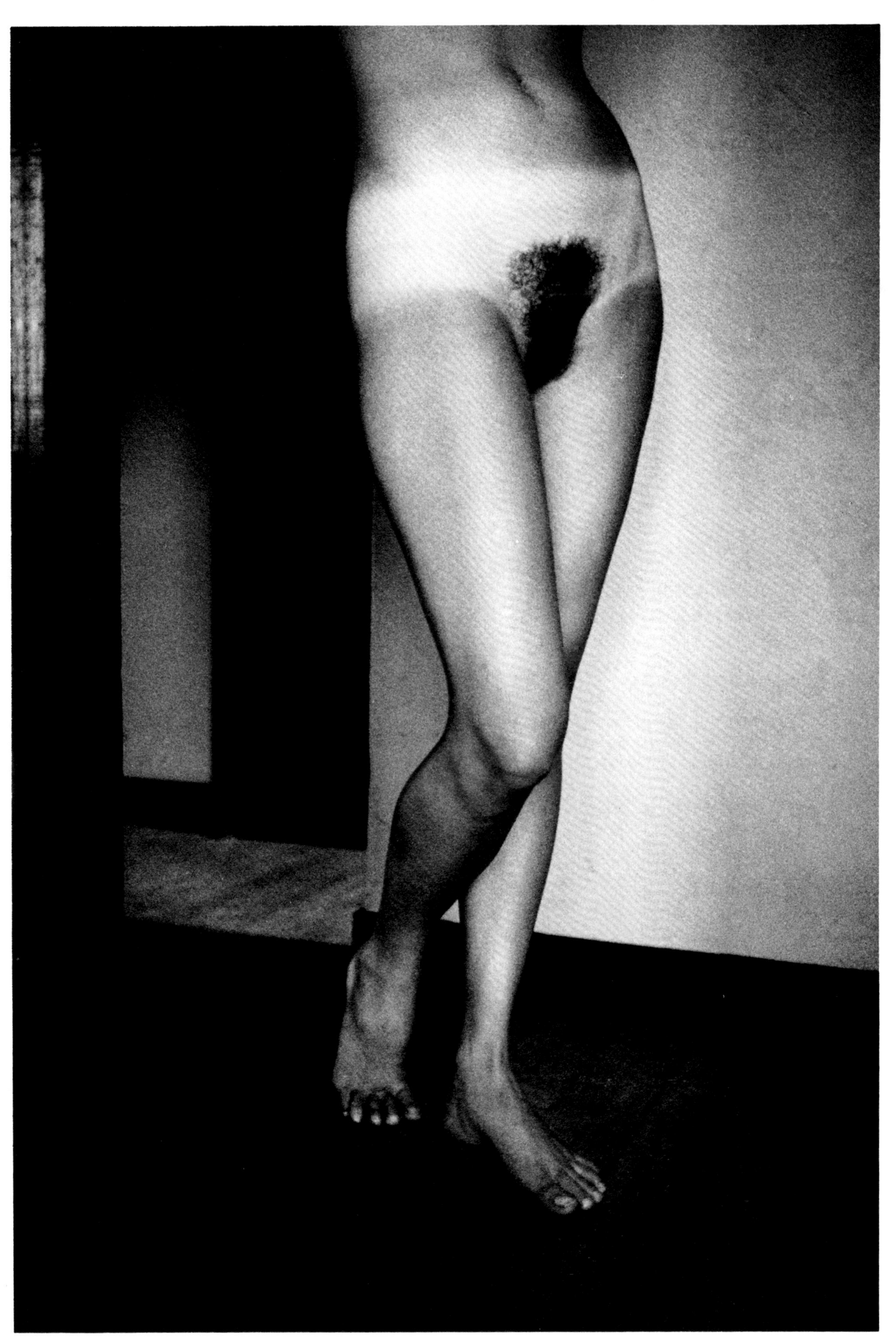

FIGURE 2: UNTITLED, 1967 (From THE SOMNAMBULIST)

I've always liked contrast in my prints because it's a way of accentuating or eliminating information. On the other hand, my prints are less contrasty in general than a year or two ago. I find that as my ideas become more abstract, I reduce information in the taking of the picture rather than in the darkroom. I'm seeing cleaner shapes with my eye, which is something that I learned from correcting my mistakes in the darkroom. That's the important thing about the darkroom; it forces one to live with one's failures.

The studies of the torso (Figures 9 and 10) are photographs made of a collarbone and throat, details of a woman's body which I deliberately set out to photograph because they had fascinated me for a long time. There is no doubt in my mind that these studies of the torso have more feeling than images in which I'm expressing more formal or theoretical concerns.

I wanted to show the substructure, the bones of the woman's body, and how the flesh covered them with signs of life and motion. For me, the significance of the photographs lie in the fact that they are virtually out of focus. The shapes were so soft in and of themselves that there was no edge on which to focus. I could have used more light and taken more time, but as I was taking the pictures I thought they <u>were</u> in focus. That is to say, they looked the way they look here on the prints, and that must have been what I wanted. When the work pleases me as much as these particular soft images, I don't consider it a mistake; I consider it the will of the medium.

The differences in the two versions are extremely subtle. The lighter version of the picture is pure abstraction, almost like a bird in flight. My concerns in photography have become progressively more formal, more aesthetic, and this aspect of my work is revealed in the first version. At the same time, I have thought that I might be losing a little of the life experience in my work, something that photography is very good at reflecting. The increase in detail in the second version is only 15 to 20%, and yet it reveals the study as a human figure. The second photograph is brought from abstraction into life. The comparison of the two allows me to consider the question: How much does one want to render, photographically speaking? I like both the first and second versions, but for different reasons.

The photographs reveal a concern that has come to me recently in the making of prints. I've become interested in letting the corners of a print flare out into whiteness, which I've never done before. In most of my work I give immense concern to every square centimeter of the paper surface; I question every area. In my work with the nude, I am interested in a less "worked over" print. If I let go a little, if I allow the negative, paper and film to express themselves, I come up with a more interesting print.

The next study of the torso (Figure 11) looks to me like a detail of a statue, except that it is living. The volume of the breast and the structure between the arms and the collarbones are clearly expressed, although there is very little information.

In the preceding three studies of the torso, I wanted the shapes to be very indefinite. Usually I attempt to delineate what could be called a cut form, as in the photograph of a woman holding a coat open (Figure 12). You can see that the black shapes are very clearly etched around her figure. The same thing is true of the nude with the stockings. The stockings create a very sharp shape. These forms are prevalent throughout my work, not just with the nude.

I knew that if I exposed for the skin of the woman, which was very white, the lining of her coat would go black. I was interested in the long wavy line that started on the right-hand side at the top of her breast and went downward, producing the cut shape. I like to look at this photograph by throwing my eyes out of focus and studying the woman's pelvic bone, the rib cage, and the shape of her stomach muscles.

In the nude with stockings (Figure 13), the angle of the back of the woman's thighs strongly reflects the angle of the upper left-hand corner, not only as a geometric form, but also in terms of feeling. I was recalling the ivory reclining figurines that women in ancient China used when they went to their physician. Rather than referring specifically to the part of the body, the women simply pointed to the figurine. I felt that this woman's body was very much in the manner of some of these Chinese figures, with the long back of the hip.

From a technical point of view, the interesting thing about this photograph is that it was made with a small lamp with a 100-watt incandescent bulb. This is my favorite artificial light source. It gives me good shadow, subtlety, skin tone and negative quality, as well as a shutter speed that I can still hand-hold. I've done portraits and figures under this kind of incandescent light; I once did a portrait under a 25-watt hanging incandescent bulb. The last thing you would wonder about is how this nude is illuminated; with electronic flash you would know instantly.

On the near leg, I wanted to use the seams of the stocking as delineation. I thought that if I took the seams away, it would look as if there were no legs because the line would be so sharp. In order to make the stocking idea work, I had to retain information in the two seams on the foreground leg. On the far leg, I wanted a black-on-black feeling; that is to say, the black stocking against the black satin coverlet. The coverlet photographs with detail in it because satin reflects highlights.

This image is extremely textural because there are four separate surfaces. There is skin tone that

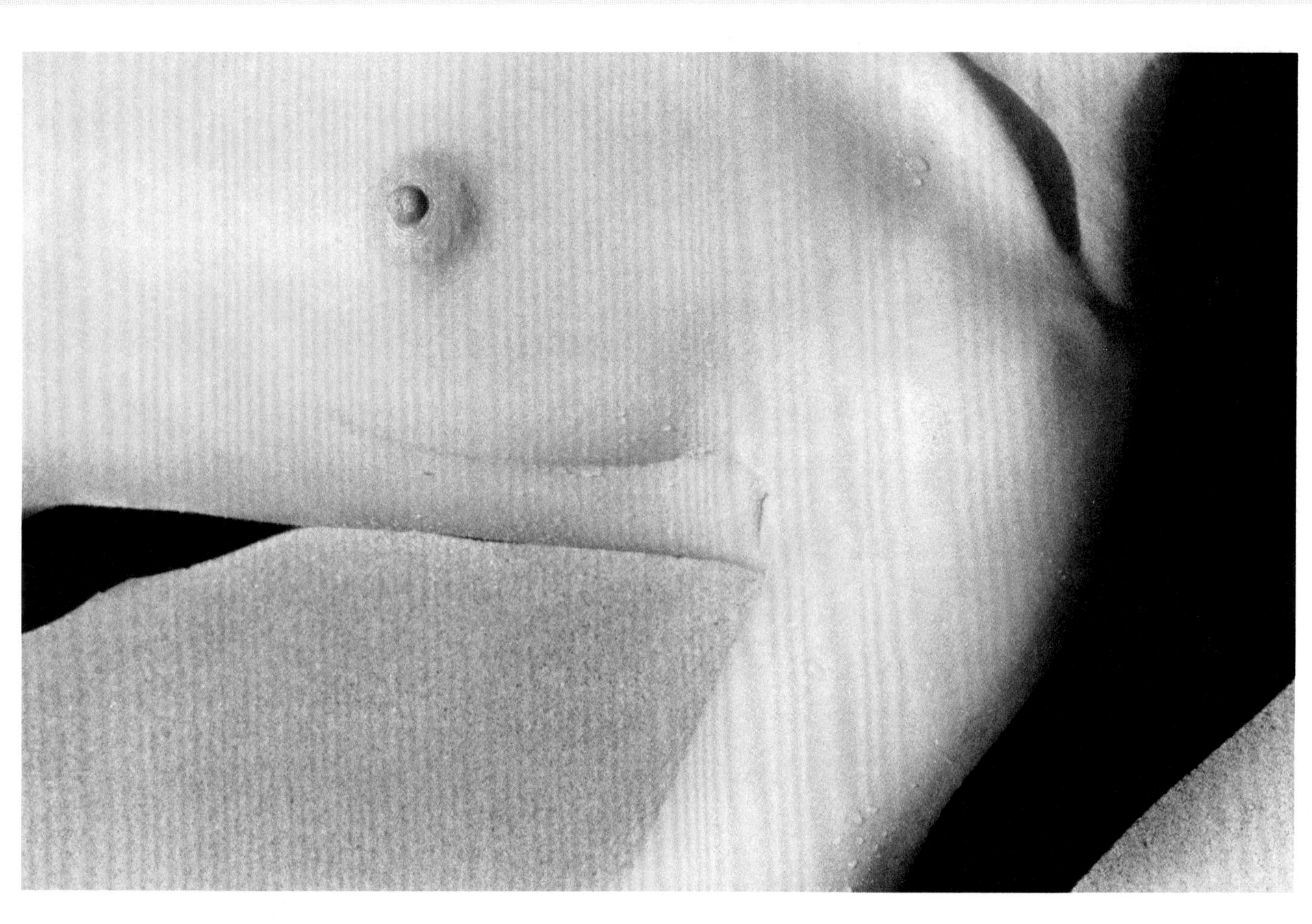

FIGURE 3: UNTITLED, 1979

is so luminous that it seems to be lit from within; one of the things I've always wanted to do with the nude is to make the light come from inside the nude out. There are also the textures of the satin, the stockings and the pubic hair. When I printed the image, I wanted to retain the slightest amount of shadow detail on the foreground leg as it became part of the pelvis and as the pubic hair became part of the section with the background light. I like to include both continuous tone and non-continuous tone in a photograph. I've done that in several of these photographs.

Figure 15 reflects my interest in flattening the figure, producing truncated shapes (the elbows, legs and black line), and combining these concerns with the model's gestural attitude to produce a kind of visual non sequitur. By this, I mean that there are many contradictions in this image: stillness and motion, flatness and roundness, a black line that is at the same time definite and yet inexplicable and mysterious (what is it? where does it come from?), and a pose that is so unusual that it shouldn't work as convincingly as it does.

Originally I was motivated to make the photograph of the seated nude (Figure 16) by the interaction between the model's navel and the lines on her stomach. I used a 90mm lens on my Leica, and I placed the camera on a tripod. I tilted the camera in increments of about 15 degrees: photographing, tilting, and discovering compositions in the viewfinder of the camera itself, i.e., the camera showed me this composition. This is the opposite of my usual method of working. Normally, I prefer to see with my eye and then raise the camera to photograph what has been seen. I find that this photograph has a somewhat art deco feeling, almost as if it had been made on a luxury liner in the 1920s or 30s.

Figure 4 is the most recent photograph reproduced here. For a long time I have been interested in working with the triangularly negative shape obtained by silhouetting the breast against the arm and the leg.

I made the photograph in bright sun with Tri-X film, which I would normally expose at *f*/16 at 1/250th of a second under these lighting conditions. While I was composing, it occurred to me to open up the diaphragm two stops, to *f*/8, to pick up more detail on the inside of the breasts and stomach and skin. There are areas in this photograph in which the detail is the most you could possibly get out of Tri-X; for example, in the wrinkles on the stomach. You can also see that the parts of the woman's body that are oiled from sunbathing have turned almost white from the overexposure. I've never before made a picture in which I wanted both overexposure and perfect exposure; I've never made a picture that modulated like this.

The suntan oil had a lot to do with it. The ambient light bouncing all over the beach also contributed to the modulation. If I had made this picture at *f*/16, 1/250th of a second, the white triangular shape of the sky would have come in as a tone, but instead it burned out into white.

This is an example of a hunch. If it had not been a photograph of the figure, I might have been much more cautious and imposed a technical prerequisite on the picture. I become very serious about my projects, but with the nude I feel much freer to experiment.

On the contact sheet you can see that I moved closer in a sequence of six frames. This is very indicative of the way I work. I start with an idea, and then I see how much I can subtract in an attempt to get to the essence (Figure 6). Originally, I thought I could allow some of the woman's hair to show in the photograph.

Figure 4 was done with a 90mm lens, which is now my favorite. Formerly, I preferred the 50mm. I think the change came about because of the evolution of my attitudes toward flatness. I learned from working with color that the 90mm lens really pulls the shapes closer to the surface of the picture plane. The choice of the lens affects the relationship between foreground and background shapes. Here the right and left arm appear to be the same size. With a 50mm, the right arm would have been smaller and the left arm bigger. The sliver of light between the arms would also have been greater.

For a long time I have felt that the space around a figure (the negative space) strongly influences the image. In Figure 4 I was initially going after a negative shape, the triangle created by the woman's arm, thigh and torso. As I was pursuing this vivid negative shape, the shape of the woman became less important than it is in the nude from the QUADRANTS SERIES.

Figure 4 shows the density of flesh, athletic, all toned up from swimming, whereas the white torso (Figure 9) is the most subtle of tissues. The triangular nude appears very warm in tonality. It is printed on Agfa Brovira No. 5, as are all the nudes reproduced here, with the exception of the nude from the QUADRANTS SERIES. The triangular nude is so silvery that it almost looks plated, an effect that I've never really pursued before.

When I print a nude, no matter how little manipulation is necessary, I always move a small dodging tool over the figure as I am exposing the paper. I feel that this produces a more interesting flesh tone. I don't know if it's a trick or a superstition or a fact. Another aspect is that I agitate the figure studies very little.

My paper developer is Kodak Dektol 1:1. I've used it for years. When I'm really refining a print, I tend to develop it longer than my usual 1½ to 3 minutes. Occasionally I use a certain technique in which I overexpose the paper and then deliberately underdevelop it with a great

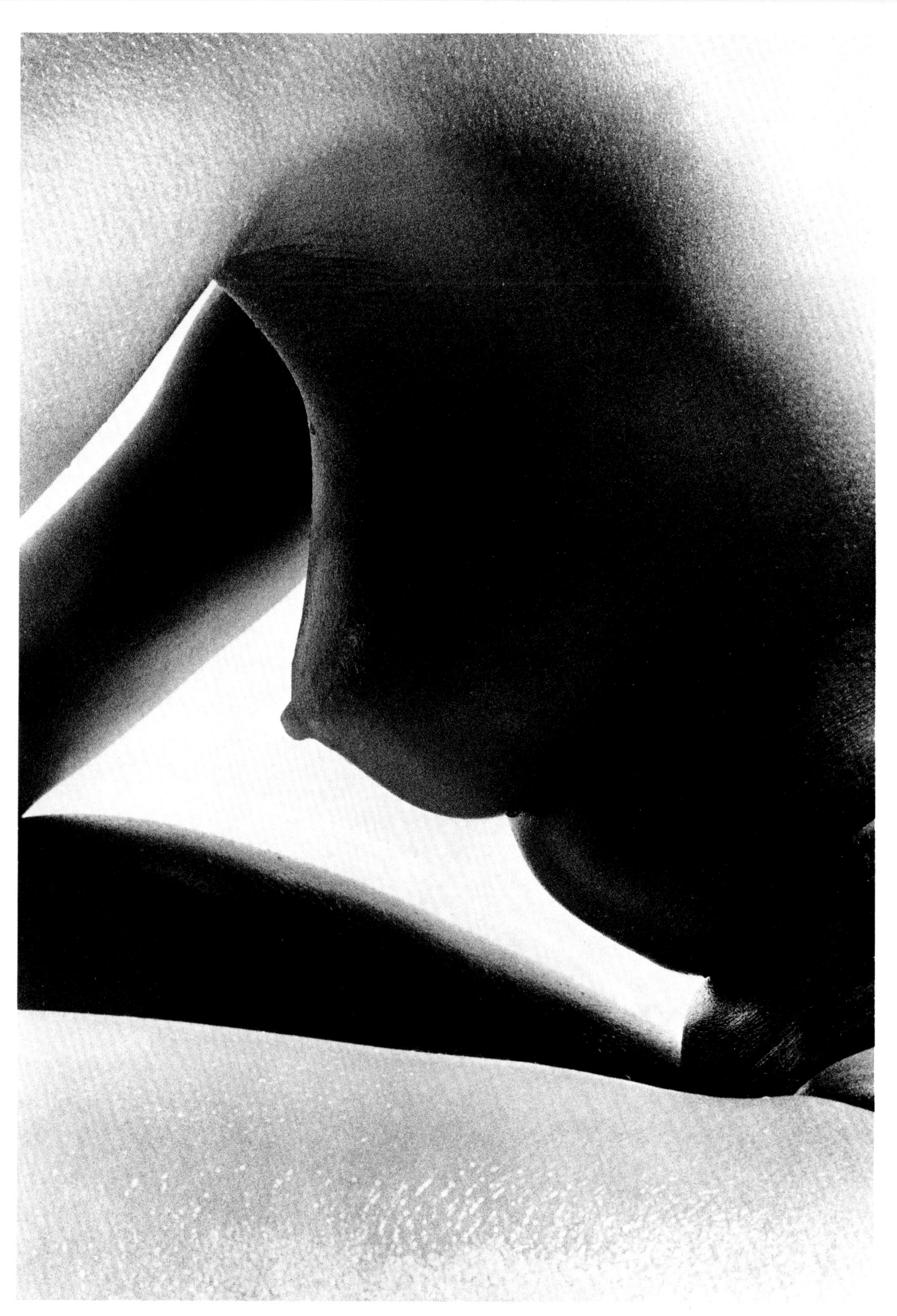

FIGURE 4: UNTITLED, 1979

deal of agitation, which is a way of increasing or decreasing contrast by a half-grade, depending on the negative.

My film developer is Rodinal, used with Tri-X. I have recently altered my dilution from 10cc Rodinal per roll of film to 7cc per roll. If I'm developing 8 rolls in an 8-reel tank, I use 56cc of Rodinal to water sufficient to fill the tank. The development time is 11 minutes.

There has always been a statement of grain in my work. I know the techniques for making fine-grain photographs, but what I really want to do is to make razor-sharp photographs that have pronounced grain.

I use only the 35mm camera, the Leica M2 or M3. I know that there is a kind of tonality that is very appealing for the figure that can be obtained only with a larger format camera, and it's fortunate that I don't want that tonality. I don't have much faith nor interest in the technical aspects of the medium because I believe that the medium is in the eye. For me, the eye resonates in harmony with the 35mm camera.

I believe that a photographer has to shoot continually. I know that I'm not going to be taking many good pictures if I'm not holding the camera in my hand and looking through it. So, like every other photographer, I have shot lots and lots of film and not gotten any pictures. At the same time, I want my film to count. Once, when I was working for Dorothea Lange, she wanted to develop her film, but there were about ten unexposed frames remaining. I said, "Let's just rewind it and soup it." She gave me a very hard look and said, "Young man, that isn't how photographers work." That was one of the lessons I learned from her: when you consider the incredible potential of every frame of film, to waste it becomes a transgression.

Another thing I've learned is that it takes me an average of ten to twenty rolls of film to get a good picture. My pictures don't come easily. I have to shoot a lot. Some photographers work completely in their heads, previsualizing and conceptualizing. But I continue to discover by looking through the viewfinder.

In recent years I have made an attempt to work exclusively on projects, to state them, announce them, pursue them, reach fruition and conclude them; and, for a while, to convince myself that perhaps I am doing exactly that. In fact, it may not be the truth. This is a contradiction that is quite interesting to me, because I realize that about the time the photographer reaches the point of producing a visual signature to his work, there are not going to be enormous differences from series to series. For instance, when you look at Harry Callahan's work, you see that it is distinctly Callahan's. One of the things I'm accepting in my work is that no matter how hard I try to change it, or how much distance I think I'm putting between my various aesthetic positions, the fact is, it's all one overall position. Each person moves in certain general directions. We might always be broadening the front of the movement, but it's basically in one direction.

As a student, I explored the concept of the figure through reading Kenneth Clark's THE NUDE (Bollingen Series XXXV 2, Princeton University Press, Princeton, New Jersey, 1956). It was here that I first learned of the golden section. A rectangle in the proportions of the golden section is formed when the longer side of the rectangle is equal in length to the diagonal of the square, whose side is equal to the shorter side of the rectangle (Figure 5). The 35mm negative has the same proportions. I love working with the golden section and finding different ways to fill this rectangle. It is what makes other formats uninteresting to me.

If you look at most of my pictures of people, especially the nudes, you will see that if an "X" is drawn through the rectangle, the center of the "X" is the focal point in almost every photograph. That doesn't mean that I put the focus of interest in the center of the picture, but I do put the origins or the vectors of thrust in the center. One of the things I learned a long time ago was that if I wanted to photograph a full standing figure, I should bend my knees and place the center of my lens at about the level of the navel, and then make any adjustments in composition from that initial point of departure.

I understood as a student of art history that there were very early solutions to a very early problem, i.e., how to render the figure. This problem has remained; it is as enduring as some of the solutions to rendering it. Marcel Duchamp said, "I have no problems, only solutions." It was Duchamp's NUDE DESCENDING A STAIRCASE that brought him to the forefront in modern art.

There are photographers who are thought to be masters of the nude. I pay homage to and admire photographers who have been working with the figure for a long time, and who at times have produced masterpieces; however, I don't think that one can ever master the nude as an idea.

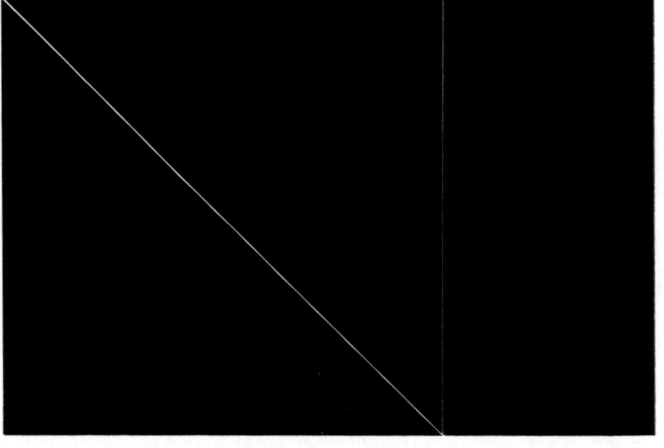

FIGURE 5

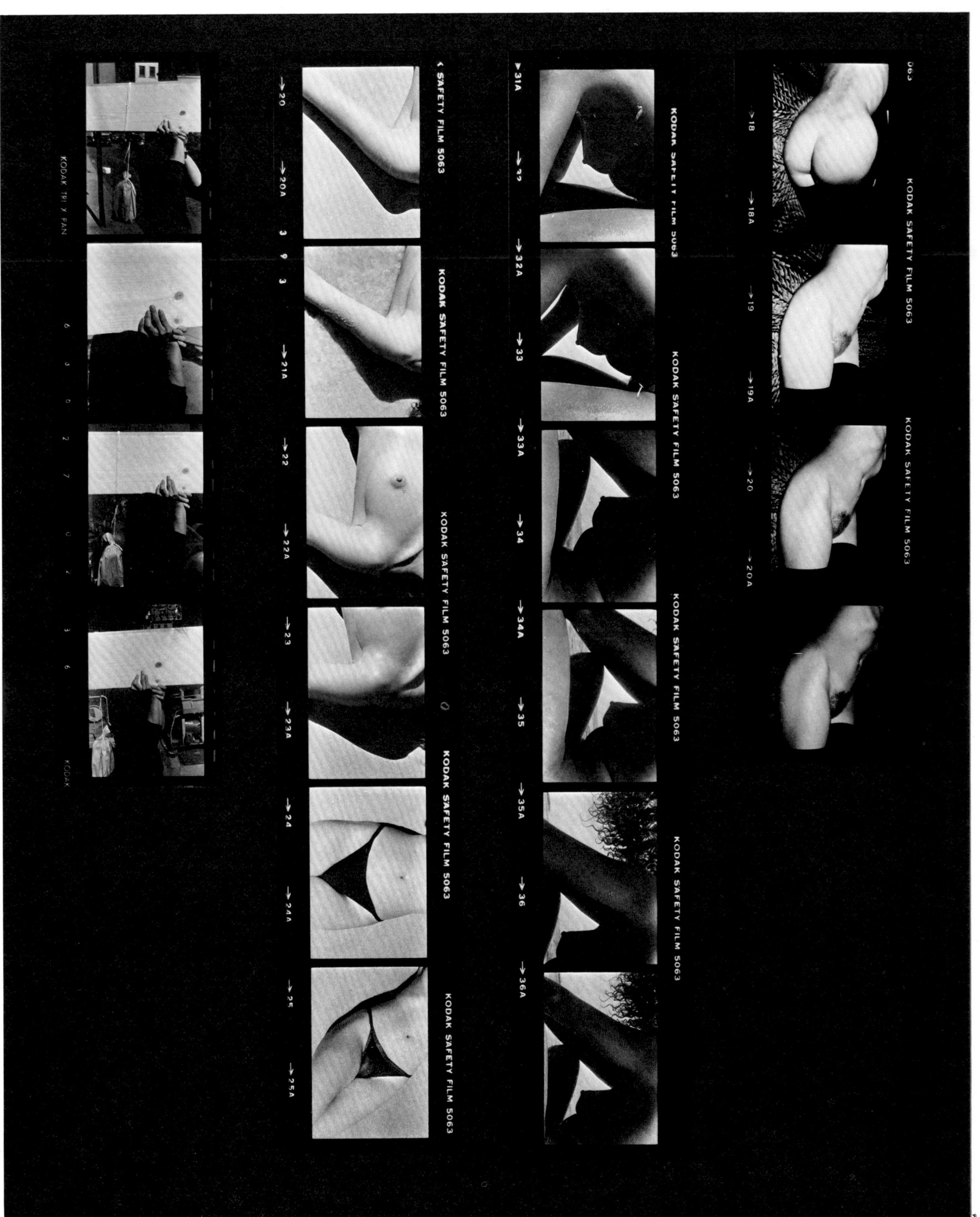

FIGURE 6

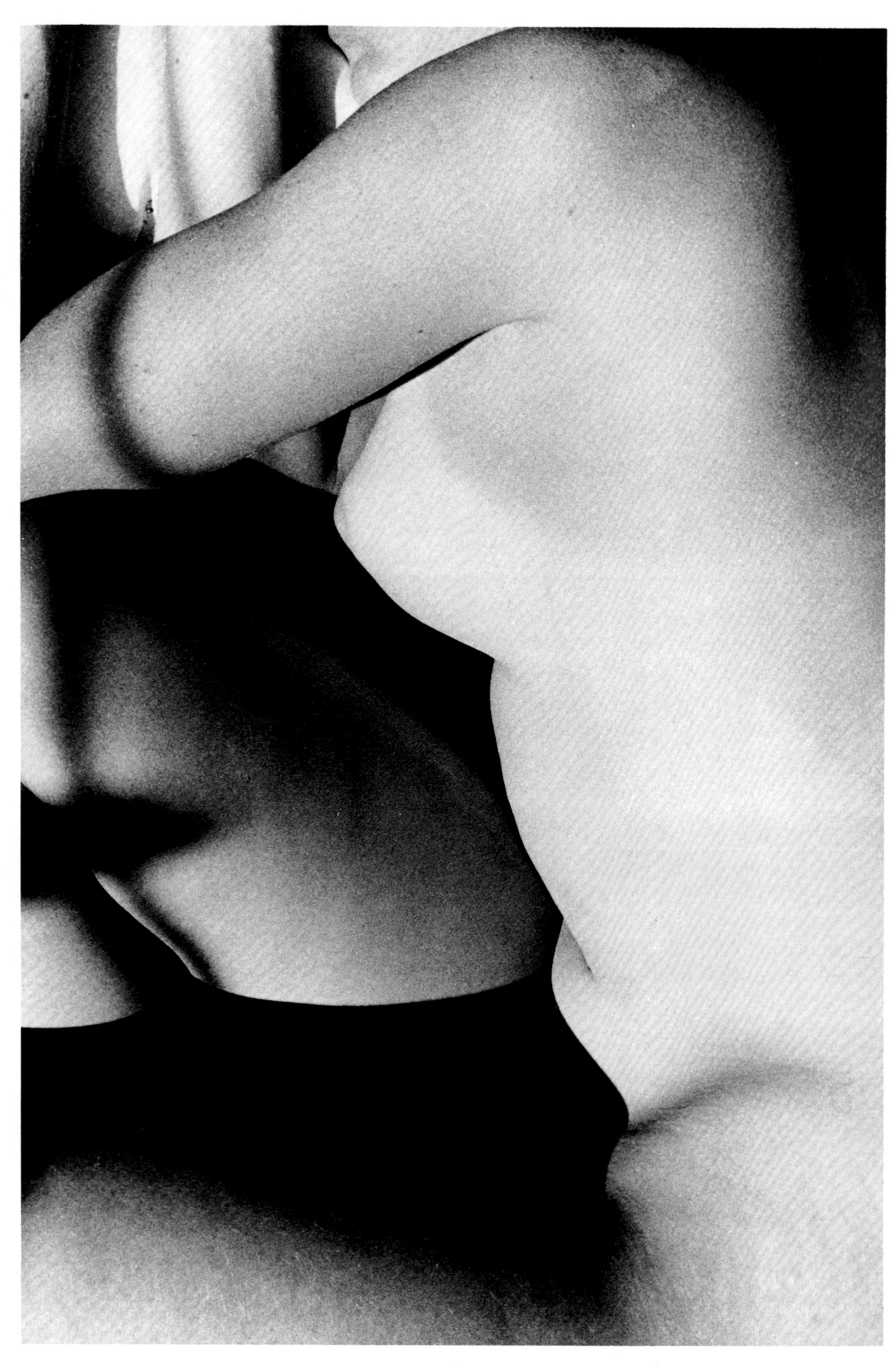

FIGURE 7: UNTITLED, 1978

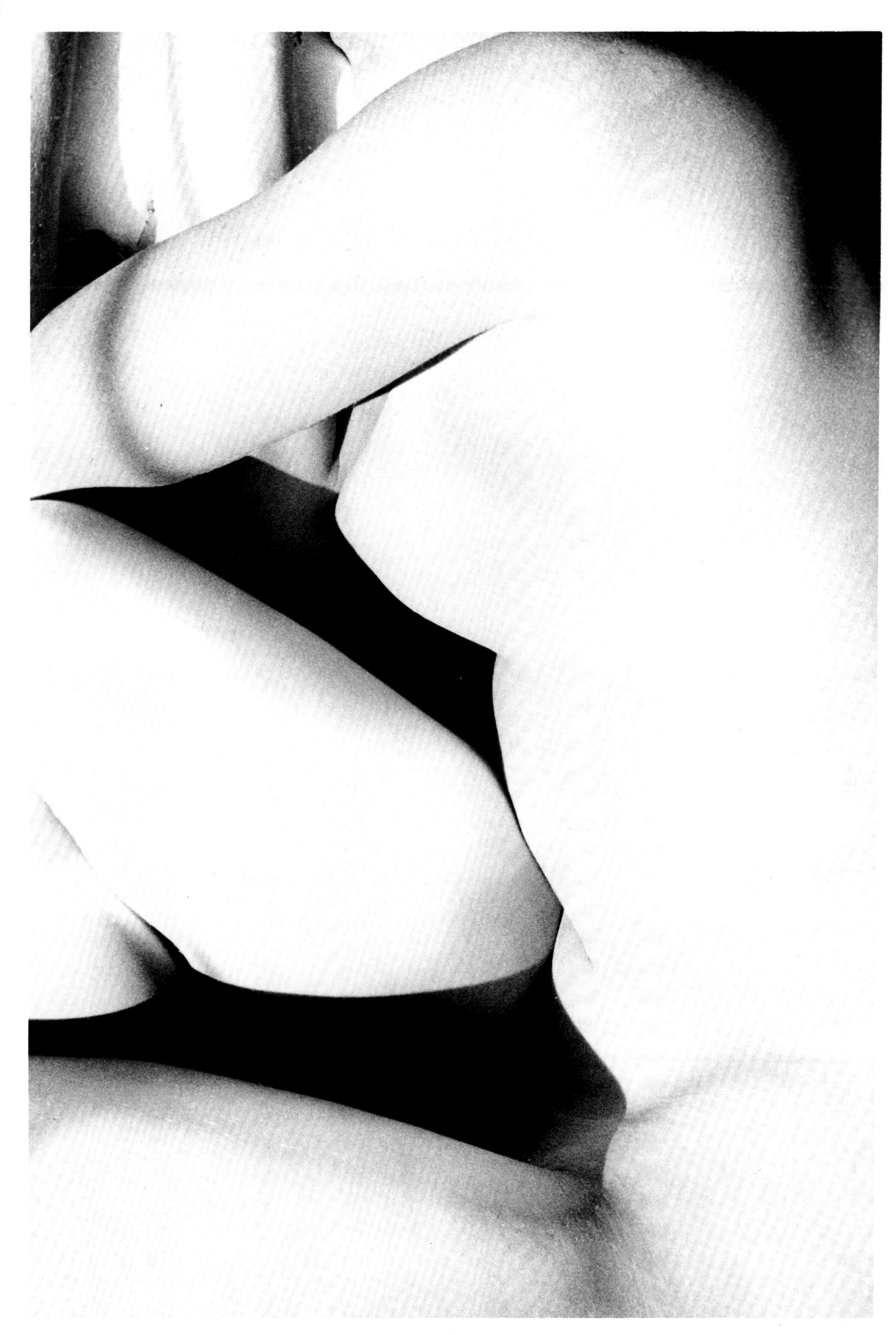

FIGURE 8: UNTITLED, 1978

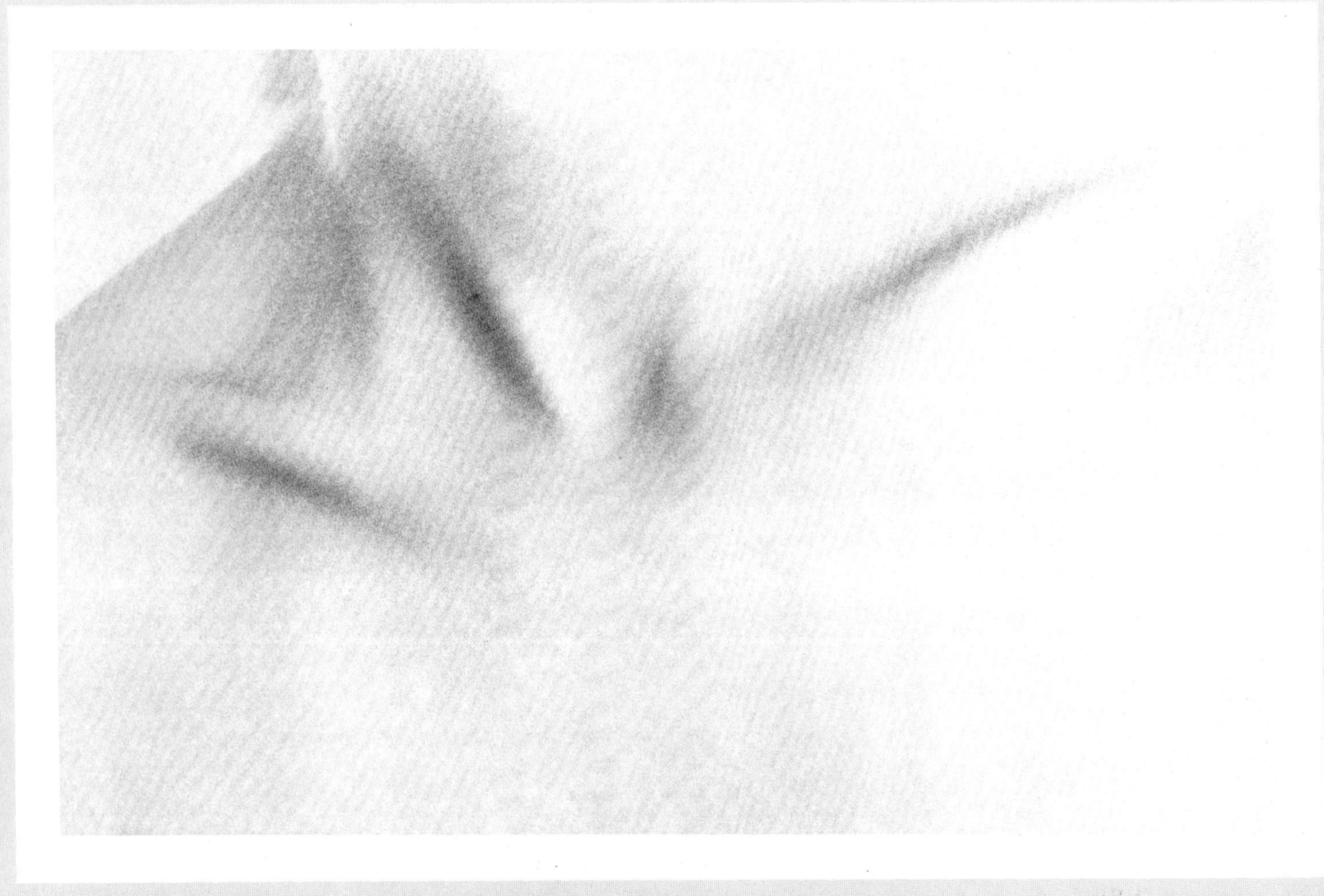

FIGURE 9: UNTITLED, 1979

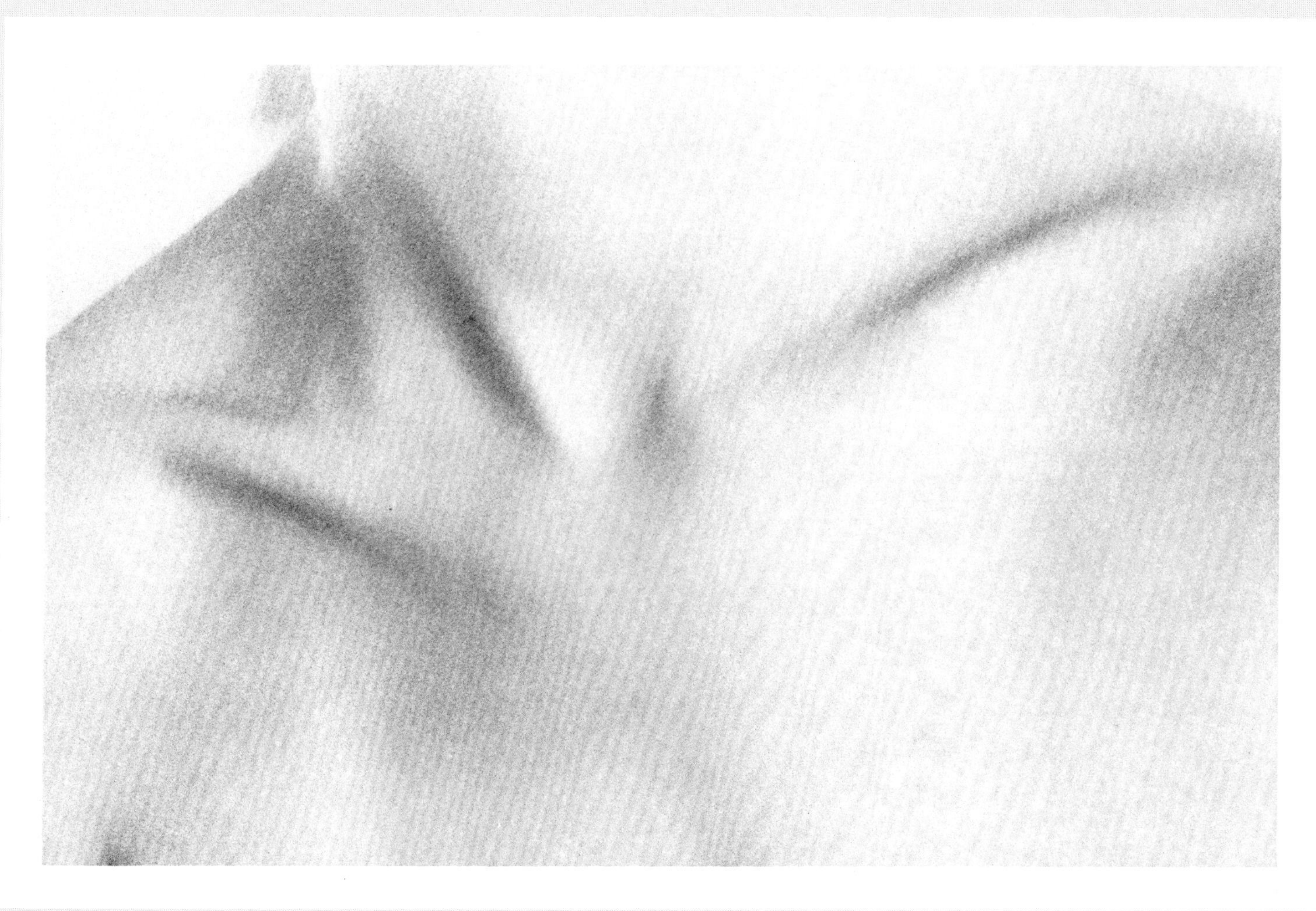

FIGURE 10: UNTITLED, 1979

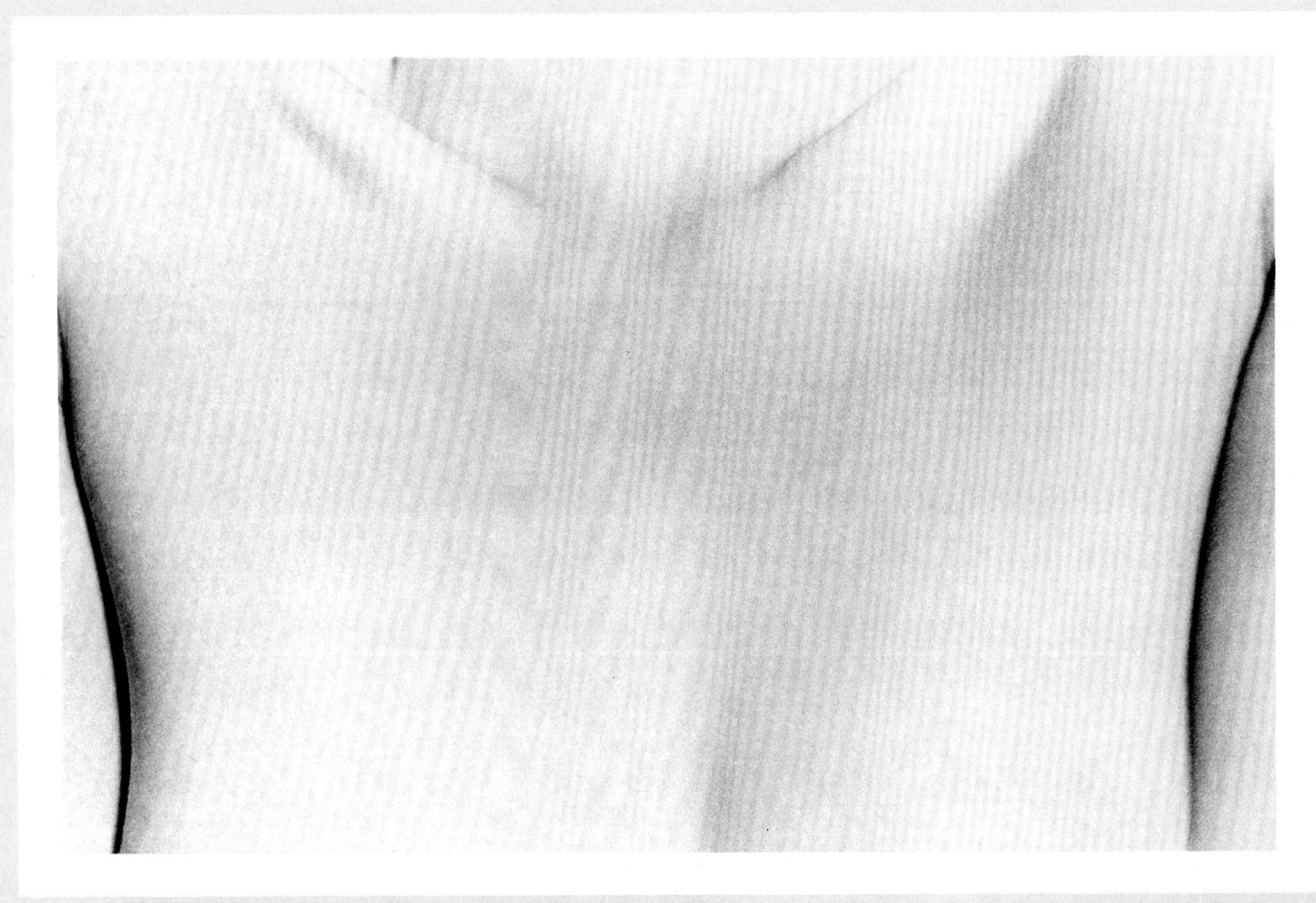

FIGURE 11: UNTITLED, 1979

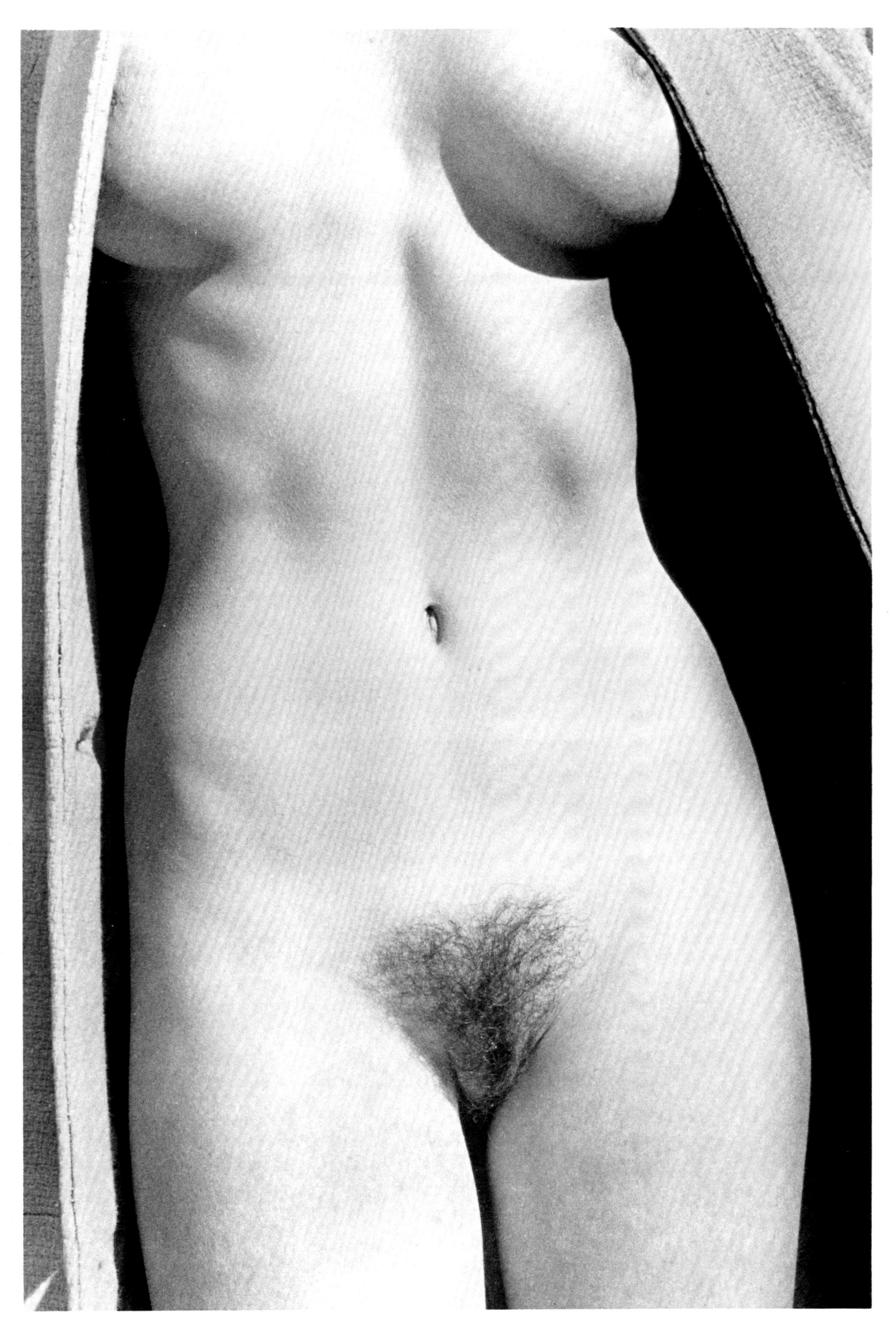

FIGURE 12: UNTITLED, 1979

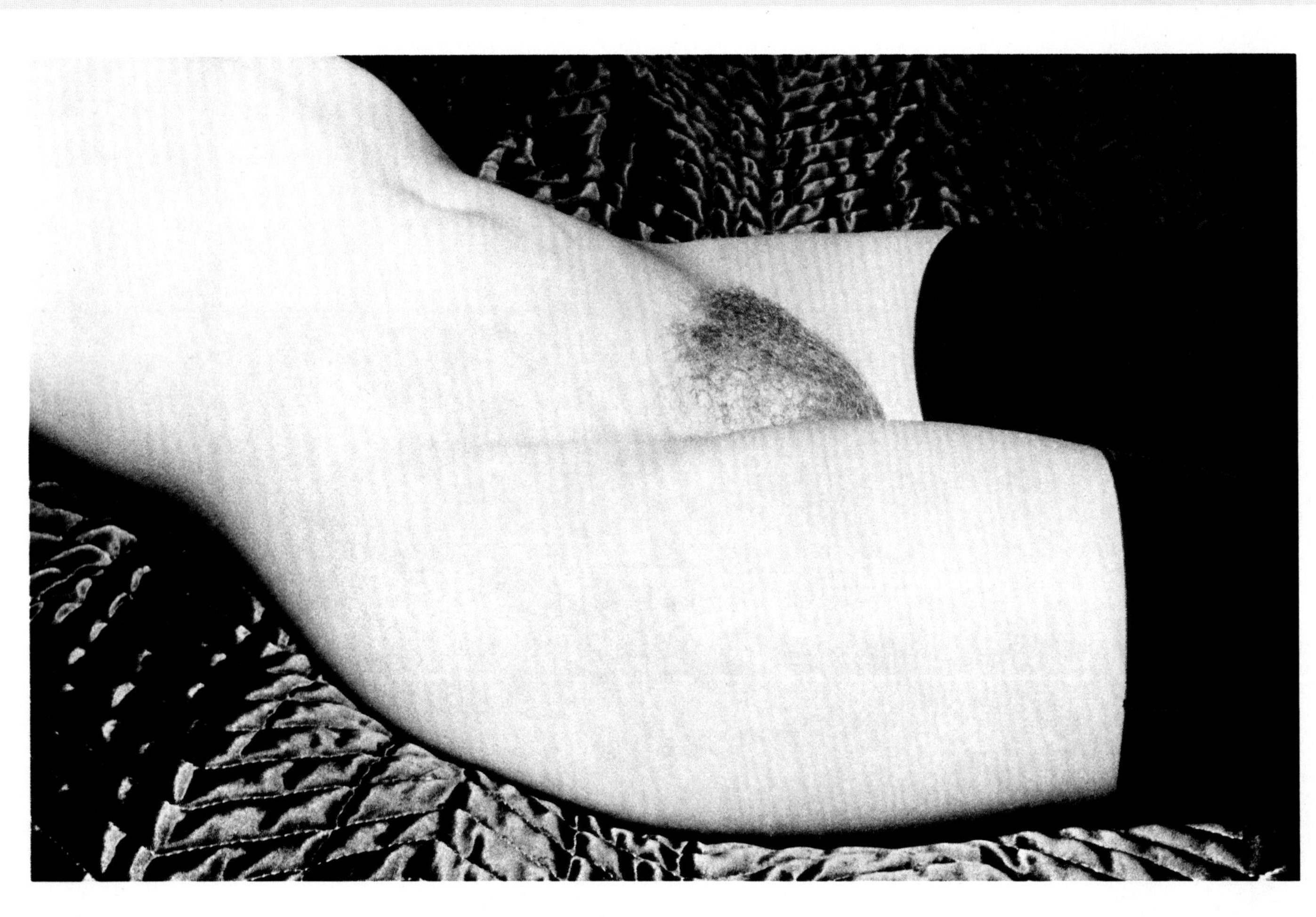

FIGURE 13: UNTITLED, 1979

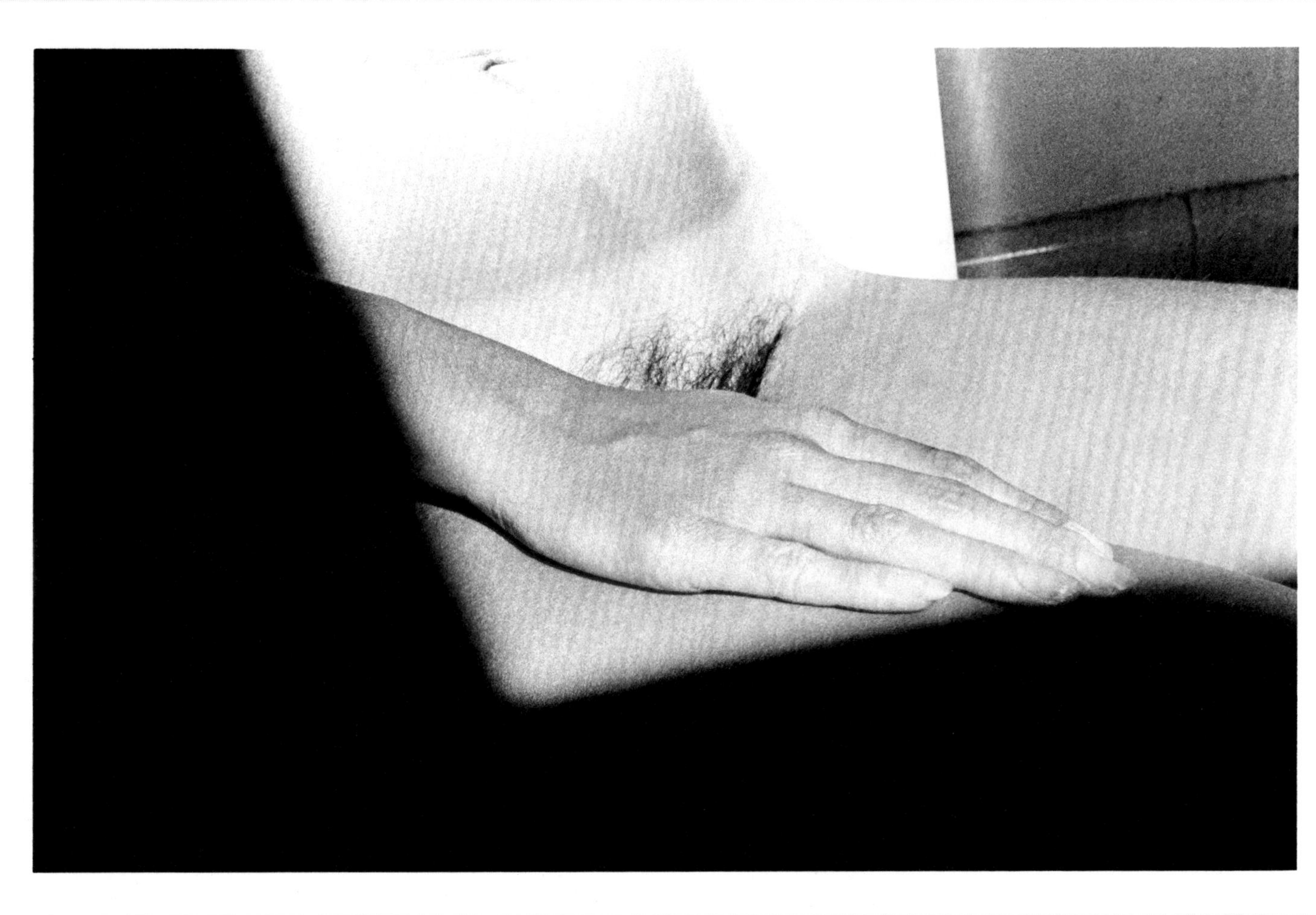

FIGURE 14: UNTITLED, 1975 (From THE QUADRANTS SERIES)

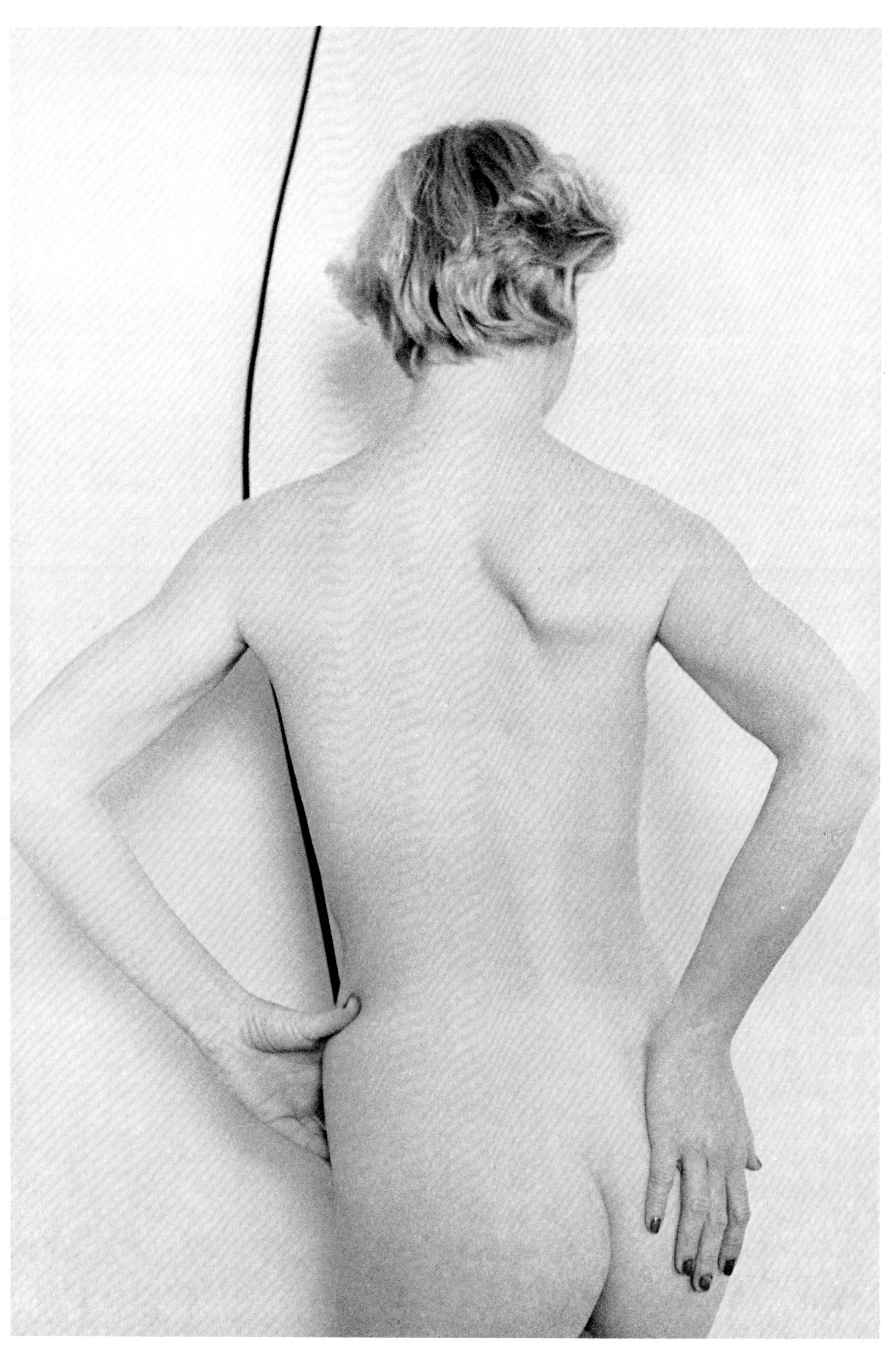

FIGURE 15: UNTITLED, 1979

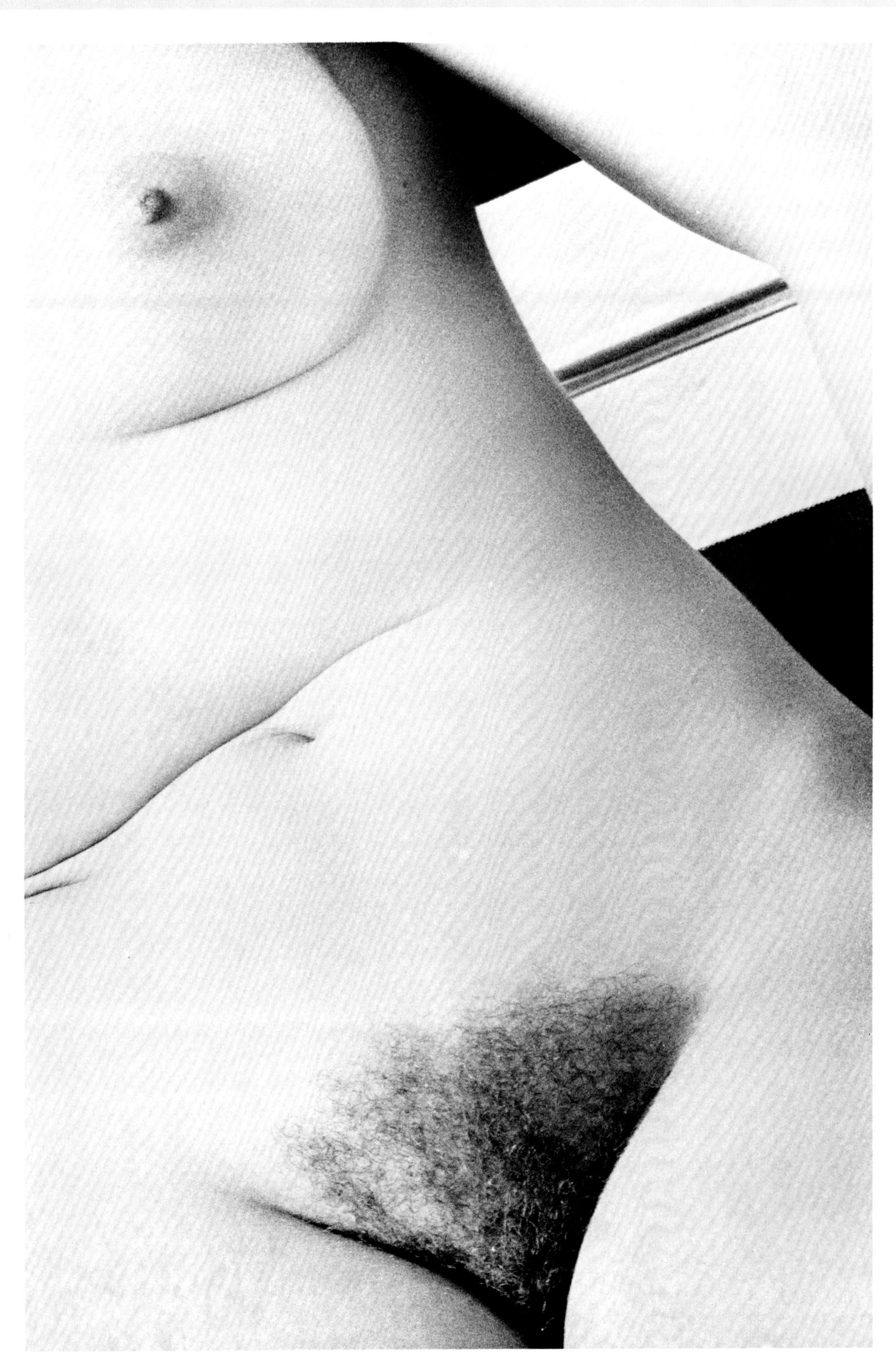

FIGURE 16: UNTITLED, 1979

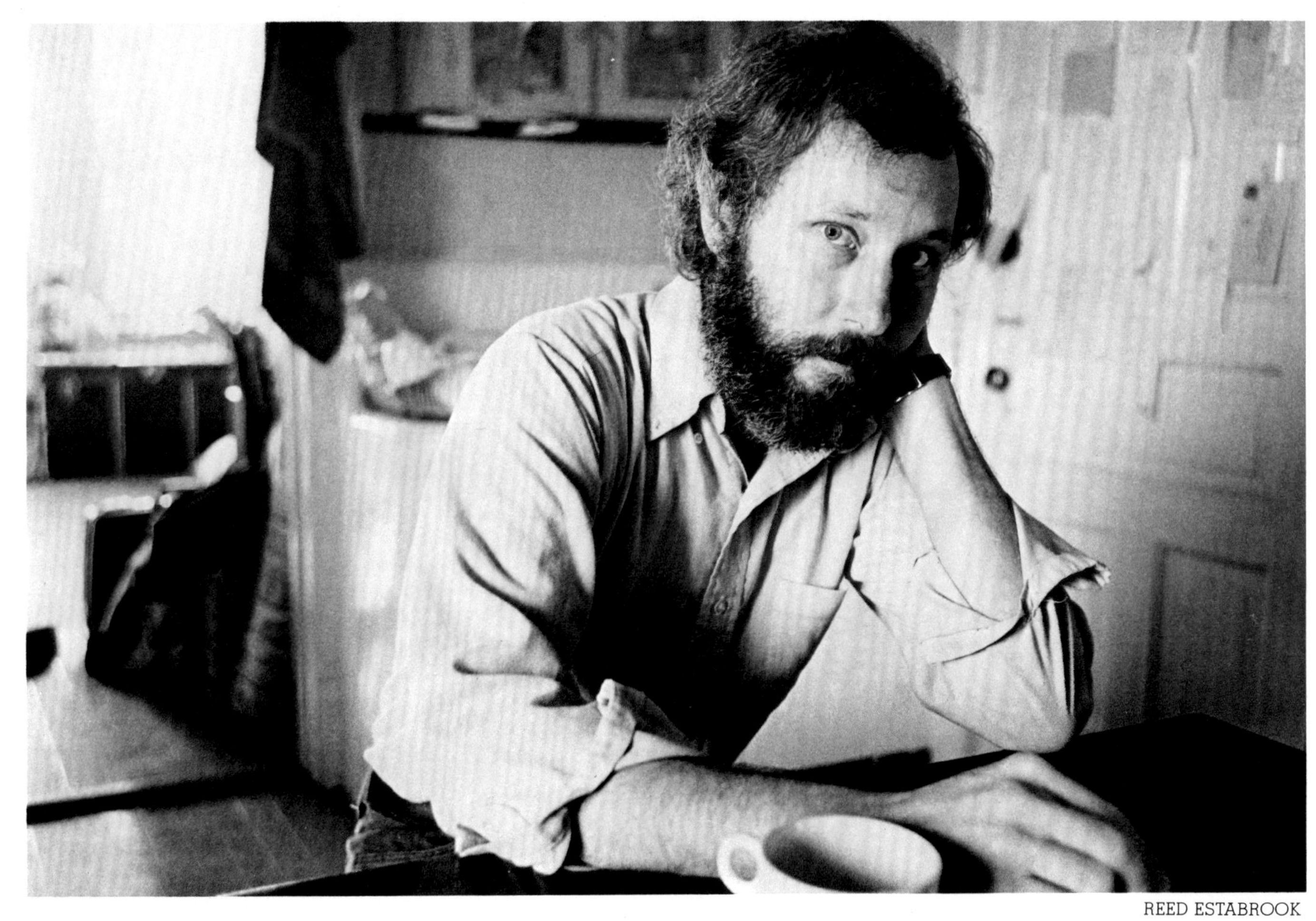
REED ESTABROOK

KENNETH JOSEPHSON: "A CLUE FROM ONE PHOTOGRAPH LEADS TO AN IDEA FOR ANOTHER."

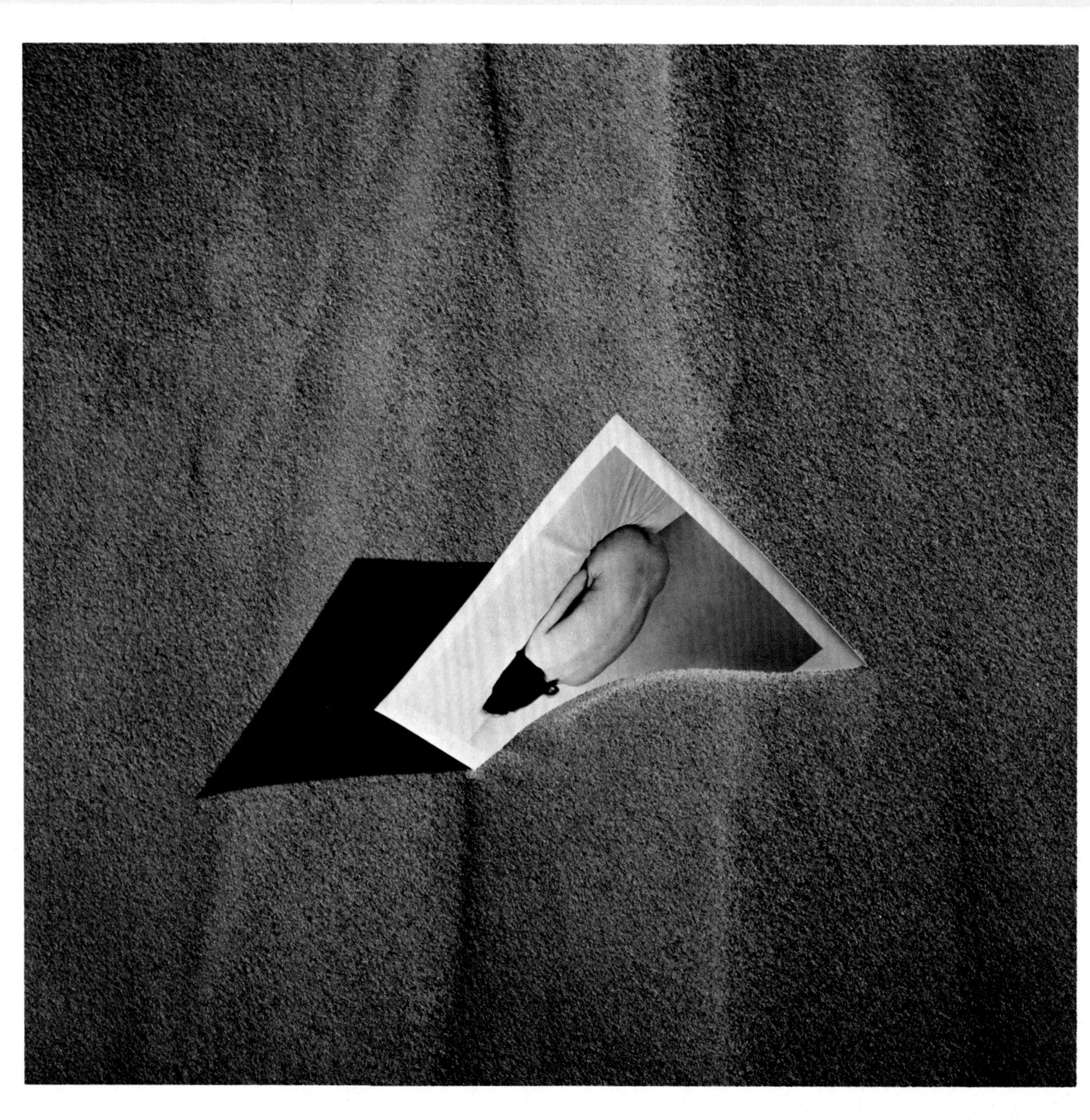

FIGURE 1: HISTORY OF PHOTOGRAPHY, MICHIGAN, 1970

The heart of my method is this: a clue from one photograph leads to an idea for another. At times the subject matter suggests a method of working and vice versa. Sometimes I seek out some specific subject matter with a planned picture in mind, but as I become involved with the subject a very different picture may result. Once the idea for making a multiple exposure of trees in motion came to me while I was working at the problem of multiply exposing trees in focus and out of focus. Through this experience I became more aware of the visual aspects of motion and its relation to time and space. This knowledge was then applied to other subject matter in which movement occurred.

While attempting to resolve an idea, I can never predict which source will supply the clue necessary for its completion. This clue might be furnished by the form and movement of the subject, a type or quality of light observed, an unrelated image viewed somewhere, some music, or a few words read or heard. The best procedure for me to follow is to involve myself completely with a number of problems, then move from one to another, and return to each for the purpose of re-evaluation. Time lapse is the most important factor in this procedure.

Lack of control is also of great value because it allows discovery to occur through trial and error and pure accident. But to understand the results, a knowledge of photographic materials and equipment is important.

The seed of the idea of re-photographing a photograph came when I was a student at The Institute of Design in Chicago. Aaron Siskind, who was teaching there at the time, often described the photographic print on a piece of paper as an object. Talking about the photograph in terms of "objectness" rather than subject matter was a new approach to me. If you speak of a photograph as subject matter you might say, "Look how high that person in the picture is jumping." But a photograph is not a person jumping. It's a representation of the event; it's black-and-white; it's two dimensional; it's on paper; you can hold it in your hand. It's an object. It's so different from the actual event that you have to start talking about it in terms of shapes that result from light striking emulsion, of illusions of spatial relationships, and so on.

I think the idea of holding a picture so that it becomes part of the subject matter of another picture may have come from acquaintance with earlier images in the history of photography. There are daguerreotypes in which a person or a couple are pictured holding a daguerreotype portrait of a deceased relative. This element in my work is a reference to that visual tradition.

Many of my photographs are about the medium of photography, about how photography works. I have a group of images called the HISTORY OF

PHOTOGRAPHY SERIES, which I began about 1970, and to which I've been adding ever since. In the HISTORY SERIES I sometimes make a picture in the style of another photographer. Sometimes the subject matter, by itself, carries the idea of someone's work. Then, too, many of the photographs have to do with photographic processes or historical movements; these are images that make a kind of off-handed reference to the evolution of the medium.

Some of these statements are the result of conflicts in historical movements. I have one photograph of someone painting a scene in Paris. You can see the brush coming into the frame and touching the canvas. The painting on the canvas is a realistic rendition of the scene. Beyond the canvas can be seen the scene itself, the subject of the painting. I was interested in the problem that resulted when photography became a substitute for painting; there was the conflict of one medium replacing the function of another.

Some of the nudes I have photographed are part of the HISTORY OF PHOTOGRAPHY SERIES; some are not. The nudes really result from the fact that I love being around women. I've always been fascinated by them and curious about them, although I don't think psychological insights into women are part of my work.

In most of my nudes you don't see the face of the woman because it never seems to work very well. The face often detracts from the figure, and I'm much more interested in the idea of the figure as a portrait. I think, also, that with this approach there is something asked of the viewer, perhaps a little work to complete the idea, to imagine the person as a whole.

There is a sense of fascination with the double image in the nude on the sand, titled HISTORY OF PHOTOGRAPHY, MICHIGAN, 1970 (Figure 1). The image and the image-within-the-image relate to each other so that there are two different spaces, two different feelings of light. Thc nude was photographed indoors and the sand is outdoors. I crossed light sources this way. I often carry photographs around with me and try placing them in various contexts to be re-photographed. In this image certain things clicked.

I was making a reference to Edward Weston and the kinds of transformations he used to make with vegetables and nudes. The very sensual feeling of his vegetables relates to the concept of the nude. Here the nude itself assumes the shape of a vegetable. Also, Weston dealt with nudes on the sand and so the sand seems appropriate. The sand is vertical, almost like a wall, and the print with the nude is stuck into it. It was late summer when I took the picture, at midafternoon, when the shadow created this particular form on the sand. Finally, the image is very carefully photographed and printed, a little bit more so than usual, so that it would approach the quality that Weston achieved.

The small photograph placed in the sand was done in 1960, when I first started working with the nude. Since then it has been part of other subject matter I've dealt with, part of everything else. For me, there has never been a long period of concentrated work exclusively with the nude. The final photograph here was taken in 1978. There is an evolution in the pictures. The later work is perhaps more romantic in feeling than the earlier images. The nude in the sand is a very hard-edged thing. Many of the later pictures get into softer line and imagery.

The photograph POLAPAN, 1973 (Figure 2) has to do with the very interesting thing about Polaroid material, that it's so immediate. You can use it in another context instantly.

One of the things I've always liked about this shot is that the insert picture is out of scale in relation to the legs and yet it appears to be in perfect scale. That's the illusion here, and I can't figure out why it works, but it does. Perhaps it's due to the continuation of the line between the legs; there's a tying in of the two images. On the contact sheet from which this picture is taken (Figure 3), the images in which the Polaroid insert does not tie in with the line do not work as well for me.

I have always liked the particular fabric that the woman is lying on. I like that kind of visual activity and the enrichment it lends to the photograph. Two years previously I had done the shooting on a plain background (Figure 3) and it looked very dull. I simply wasn't very satisfied with the series done with a plain skirt and background and so I redid it. I repeat an idea until I get it right, going back and re-shooting. Three shootings were involved in the Polaroid sequence. In frames No. 11 and 12 on the contact sheet there was a sunlight pattern. The light made the images too disorganized. It chopped them up too much and the clarity was lost. The flatter light on No. 13 was better.

The Polaroid insert in this series introduces another idea. I think of photographs as representations of windows. The Polaroid makes the picture intrinsically voyeuristic. People are always covering themselves up in public situations, but here it's almost as if the viewer has X-ray vision. I often wondered as a child if some people could see through clothes. That possibility really intrigued me. I don't think that voyeurism as a concept has influenced my work overall, but here it is definitely a factor.

I also like the row of three photographs with the Polaroid on the floor (Figure 3). The photograph can be a window, but here it becomes something else. I've always been intrigued with Oliver Wendell Holmes' description of the daguerreotype as a mirror with a memory. I guess I was thinking of the Polaroid

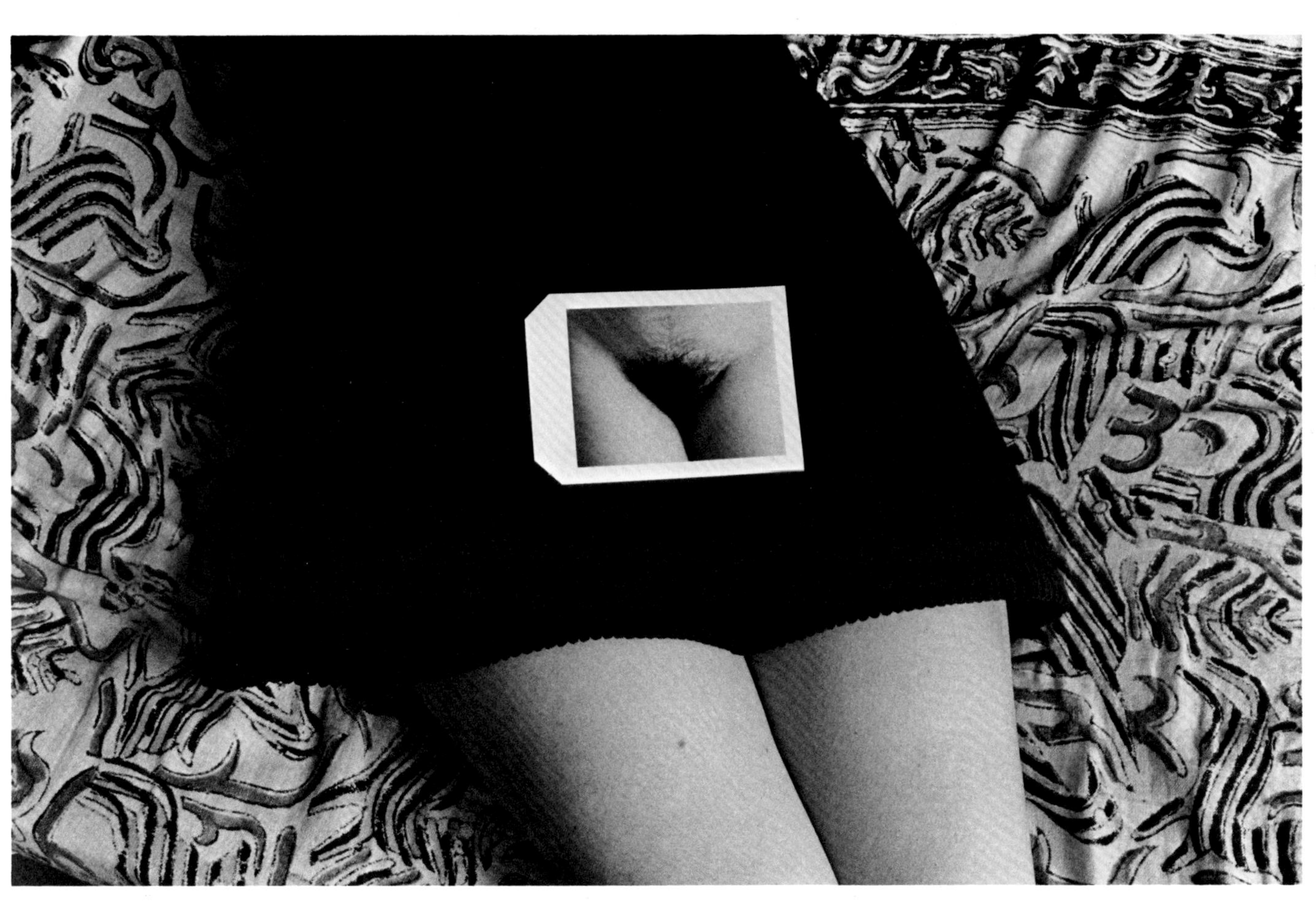

FIGURE 2: POLAPAN, 1973

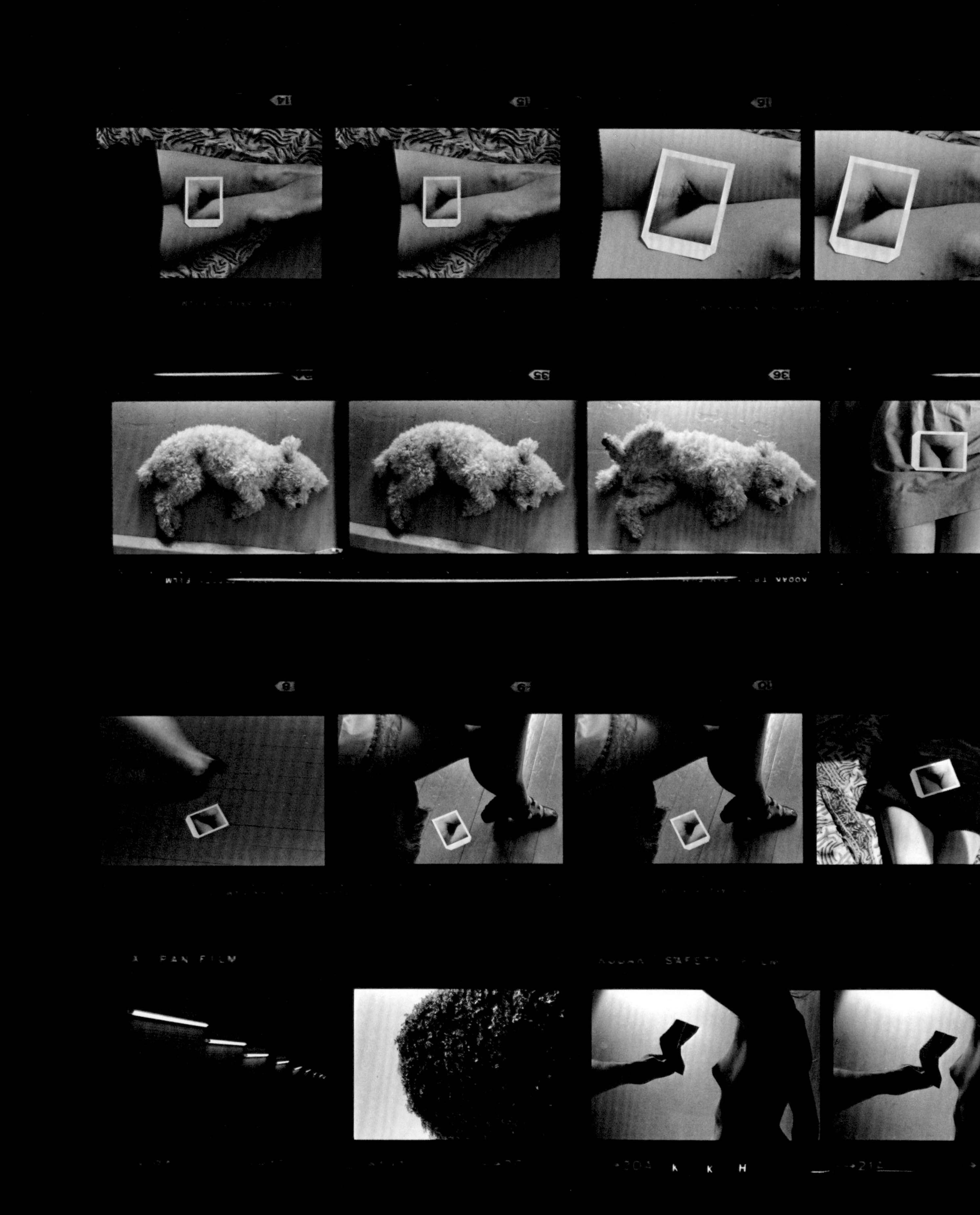

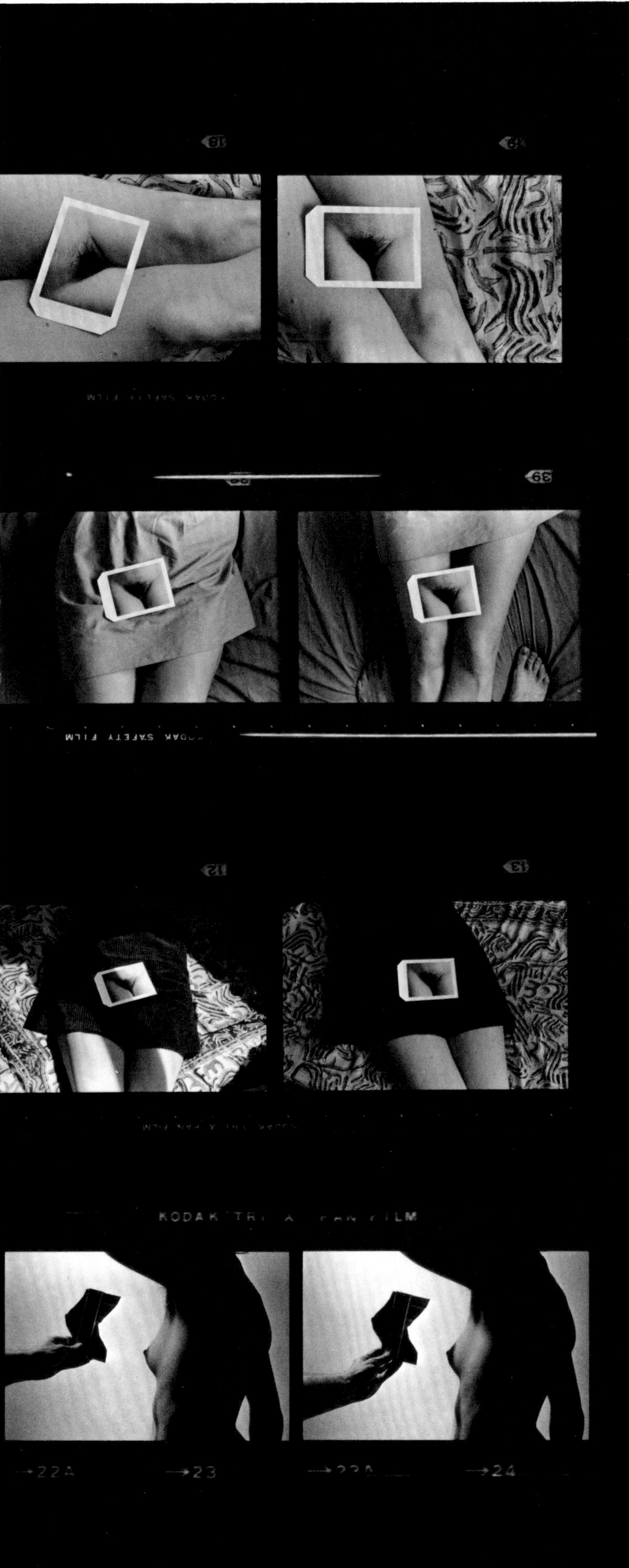

FIGURE 3

as a mirroring device, and there it is underneath the model's body. Students had told me that in the 60s on the subway sometimes men put mirrors on their shoes, which seemed quite bizarre. So maybe voyeurism once again crept into the concept underlying the photograph. Voyeurism may also have a little to do with frame No. 8 in which the Polaroid is on the floor and a leg is passing by. Also, there's a visual contradiction here in that the Polaroid is stationary and the body is in motion.

In the photograph SALLY, 1976 (Figure 4) there's a visual question of whether that's a photograph inserted in a matte, or a person. Of course, it's actually a person. There's another element. We've all seen pictures in which an extra hand or some part of the body has been introduced into the frame of the photograph, seemingly coming from nowhere. I'm intrigued by that sort of thing, but it's not the reason I took the picture. I'm just saying that the hands holding the matte remind me of it. Then there's the idea of taking a rectangle out of its normal reference, out of reality. That rectangle becomes a defined picture inside the larger picture.

In Figure 5 there appears a sequence of nine photographs taken with the nude and the matte board. In every frame but No. 42, the figure appeared above the board. It just seemed that the image that gave the illusion of the framed figure worked best. The photographs in the top row of mattes are of gas tanks at a storage area. The gas tank has a very round shape, a very feminine quality, and this is why I used it with the nude. Then I changed photographs in the matte, experimenting with a picture of a reflection of a white pole on water, with my finger pointing to the reflection.

The last two frames on that contact sheet are there simply because they were the next two pictures I made. The figure in the photograph appears to be nude, but actually the giant book covers her clothing. I checked out the largest book The Art Institute of Chicago had. I liked the idea of that big book being carried around by that figure. I thought of it as a book with legs.

In the second SALLY, 1976 (Figure 10), the television relates to the concept of a rectangular opening similar to that of an overmatte. Normally, we use TV as an image source; here it becomes a light source to illuminate subject matter outside the rectangle. I have often watched the light on people's faces as they gather around a TV in a darkened room. This remembrance was one of the stimuli for the photograph.

I thought the silhouette effect of the lighting in CHICAGO, 1976 (Figure 8) was most appropriate to show the objects in the photograph and how they interrelate. I like the shapes in this photograph. The object held in my hand is a contour gauge. It's used by archaeologists and

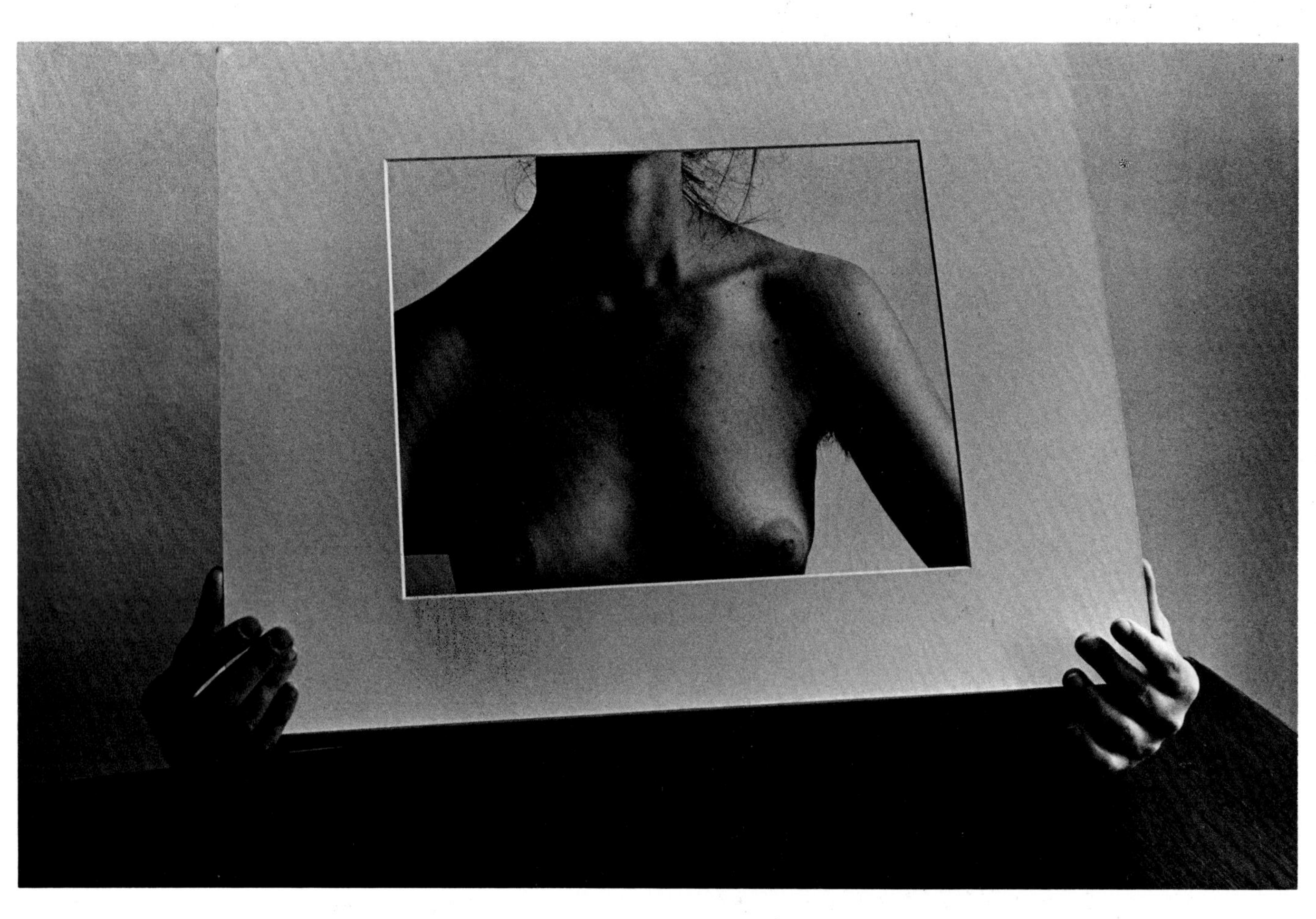

FIGURE 4: SALLY, 1976

carpenters. You press this tool against something hard like a molding to get the impression of its contour. The tool consists of tiny rods that travel, duplicating the shape. It's not possible to make an impression of something soft, like a breast. I had to create that shape by pushing the rods.

On the contact sheet (Figure 3) Nos. 21 through 23 were off in the framing. I used a Leica M4 on this series and I often have to make several pictures to make sure I have what I want. If I used a single-lens reflex there might be less of a problem because you can see exactly what the camera sees. However, in this case I was holding the gauge and I couldn't look through the camera as I was taking the picture. It was physically impossible. And so I took several, hoping one would work out. In the one I selected (frame No. 24), the gauge and the breast seemed to line up more convincingly. There was a more direct translation of the shape of the breast to the object.

In Figure 6 there are some more versions of the contour gauge series, done in the 2¼ format. I don't like the angle of most of these pictures. The shadow is bad and the suggestion of a very large stomach is here. This wasn't really the case, and, also, I don't particularly like the shapes that result in the lower white area. The final selection seemed to have more drama to it.

CHICAGO, 1976 (Figure 7) is, in part, a reference to commercial photography. I've always been intrigued with the real hard-core commercial picture done when an employee retires, the cliché type of thing that overdoes a point. This relates to the obviousness of pointing to something, in this case marks left on the skin by underclothing. The pencil exaggerates and overdoes the making of a point. I also like the idea of its being there to give a sense of scale.

Of the pictures on this contact sheet (Figure 6), the one with the pencil pointed horizontally is the only one I would use. The others don't seem to be as successful. You go about choosing pictures on a contact sheet in a very subjective way. I don't like the angle of the pencil on most of the pictures. On No. 7, my fingers were out of the frame, and the form of the woman was not as interesting as in the one selected. I thought the final choice had a more interesting shape, and I like the suggestion of a hand coming into the frame. I like the wrinkle marks. Most photographers wait until those marks go away before they start shooting. Usually the model waits for half-an-hour in a robe.

In the photographs with the bra marks, I didn't make the marks as visible as I should have. In one picture the pencil is actually making contact with the skin. It really bothered me. It looked painful and I didn't like that.

The black line around the figure in CHICAGO, 1977 (Figure 9) is a sealer that you put around doors and windows. I made this picture because I wanted to deal with the idea of a pseudo-flash. I wanted the effect of a modeling light and of that hard shadow that flash creates when a three-dimensional object is close to a background. Also, I have always been fascinated with Weston's use of that hairline shadow at the edge of the figure. I was thinking of both things when I took this photograph.

I'm also very interested in this particular woman's figure. Quite beautiful. She's not a large woman, but here she appears much fleshier. I think some lenses have a tendency to do that, to make the body look fleshy.

NEW YORK, 1978 (Figure 11) refers again to the idea of mattes and images-within-images. I wanted to use the matte to give the feeling of a window being present. At the same time it becomes a way of creating a shape that influences the three dimensional quality of the nude. The flatness and two dimensionality of the rectangle of light create another shape on the hips, and the matte blocks the light from spreading beyond the rectangle. I held the matte and I asked the model to hold the flash. This lighting is atypical in my work, but it's characteristic of a kind of quality you get when you work with flash.

When I photograph the nude, the length of the shooting and the number of photographs taken depend on how many ideas I have on that particular day. I usually take two to three rolls of film in an hour-and-a-half session. As I have indicated, many times I reuse photographs or ideas that are the result of previous work. In some cases, a shooting might last only 15 minutes or so. Most of my models are women I am close to. When you have the same model around all the time, it's a different situation than when you hire one. With a hired model, you might do a lot of work all at once. When you are photographing a wife or friend, the work usually extends over a period of time. Also, you are in a position to observe interesting things when you are around a person in a day-to-day living situation. You can enlarge on the observation photographically. For example, the underwear marks on skin: that was something observed in a day-to-day situation and then referred to in my work.

In terms of technical approach, I want a very uncomplicated way of working, a standardized procedure. It relieves me of all the fussing around that can go into the process, but which doesn't interest me very much. It seems to sidetrack me and impede the amount of work accomplished. I don't want to have to think about making adjustments in what I'm doing all the time. I concentrate all my work within a controlled technical framework. I'm interested in the idea, the visual image, and I want the procedure very clean.

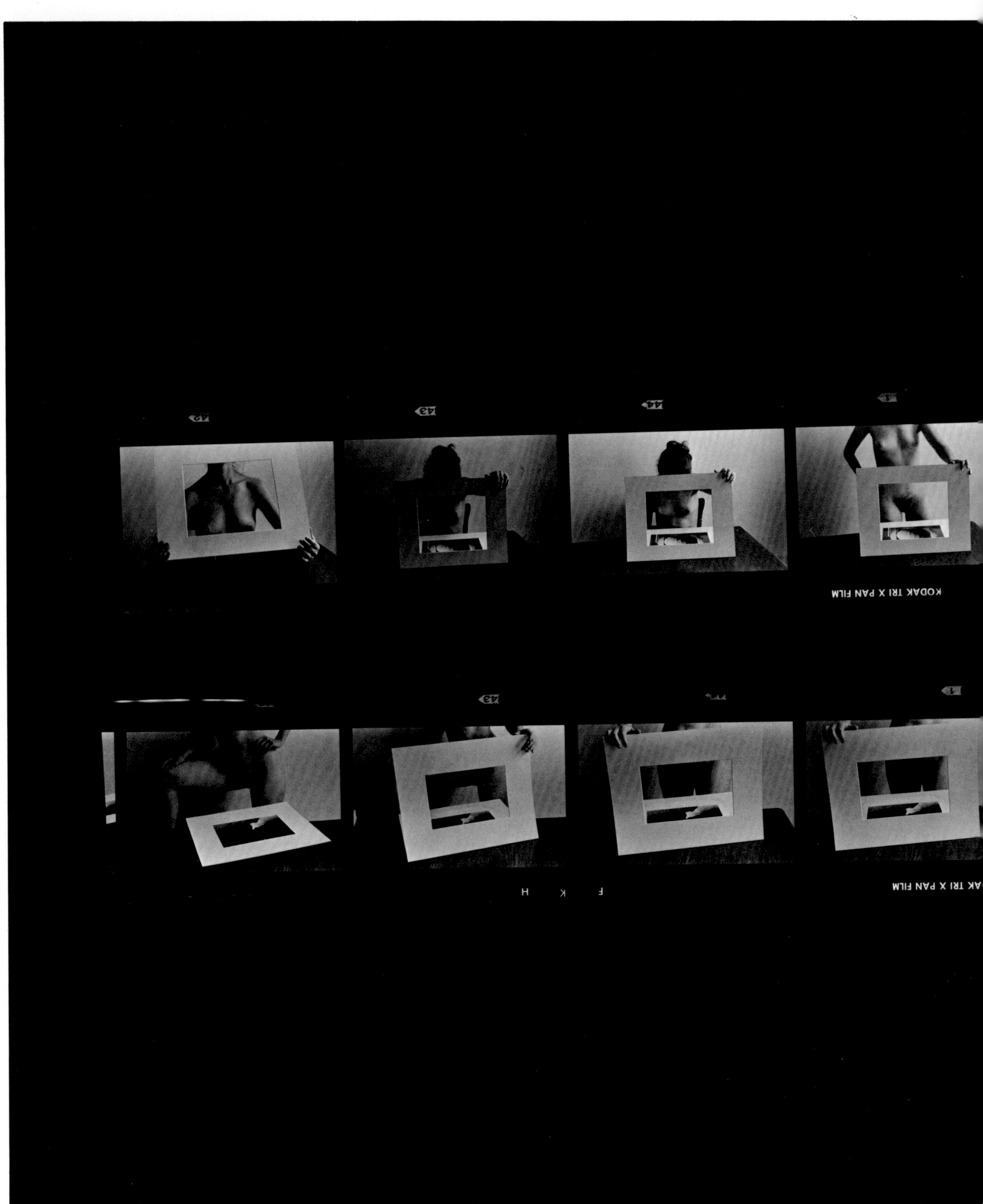
KODAK TRI X PAN FILM

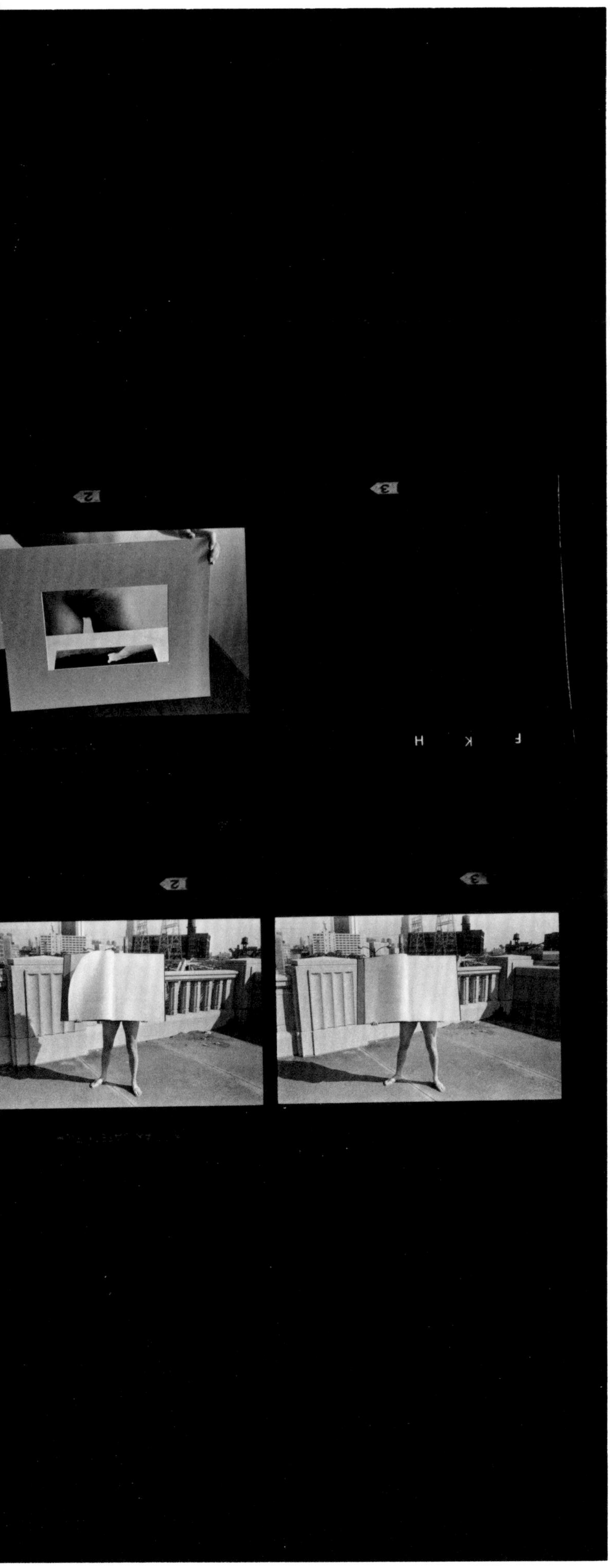

FIGURE 5

I have purchased a great deal of photographic equipment through the years. I find I like the kind of quality I get from the Leica M4, the way it operates, its reliability, and its lenses. I do perhaps 70% of my work with a 35mm Leitz lens, but I also use a 50 or 90mm when appropriate. I would use a 90mm with a nude if there were a small area I was really trying to concentrate on, or if I wanted to flatten space somewhat. I might also use the 90mm if there were a reason for keeping distance from the model.

The other camera I use a lot is a 2¼ x 2¼, an old Rolleiflex from the 50s. It has a 75mm Tessar lens, which I think is a really beautiful lens. It describes the subject matter in a very nice way and it's extremely sharp.

If I had to take a particular picture, I would just pick up whatever camera was nearby. However, certain pictures just seem more appropriate to certain kinds of cameras. I don't think about this too much. The nude with the pencil was done with the 2¼. The skin quality produced by a 2¼ Plus-X negative seems very appropriate for this particular image. All the 2¼ work is done on a tripod, and some of the 35mm work is done this way, too.

I also have other format cameras, including an 11 x 14 view camera that I use from time to time. I've never done any nudes with this camera, but I really enjoy photographing with it because it seems to me rather a primitive way of working. I like the fact that I can make 11 x 14 contact prints with it.

I use Tri-X film for 35mm photographs and Plus-X for 2¼ work, and normally I print the full negative. The quality and speed of Tri-X are very suitable for my work. I expose it at about EI 500 or 550 rather than the manufacturer's recommended 400 ASA, and this seems to work very well with Ethol UFG developer and Agfa Brovira paper. I expose Plus-X at 125 ASA. I usually don't under or overdevelop my film, except in some rare instance in which the lighting is so unusual that I have to use a different exposure index. I just give the film a standard development and I know that my paper contrasts will allow me a certain range of over and underexposure in printing.

I have gone through periods of testing photographic materials to establish the film, film speed, developers and paper that provide the best results for my work. Ultimately, Ethol UFG film developer gave me the grain pattern and rich tonal scale that other developers didn't seem to provide. My normal development time is 3¾ minutes for Tri-X and 3 minutes for Plus-X. Ansel Adams' Beers formula was among the paper developers I experimented with, but it was much too time consuming to mix the chemicals. It seemed that Kodak Dektol provided me with a very satisfactory print.

My aim is to treat my prints archivally. For example, I use two hypo baths and a hypo clearing agent, and I'm careful about the number of prints I put through the hypo.

I strive for a fairly standard full tonal scale. This is what I like best and it is the way I see. A typical print would be the nude with the contour gauge. It was a fairly straight print with a little burning in at the upper left-hand corner, where I wanted to get some additional separation and tonality.

I work on some part of my total involvement with photography every day. I may be photographing one day and the next day I may be processing, or reading books on photography, or just sending out bills. There are periods when I shoot a lot more; periods when I print a lot more. It's not like being a writer. I'm mystified that a writer can create a schedule. I don't know how many writers actually do it, but I've heard about it from several people who know that at a certain time of the day, every day, they're going to be writing for several hours. I couldn't do the same thing every day.

Basically, I earn my living as a teacher. I really enjoy teaching and the contact with people who are learning and growing very rapidly. In a school there is concentrated effort. It's not like the "real world;" it's an artificial environment in which there's rapid growth in people's ideas. I like being part of that process and observing it. It's very enriching and exciting.

The teachers who were most important in my development were Aaron Siskind and Harry Callahan. I studied with them both at The Institute of Design in Chicago. I think Callahan's nudes had somewhat of an influence on my nudes. My photograph of the nude with the contour gauge reminds me of that heavy silhouette Callahan did of Eleanor with her arms up, ELEANOR, 1948. It's a transformation and I'm interested in the idea of transformation. I like the shapes that result in Callahan's nude and I think that unconsciously they are reflected in my images. I know his work very well; I know Siskind's, too.

The biggest change in my photography took place when I went to The Institute of Design as a graduate student in 1958. Ever since then, I've continued building on and expanding certain key ideas. I'd like to go back to some ideas I haven't dealt with for a while and re-explore them. For example, I haven't made collages for a couple of years and I intend to go back to them again.

I would like to point out that I approach some of my work from a somewhat humorous point of view. I think that's been lacking in the history of photography. It's all too serious. Ultimately, my aim is to make a visual statement rather than a verbal statement about our medium because I think it is an important thing to do.

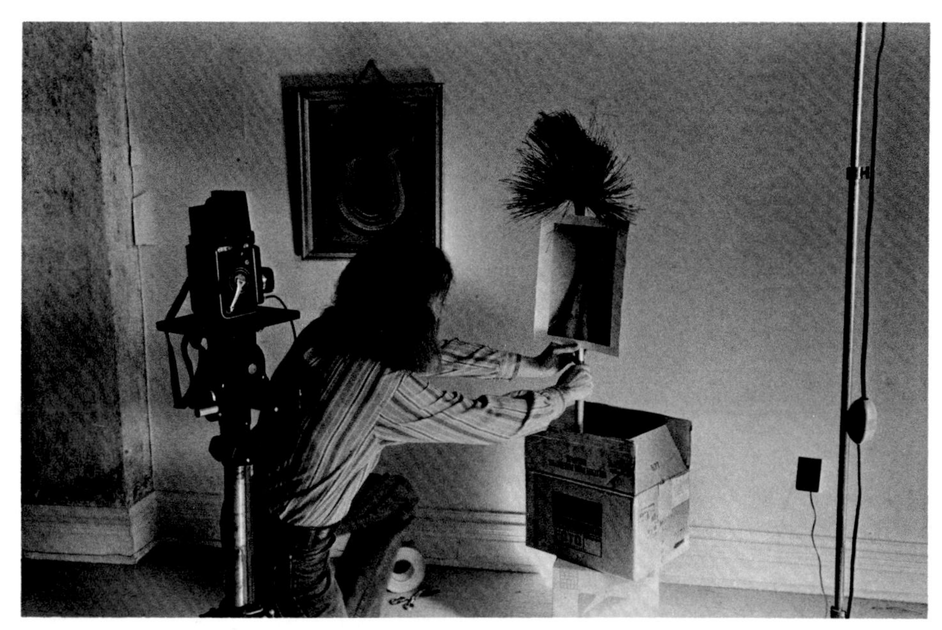

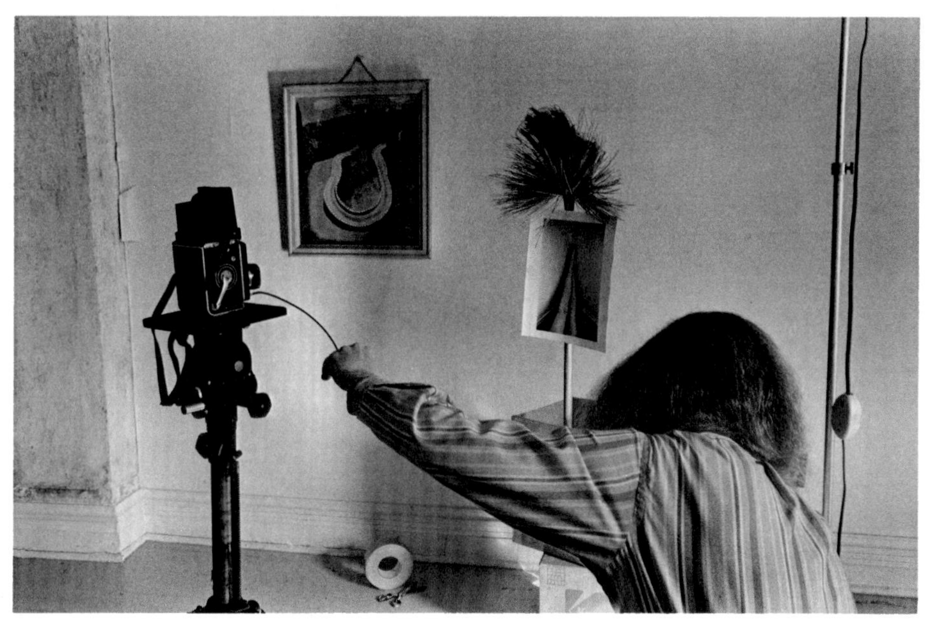

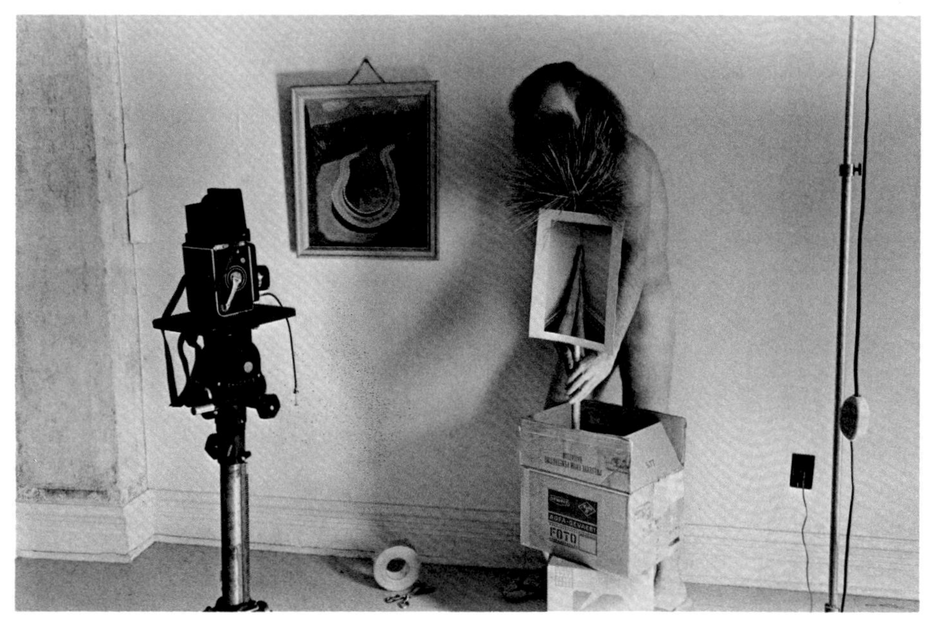

SELF-PORTRAIT OF THE PHOTOGRAPHER AT WORK.

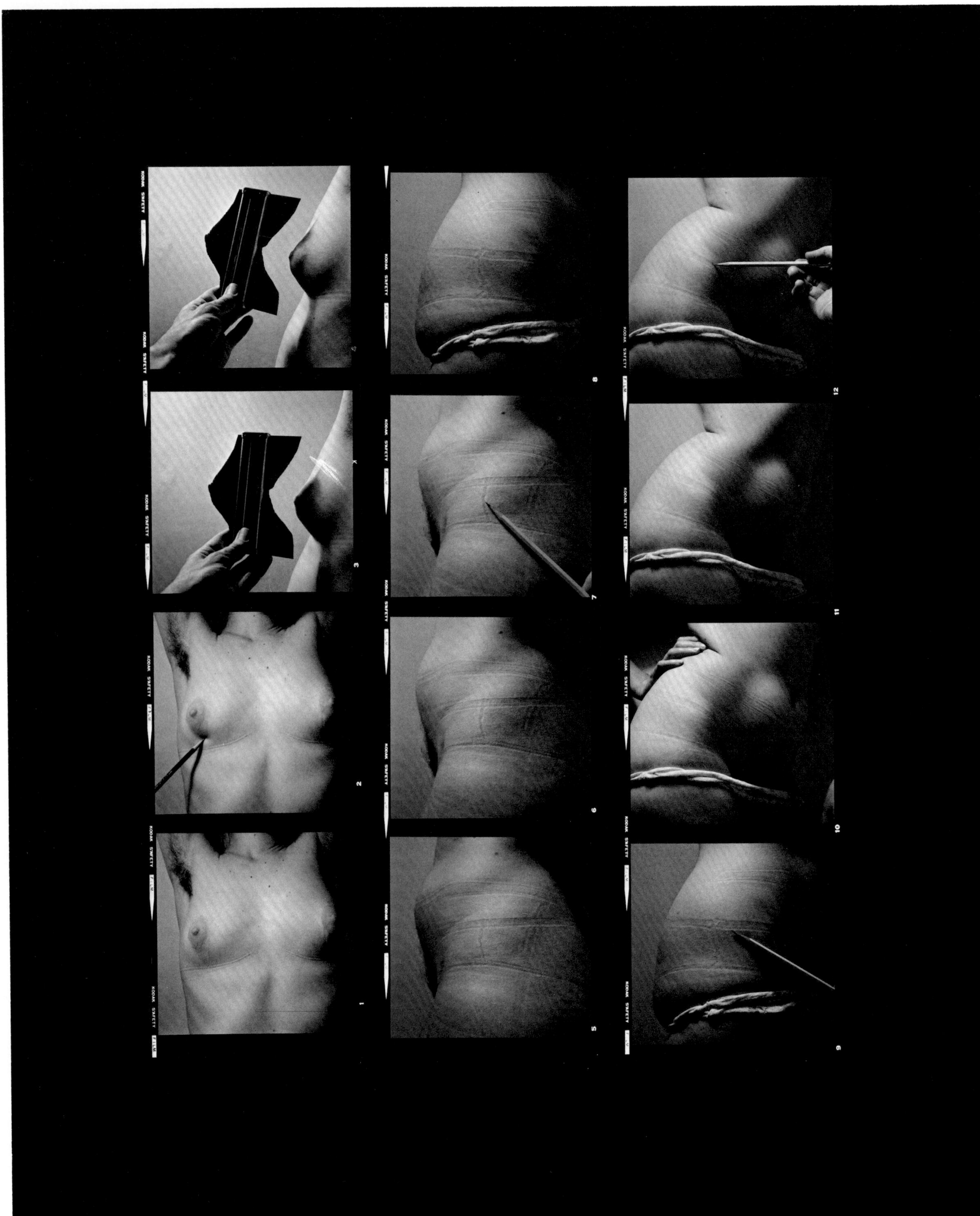

FIGURE 6

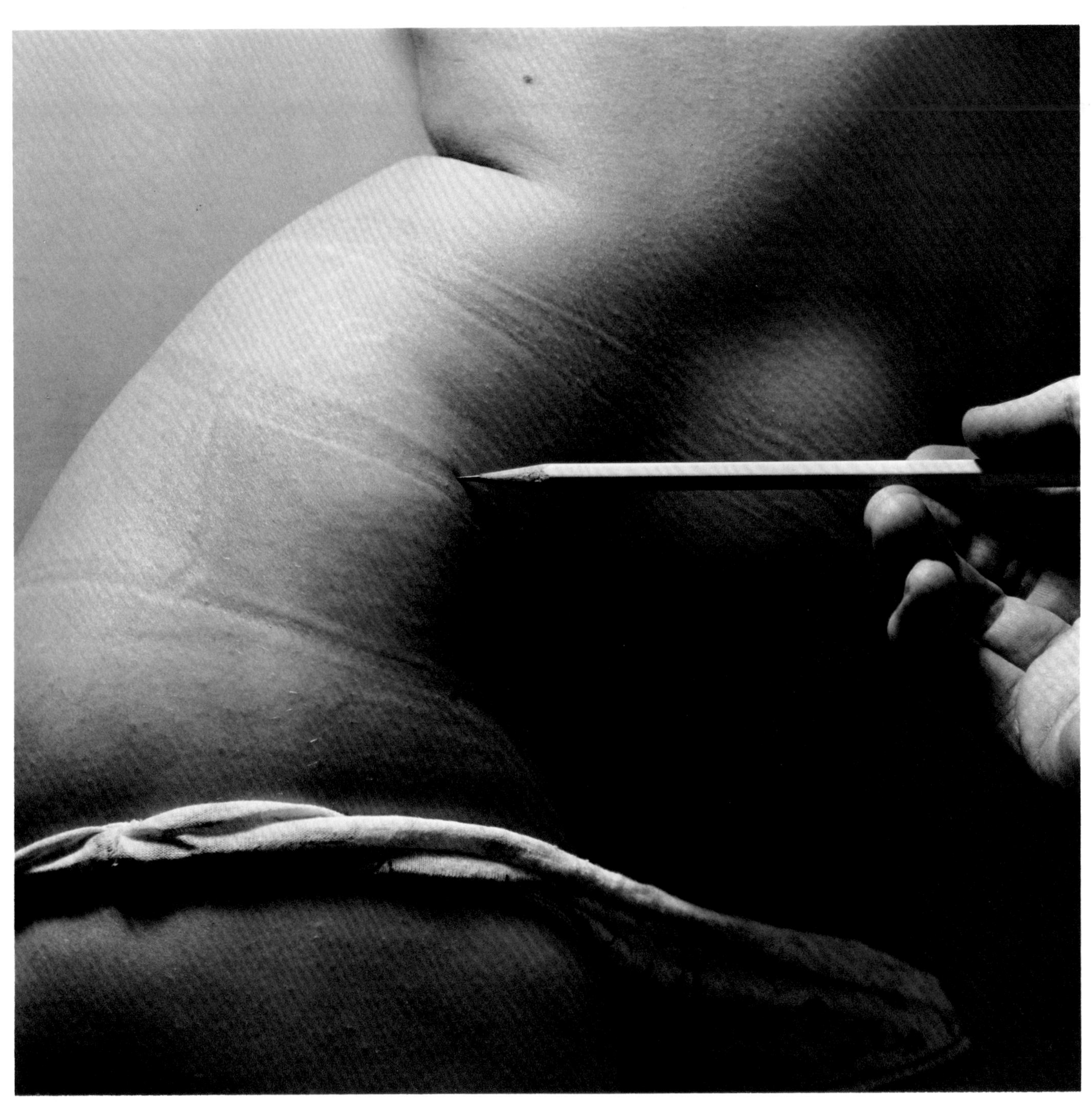

FIGURE 7: CHICAGO, 1976

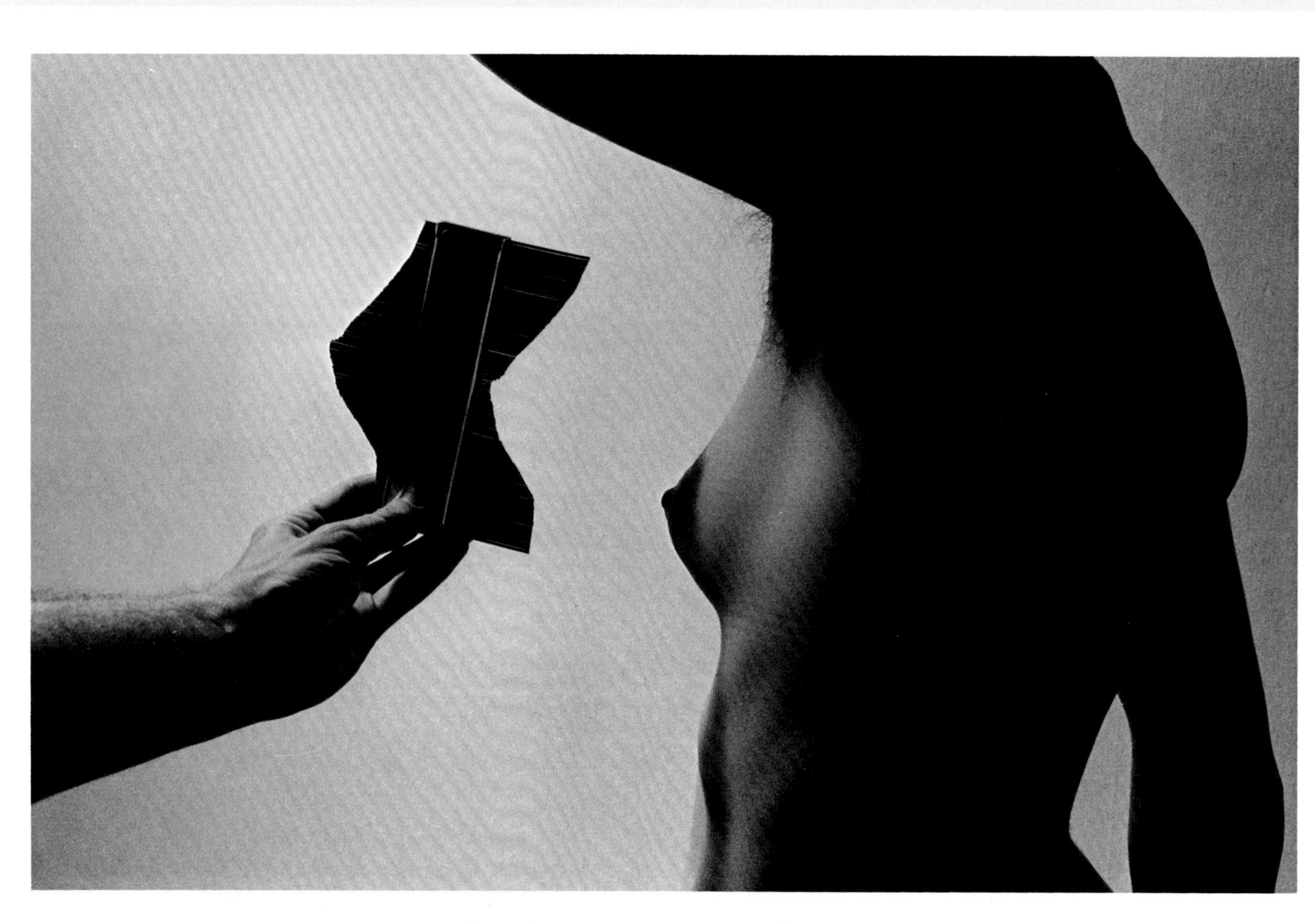

FIGURE 8: CHICAGO, 1976

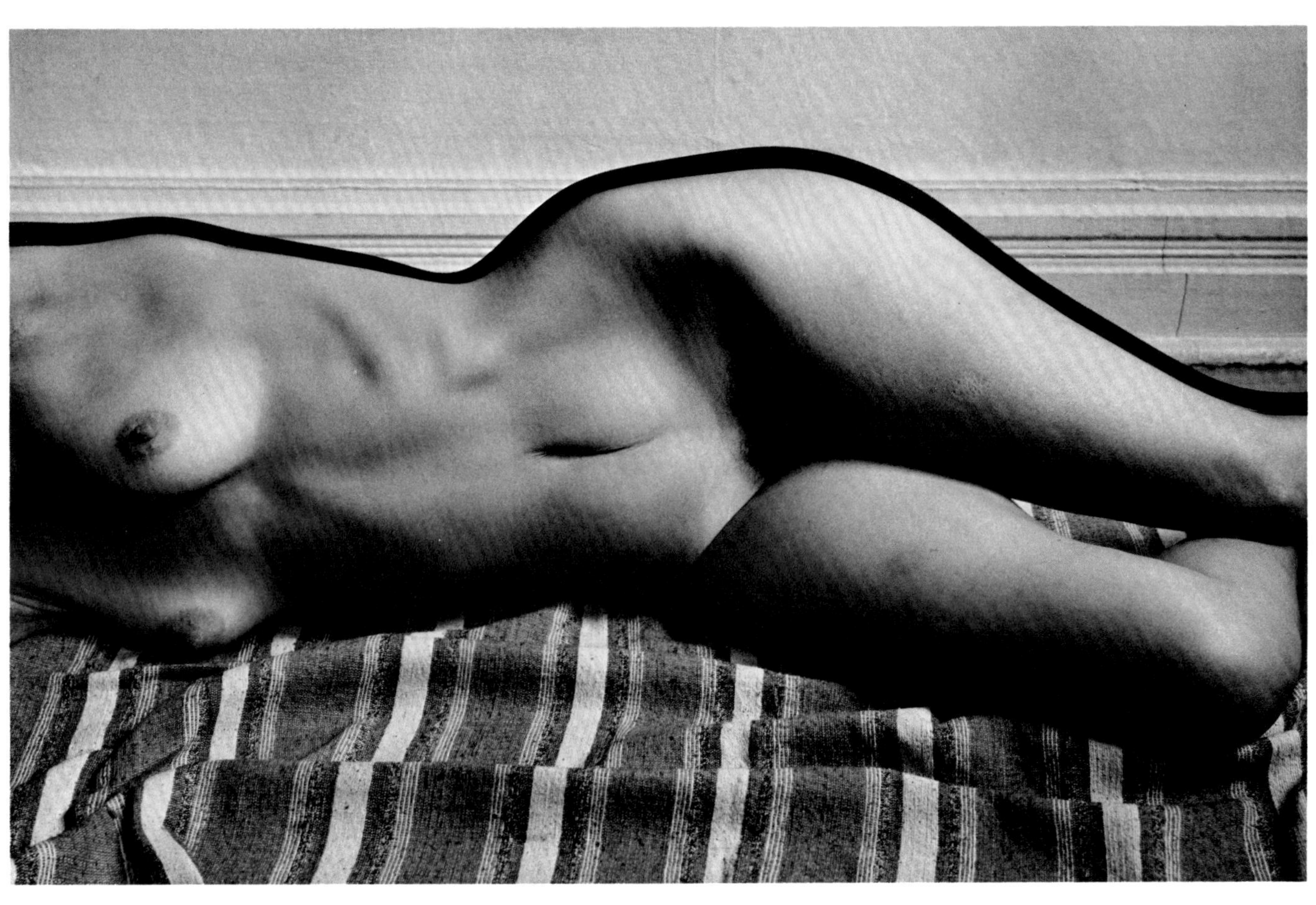

FIGURE 9: CHICAGO, 1977

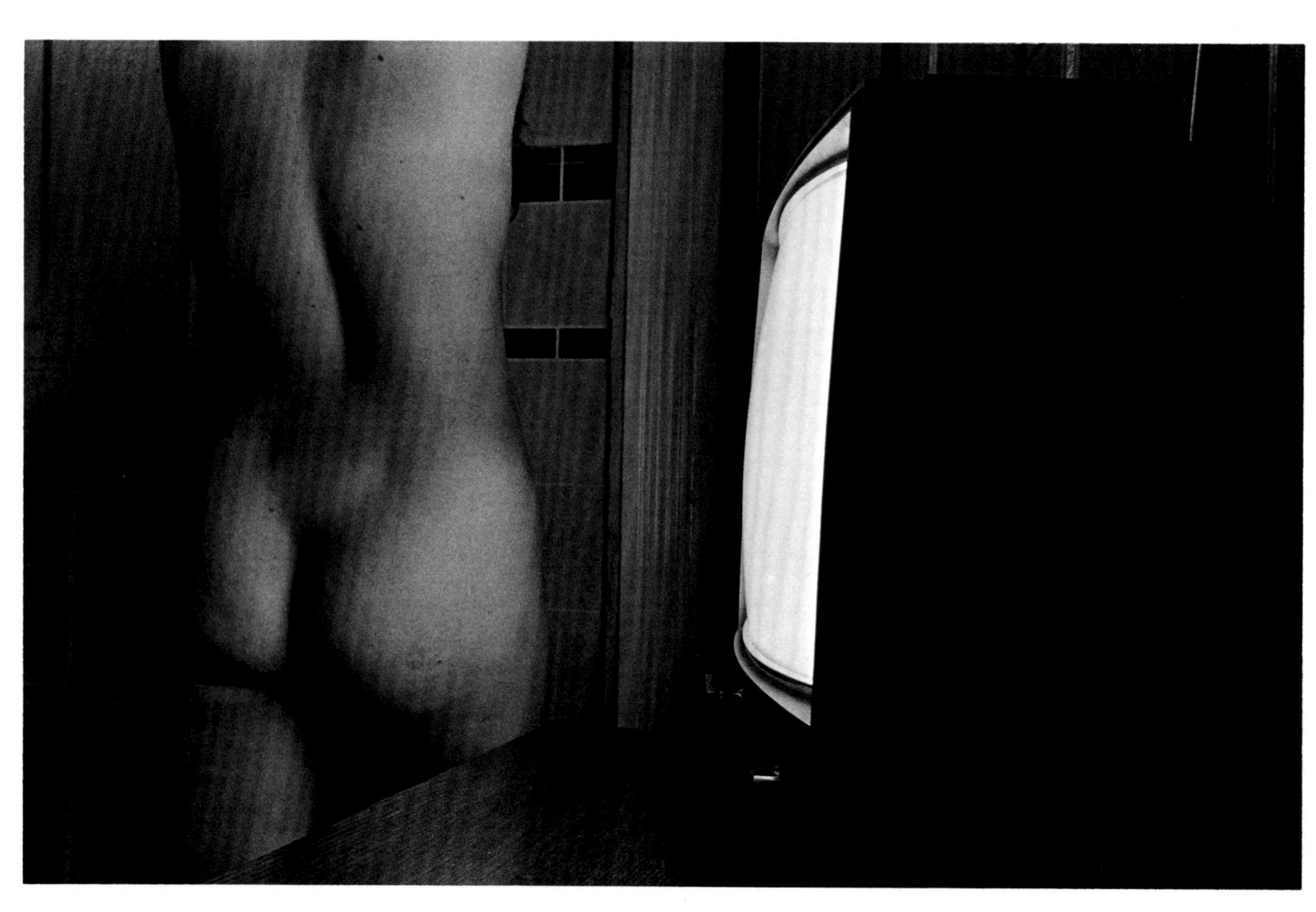

FIGURE 10: SALLY, 1976

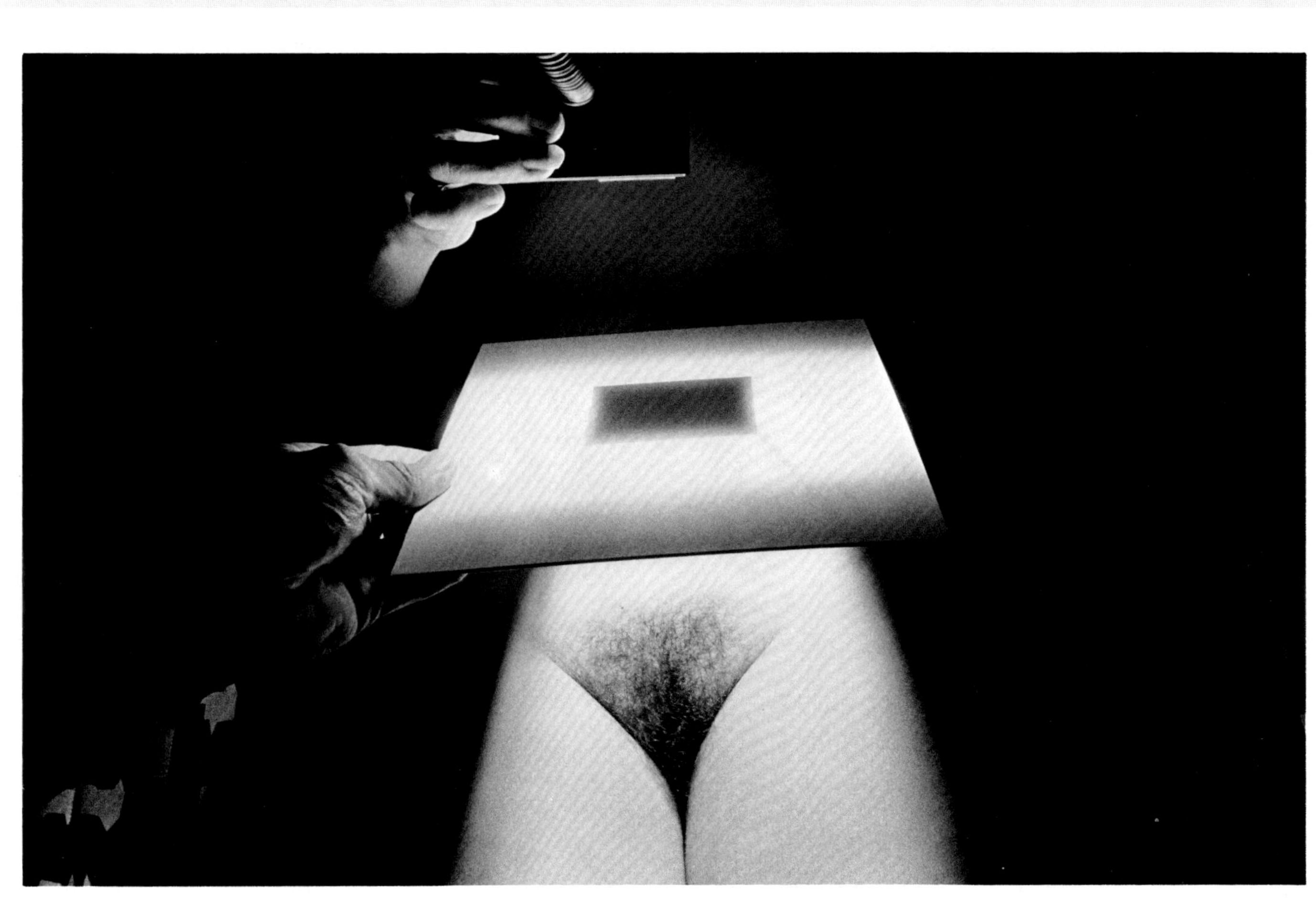

FIGURE 11: NEW YORK, 1978

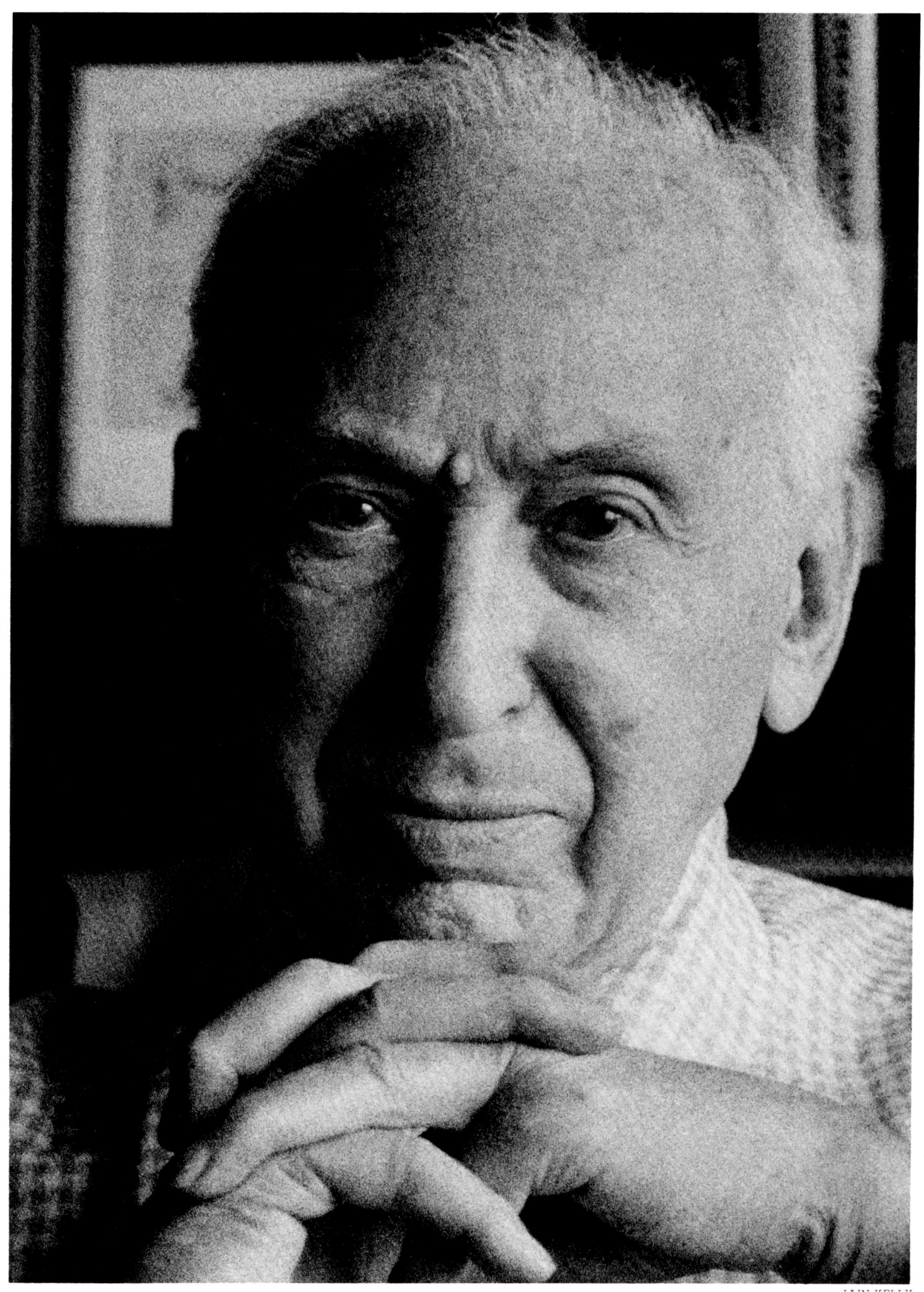

JAIN KELLY

ANDRÉ KERTÉSZ: "IN EVERYTHING I PHOTOGRAPH, THERE IS THE HUMAN TOUCH."

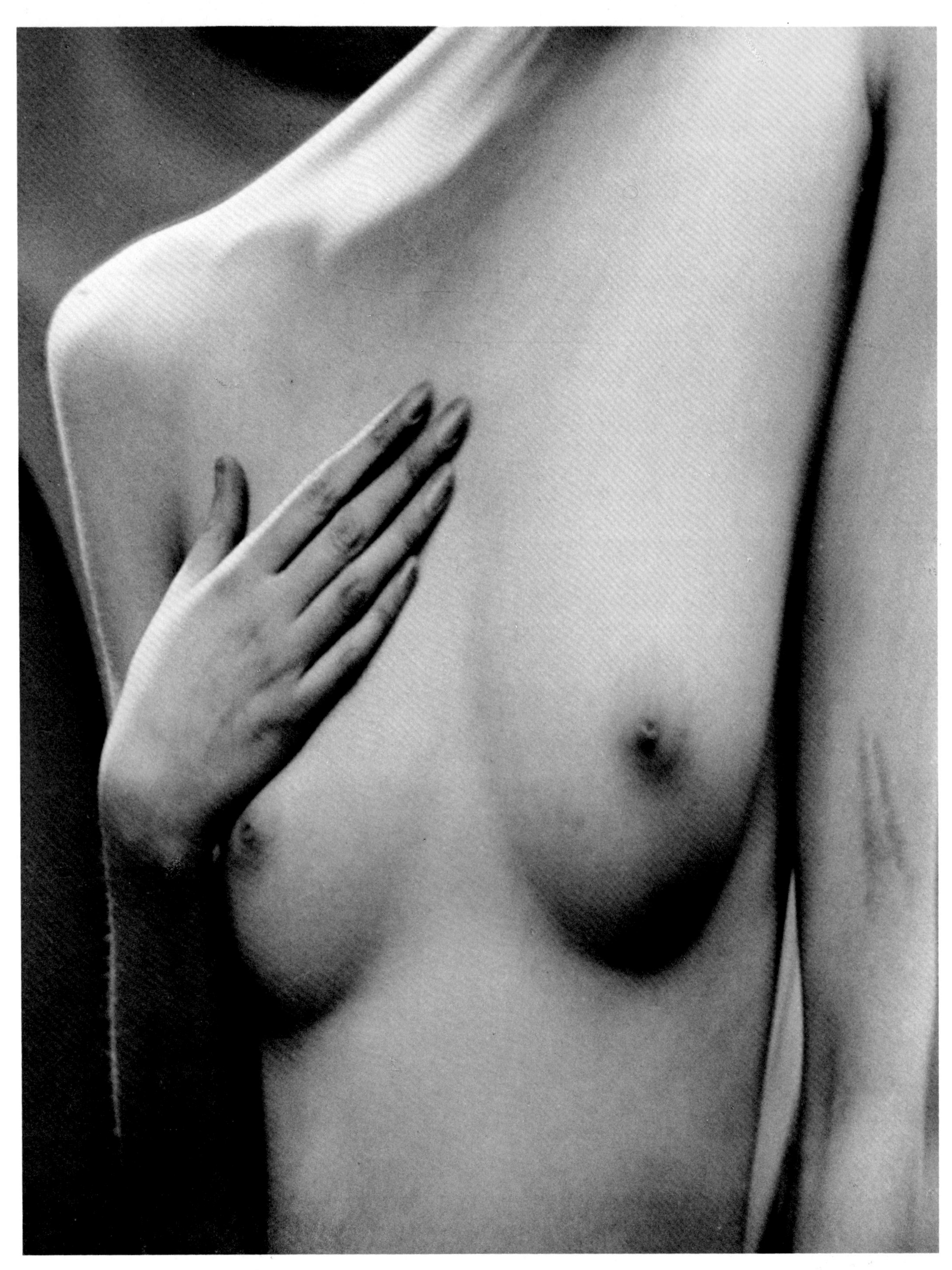

FIGURE 1: DISTORTION NO. 68

When I was a child about five or six years old, I visited my relatives in the countryside of Hungary. In the attic of their farmhouse, I found Austrian and Hungarian calendars and magazines illustrated with wonderful woodcuts. Some of the woodcuts were of things happening in the world, but most of the subjects concentrated on family life. These beautiful and sentimental family themes, as well as my comings and goings in the country and in the town, influenced me greatly. As I was growing up, I thought that perhaps someday I could do something with all the things I saw, and eventually photography came to me.

I was sentimental; I am sentimental. In everything I photograph, there is the human touch. I have never wanted to liberate myself from this approach. There is no reason. I am the way I am. Trying to change myself would not be natural; it would be counter-myself.

Photography has not influenced my life; my life has influenced my photography. Photography became the instrument through which I expressed myself, rather than painting or gravure or writing. When I began to photograph, my pictures did my talking for me. I am a lucky man because I can do something with almost anything I see. Everything is interesting to me. There is no explanation for this. I was born this way. I am not saying that God gave me this. For me, there is no God. It was something in my nature.

In each country in which I have lived, I have used the atmosphere of the country itself in my photography. In Hungary, there was a certain atmosphere and certain things were happening all around me. France was a new country for me, with a new atmosphere. I used the atmosphere, but I didn't push myself into anything. I never tried to analyze or speculate on what I was doing. Later, when I came to the United States, the situation changed again. Here the atmosphere was less warm than in Paris or Hungary, and the times were difficult. All my experiences here instinctively gave me a feeling that was not similar to my feeling on the other side of the ocean. The photographs I make today in New York can never be as warm as the ones I made in Paris in the 30s. Everything in the United States is different. The people are different, even the streets are constructed differently. In Paris, everyone is an individual; here are only the masses. I do not pass judgment on this. It is simply that life here is different. It is important to comment on this, because the photographer's experiences and feelings dictate the way he sees.

In 1933, while my wife, Elizabeth, and I were living in Paris, I received a phone call from the artist and designer Marcel Vertés, who was a Hungarian compatriot of mine.

Vertés said, "The publisher of SOURIRE Magazine, Querelle, asked me to call you. He wants to know if it is possible for you to do some work for him."

I was surprised. Querelle knew me. Why didn't he ask me himself?

The next day, I phoned Querelle and asked him what he wanted.

He said, "Is it possible for you to do something for my magazine?"

"Of course," I replied. "Why didn't you phone me yourself and ask me directly?"

"I didn't want you to refuse me."

Very delicate and very French.

Now, the situation was this: I had my reputation as a photographer in Paris. I could work seven days a week or not, as I chose. Querelle's magazine, SOURIRE (TO SMILE), was a girlie magazine. This was not a vulgar publication. It was "piquant" in the French sense of the word. Vertès worked for SOURIRE at this time and so did many other artists. But Querelle thought I might look down on his magazine, might not want to touch it.

Querelle asked if I had some idea for working with the nude. I replied immediately that I would like to photograph the nude done in distortion with a curved mirror.

"Wonderful! Do anything you want. I will get you anything you need: models, a studio, anything," he said.

I went around to look for the mirrors I needed, and I found two large ones and a small one in a junk store. Querelle had a small studio, which we used for the sessions, and he arranged for two models. One was a young White Russian girl, Najinskaya, and the other was an old show girl, a dancer. I'm sure his idea was to show the contrast between the two women.

Najinskaya was rich and spoiled, but completely charming. She was not intelligent, but she had intelligent feeling, and she understood what I was doing and helped me many times. We collaborated very nicely.

She said, "Don't tell my parents!" Of course, I never even met her parents.

There was the question of the camera and lenses to be used. In the beginning of my work in photography, I had had a small, ordinary box camera with glass plates. There was only one shutter speed, so I could not always be sure how my pictures would come out. It was very primitive. Next I had a camera that was handier because it was possible to regulate the shutter speed. Then I got a better camera, and a better, and so on. They were small, always small. With them, I made "Leica pictures" long before there was such a thing as a Leica. Once my brother bought for me, as a surprise, a 9 x 12cm glass plate Voigtlander camera (this was approximately the equivalent of a 4 x 5). The larger format camera confused me at first because it could not be handled like a small camera. I got around this problem and began working with the 9 x 12cm in addition to the small cameras.

I had started to use the Leica about 1928, but it would not have been possible to make the distortions with it. At that time, Leicas had noninterchangeable lenses. The lens on mine was the Elmar 50mm *f*/3.5. Working with only one lens, one perspective, was a great limitation.

With the distortions, the technical problem was this: from my perspective, standing away from the mirror, I could see a particular image of the woman in the glass. Perhaps I wanted only a little section of that image, something in the middle or in the corner. With the 50mm lens of the Leica, I would have been forced to walk closer to the mirror. But in going closer, I would have lost my perspective, lost the image I wanted.

The solution was the 9 x 12cm glass plate Linhof with "combination" lenses that were the forerunners of the zoom lenses. These were called Hugo Meyer Plasmat Satz lenses. A set of two lenses could be purchased. Each lens could be used separately, or they could be attached together in several different ways to give various focal lengths. In effect, I could go close by using them or stay back. I still have them today. For another variation, I used a Tessar lens.

One of the outstanding qualities of the Hugo Meyer lenses was that they conveyed a sense of dimensionality, of plasticity. It was a revelation to me when I first saw the results. The lenses were sharp enough, but they were not designed to be sharp enough to kill. In the sharpness, one always felt the form itself.

Even with the combination lenses, I could not always get the image I wanted in the distorted nudes. Perhaps 80% of the nudes are printed from the entire glass plate; the rest are cropped in the printing. From some glass plates, I make up to three variations through cropping. Even today, I see new images, new croppings, when I look at the distortions. This is why the artists of the time, the painters and sculptors who were my friends, asked for my prints. They recognized that the possibilities were endless.

The lighting wasn't complicated. I had window light and one ordinary flood light to use when something went a little dark for me. We left the large mirror in one place because it was big and difficult to move. It was easier for the models and me to move around.

I did the first session with both women. When Vertès and Querelle saw the material, they were surprised and delighted. They immediately spoke of doing a book in addition to the spread in SOURIRE Magazine.

Najinskaya's response was, "André, this is not me!" She was quite upset.

I laughed, "Yes, this is you! You do not recognize yourself! My camera does not lie!"

I worked with both Najinskaya and the older

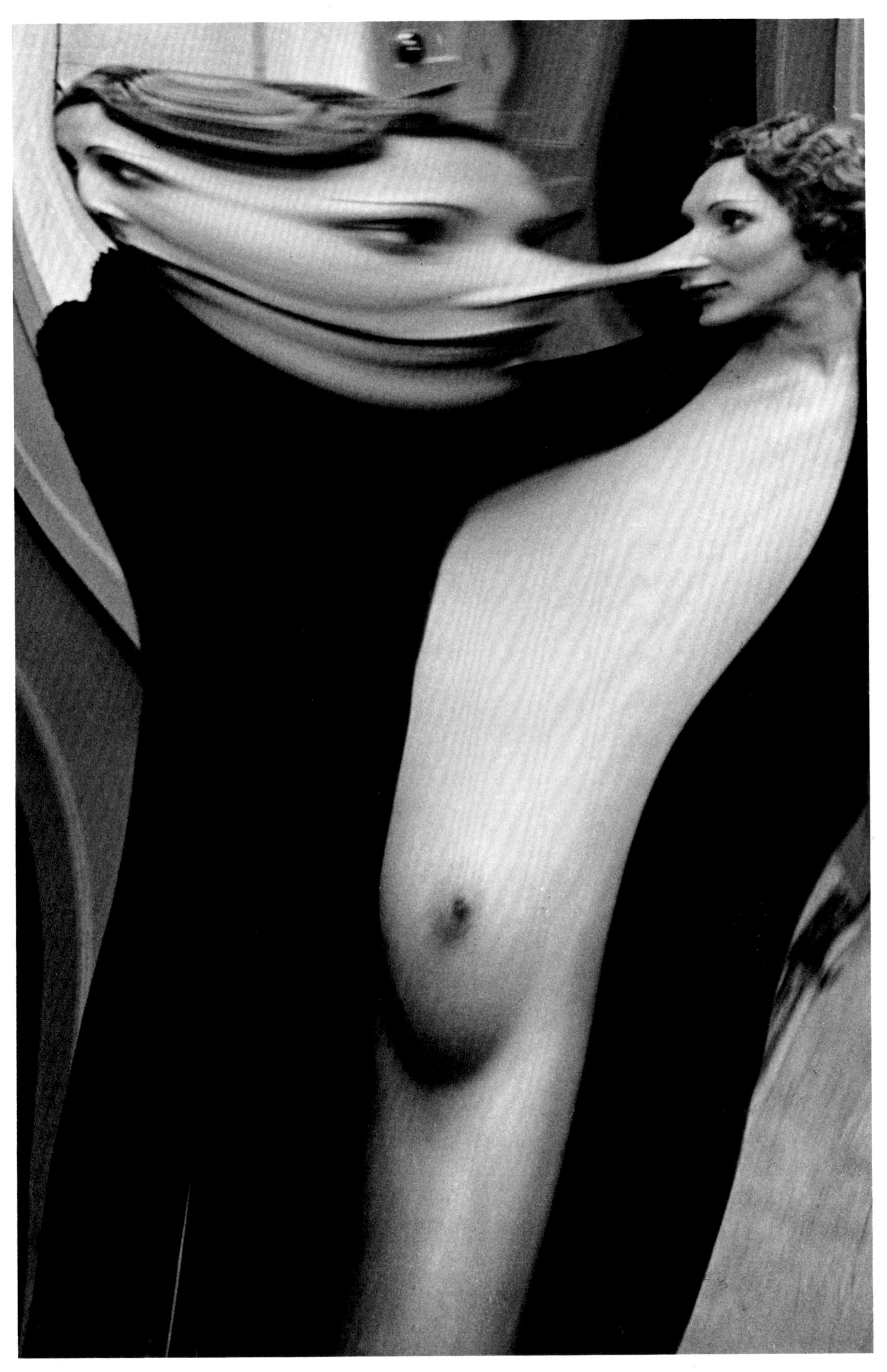

FIGURE 2: DISTORTION NO. 70

woman, together, for a session or two, but I didn't need the older woman after this. I have about five or six photographs of her. I returned the second large mirror, which was no good, but I kept the first one, which was fantastic. For the next four weeks or so Najinskaya and I worked once or twice a week. There were about eight or nine sessions, no more. In total, I made about 160 photographs (Figures 1 through 8).

At the time I made the distorted nudes, it was great amusement, absolute fun, and we didn't force anything. With every movement of the model, there was some interesting transformation, some fantastic design. Sometimes the forms were sculpturesque, sometimes horrible and cadaverous. The curve of the mirror gave the inspiration for the photographs. With my lenses, I took from the mirror the form that I wanted. In every photograph, I saw more ideas for the next picture. It is possible for critics and writers today to give any theoretical aesthetic or psychological explanation of these images that they want, but for me the explanations are too "high." They had nothing to do with the photographs in the time they were done. They were just wonderful fun.

I had photographed many nudes before, but not in distortion. In Hungary, I had worked with artists' models and friends. These pictures were also done with 9 x 12cm glass plates, but they were destroyed during the breakup of the Austro-Hungarian Dual Monarchy in 1918.

My work with distortion goes back to 1917, when I was wounded in World War I. After I left the hospital, but while I was still recuperating, I used to sit around the swimming pool with the other wounded men, talking and swimming a little before we went in to eat. A man was sitting in the water, moving his leg and hands, and I began photographing this. The men thought I was crazy and asked me what I was doing. The distortion existed; I liked it; I photographed it. I have only one of these pictures left, of a man swimming underwater (UNDERWATER SWIMMER, AUGUST 31, 1917, ESZTERGOM, HUNGARY).

After the distorted nudes, I was asked if I had an idea for making a photographic introduction of Carlo Rim, the new chief editor of JOURNAL VU, to the public. Rim was a wonderful guy, a caricaturist. Once again, I used the idea of the distorted mirror (Figure 9). For the cover of JOURNAL VU, I photographed Rim as a short, fat man. Inside there was reproduced another picture of him, this time as a tall, thin man, to show a contrast.

Years later I used the small mirror, which I still have. With it I photographed a drinking cup and the MELANCHOLY TULIP, 1939. I still have ideas about doing some work with the mirror, but, unfortunately, a small mirror is very limited.

A two-page spread of the distorted nudes was published in SOURIRE, with perhaps eight or ten photographs. In this time, magazines did not publish 20-page portfolios. A two-page spread was a big thing. In addition, a layout for a 60-photograph book was prepared. Carlo Rim wrote little titles for the book, rather than a text. I remember that one of the titles was "Twenty years later." It illustrated a photograph in which Najinskaya appeared in the foreground with a good-looking, healthy body; and in the background, as reflected in the mirror, with a body that looked 20 years older.

Querelle planned to sell the book not only in France, but also in Germany and Central Europe. Everything was ready to be printed, but before printing began, Hitler came to power. Querelle decided to wait.

"How long?" I asked.

He replied, "Until this little man is finished. Two months."

We all know what happened. And this is why the book was never published.

In 1934, a selection of ten distorted nudes was shown at a group exhibition arranged at Leleu's, the establishment of the noted decorator. The nudes were very well received by the public.

In 1936, I accepted an offer from Keystone News Agency to come to the United States for one year only. At the time, my wife and I could not guess that we would remain in America.

Querelle returned the distorted nude photographs to me, expressing the hope that I could do something with them in America.

At the very time that Elizabeth and I were crossing over on the ship, the first curator of the department of photography at The Museum of Modern Art was in Paris trying to find me. Upon his return to New York, he came to our hotel room. He was arranging a major international exhibition of photography at the museum, and he wanted some of my photographs. He chose four or five photos, including a distorted nude.

"I'd like to use this nude," he said, "but I must ask you to do something."

"What is that?"

"Can I ask you to crop out the pubic area?"

He explained that with the pubic area, the picture was pornography; without it, the picture was art. This was my introduction to American taste in this epoch, as explained to me by the curator of photography at The Museum of Modern Art.

I asked, "How would you like somebody to cut a little off the top of your head? And take away a little section of your foot? The way you are, everything is complete, as the photograph in your hand is complete. No, you can't crop it."

I was too green. It was too soon after my arrival. In the end, I gave in. This was my welcome to America.

At the time I arrived, the most highly regarded photography was done by the Group *f*/64. Their

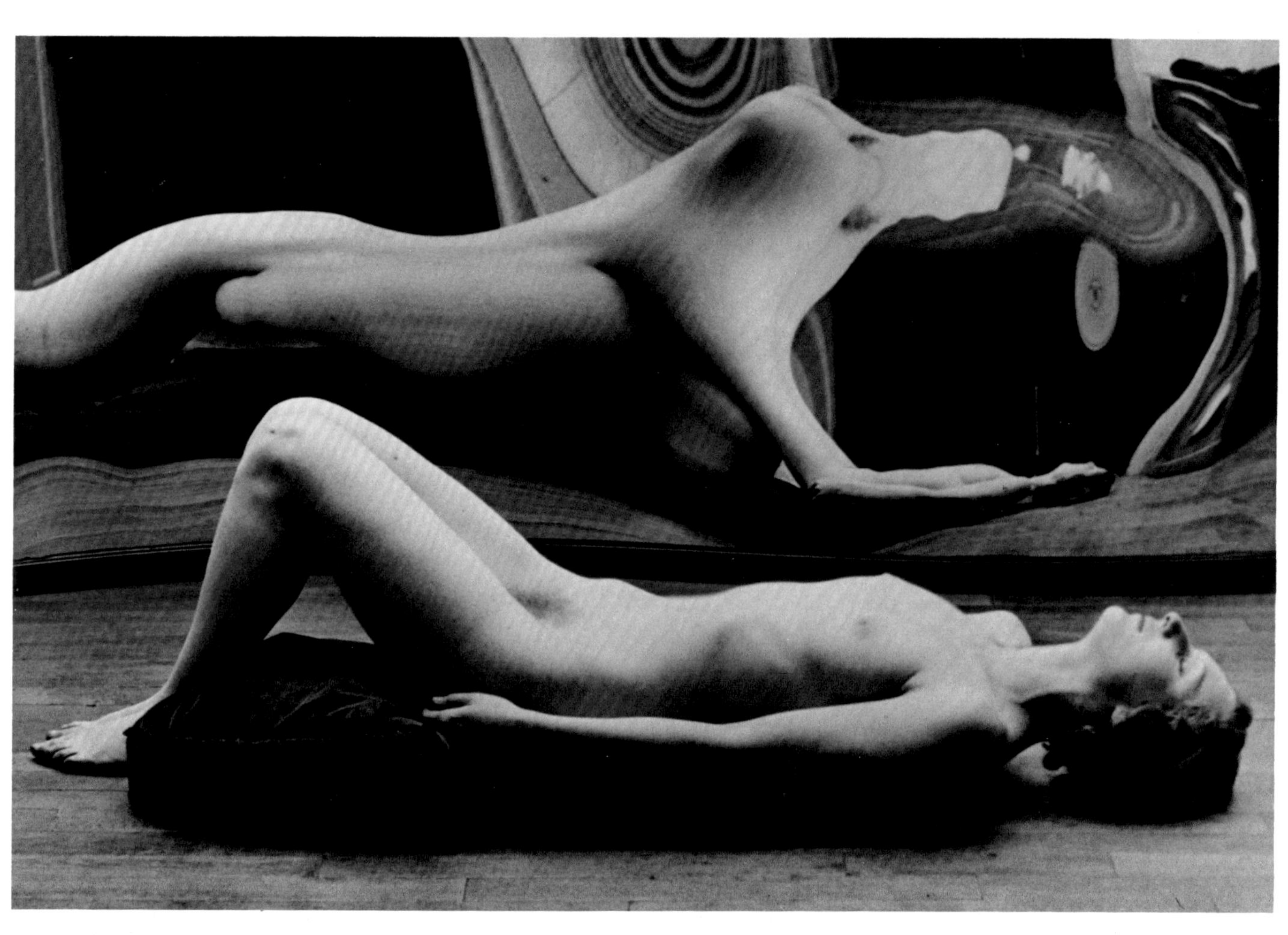

FIGURE 3: DISTORTION NO. 45

idea of art was to make everything technically perfect, everything sharp from foreground to background. Art was killed by supertechnique. Every detail that the eye never sees was revealed. This is all right if you are an artist who wants to work with an idea for a while, but it is not right for everything. In reality, your eye adjusts itself to the thing you see. If you look at something close to you, then other things around it are not sharp. Or if you look at something far away, the things close to you are not sharp. A photograph should correspond to the reality of the way we see the world.

Only six or seven months ago I reused the very photograph that the curator had mutilated. I found a little tourists' sculpture of Leonardo da Vinci's THE LAST SUPPER in a junk store. I placed the sculpture in front of the same print he had used in the exhibition. The expression on the woman's face is pitiable as she looks at Christ and the Company.

Symbolically, perhaps she is desperate because her pubic area has been cropped out.

A friend of mine, a painter named Julius Zilzer, told Alfred Stieglitz that I was in the United States. Zilzer had shown him a few of my distortions, and Stieglitz asked to meet me. I took him a group of distortions, and his reaction was, "Very interesting. But I must tell you something. If you exhibit these, tomorrow everyone will be doing the same thing."

He did not understand how difficult it would have been to imitate them, from the technical standpoint alone. At this time, most photographers did not know about the combination lenses, and would not have been able to figure out how to duplicate what I had done.

Other friends sent me to publishers with the nudes, but the response everywhere was the same. Publishers liked the work, but they called it pornography. They were afraid to make a book because they might go to prison.

Then Frank Crowninshield was introduced to the material. Crowninshield was the creator of the magazine VANITY FAIR. He was visiting the studio of the painter Sári Dienes one day, and upon seeing my nudes there, he asked to meet me. I went to see him and told him the whole story.

He said, "I would like to do a book, but it is impossible. But, look, I have an idea, a proposition for you. I am the president of a private club. If an offering is made to the members, it doesn't go outside the closed circle. If you like, I can make an arrangement for you to sell portfolios of these photographs to members and their friends. This way, the public has nothing to do with it."

I accepted the offer.

Crowninshield was to give me a list of members to contact about the portfolios. The next week I received a phone call from him. He was sick. We would have to delay our next appointment by a week. The next week, the same thing happened. Shortly thereafter he died.

In 1976, a book on my distorted nudes was finally published, 45 years after the photographs were made (DISTORTIONS, with an introduction by Hilton Kramer, Alfred A. Knopf, Inc., New York).

I have never gone back to photographing the nude in distortion. However, a few years after I came to America I did a handful of photographs of the nude without distortion, a few of which have been published.

Over the years I began to have trouble with oxidation of my glass plates, not only of the distorted nudes, but of other subjects, too. For a while, I asked various technicians to look at them, including representatives of Eastman Kodak. Everywhere I received the same answer. "We can't touch them. We might make a mistake. We could ruin them."

It happened that a young German photographer knew of my problem, and one day he brought August Sander's grandson, Gerd Sander, to visit me. The young photographer thought Sander might be able to help me. I have duplicate negatives on film, but, of course, I wanted to save the originals. To my complete surprise, Sander returned with a group of the glass plates completely cleaned. No one else had been able to do this. All my respect goes to this man. He has cleaned about 250 glass plates for me so far, and little by little he is accomplishing a miracle for me.

From time to time I am asked for advice on how to photograph the nude. I give the same advice to photographers of the nude that I give to photographers of other kinds of subject matter. Do what you like and what you <u>feel</u>. Liking something, of itself, is not enough. You can touch on the subject matter only if you really feel it. A young fellow came to visit me recently, and he told me that each morning when he leaves his home he takes with him three rolls of film. He does not return that day until he has finished the film. I asked him what he photographs. He replied, "Anything. It's not important." This was the attitude of LIFE Magazine photographers. Take 1,000 photographs and use only one. There is no human feeling, no artistic feeling in this approach. It is only shooting, shooting, shooting like a machine. This approach does some good for film manufacturers, but not for anyone else.

The young photographers I see are usually trying to play themselves up for the public. I never went in for this in my life. You do not make yourself more by doing this. You should try to be honest with yourself. Do your work for yourself and not for anybody else. Do anything you <u>like</u>, I repeat, <u>like</u> to do. And, with mistakes, discover what is right and not right for you.

In terms of making a living, probably the best

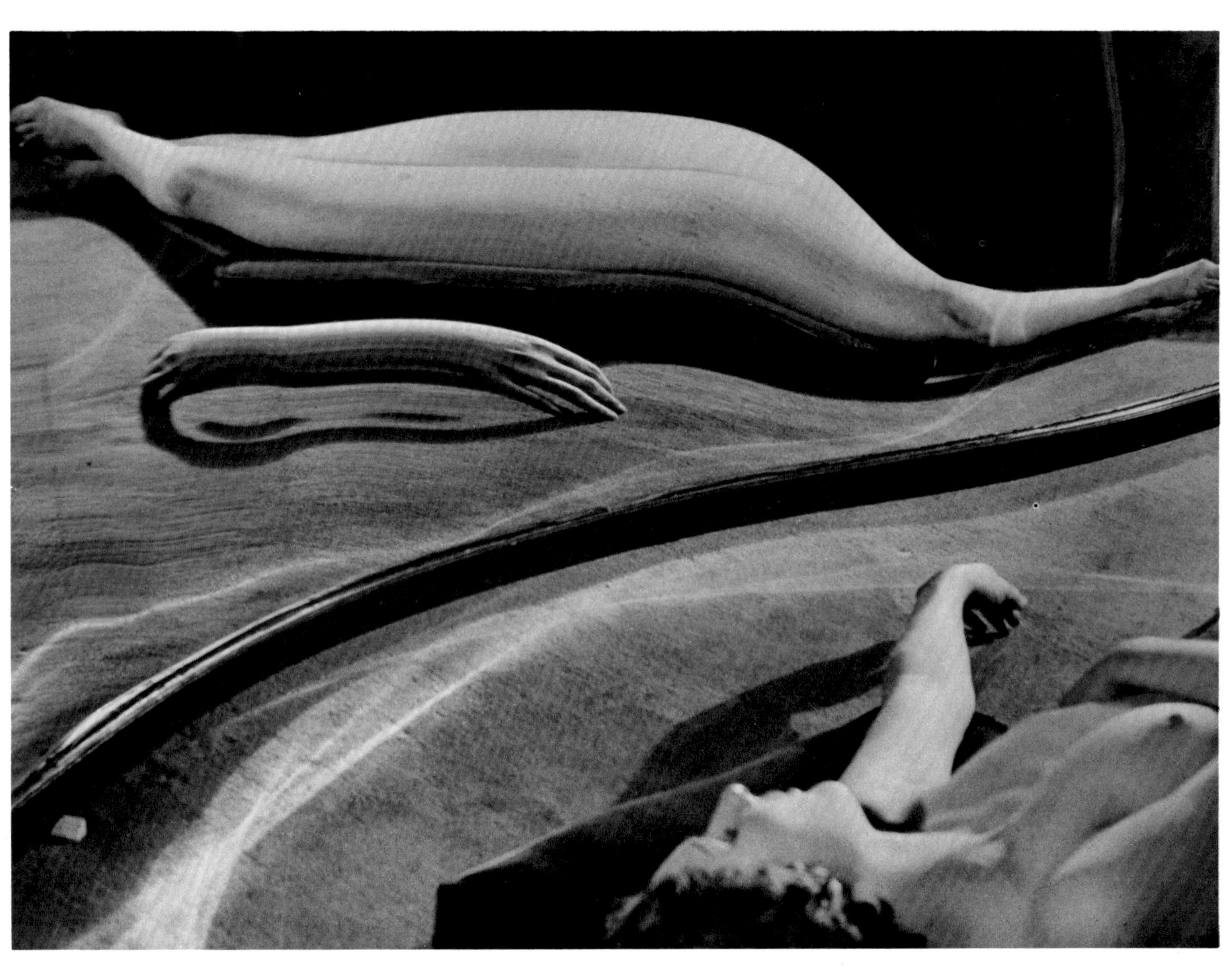

FIGURE 4: DISTORTION NO. 49

solution for the young photographer is to take a job unrelated to commercial work. If you have enough money to live on, you can spend the rest of your time and energy on taking pictures. If you remain an amateur, you don't have to make compromises in your work. It is impossible to avoid compromises if you become a professional photographer. In commercial work you have to satisfy your client, not yourself. The camera is a very frank instrument of expression; if you are attempting to satisfy someone other than yourself, this approach shows in your pictures. If other people like your pictures, this is good, but your expression of your individuality is far more important than others' reactions.

When I take photographs, I never document. I always interpret what I feel at the moment. I have a sense of balance about life; I perceive its tragic aspects as well as its beauty and richness. My photographs say something about the human condition. Every minute is important to me, and I live every minute intensely whether I am taking pictures or not. Intensity of feeling comes first; recording what we see is secondary. Many photographers can see, but seeing is superficial without the stimulus of feeling.

Naturally, the first thing to do is to learn technique completely. After that, forget technique. You should use the minimum that you need to express yourself. This is the way in which you learn the alphabet and how to use it. After you learn the alphabet, what do you write with it? Is it a poem or a scientific treatise? What you write with the alphabet is the important thing, not the technical perfection with which you form the letters. A photograph can be killed by too much technique. In writing, the equivalent to this approach would be calligraphy. For many years, "calligraphy-photography" was all that was appreciated in the United States.

My belief is that a photographer should avoid a complicated approach and express his own feelings. There is a charming story that took place in Paris in the 30s. The people from the Bauhaus used to visit me when they came to Paris. I remember that one visitor from the Bauhaus told me, "You are not 'witziger' enough." "Witziger" means that when you have an itch, you scratch around it first, instead of going directly to it with your hand. He meant that my work was not indirect enough, not amusingly complicated enough.

I feel that the photographer should try to be as direct as his eye sees, without a lot of ridiculous playing around. For me, this is only natural. The Bauhaus approach was to make art "interesting." I feel that if something is interesting, then it is interesting; if it's not, then there is no reason to force it to be interesting. Your photographs should reflect what is truly interesting to you.

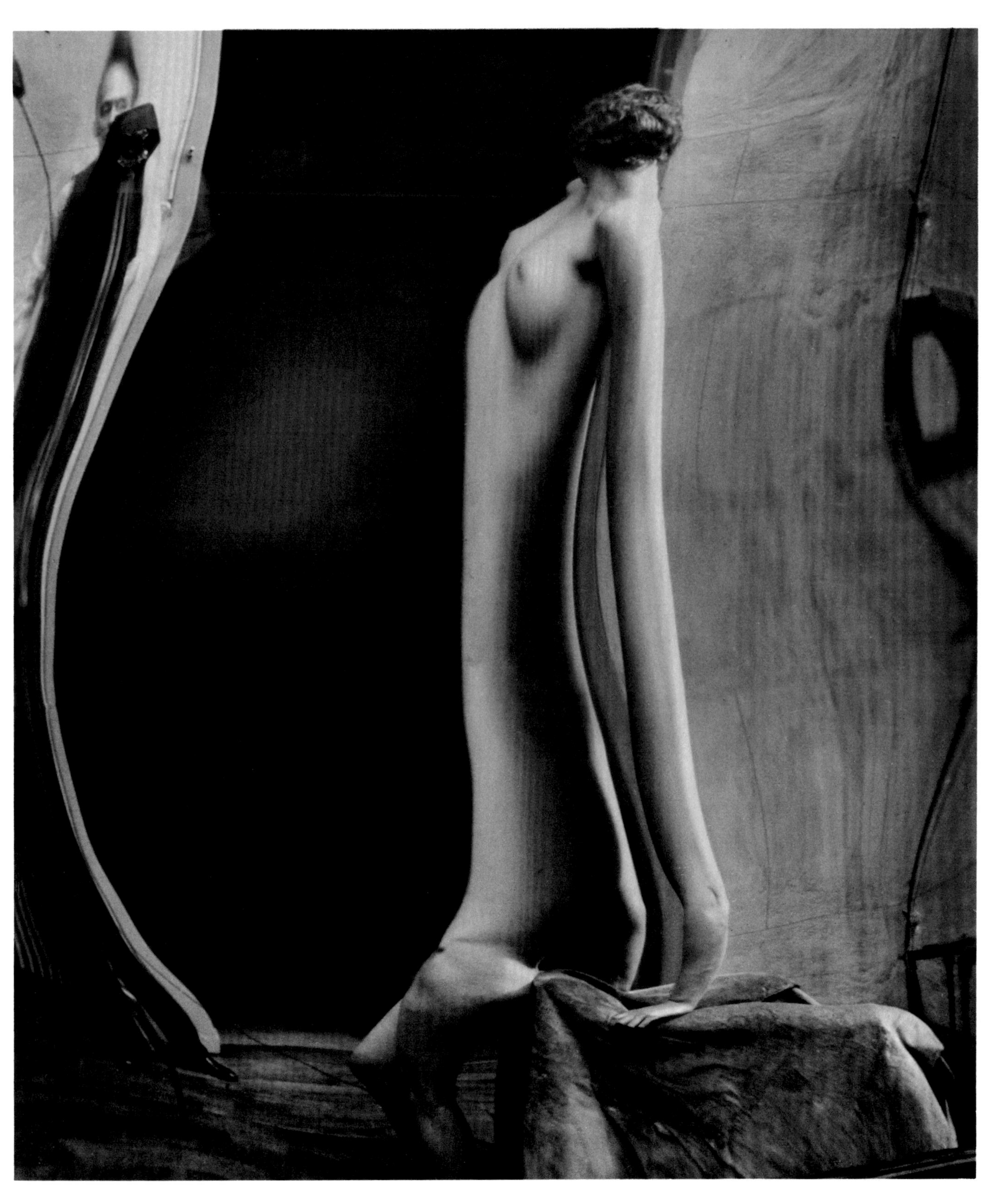

FIGURE 5: DISTORTION NO. 113

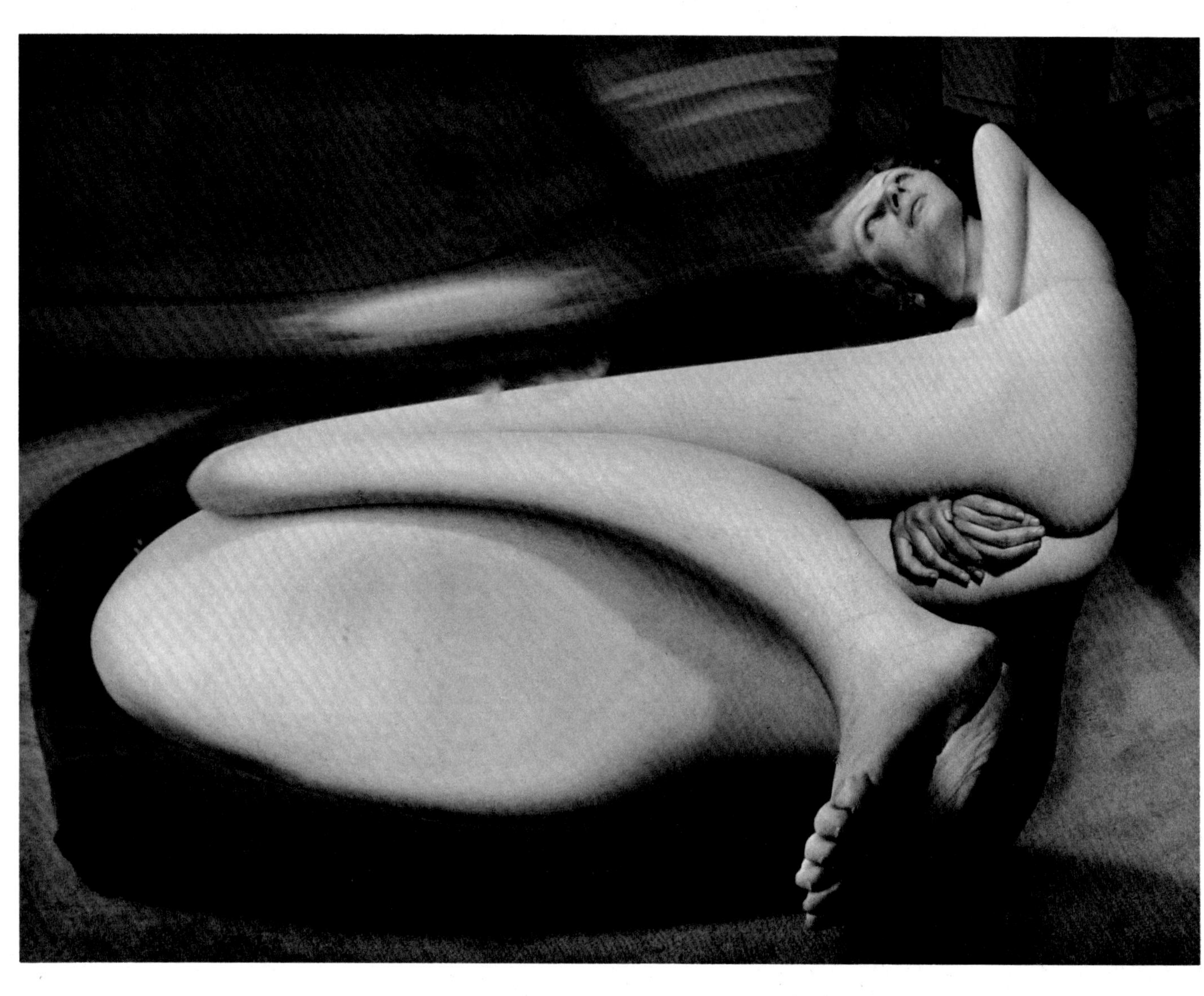

FIGURE 6: DISTORTION NO. 40

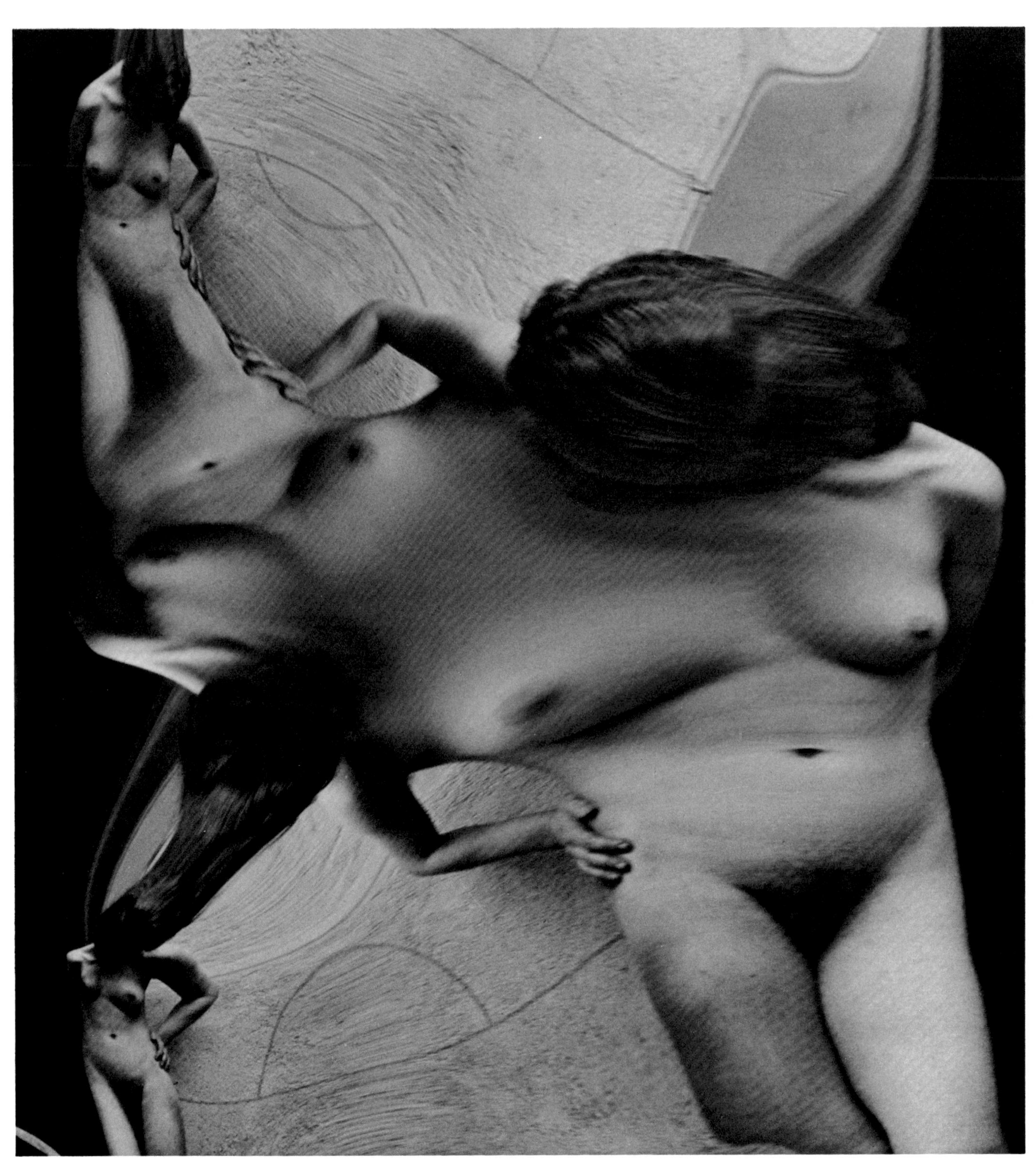

FIGURE 7: DISTORTION NO. 91

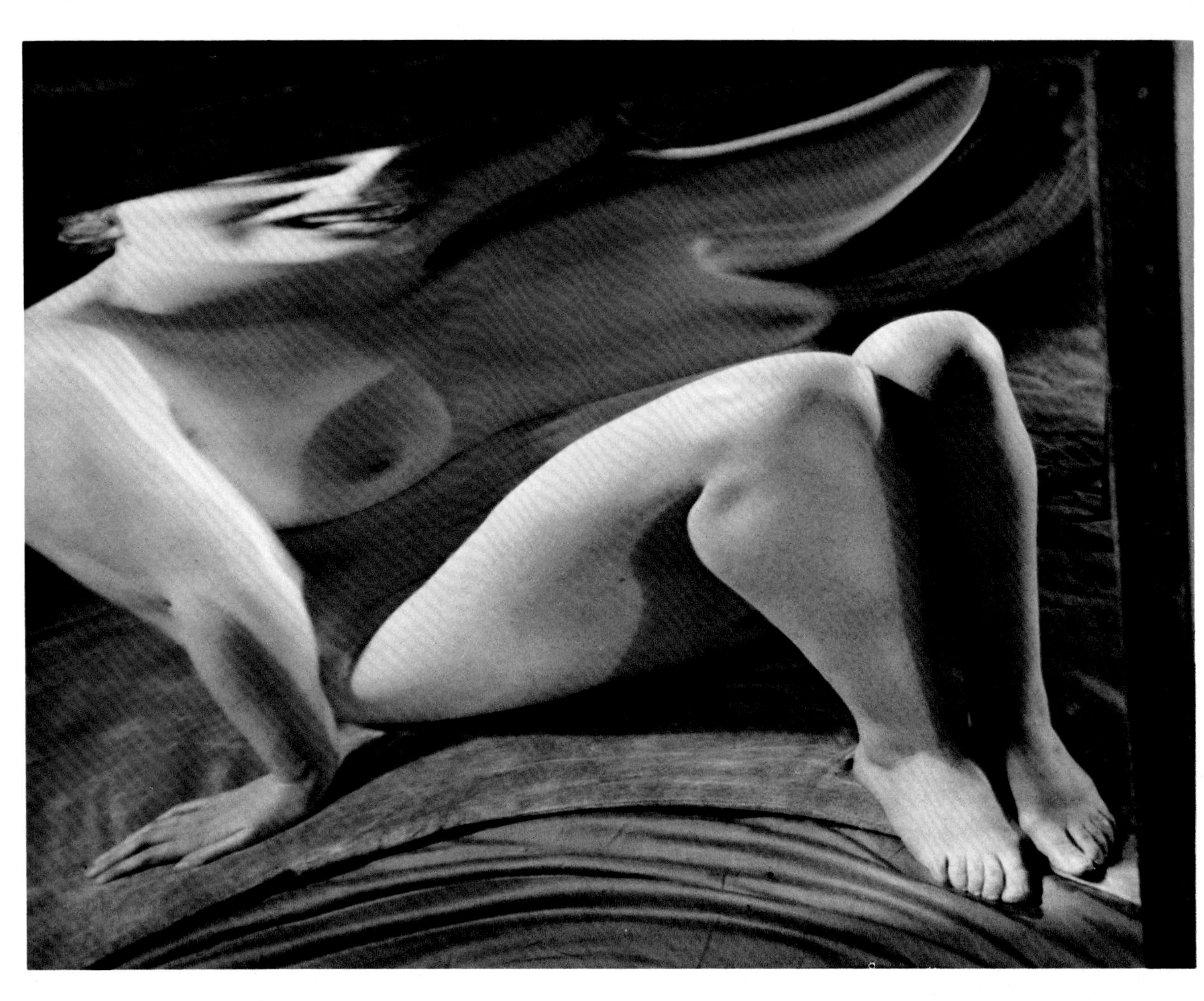

FIGURE 8: DISTORTION NO. 130

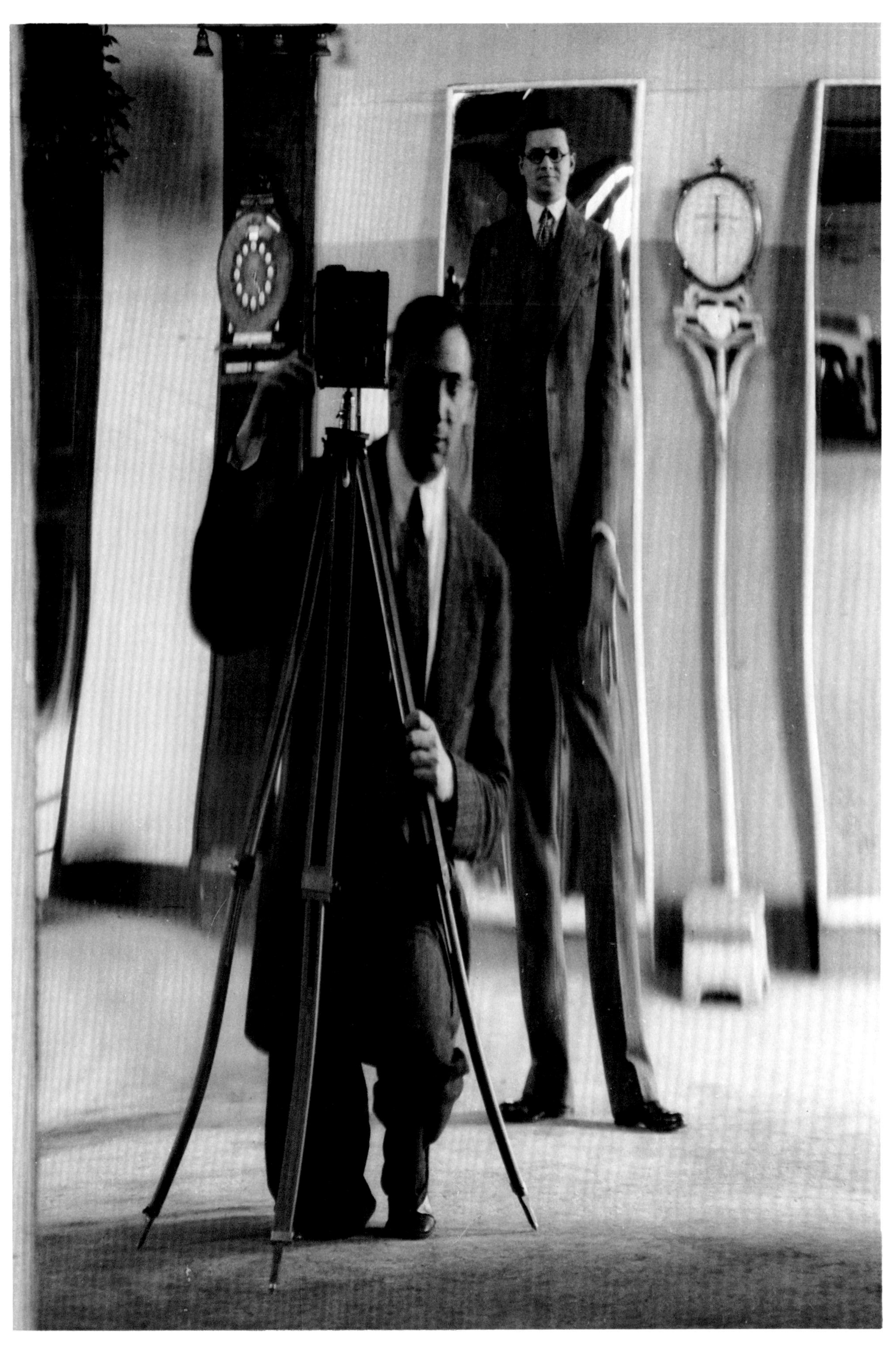

FIGURE 9: ANDRÉ KERTÉSZ (SELF-PORTRAIT WITH CARLO RIM IN BACKGROUND)

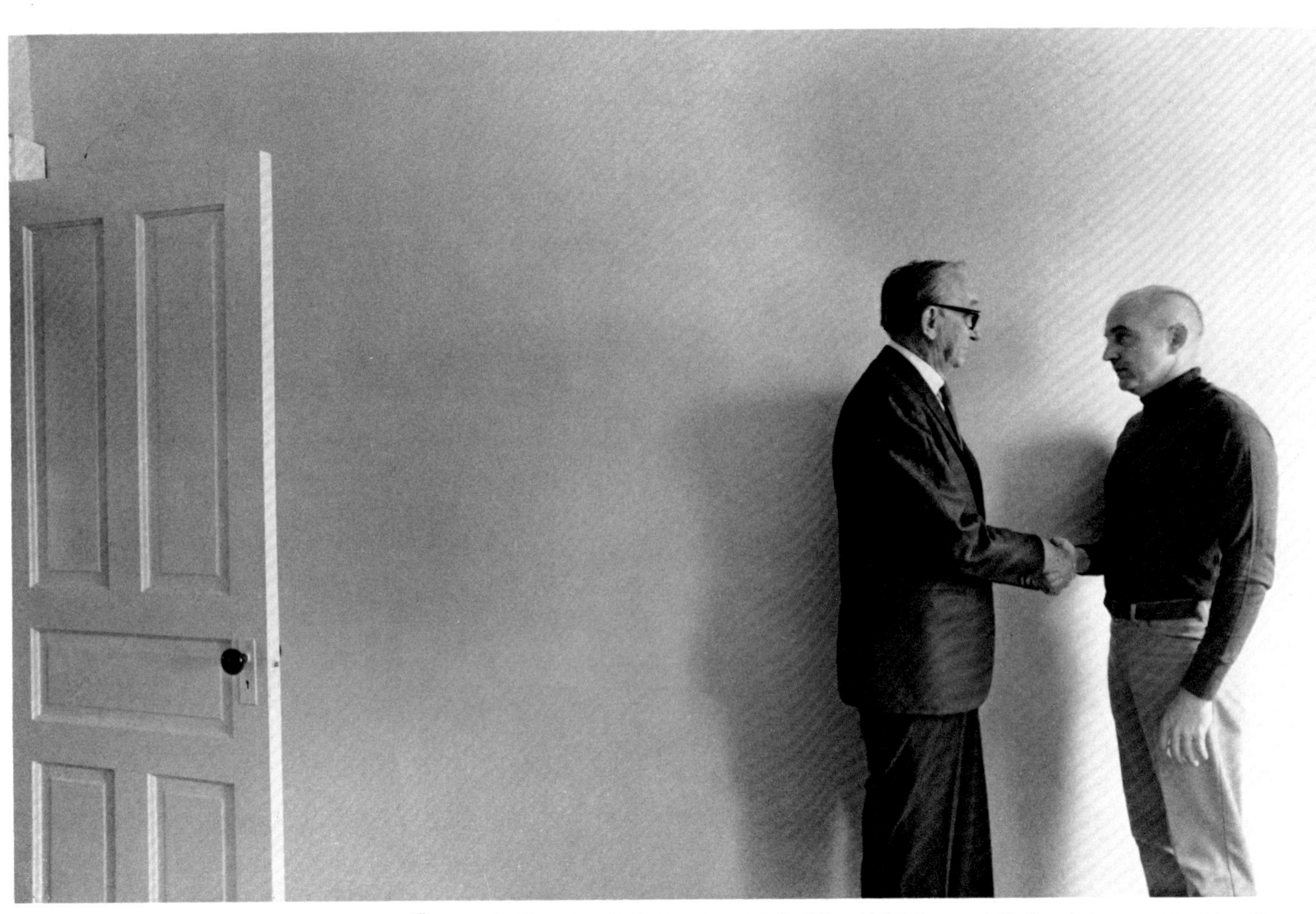

SELF PORTRAIT SHAKING HANDS WITH MY FATHER

DUANE MICHALS: "MY MIND IS ALWAYS THE SOURCE OF MY WORK, NEVER MY EYES."

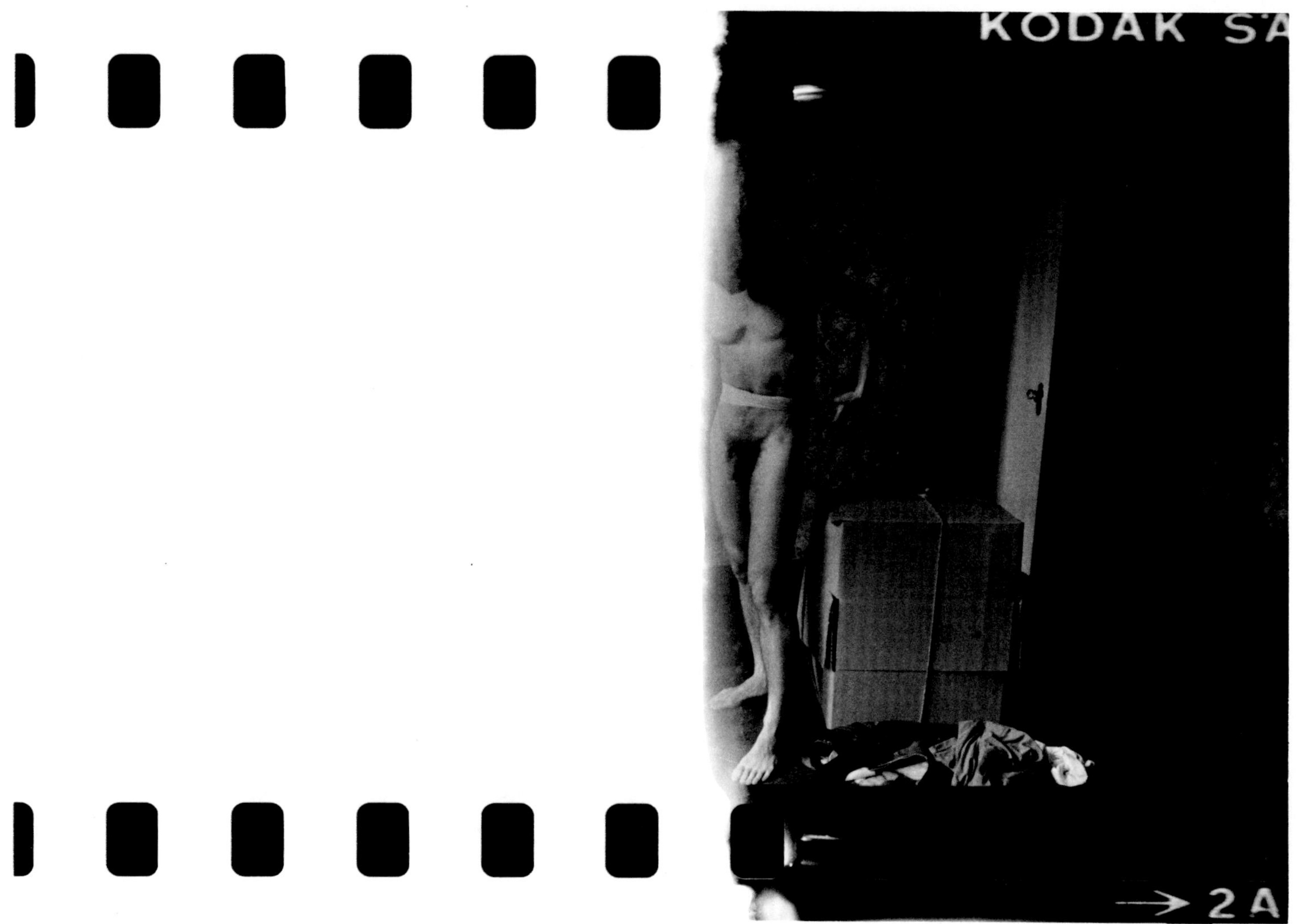

FIGURE 1: UNTITLED, 1977

The nude has always been part of my work; all my early sequences were done with the unclothed figure. There's something about the nude body that makes the person "nonspecific," universal. The moment the person puts on clothing, a point of view is defined, a social class is established.

When I work with the nude, I prefer the figure to be traditional and classic. I am a victim of the Greek ideal. I like the idea of searching for perfection, the idealized form. I don't like the women to be too voluptuous or the men to be too muscled. The figure that is unexaggerated in proportions is very beautiful and it has great potential for mystery and tension in a drama.

The nude figure implies both vulnerability and sex. I would say that the nude woman is more vulnerable then the nude man. One of my early sequences, titled THE GIRL IS HURT BY A LETTER, 1968, showed a nude woman seated at a window. A clothed man entered the room to deliver a letter. The woman read the letter and wept. The woman's nakedness emphasized her vulnerability.

Through the years, the role in which I have cast the nude has changed. Recently, I have been photographing the male nude more than the female nude.

As far as the sexual aspect of the nude is concerned, there is no such thing as an innocent nude, even in a photograph of a 97-year-old person. The viewer still responds out of sexual curiosity. In the case of the old person, there is always the sense of physical loss. The older you become, the more you experience this sense of loss. I'm working on a book now on change and transition upon aging. I did an entire section on myself, photographing myself over the years, seeing my own death and experiencing myself as part of a cycle that is completely fascinating. We do not often think of ourselves in these terms, but now I have enough of my life behind me to see how I fit into the cycle.

It's always been a problem for me to find models, both male and female. Perhaps I make it a problem. Someone from my generation doesn't simply go around asking people to pose in the nude. I would never stop anyone on the street to ask him or her to pose. Recently I was photographing a man who was doing me a favor by posing. I'm almost embarrassed to publish the photographs. I keep thinking he's going to be upset, and I don't like to upset people.

One of the things a photographer should talk about is the pleasure it gives him to photograph the nude. No one can tell me that the photographer of the nude doesn't enjoy his work. There is a pleasure in looking at the body, being aware of the presence of the body, of working with the choreography of the figure in motion. It is even possible to make an ugly body beautiful, merely by finding the right angle.

I'm always amazed at the response to the

human body. The body is such an important part of what we are, and yet in most cultures it's something to be ashamed of. It's always hidden under clothing and yet it's the ultimate curiosity. Because we have lost a lot of our naturalness about the body, many of our responses are artificial. We seem to forget that it's all right to look at bodies, it's all right to enjoy another figure. We are embarrassed about what we should be proud of. Instead, our interest in looking at the body, in admiring the body, should be expressed with an openness and joy.

For a long time it was definitely considered poor taste to describe a male nude as being beautiful. Men have always been very nervous about this type of reference. Yet, gyms are filled with men developing their bodies, making themselves beautiful.

I am very aware that there is a certain wonderful moment in which a young man comes into full possession of the physical power of his body. At that moment, he is separating himself from his family; he is beginning to establish his career; he is starting to make erotic gestures toward women or men. This is the great point of potentiality that he passes almost without realizing that he has left it behind. I remember talking with a friend when we were both 18 years old. We were saying how wonderful it was to be a man, that it was in such a strong tradition, that there was great strength and potentiality in manhood. As I've grown older I've seen youngsters with that quality of potentiality, but when I was the same age I didn't recognize the transition moment, the moment of coming out of a cocoon and stretching one's wings. The young man's father is still there, but the son is now also an adult, the same as his father. They have become "unequal equals." It's something like the day that the pear becomes perfectly ripe; the next day it's still ripe, but it's too ripe. Ten years after the transition moment, the young man's potential has matured and he has fulfilled his promise.

I thought that a very appropriate way to begin an article on the nude would be with the series MAN UNDRESSING, 1979 (Figure 2). At first the man simply stood for a moment, very naturally, and then he brought his hand up to begin undressing. As he took his clothing off, the movements of his hands and body created many blurs in the photographs. The blurs are very beautiful and create different shapes. They contribute to the feeling that this sequence is a little movie that examines what people do when they take off articles of clothing.

This series was done with a 35mm Nikkor lens, which I use for most of my work. My figures are usually placed in a room. They are always figures in a space, and the relationship of the figure to the room is extremely important. With a 35mm lens I can include both the figure and the room, with relatively little distortion. The type of room I like is very spare and light-filled. I like rooms that look like my grandmother's house, with solid, old-fashioned furniture.

My camera is a 35mm Nikon, usually set on a tripod. Sometimes I feel that I should really be using a view camera. A contact print from an 8 x 10 negative is gorgeous. An enlargement from a 35mm negative is never going to be as beautiful. However, the 35mm camera gives the photographer much greater freedom. With it, you can get a very acceptable, viable result without dragging around a heavy view camera.

The mechanics of photography should never get in the way of making the photographs. The act of taking the picture shouldn't be so cumbersome that it removes the joy from working. You should know your camera and equipment so well and move it so quickly that it's like working at a typewriter. If the photographer is completely at ease with his equipment, his energy goes into what he's looking at.

I use only Kodak Tri-X film rated at 400 ASA. To determine my exposure, I use a Brockway incident light meter. The light I like to work with is a soft, natural, window light, which gives a beautiful chiaroscuro effect. I place the meter in front of the model's face and take a reading of the light falling on the model. In general, I tend to overexpose a stop because I feel that overexposure gives me a better black in the final print. With the MAN UNDRESSING sequence, the exposure was 1 second at *f*/16.

My prints are made on Kodak Polycontrast paper, usually with a No. 4 filter, or on Agfa Brovira. The prints are usually 5 x 7 in size because I like the one-to-one relationship between an intimate idea and an intimate scale. Some people think that a bigger print makes a more impressive photograph. I don't agree with that at all. I like small rooms, small people, small prints and small cameras.

My photographs of the nude don't have to do with a beautiful physique or a beautiful pair of breasts. There are valid reasons for such photographs, but to me they are not satisfying. I think the nude must transcend itself: the problem is how to deal with the "body beautiful" as something other than what it is by its very nature. I like to use the body as a vehicle in a drama. I think the real strength of my work is in the establishment of tension in a relationship. Ultimately, photographs of the nude have more meaning when a second and third layer of tension are revealed.

The MAN TO MAN series (Figure 3), done in 1977, is a precursor to the HOMAGE TO CAVAFY series. MAN TO MAN has to do with the relationship between an older, dressed man and a younger, nude man. There's always a great deal of tension in a relationship in which one

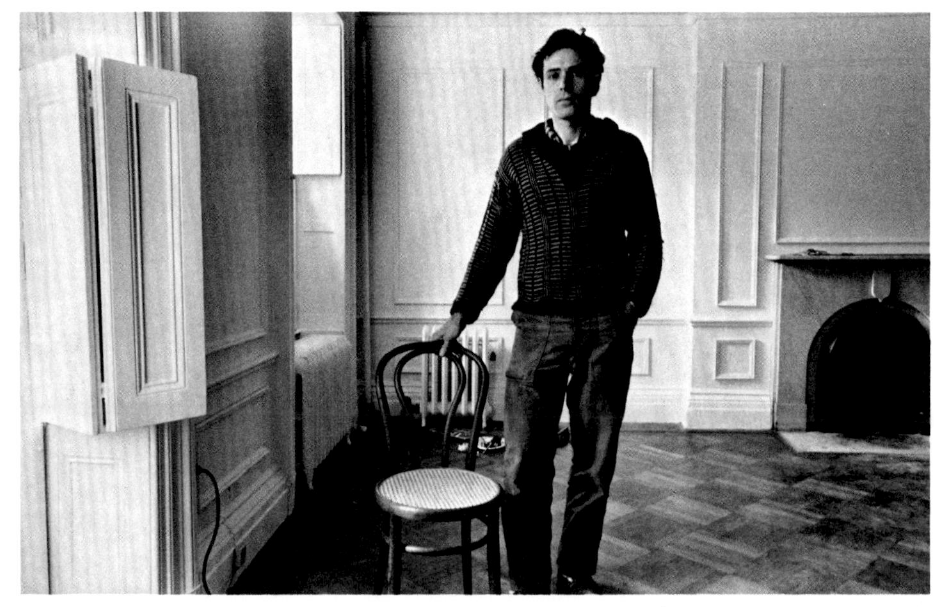

1

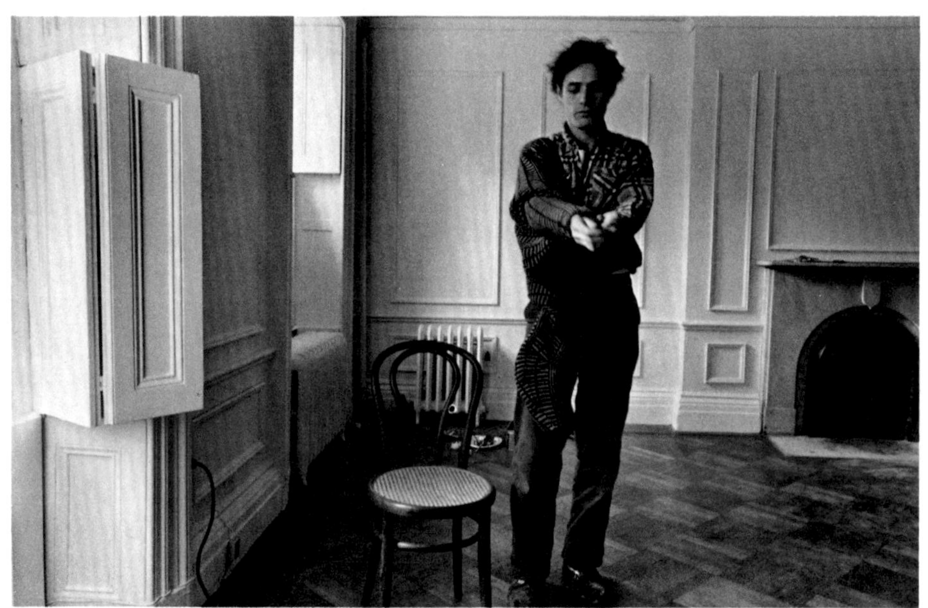

2

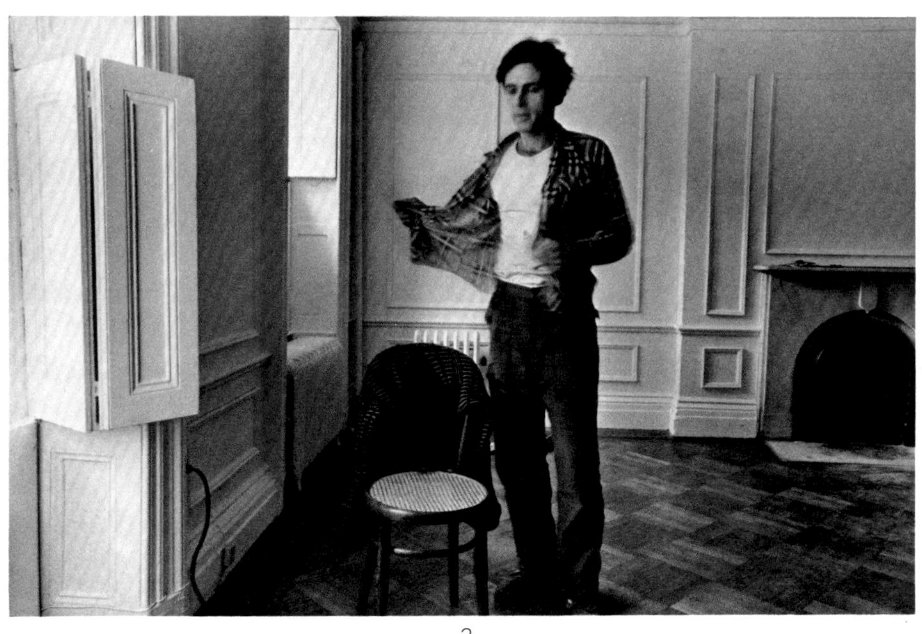

3

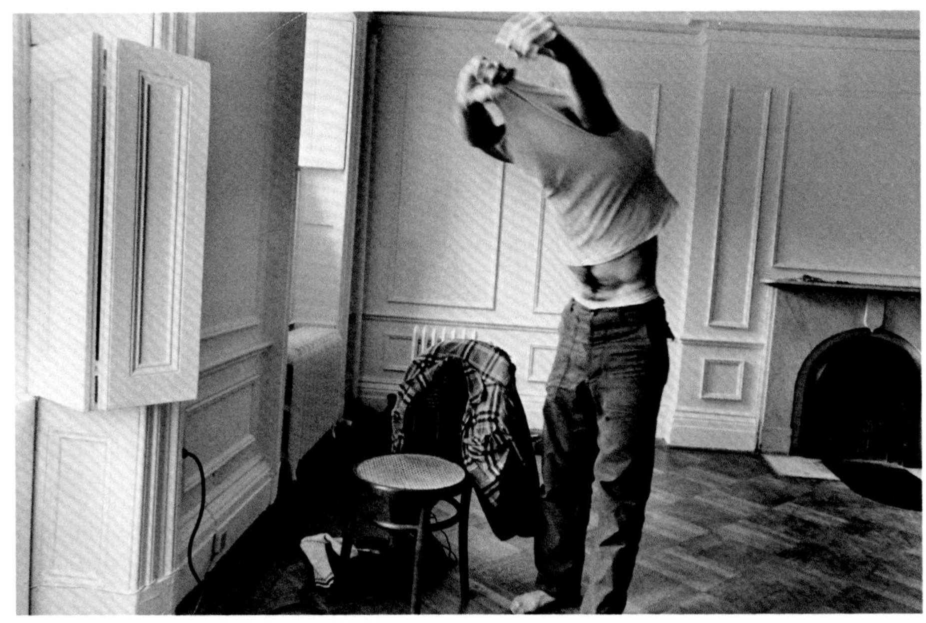
4

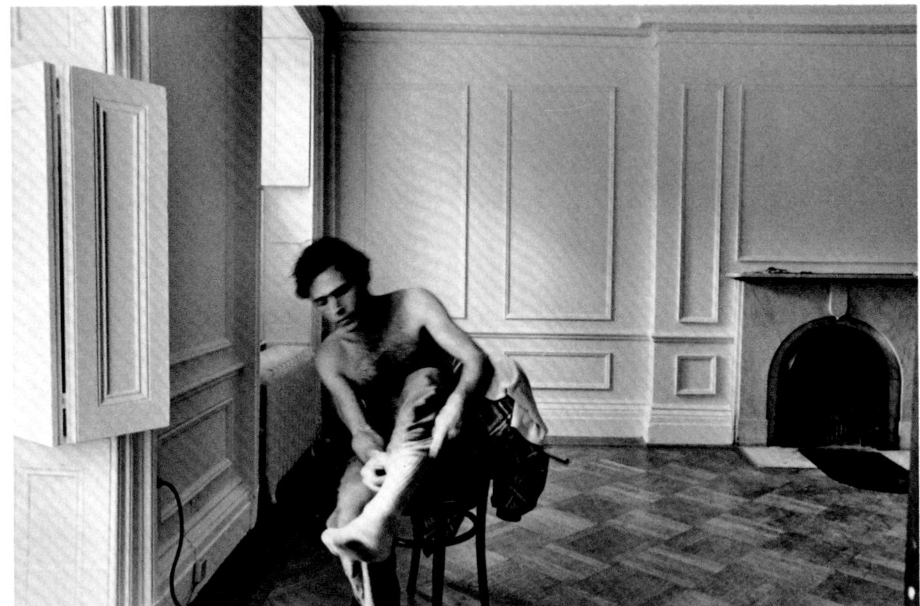
5

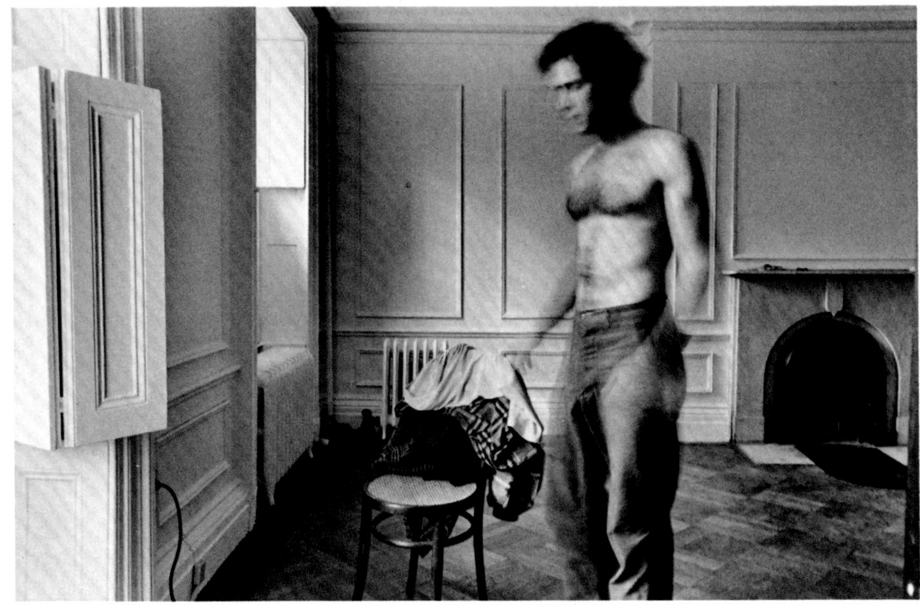
6

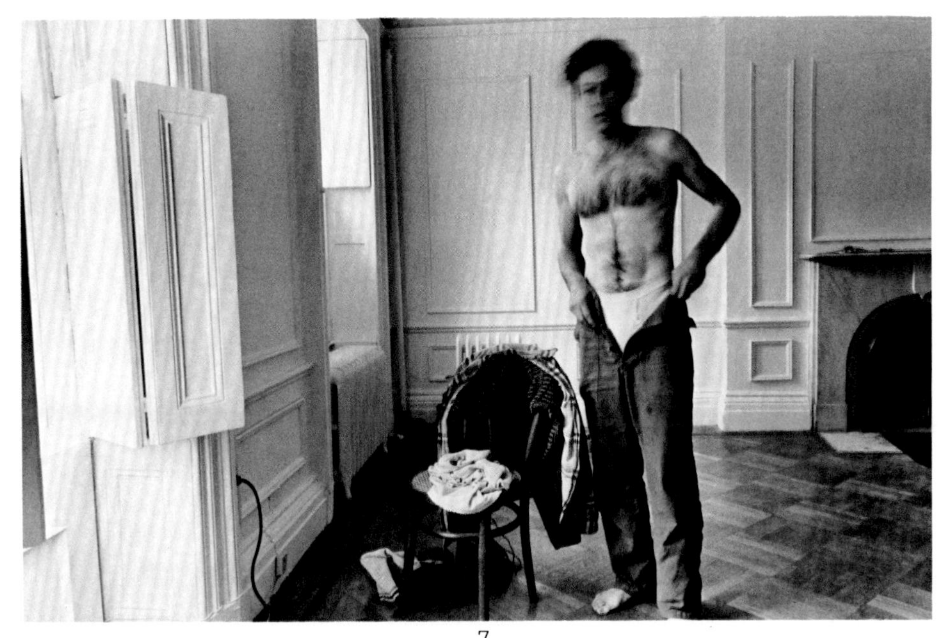

7

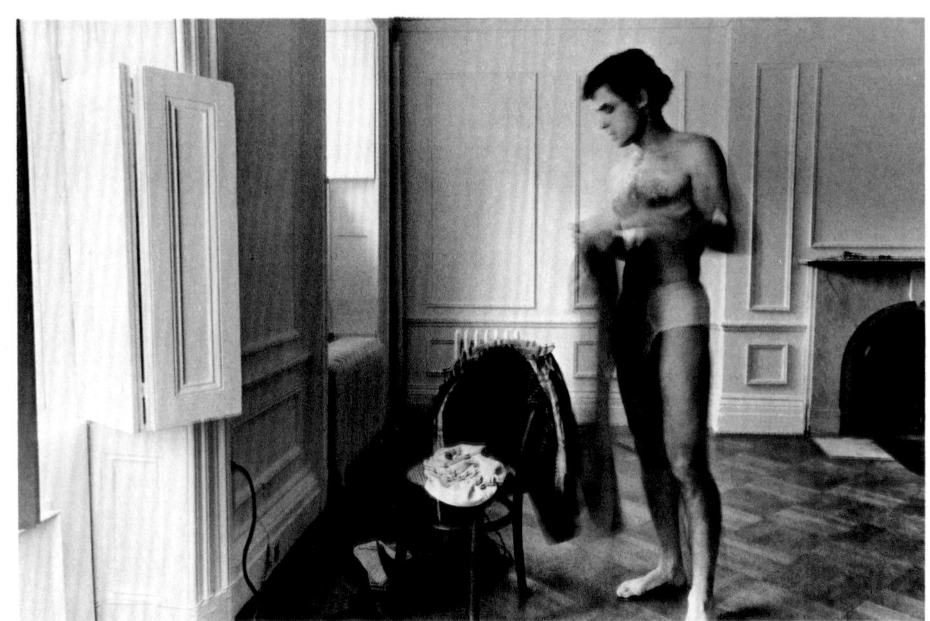

8

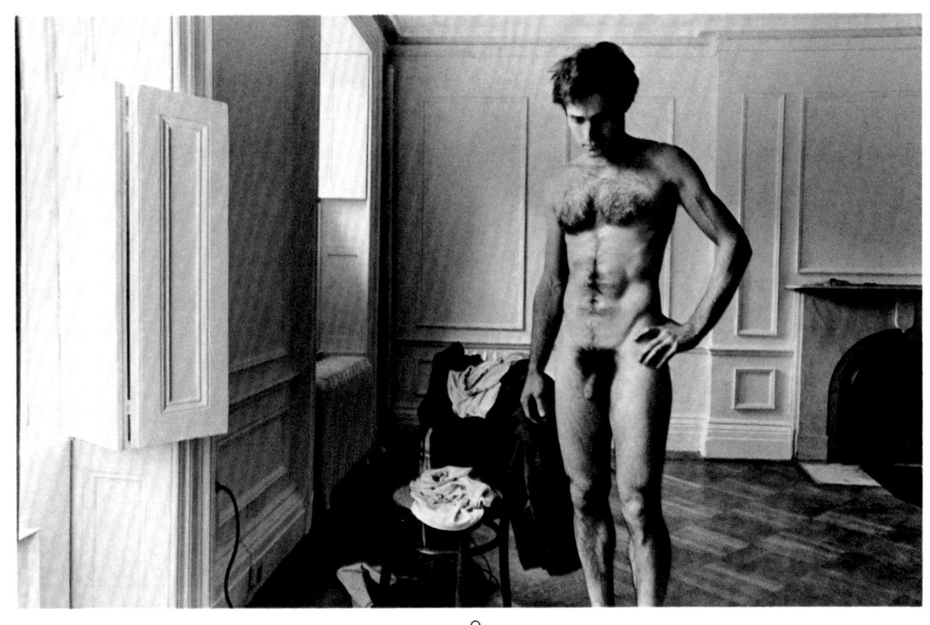

9

FIGURE 2: MAN UNDRESSING, 1979

person is clothed and the other is nude. Again, the use of the nude figure implies vulnerability. For me, this is a very charged series because there are so many possible interpretations of the relationship between the two. There are many ideas operating here: the mentor-student, father-son relationship; an erotic relationship; the concept of lost youth; role-changing between members of the same sex, etc.

In the first image, the younger man is putting his fingers in the mouth of the older one. This is an incredibly erotic gesture and it sets up a premise of some sort of erotic relationship. At the same time, the hand in the mouth is also a kind of male umbilical cord from the father to the son. I am very conscious of the use of gesture in my work. I think wonderful things can be expressed between two people simply by where the hand is placed, or by how a hand is reaching toward (or pulling away from) a figure. Paying attention to gesture is paying attention to detail. I like trying to reduce a very complicated notion to the simplest gesture possible. The gesture itself expresses feeling between two people, or lack of feeling, or tension. When photographers deal with the body, they often deal in cliché gestures and poses; a restrained gesture, a delicate touch, like a hand on the shoulder, can be a more powerful thing.

The second image reminds me of the game of "wheelbarrow," which we used to play as children. But there is also the concept of the older man supporting the younger man.

In the third photograph, the older man is holding a book and he appears to be teaching or preaching to the younger man. Any relationship is some kind of exchange. A relationship, by its very nature, has to have something happening, even if one partner is not participating, even if something is going wrong. The important questions here are: What is being exchanged between these two men? Are they really two separate men, or is this a case of one man seeing himself in various roles? Is this the father-son relationship? Ultimately, the father cannot protect the son. The son must go through painful personal relationships, through war, through danger. The son cannot be saved from his own pain; he must experience it himself; and yet the father can offer wonderful gifts of love and knowledge to the son to prepare him for life.

In the fourth photograph, the older man is sitting on the back of the young man, who is supporting him. For whatever reasons, the two men must support each other in the relationship.

In the next image, a mirror reflects the face of the younger man where the older man's face should be. Here we could be talking about the older man's youth.

The older man covers up the younger man with a coat, causing the younger man to vanish. Of course, the young man could be the older man's own vanishing youth; the older man is saying good-by to his youth. You mustn't forget that everything I do is from the point of view of a 47-year-old man who's quite aware of his own vanishing youth. I'm not old, but I'm not young anymore, and that's a very interesting transitional place to be in.

In the final picture, I blurred the older man. I love the blur because it makes a second shape, a shape that could be described as erotic.

There's not much difference between doing an erotic sequence between a man and a woman and an erotic sequence between two men. The same ingredients are there. To me, the important thing is not what you see; it's what you don't see. The strength of my work is in the restraint. I would never do photographs in which explicit sex is involved. The exciting thing to me about sex is that it's all in the mind, just as all our experiences are in the mind. Sex has to do with fantasy, with role-playing, to a very large extent. It may be that one person finds breasts beautiful and someone else happens to find a man's chest beautiful, but it's all the same impulse operating. The psychological needs and physical desires are universal. It's just that the object of desire differs.

My mind is always the source of my work, never my eyes. I don't know how the ideas for my work come to me. Everybody has ideas constantly. What I do is to pay attention to them, and in paying attention I don't dismiss the things that most people do. When I'm working on specific ideas for sequences, I piece all the parts together in my head very carefully, like learning all the lines in a part for a play.

The longer I have worked in photography, the more depressed I have become by the way most photographers work. They are so dazzled by looking that they seldom exercise any other faculty, and it's a shame. With the proliferation of photographers now, you would think there would be more interesting ones than there are. So many of them merely repeat the old familiar clichés.

UNTITLED, 1967 (Figure 4) is a study of a figure moving in space. Usually we see the body from only one point of view, as when we are talking to someone seated in a chair. I had the model move in a circle here while I hand-held the camera. In some frames the body is in focus and in others the figure moves out of focus. I like the idea of publishing the entire contact sheet, rather than enlarging one selected image. The contact sheet has a wonderful rhythm to it. I was interested not in the mechanics of how the legs and arms operate, but in the aesthetic quality of what the body does, in the sheer pleasure of observing the body moving in a circle. Each photograph is reinforced by the photographs next to it. There is a subtle transition in rhythm in the movement of the shoulders to the left, to the right. I have photographed this particular man through the years, and it is interesting to see how his body developed after he began to work out. Here you can see the potential; step by step he matured and fulfilled that promise.

People always respond to the photograph of the woman on the bed (Figure 5), partly because it has great erotic impact. A photograph of a woman standing in the nude is not necessarily erotic, but a photograph of a dressed woman exposing one breast can be incredibly erotic. It's not a question of the amount of flesh shown; often what is not shown is more exciting than what is shown. The important thing is the attitude expressed by the figure; the most innocent gesture can become an erotic experience. It all goes back to the point that eroticism is always in the mind. In this case, the woman has clothing on, but she is pulling her skirt over her head and her silk stockings are pulled down. One of the feelings conveyed is that of embarrassment or shame about what she is doing.

On the bureau behind her is a photograph of a little boy and his mother. I like the idea that possibly the woman with black stockings is in this little boy's room, but now the boy is a man. There's something vaguely perverse about "being bad" as your mother is watching you.

BEAUTIFUL LEGS, 1971 (Figure 6) is another example in which the nudity is not complete. The body of the woman is almost entirely covered and yet it is an extremely erotic photograph. The textures of the rug, sofa and wall are extraordinarily beautiful. Your eye follows the line of the back of the sofa, which is interrupted by the white of the woman's thighs. The back of the sofa is a kind of abstract line that runs through the center of the picture. The sense of scale is very interesting here: the sofa looks very small in proportion to the figure of the woman.

I like UNTITLED, 1977 (Figure 1) because it says quite blatantly: this is a photograph, not a painting. The cutting off of the figure was an accident, the type of accident that could not have happened in a painting. You can tell that this frame was located at the beginning of the roll of film. An air of mystery is lent by the white, torn edge of the image. There is no way of knowing what the first half of the image was supposed to be like. The sprockets make us aware of the presence of film in the image-making process.

Although the image is very "photographic," the figure is very "classical" in the sense of coming out of the painterly tradition. Here is a beautiful figure in mysterious circumstances. Why is the box in the photograph? What is the band around the man's waist? The man is tying his wrapped undershirt around his waist and the band reminds me of Michelangelo's BOUND SLAVE. I've always found the idea of Michelangelo's sculpture with a band across the chest incredibly erotic.

UNTITLED, 1979 (Figure 7) was made in a loft that the two men in the photograph were moving into. In the loft was an old display case left by a previous tenant. The case had sliding glass doors in front and a mirror inside. After I looked into the cabinet and saw the reflections in the mirror, I asked the two men to pose.

It was a very gray day. On a sunny day, making the photograph would have been much more difficult because of all the sunlight bouncing around. I made an exposure reading in my customary manner, by holding the incident light meter in front of the men, and then I overexposed one stop. The exposure was 1 second at *f*/16. I used a tripod.

I focused on the mirror, shooting through the sliding glass doors. What the viewer sees are reflections of the men on the glass, as well as the reflections in the mirror. I love the feeling of layers of light and layers of images. It was hard to pick which frame I preferred on the contact sheet. I chose this one because of the way the double image of the man on the left appears to be moving out of the frame.

MAN WITH A KNIFE, 1979 (Figure 8) is a reference to St. Sebastian, a wonderful classic male nude subject. St. Sebastian was martyred by being tied and shot with arrows. Mantegna, Botticelli and many other major artists of the Renaissance did versions of St. Sebastian. Here the skin is being dented with a knife (which also serves as a phallic symbol), rather than pierced by arrows. There's a tension in the fact that the man is restrained in some way, with his arms behind him, and that the knife in my hand is really pressing the skin. I felt the little edge of nervousness and yet fascination associated with the possibility of danger. It is the same with fire; I like to photograph it and yet I am afraid of it.

About a year and a half ago I began to paint on photographs. In the beginning I wasn't very happy with them, but I felt it was a wonderful area to work in. I'm nowhere near the end of my explorations, and I don't know what the solutions to all the problems will be. The first time I put paint on top of a photograph, I realized that the gesture alone meant that I had "disrespected" the traditional photograph. This was upsetting, yet terribly exciting.

When painters use photographs, they transcribe them into paintings, but they don't transcend any element of the photograph. They are simply making a bad (usually) photograph into a bad (usually) giant painting, while displaying a lot of painting virtuosity. But the information in the original photograph has not been changed; nothing has really been changed. When photographers, in turn, have borrowed painting techniques, they have usually done it by tinting the surface of the photograph. They paint in blue skies, green grass, pink cheeks and lots of rainbows. I felt that there had to be another approach. I think of my own approach as a collision between photography and painting.

UNTITLED, 1968 (Figure 9) is a painted image from the sequence THE YOUNG GIRL'S DREAM. I love the white paint and the scratchiness of its texture on the black of the photograph, and the way the black shows through underneath the paint. On the outer edge, I like the tension between the ragged pattern of the paint and the straight edge of the print.

The figure of the man becomes very menacing here. This is not the case in the original unpainted version, in which he is lighter, and appears merely to be leaning over the woman. The woman is very vulnerable, lying horizontally on the sheets. I like the white sheets, which remind me of a bed or a coffin. There is always a sense of ambiguity about a horizontal figure. Is she asleep or is she dead? Each night we stretch out horizontally, we cover ourselves up with layers of sheets and then we drift off into another state. Each night we are rehearsing for death.

In my work with the nude, I try to deal with my feelings as openly as I can. All we can know for sure is what we feel; all else is assumption. It is often painful to be honest in our response to the body. There are some aspects that make us uncomfortable, that we have difficulty making public.

Usually in photography we must deal with the nude body in a very structured way, as in a figure study or sequence done indoors. It's very seldom that the photographer encounters a naked person running down the street. It has occurred to me that I would like to photograph the nude in the forest, to create a kind of A MIDSUMMER NIGHT'S DREAM by moonlight. One problem with this idea is that the insects are ferocious. It's very difficult to persuade people to come into the woods and to stand still for long exposures without wiggling too much. This creates a technical problem, but the concept is quite beautiful.

It is amazing to me that I never run out of ideas for photographs. My attitude is that I can hardly wait to see what will happen next in my work; I love the fact that next year I will be doing something that I cannot even conceive of this year. At this point in my work I have fairly well defined the concept of the sequence and have worked a great deal with writing to accompany images. I feel that now the potential for my work with painting is enormous. I haven't painted in 30 years, so I find it frightening, but I also realize that the creative act is always difficult and complex. By its very nature, it is risky and upsetting. I'm discovering what I am doing with paint literally inch by inch, and there's a sense of wonder about finding an entirely new area to explore in my work.

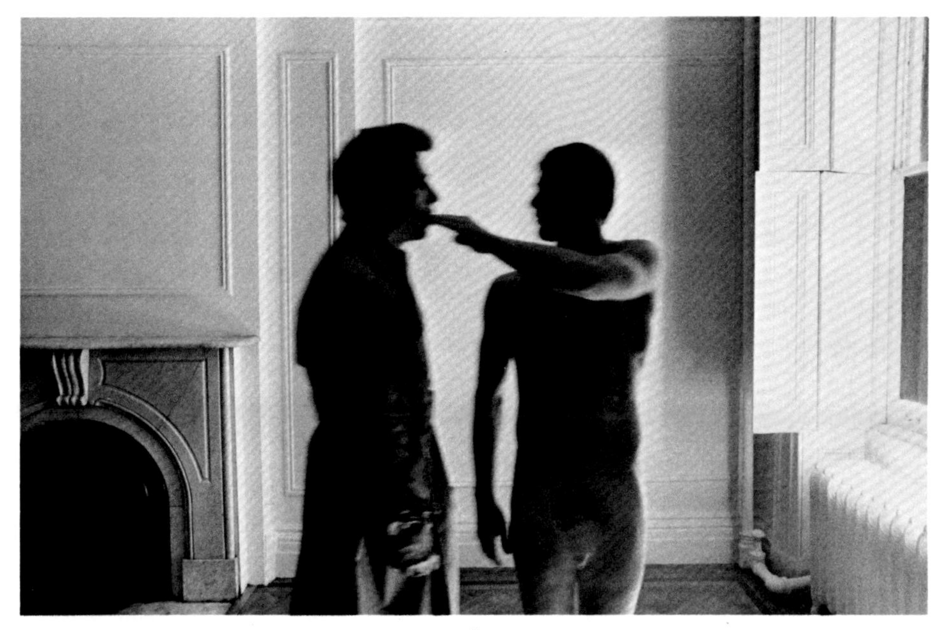

1

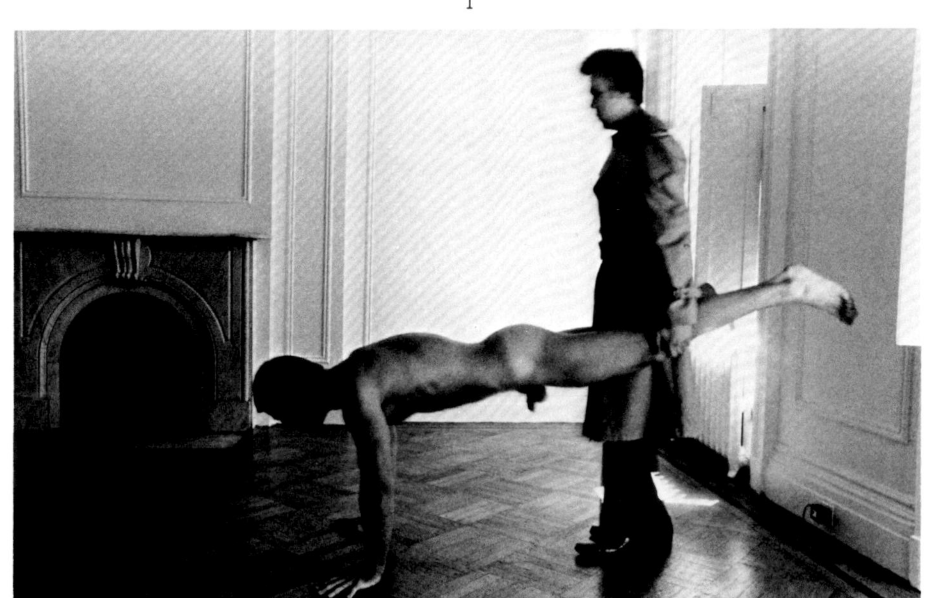

2

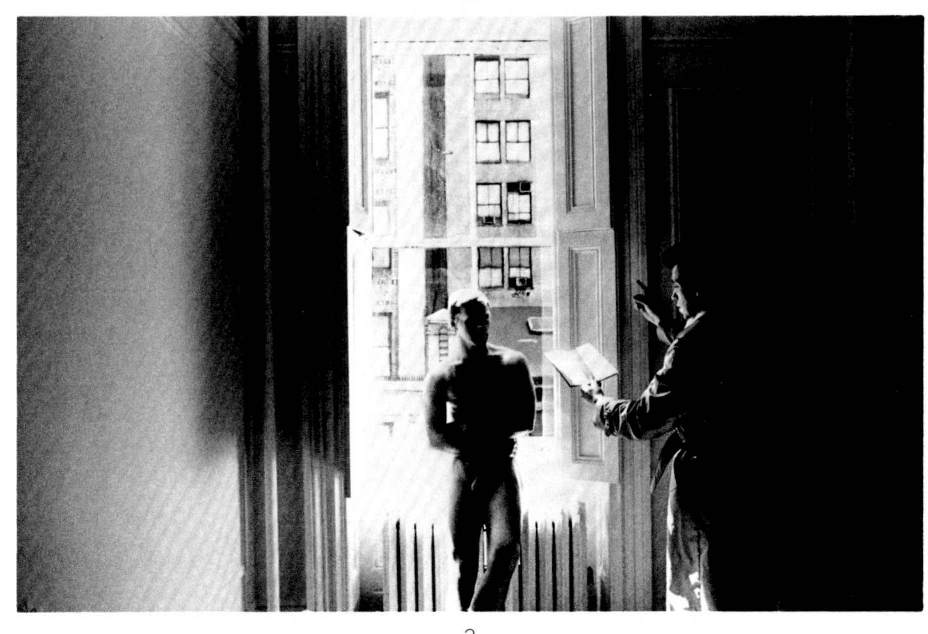

3

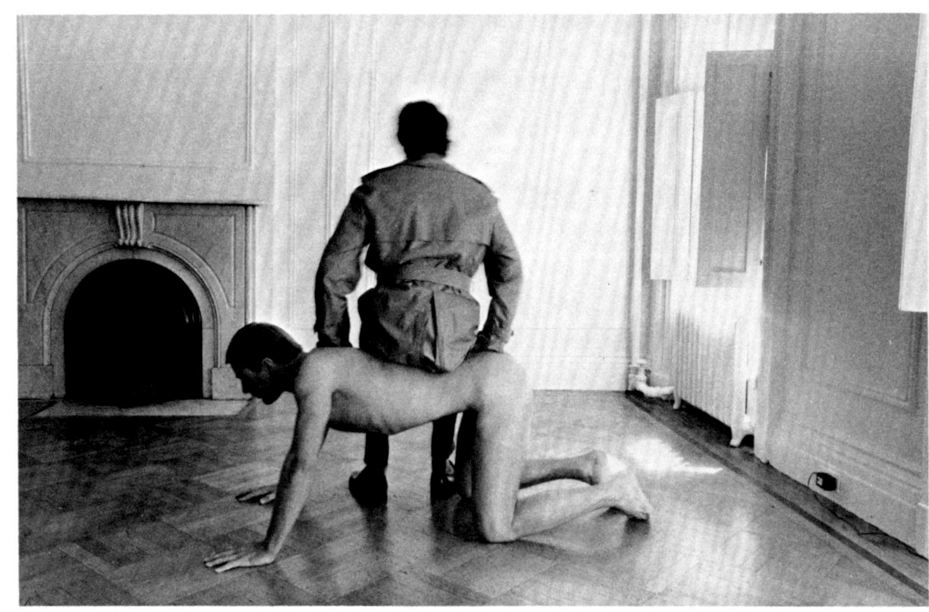

4

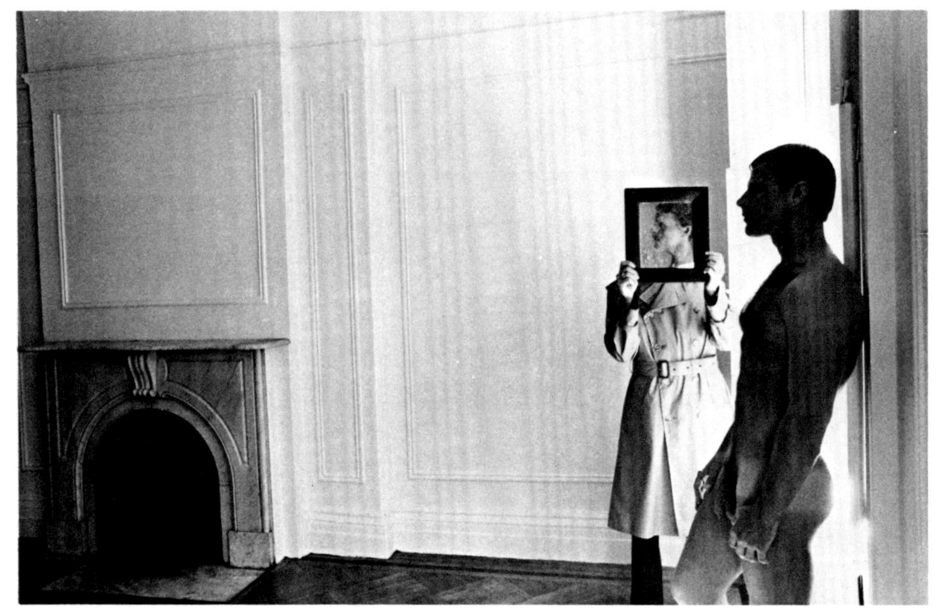

5

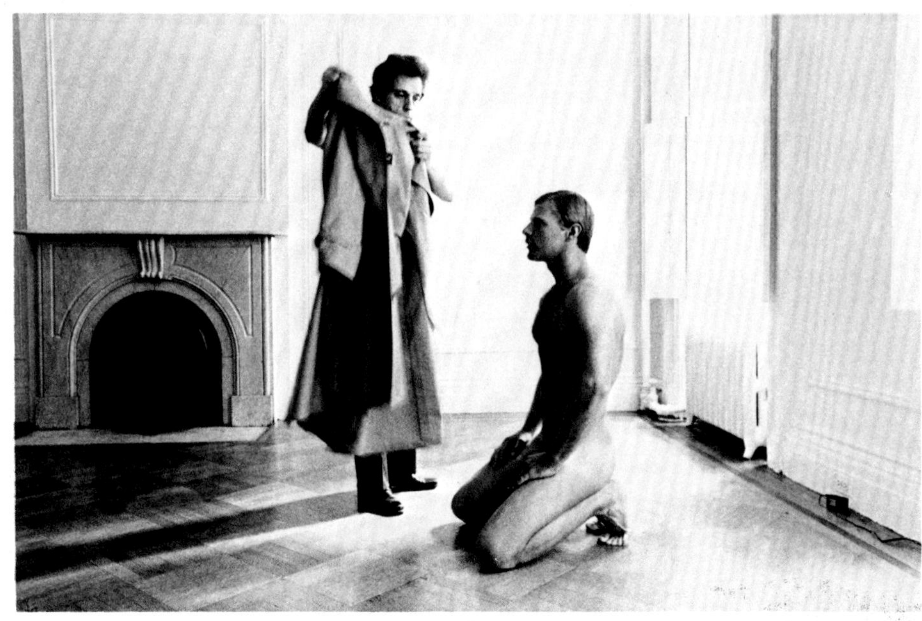

6

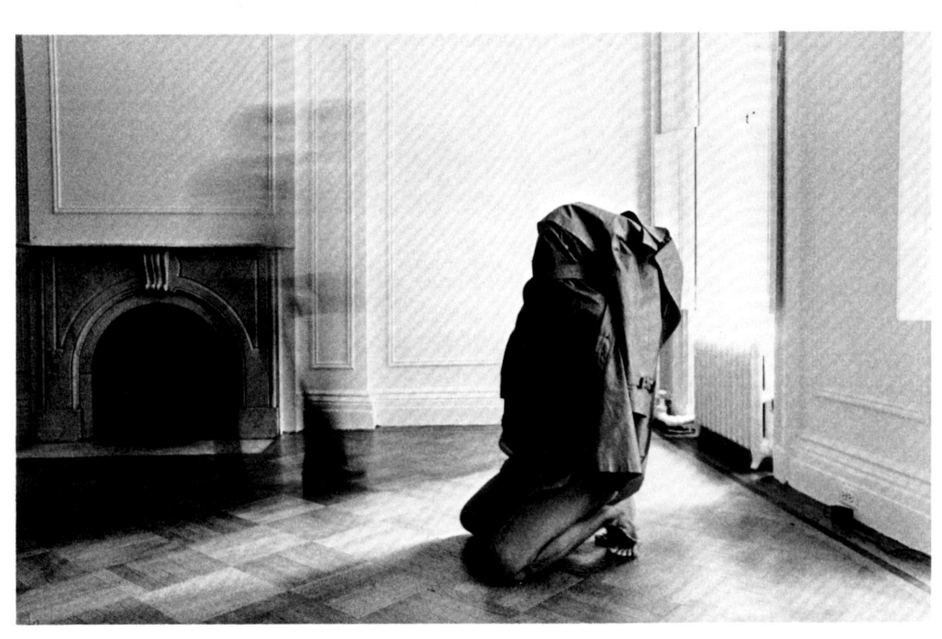

FIGURE 3: MAN TO MAN, 1977

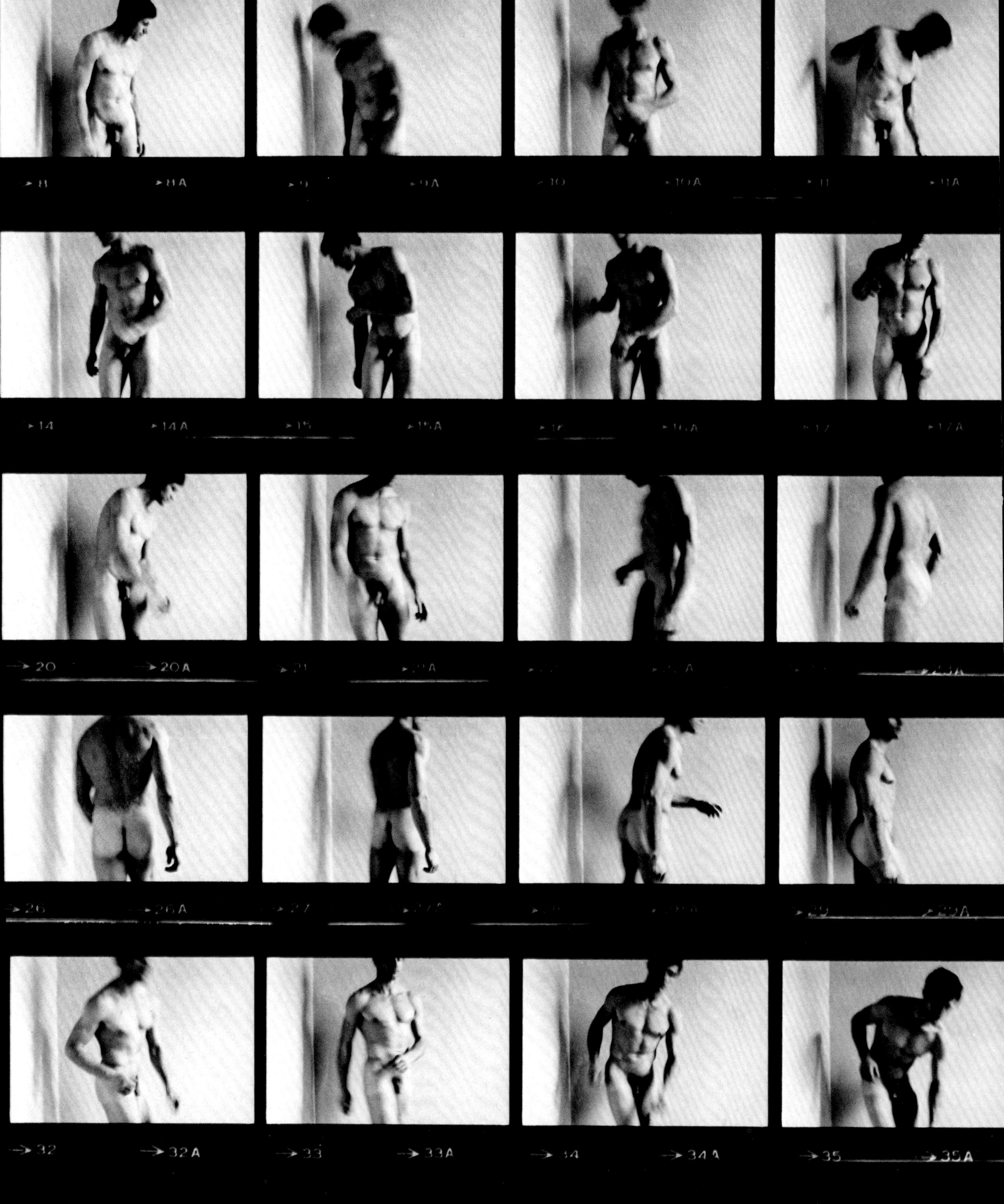
→8A
→10A
→14
→14A
→15A
→20
→20A
→26
→26A
→32
→32A
→33
→33A
→34A
→35
→35A

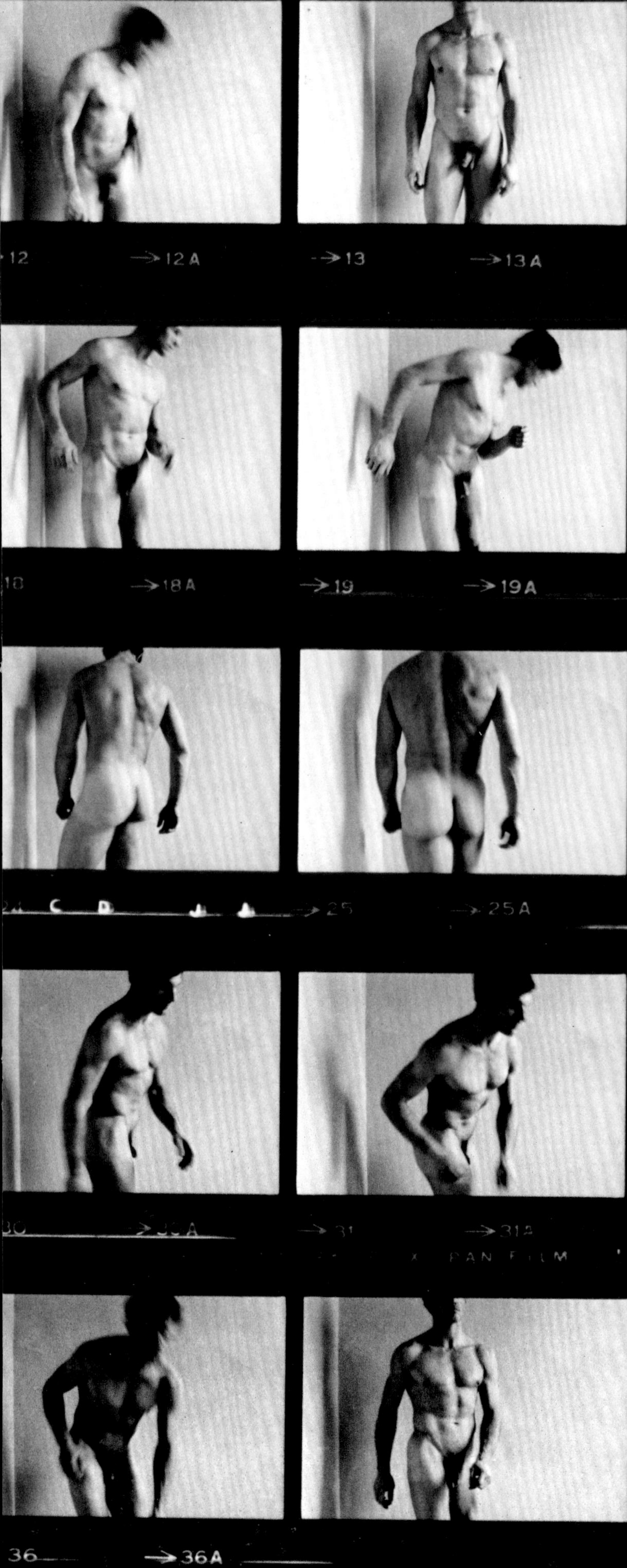
12
12A
13
13A
18A
19
19A
25
25A
PAN FILM
36
36A

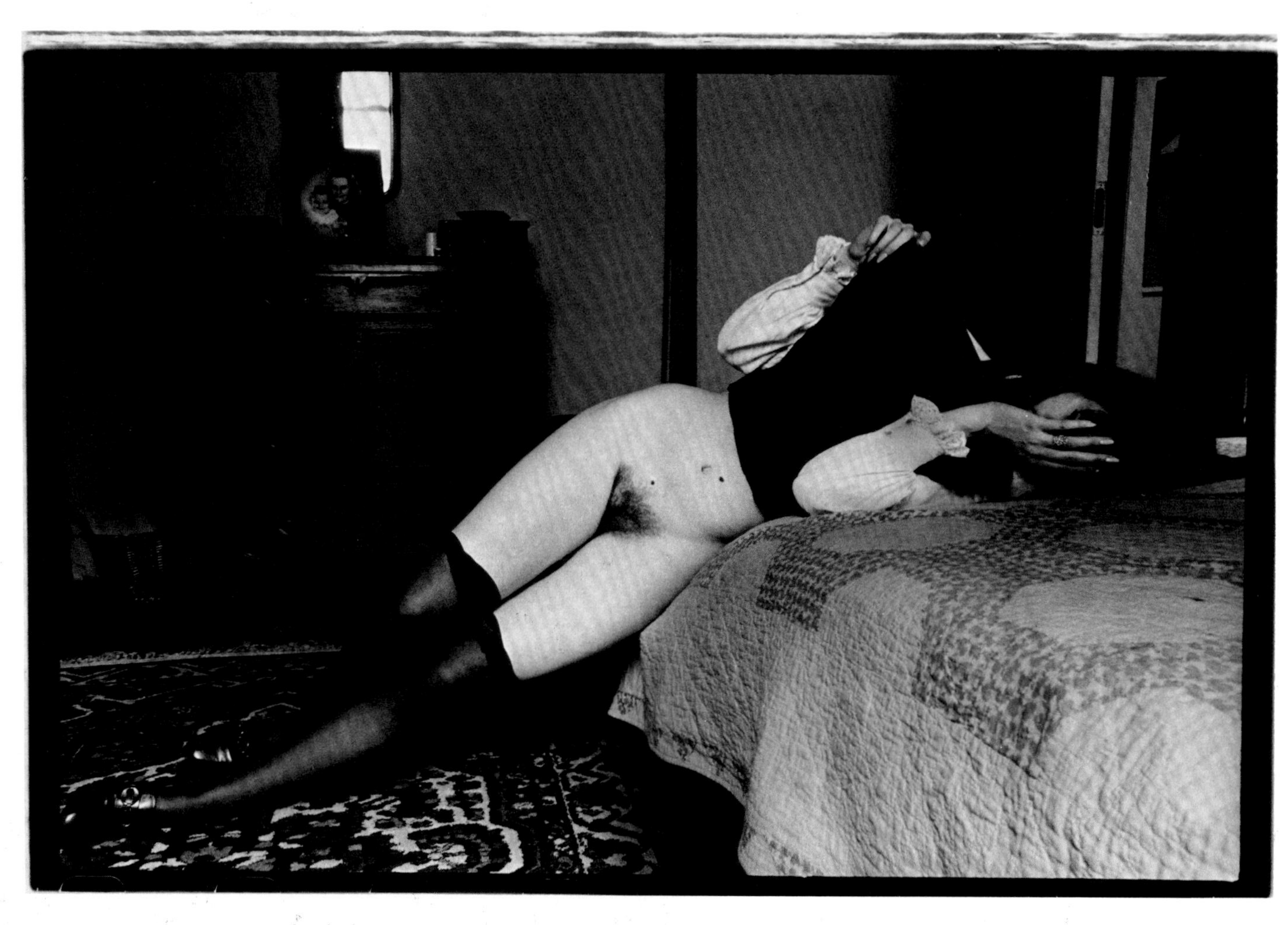

FIGURE 5: UNTITLED, 1969

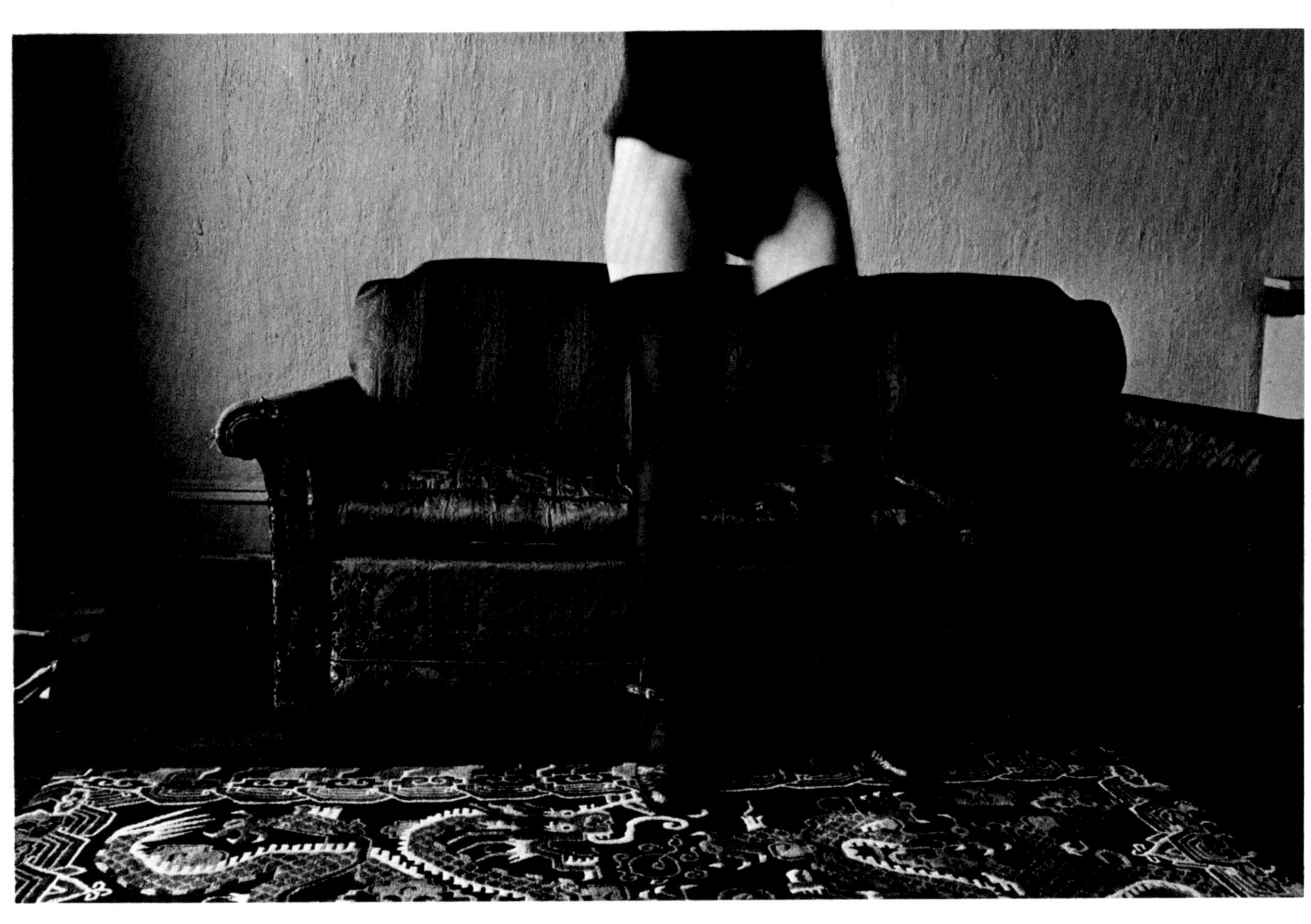

FIGURE 6: BEAUTIFUL LEGS, 1971

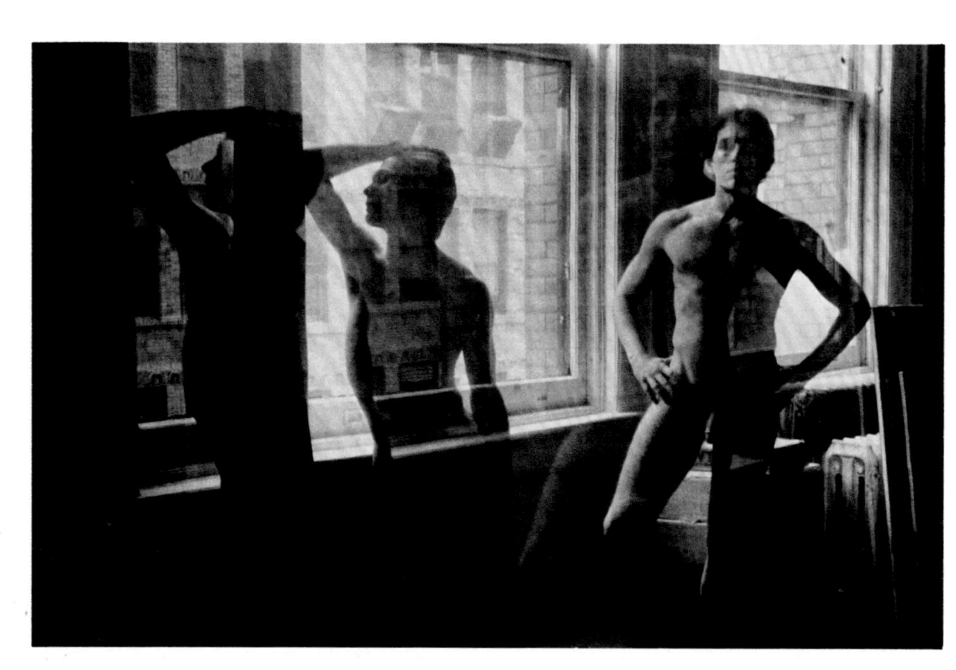

FIGURE 7: UNTITLED, 1979

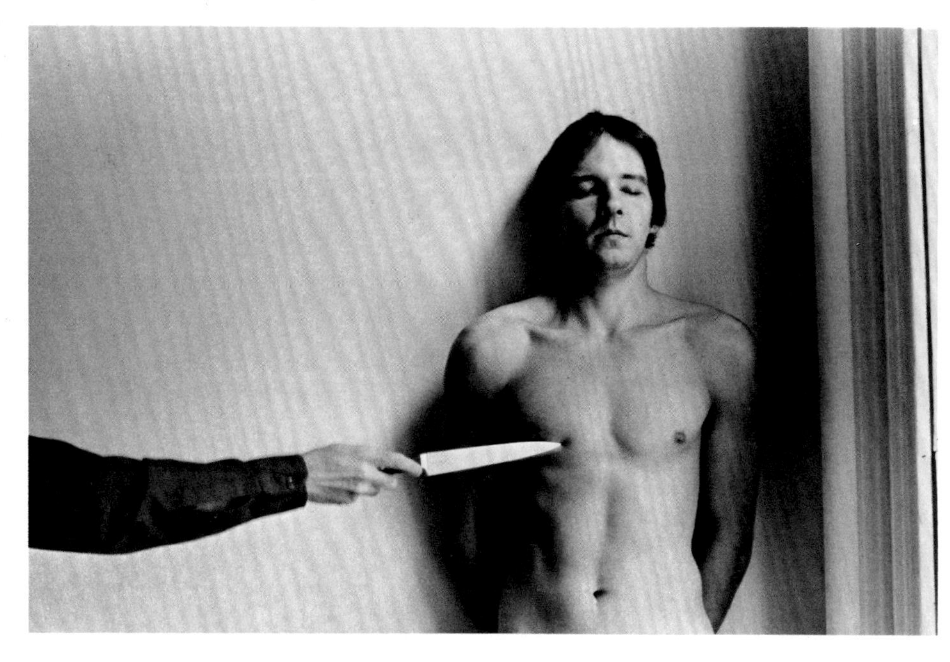

FIGURE 8: MAN WITH A KNIFE, 1979

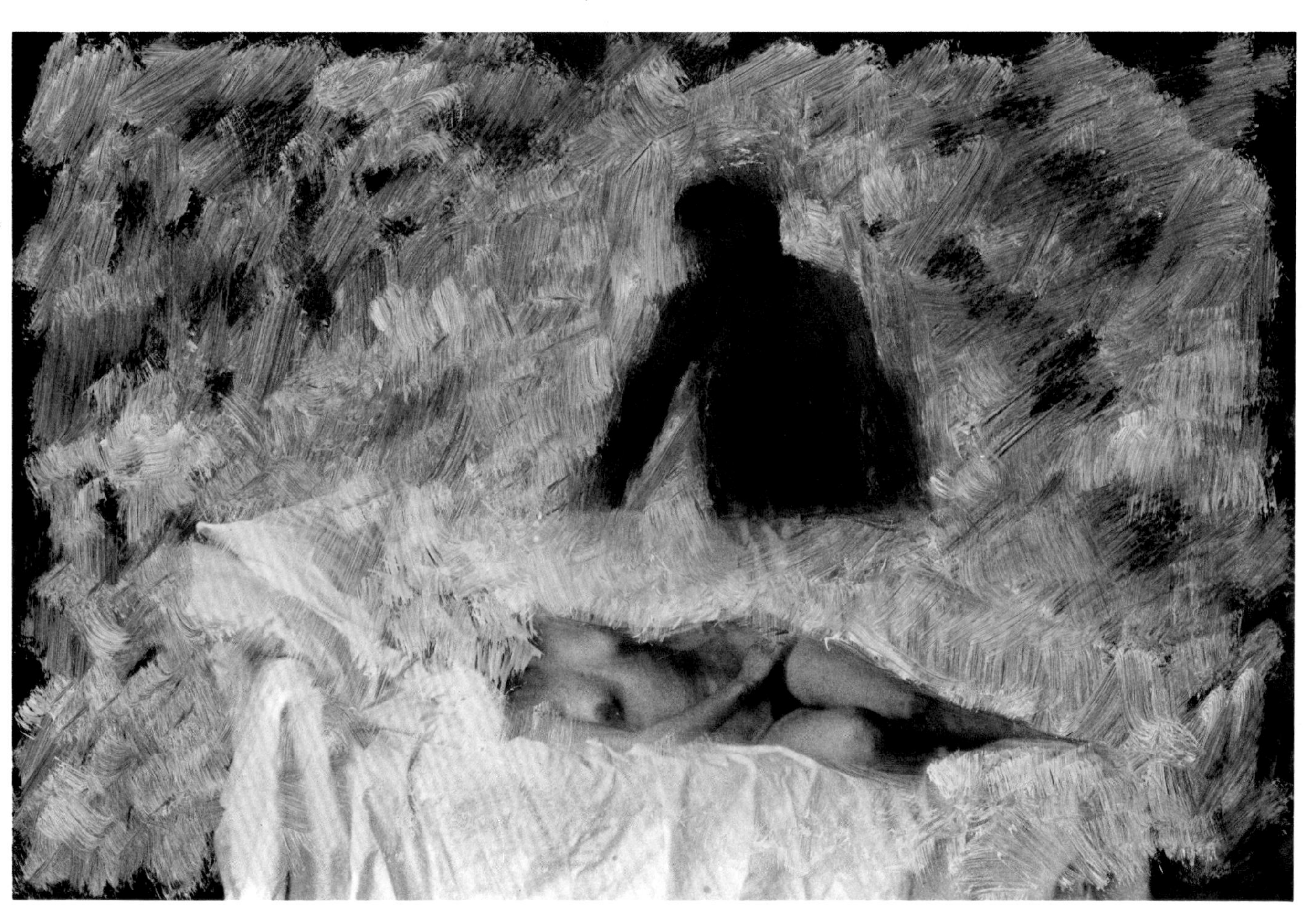

FIGURE 9: UNTITLED, 1968 (From THE YOUNG GIRL'S DREAM)

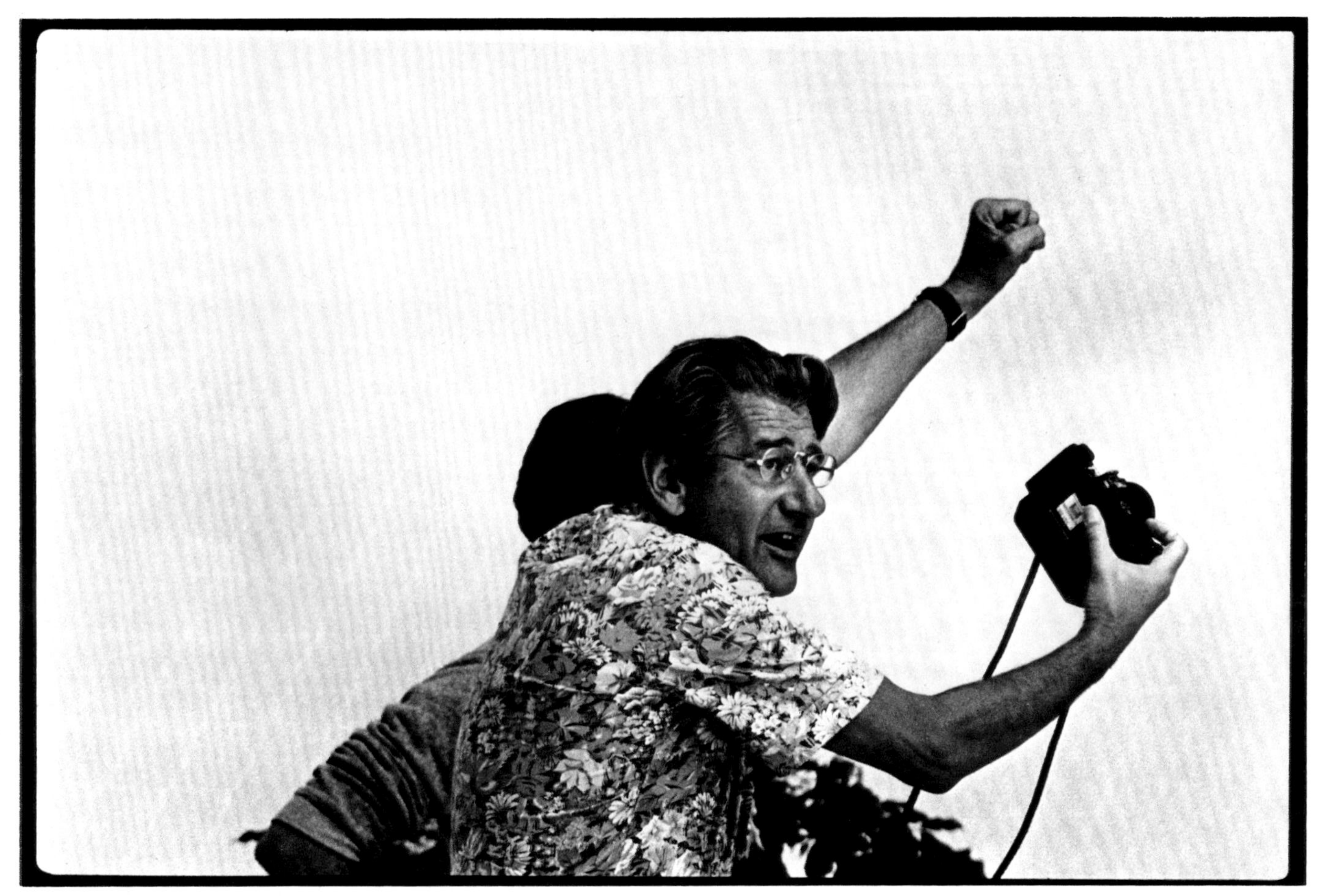

ALICE SPRINGS

HELMUT NEWTON: "I THINK THE <u>IDEAL</u> NUDE IS EROTIC."

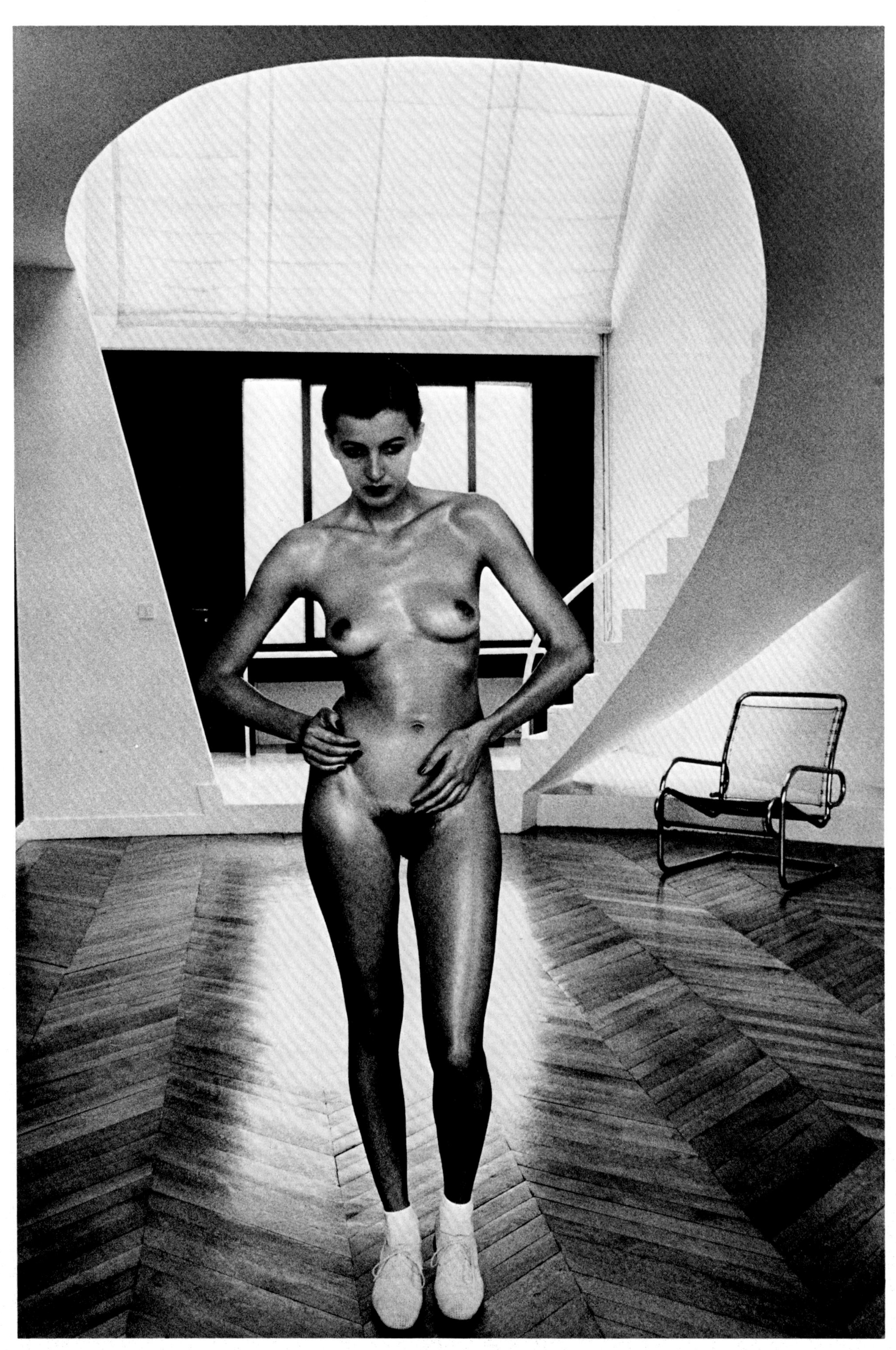

FIGURE 1: IN MY STUDIO, PARIS, 1978

There was a moment in the late 60s when I was fed up with fashion photography and I started working for girlie magazines. At that time they were quite an adventure. I began by doing "dressed nudes" with only part of the body revealed. Only much later did the nude in the classic sense become more serious for me. In fact, my attitude has changed tremendously over a 10-year period.

Eventually, I got fed up with girlie magazines because they became completely standardized. Now they are worse than a mail order catalogue. The attitudes are the same and there are about five basic poses. What is published in girlie magazines is more traditional than what is done in fashion. These magazines have destroyed a kind of mystery, a kind of secrecy that I think is important. The only thing left is to go inside the vagina with a clinical camera, and I find that sad.

It is only recently that my nudes have become very, very naked, even to the point where I sometimes discard shoes. For me that's hard, to discard shoes. A barefoot woman and a woman in shoes stand differently. There is a certain strength, a certain tension in a woman's legs and back when she wears high heels: the muscles work, they're not at rest, they stand out.

What I want now is a model in no way reminiscent of girlie magazines. I want a woman who has personality, who is the real thing. She may have a less than perfect body because a perfect form is not interesting by itself. In fact, it is a turn-off. To me, imperfections are much more attractive. Other people may say that women I find marvelous are too fat or too big. I love the forms of beautiful buttocks and beautiful legs. Everybody has a different idea about the shape of the buttocks, of the breasts. Personally, I like a big back. When it comes down to a narrow waist, that's lovely.

Sometimes I have a model who does not have good breasts. I try to camouflage this because it is offensive to show parts of the nude that are not the best parts. I would never do a caricature of a woman or make fun of her. This is one of the reasons why women like me to photograph them. They can give themselves completely to the camera, knowing that nothing ugly will be shown. I've seen nudes that are not beautiful, and at times they may be valid photographs, but they are not the kind of thing I want to do.

I chose the model for this particular series of photographs because her body is sensational. It's very much a fashion body. It seems to be made to draw or to put an elegant dress on. It wouldn't have done to use a woman with a very lush body. I was interested in the architecture of the studio where I made the pictures, and this woman fits the architecture. Spare, very spare. The shape of the body and the shapes in the studio reflect each other. She is the antithesis of a model in a girlie

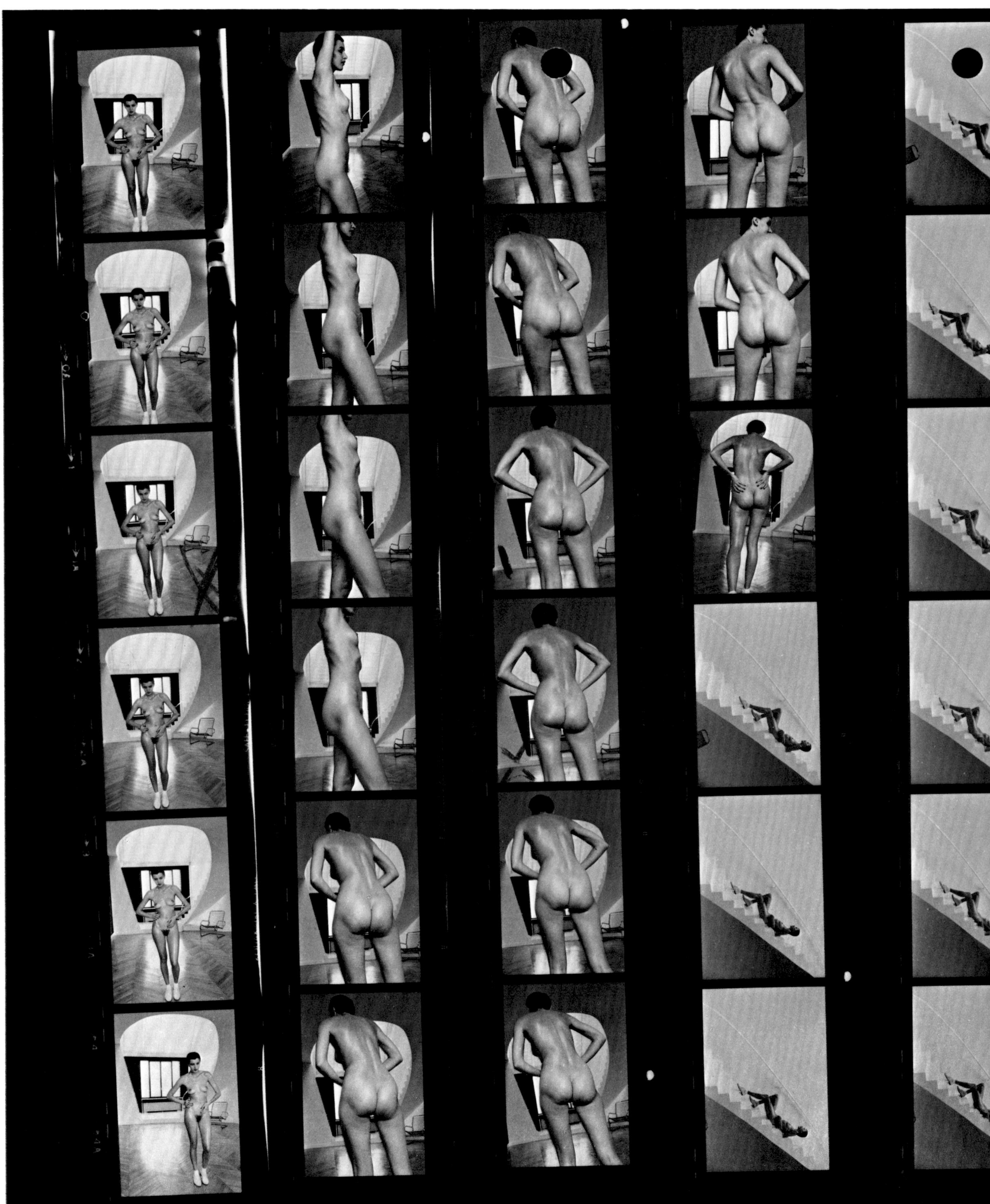

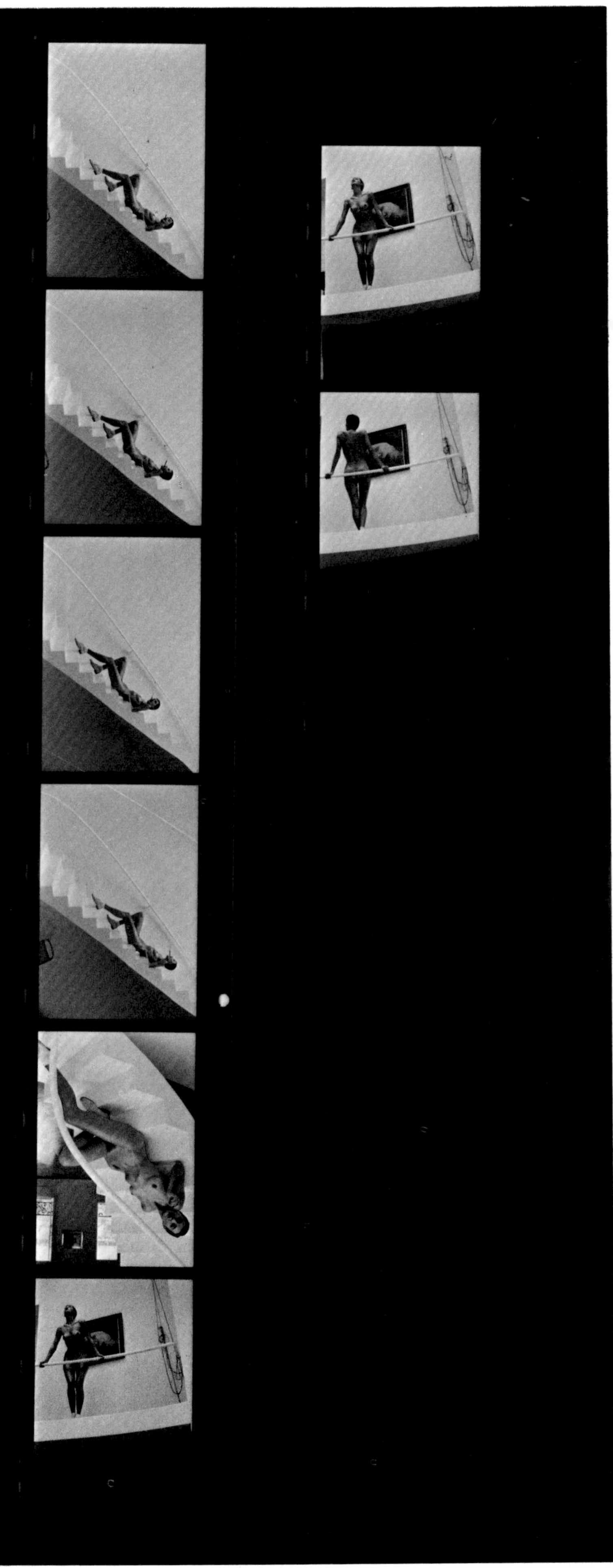

FIGURE 2

magazine. I've known this woman over three years. She tried to be a professional model and it didn't work for her, so she became a fashion editor. I photographed her in Berlin last year for my book SLEEPLESS NIGHTS (Congreve, New York, 1978). I saw her again after Berlin and decided to do this series with her.

There's something boyish about her body and face, and the short hair enhances the effect. I like very short hair on women with well-shaped heads. I think it's quite beautiful. The model's hair has cream on it to smooth it and keep it down. It was standing up too much. It's much neater this way, and with a part added on the side.

The shooting was done in winter, when her skin was very white. Whenever I do fashion photographs, I have a make-up artist put cream on the women wherever a bit of shoulder or arm is exposed. We got an extra glow to this woman's skin by creaming the entire body, even in the daylight pictures. The cream gives a kind of richness to the skin, a luminosity.

The setting is the studio in my new apartment, where I've been living only six months. I've seldom used the studio professionally because I usually shoot on location. I love this apartment. I've taken lots of pictures of the place empty, for myself, because the play of light and shade in the summer and winter is extraordinary. There are windows everywhere. The whole studio is skylight. I put in a staircase that looks entirely different by night, and I wanted to play with that difference in the pictures.

I have the feeling that these photographs represent a big departure for me. There are a million pictures that go up a blind alley and don't lead the photographer anywhere. When I began work, I didn't have the sensation that these were different. But when I saw the contacts, I realized that they were. The work went over three sittings. The first sitting wasn't that good; I did only a few pictures because the model's hair was all wrong and the lighting was off. I can't tell exactly why the second and third sittings are important; I can't give you the reasons. I just feel positive that they serve as a springboard and it would be exciting if I could go further. We'll see.

In the first nude (Figures 1 and 2), there was a very interesting problem both in exposure and printing. How to get good backlighting and also complete detail in the figure? The apartment has north and south windows, but no east or west windows. I wanted to use only natural light, although it was not a bright day. I placed the model so the north window was behind her. The figure itself was lighted from the south window. I took the photograph while sitting on the window sill, within seven feet of her. The right leg is dark because the light from the window fell off. The left thigh was lifted toward the light source and caught the same amount of light as the torso.

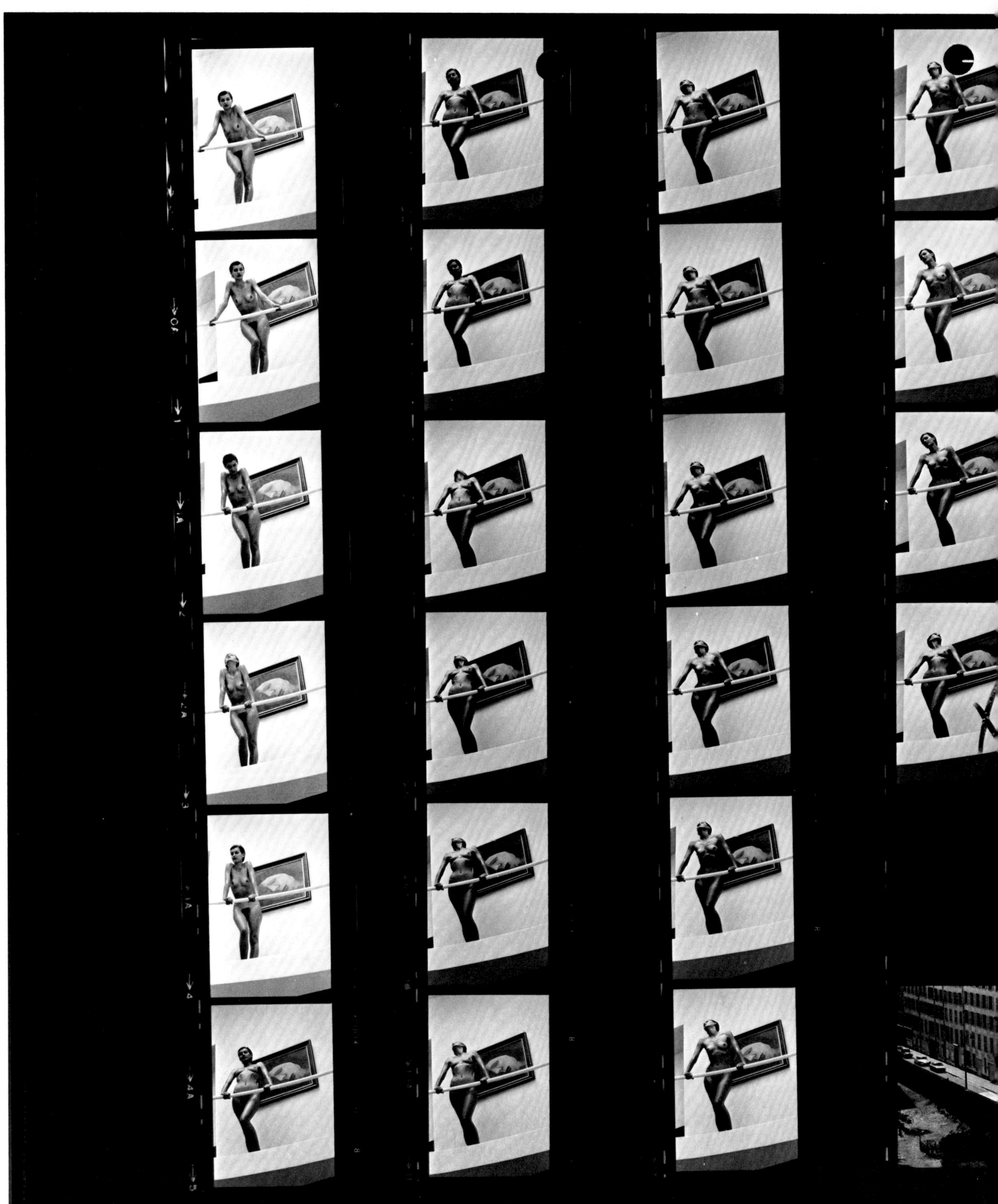

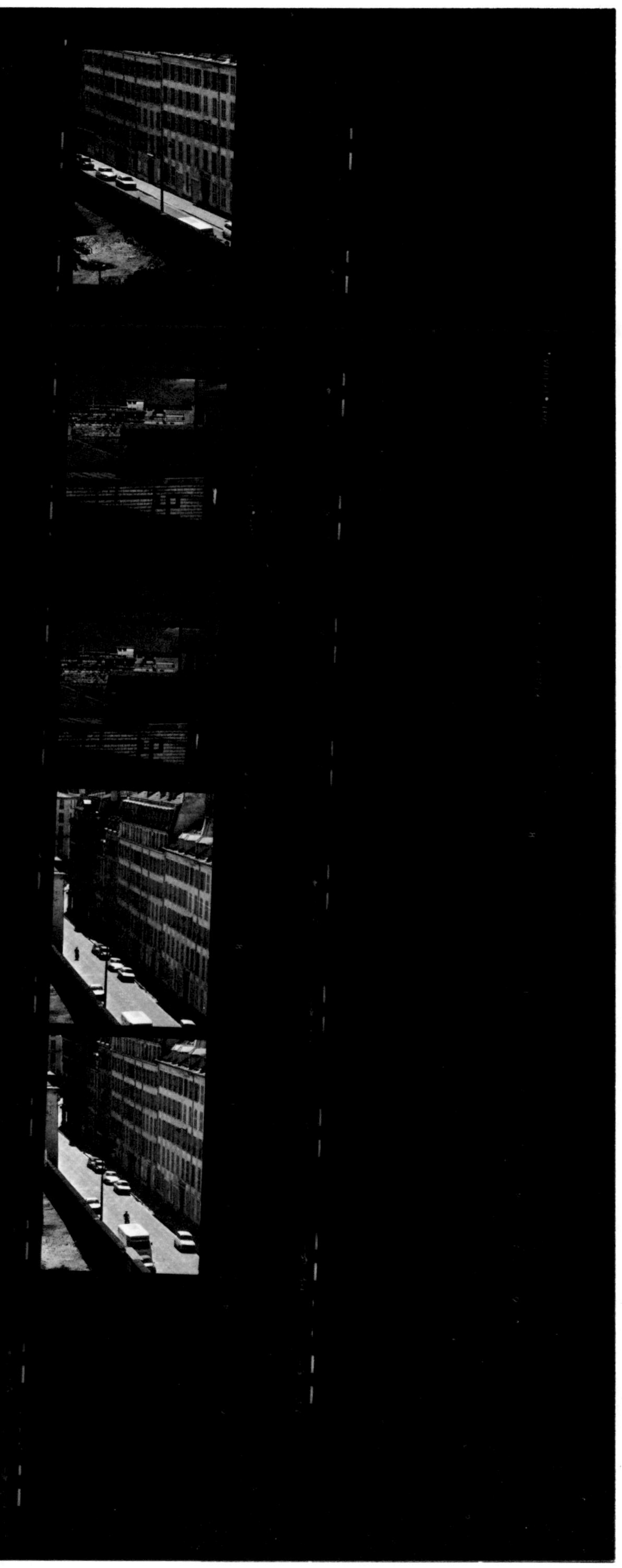

FIGURE 3

I used a Pentax with a 40mm lens, which I consider a perfect focal length. There's no distortion because the center of the lens is about the level of her belly button. Generally I use either a 50 or 40mm, but nothing shorter. Sometimes I go up to 100mm, but I rarely use very long lenses, even at a fashion sitting, because I lose contact with the person.

The film is Tri-X exposed at 400 ASA. If I have very bright sunlight with a lot of speed left over, then it is beautiful to make negatives at an exposure index of 200, which is much better. Personally I don't like to see grain in a photograph. I hate it, especially on nudes, because I like to see the quality of a woman's skin rather than the grain in the film. But I can't use slower film when I'm shooting at a low light level without flash. The reading here was something like *f*/5.6 at 1/60th or 1/125th of a second.

Besides speed, Tri-X is good for the shadows. They don't get too hard, too contrasty. If I do need a little contrast in the shadows, I can always get it back in the final print.

I like to expose and develop normally. Everyihing is done by the book. My negatives are developed in a custom lab, the same one that I've been using for many years. The negatives they develop are extremely good. I don't like thin negatives; I think they are a problem.

When I placed the model in front of the painting (Figures 3 and 9), I crouched down with my back against the wall to get the right angle. I used an 85mm lens on the photograph. From this low angle, anything shorter would have been a disaster. You would get absolutely nothing with a 40 or 50mm because she would be much too small and distorted.

The positioning of her legs here is typical of classic fashion poses. They are also poses that Varga used in his pin-up girls. There's always that knee that goes slightly across the other knee to get a certain shape and fullness in the hips. Then the figure narrows downward, flaring out at the feet. This goes through the series.

The poses of the nude must be controlled and corrected because so many ugly things can happen. For example, shoulder blades sticking out in the wrong places can become unacceptable. I don't think this is a question of whether or not the model looks natural. Women often get themselves into positions that I don't think are natural at all, but they do it. They do it automatically, and it is for the photographer to choose the moment to take the picture. Naturalness is not too attractive to me. I'm much more interested in manipulation than naturalness.

You see another typical fashion pose in the nude with a cigarette, who stands on the staircase (Figures 4 and 10). This is rather extravagant. In a dress it wouldn't work. It would be too "démodé," too dated. But here it works for

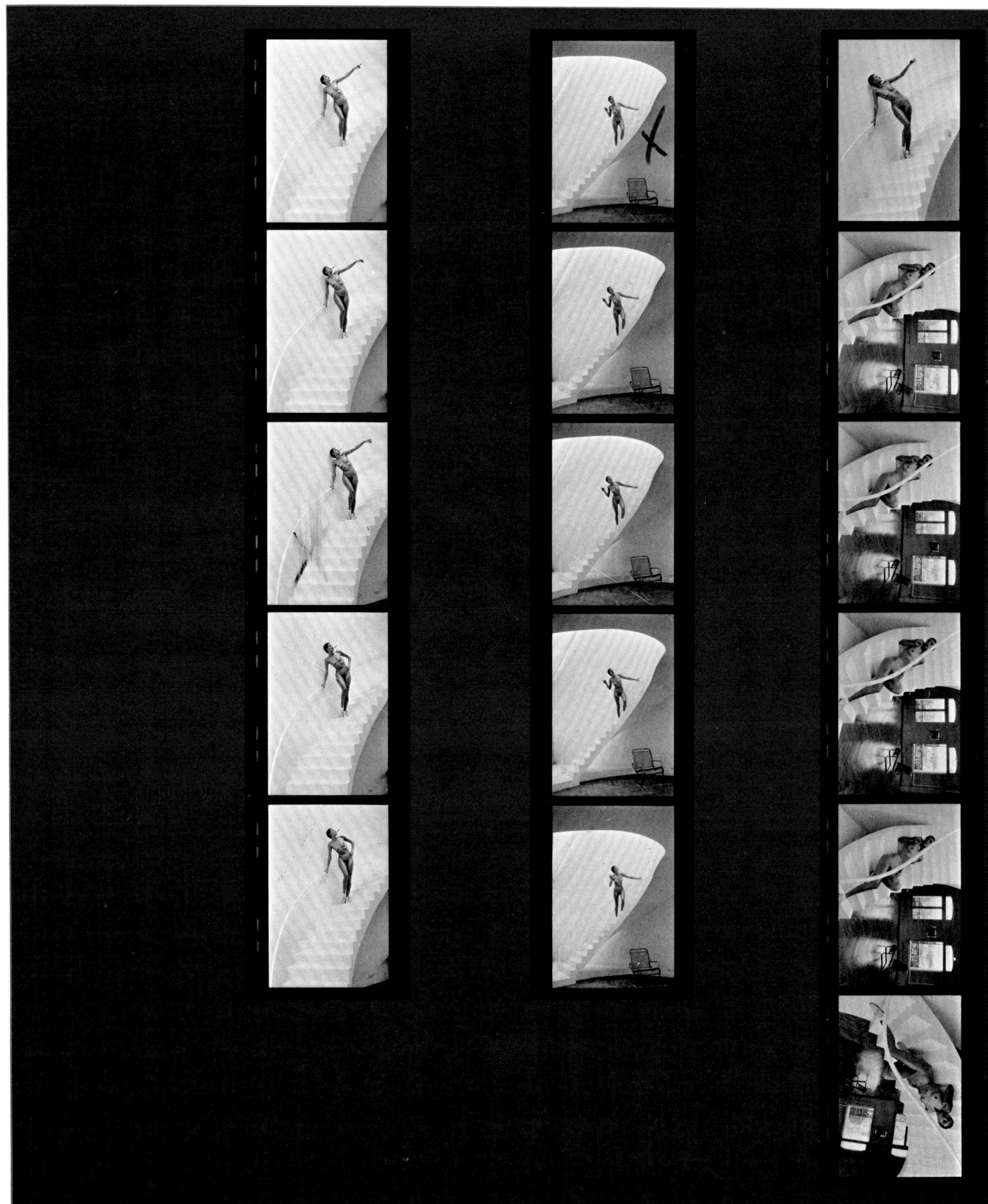

FIGURE 4 FIGURE 5 FIGURE 6

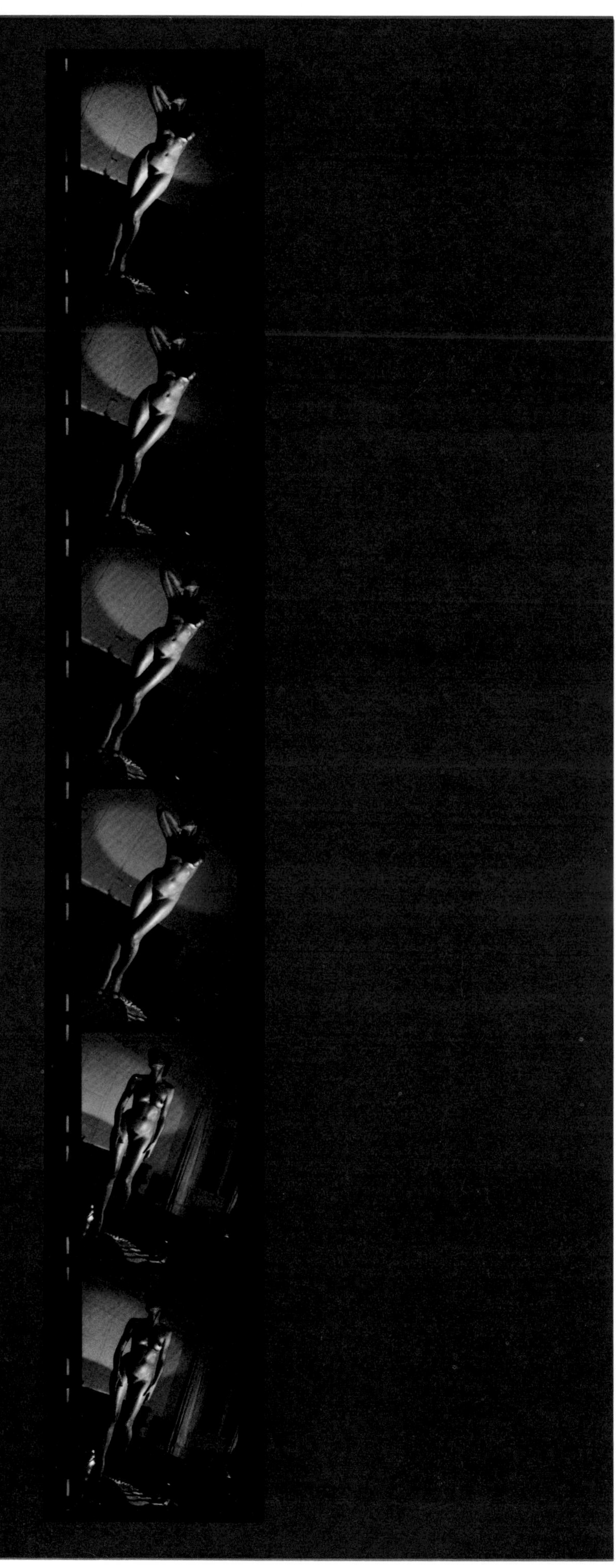

FIGURE 7

me. The thought behind it is that what attracts me is to photograph a woman in the nude doing exactly what she would be doing in an elegant dress. This is not satire of fashion photography. Not at all. It's a consciousness within myself.

The shoes also contribute to the mood. It's very thought out that she wears sneakers in the day and high heels at night. Here the sneakers work well because the woman's got such terrific legs that she can look good even in low heels.

In this variation of the nude on the staircase (Figures 5 and 11), I used a chair designed by an Italian architect. The chair is always in the same corner of the studio. For this picture I moved it a little bit to the left because I like the electrical outlets and wires. The chair is very important to the picture because of its design and the way it fills out the corner.

Next, I used the handrail as a device to cut across the body because I like the effect (Figures 6 and 12). The view outside the windows was at least three stops brighter than the model's skin. Burning in the window area on the final print was not easy. One doesn't want to overdo it, but at the same time one must have the right amount of detail. Also, burning in the window area established the geography of the location, and I like this idea.

Over the last year or so, I've started to tilt the camera to make diagonal compositions, and now I do it quite often (Figures 7 and 13). It makes control of the background possible. There may be certain things I don't want to show in the background, or certain things I do want to include. When I place the camera vertically or horizontally, sometimes I think I've cropped off too much. Since I've started using the diagonal again, I've noticed that French television has picked it up on some of the camera work. Not that what I'm doing is an innovation; it's just a memory of my past. Around 1936, it was quite the thing in fashion and even in portraiture. My boss at the time worked with big plate cameras, and it was a big struggle to get the tripod tilted just right so the camera didn't fall over. We couldn't use a tilt head on the tripod. The camera was too heavy for that.

The diagonal picture was taken in my living room. There are triple doors that open up and go into the studio. The elliptical light effect on the back wall is caused by the mirrored, round coffee table picking up the light of the 500-watt flood used on the model.

I often use artificial light because I like to photograph at night. Generally I use 100- or 60-watt bulbs because I hate burning in a print. I am very careful about artificial light, particularly a 500-watt bulb, because it can become too crude and impossible to control. The hardness of sunlight is another quality because it is purer, easier to control, and has much more "bounce."

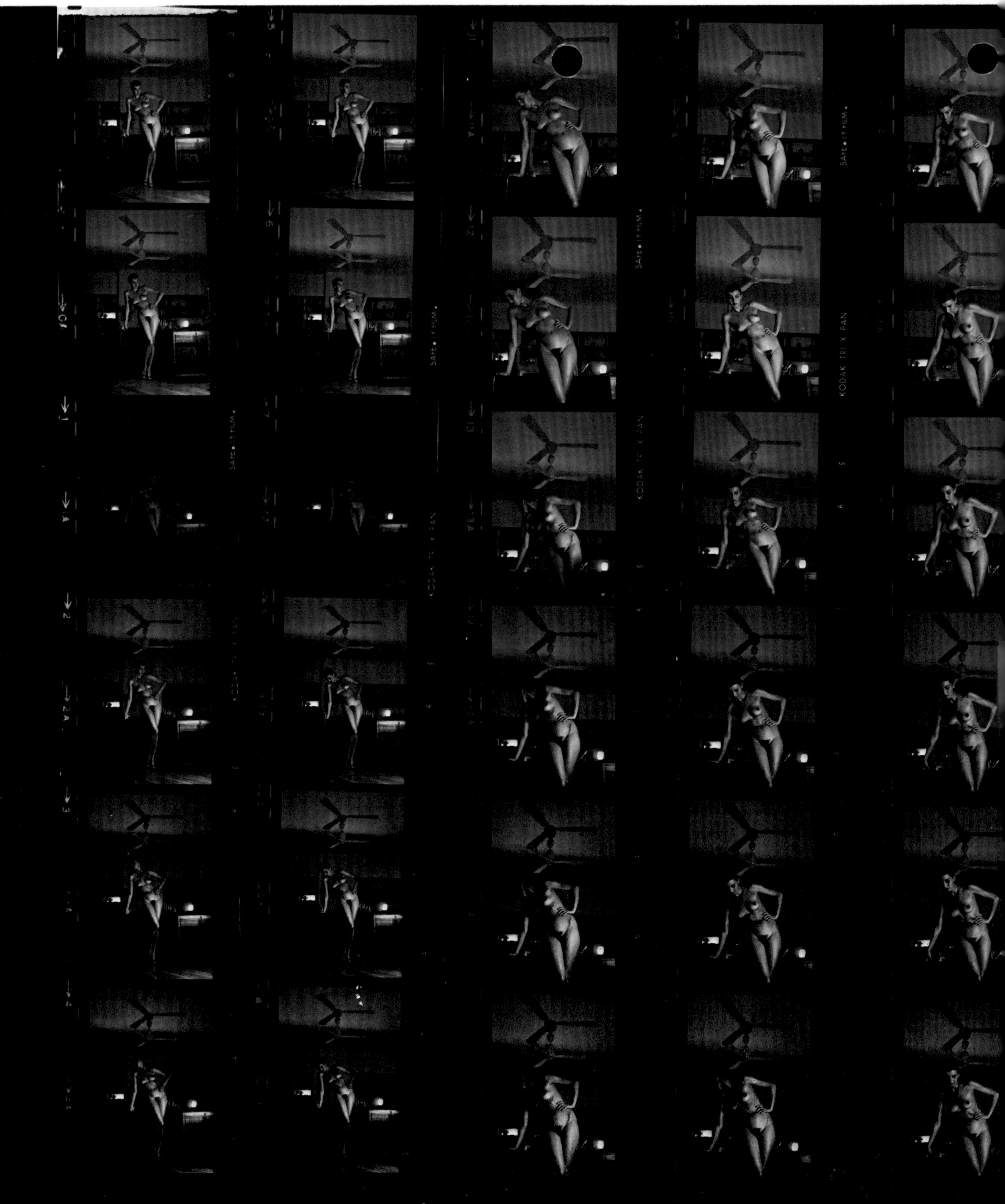

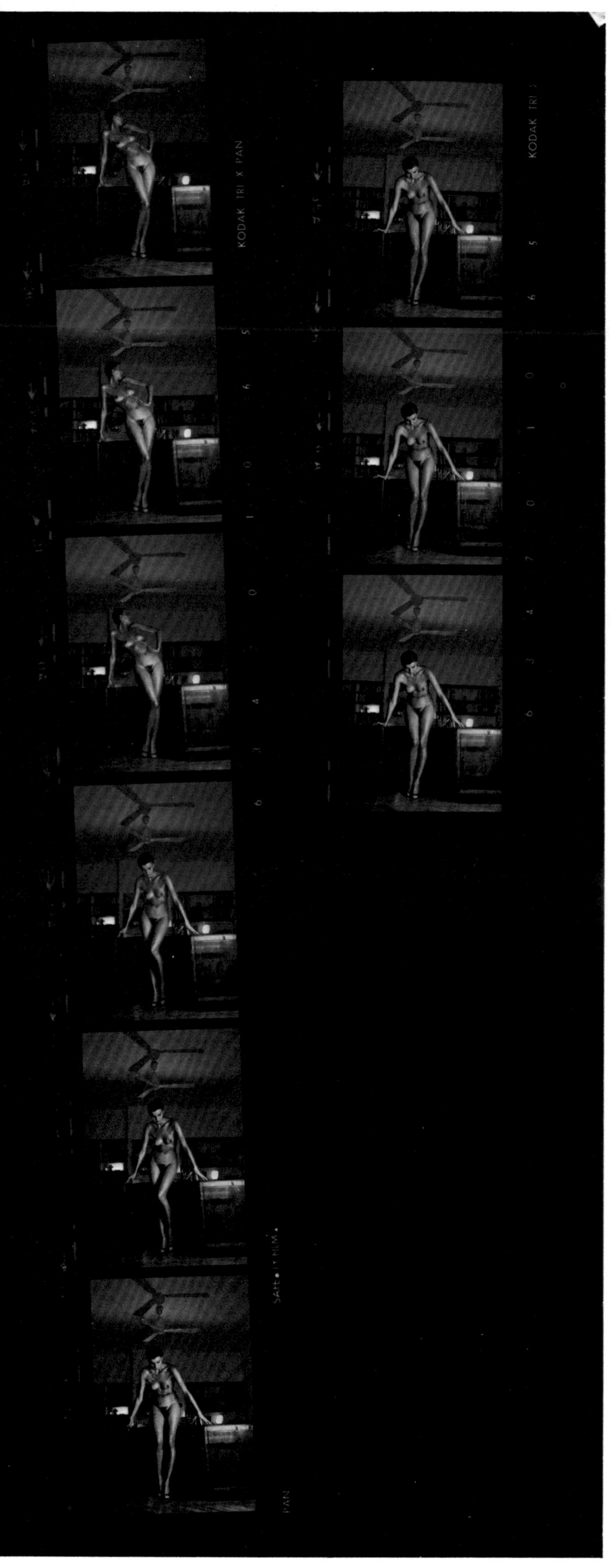

FIGURE 8

Figure 14 has only a small condenser spotlight, permanently installed to light up the staircase. Originally, I put in the light to show up the beauty of the staircase. When I saw what that spotlight did in my apartment, I bought another one to take with me on location. It's really sharp, like a projector. You'd never get that quality with a regular flood light.

The model's face, I think, changes from photograph to photograph, and is sometimes partially hidden by shadows. It's not that she is ever anonymous. Not at all. Some of the daylight pictures could almost be portraits of her. But my studio takes on an entirely different character at night. The difference in mood is striking, and the model's face becomes much more mysterious with the shadows.

The last set of pictures (Figures 8 and 15) involves a more difficult lighting situation. This is in the living room, with a flood light on the right, and then a light on the floor behind the desk. The flood light is stuck inside the transparent lamp shade. The woman stands in front of the desk, and the light falls from the right onto her body. The light is shielded so it doesn't reach the ceiling. I wanted the shadow of the ventilator and I got it from the light behind the desk, which shoots up to the ventilator.

I like the fan in this picture. It hangs in my living room permanently. The shape of the fan relates to the shape of the model's left arm, but I didn't think of that when I made the picture. I simply decided that I liked the look of the ventilator. There are things I <u>don't</u> like about the picture. I don't like the knee shadows; somehow they're not quite right.

I think of all the photographs the only one I find erotic is the diagonal nude (Figure 13). That I find erotic indeed; don't ask me why. The others are really very sporty. They're very cool. Not cold, but cool. I think the <u>ideal</u> nude is erotic. It doesn't always happen, but it's the ideal. Getting an erotic feeling and retaining a highly aesthetic figure is a big problem.

There are a lot of nudes in the history of photography that are successful for different reasons. Brassaï's women in the brothels are highly erotic. To me, they are incredible. Bill Brandt's nudes are beautiful, but I don't find them erotic. His photographs of clothed maids are much more erotic.

I am often asked about the role of erotic symbols, like whips and corsets, in my fashion and other work. I don't consider these elements of violence. Every erotic device I use goes back at least two centuries, back even further than that. I've got books of illustrations of paintings and drawings depicting women pretending to be horses, carrying men, and so on. This is a kind of pornography that has nothing to do with girlie magazines; it has to do with erotic symbolism.

I don't know if I was the first in fashion photography to introduce these elements. I would hate to try to answer that. Maybe it was the first time it was remarked upon. A lot of the pictures I did in the 1960s were rejected by fashion editors as unprintable.

But what makes fashion so significant, perhaps, as an art form, is that it reflects the times. And the times have changed. Look at the way young women walk around now. Women who I laughingly refer to as coming from good families wear see-through blouses and split skirts on the street. Many of today's fashions make women look like hookers from the 50s.

When the fashion I am photographing is really interesting (and this is rare), I can concentrate on the fashion itself. What often is the case is that it's not very interesting, and then I have to cover it with a lot of devices.

Many pictures of the nude go beyond the erotic and are pure beauty. I'm much more interested in a kind of abrasiveness which is at its most exciting in spontaneous circumstances. I saw a woman on the beach who was very exciting in the way she moved. She had no idea she was being observed. She was relaxed. It was totally erotic. With me there is a voyeuristic element involved. Of course, the trouble with a very controlled nude is that it is not voyeuristic anymore. The immediacy is lost.

It might be a good idea to say to a woman, "Go out in the backyard and sun yourself or do whatever you like. You won't even know where I am." You would lose control completely, but you might gain something else. It might be even more interesting to have a friend who suns herself every day and who leaves the key in the door for you. To do the backyard photography would be a little bit dirty. It's not classic; it's a little forbidden; there's a feeling of secrecy. The moment it becomes forbidden, it is the ideal, not only in the nude, but in any photograph of a woman.

I've always thought the most extraordinary photographs of the 70s were the nudes of Jackie Kennedy Onassis. To me, they were one of the greatest feats of photography. They had all the elements of forbiddenness, of voyeurism. They were terribly well done. I've heard a lot of stories about how the photographs were made but I don't know if any of them are correct.

I do a lot of my work at midday, even in the desert, because I adore hard light, whether I'm working on fashion, portraits or nudes. With the nude, hard light brings out those muscles. The back of a woman shows a tremendous amount of sculpting and modeling.

I love Vaseline on the eyelids when it is very sunny because of the shadows cast by the lashes when the eyes look down. With eyeshadow and Vaseline you get this marvelous, slightly old-fashioned glamour look. I think it is wonderful.

As a rule I use an orange filter the moment I get sunshine. In the old days, I used a lot of red filters. My filters are not very dark, about one stop. The orange filter helps the skin. It makes the skin look smoother and suppresses minor blemishes. I just have to be careful that the lips don't go too pale. You can compensate with lipstick, but with a red filter the lips go completely white. I don't think there is ever any point in putting a filter on when there is flat light.

Sometimes, even in broad daylight, it is easier to use a tripod when you want a very exact composition. The only thing is, the mistakes can be a great help. At times you get something in that you think you shouldn't have. At the moment you take the picture, you say, "Damn, I got that in. It would have been better had I been very exact in my framing." When you see the contacts again six months later, you may find your point of view has changed completely.

More often than not, when I've been in close on a subject, I'm sorry. I've never been sorry when I've been too far away. I can always crop, although it is only rarely that I do crop. This is because in the end I would prefer to have everything that was going on in the picture.

I shoot very slowly. It's a matter of upbringing. I apprenticed with a view camera, and you can't shoot very fast with a large format. It doesn't work.

I am a stickler about exposures. I am not capable of guessing them; I would probably be wrong, and so I have always worked with a meter. I would never trust myself without the meter because I am a very bad printer. I printed when I was young, mostly because I couldn't afford a lab, but now I supervise the lab to the last degree. It is a big sweat to get the prints I want.

The lab that printed the series for this book has been printing for me in Paris for the last 10 or 12 years. The lab men know exactly what I want. Or perhaps I should say they think they know, but as I change, the printing obviously must change, too. But they're not aware at what points I change. It's not possible. If I say the print is not quite what I want, they say, "I've always printed for you like that." I just have to say, "I know, but please try it a new way this time."

I don't think in terms of a different kind of print for a nude. To me, the quality is the same whether it is a nude or a fashion photograph. The only difference is that skin is more delicate than a black-and-white dress.

When I look at my photographs, I would say that generally my shootings are completely controlled. Again, I think it is my upbringing in fashion photography. The perfect picture is a controlled snapshot that does not look as if it is controlled or contrived. Otherwise, it becomes stiff and completely unacceptable. So, whatever you do, you must keep a spirit of freedom. If not, the purpose of the photograph is defeated.

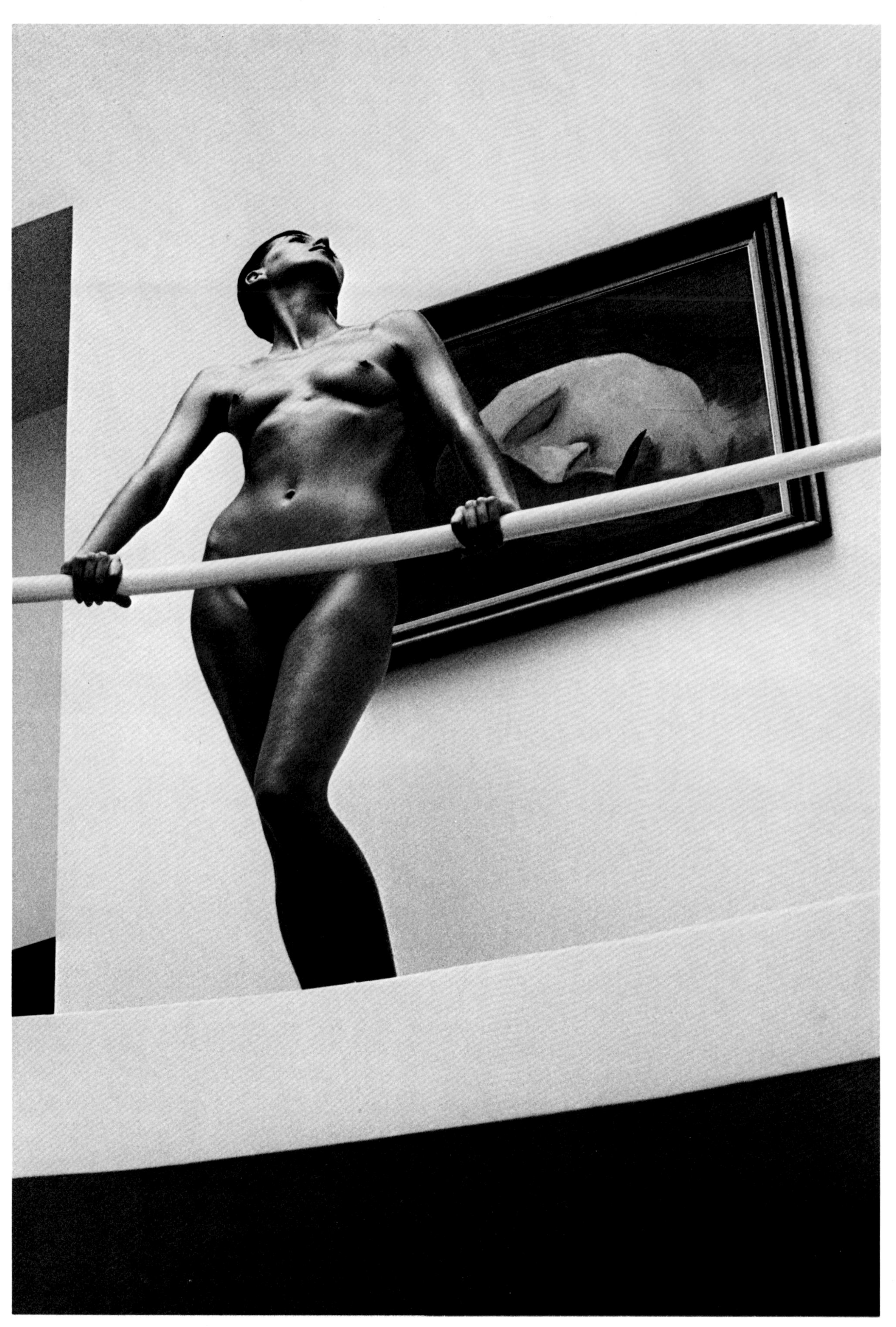

FIGURE 9: IN MY STUDIO, PARIS, 1978

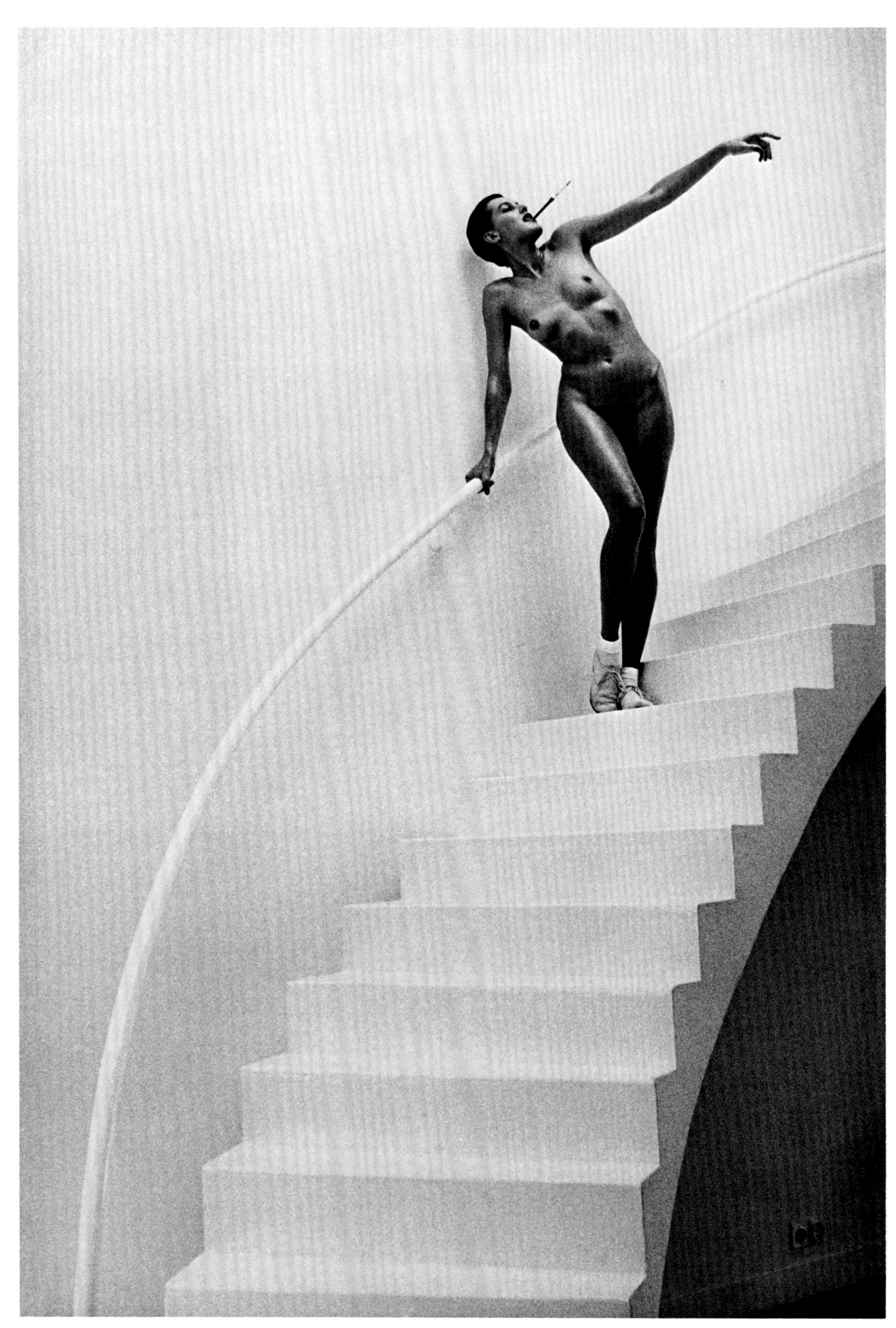

FIGURE 10: IN MY STUDIO, PARIS, 1978

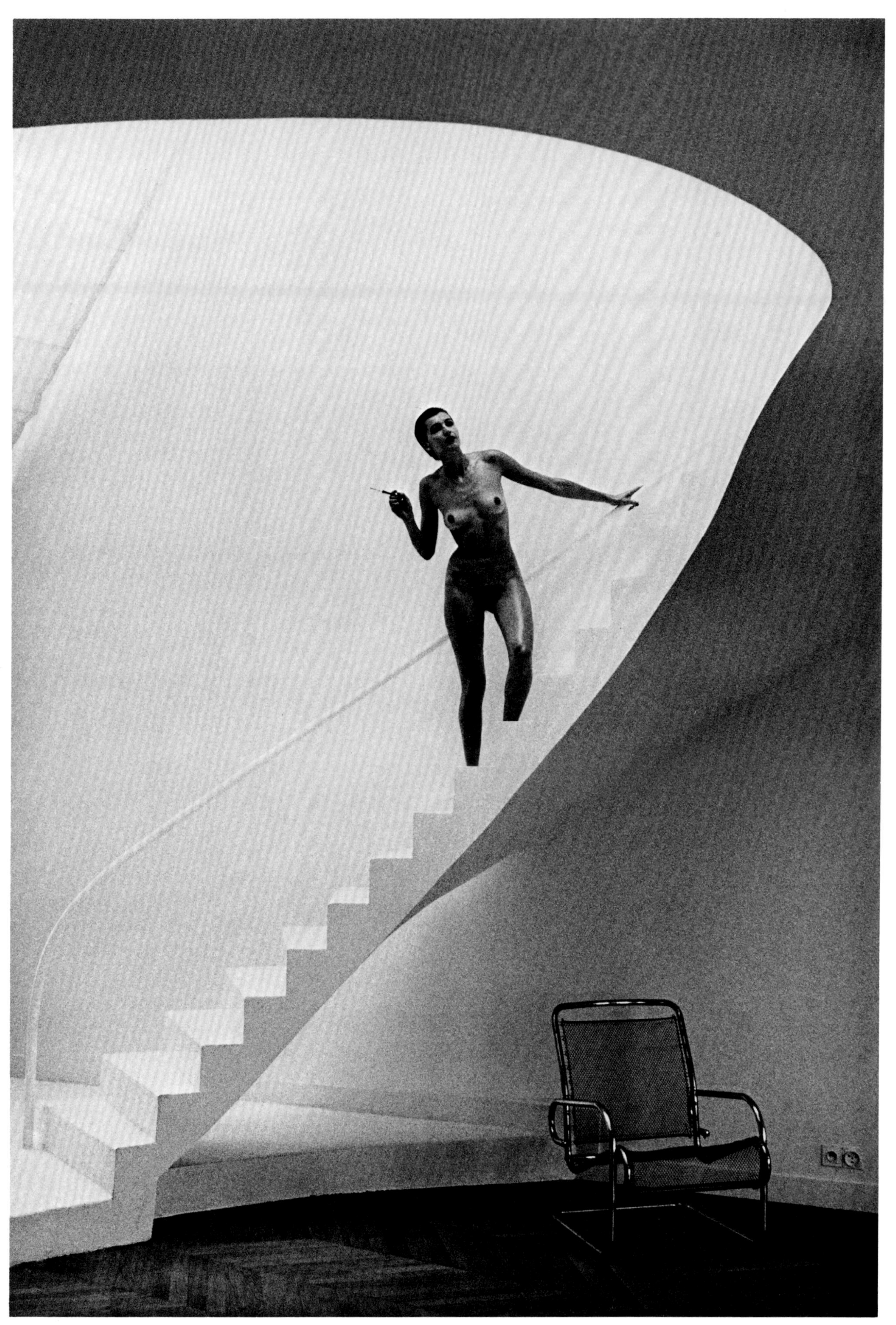

FIGURE 11: IN MY STUDIO, PARIS, 1978

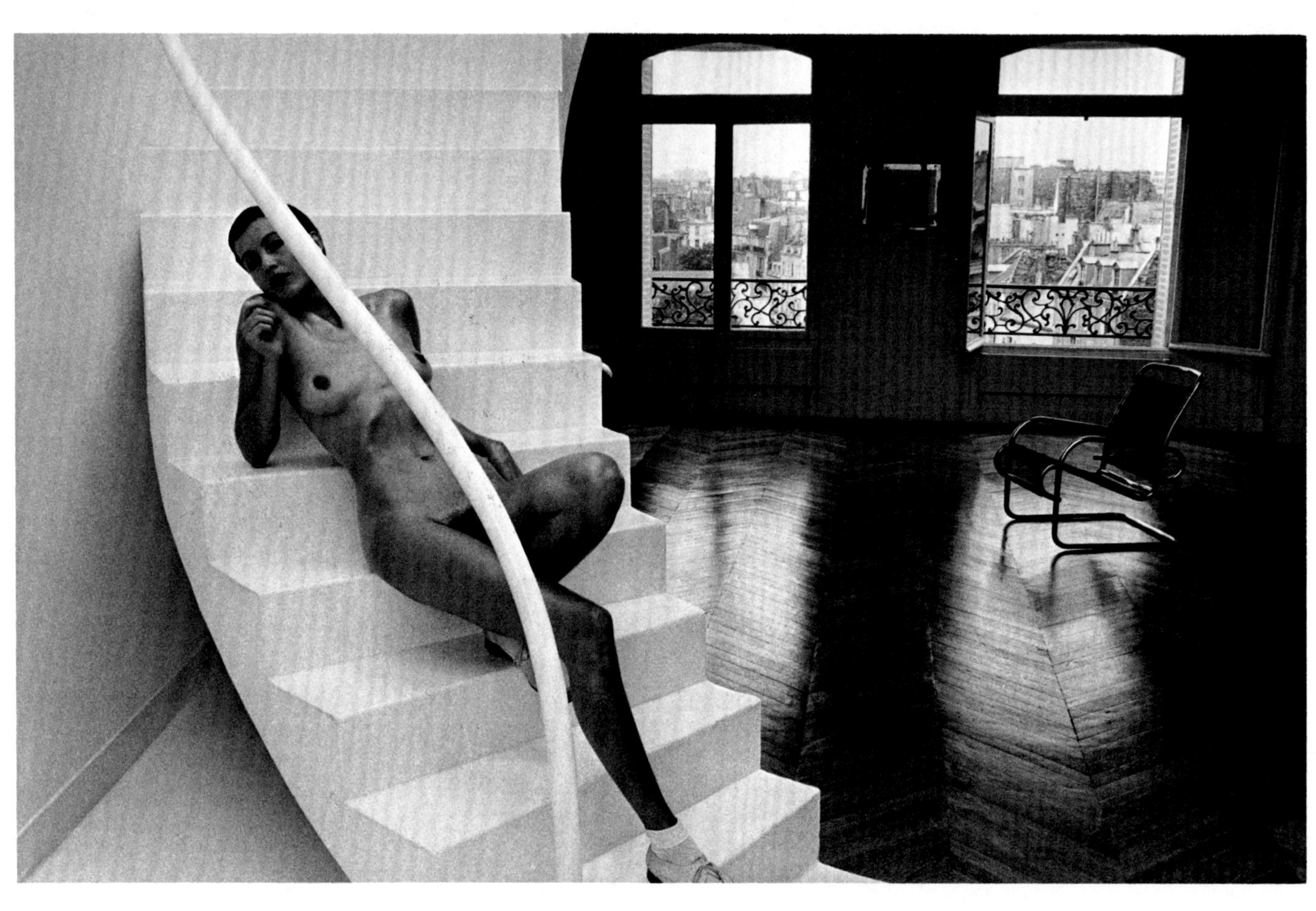

FIGURE 12: IN MY STUDIO, PARIS, 1978

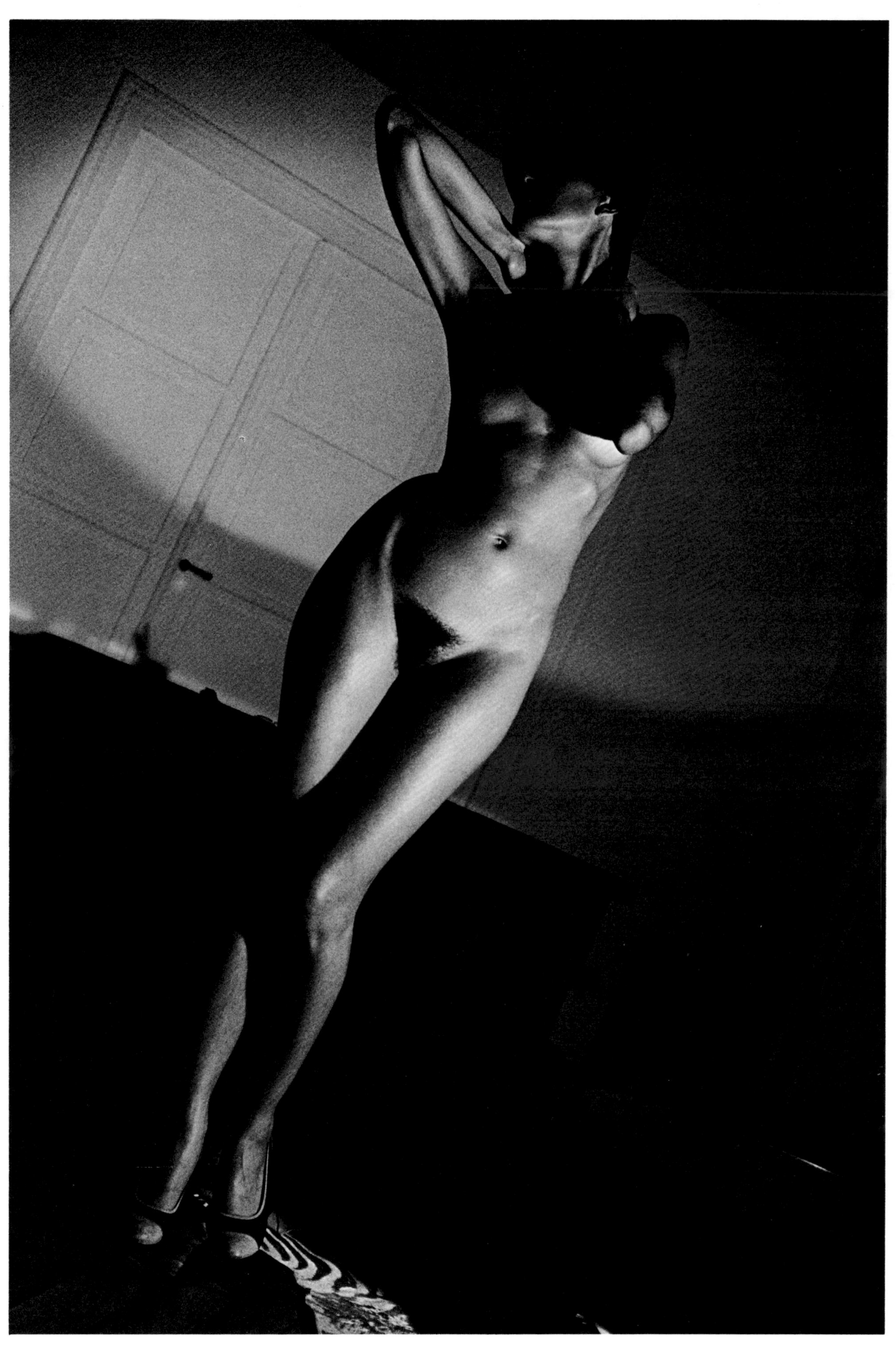

FIGURE 13: IN MY STUDIO, PARIS, 1978

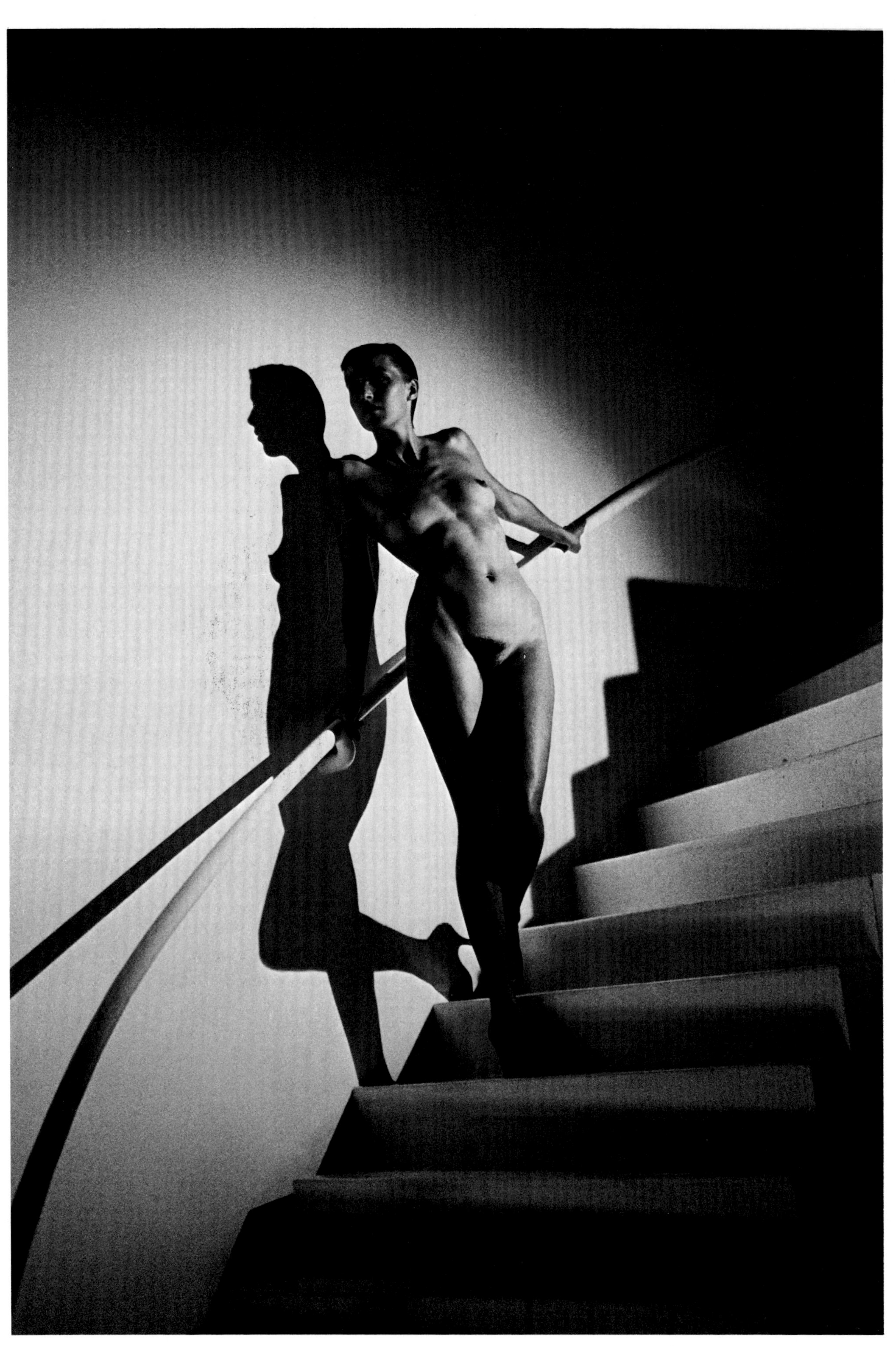

FIGURE 14: IN MY STUDIO, PARIS, 1978

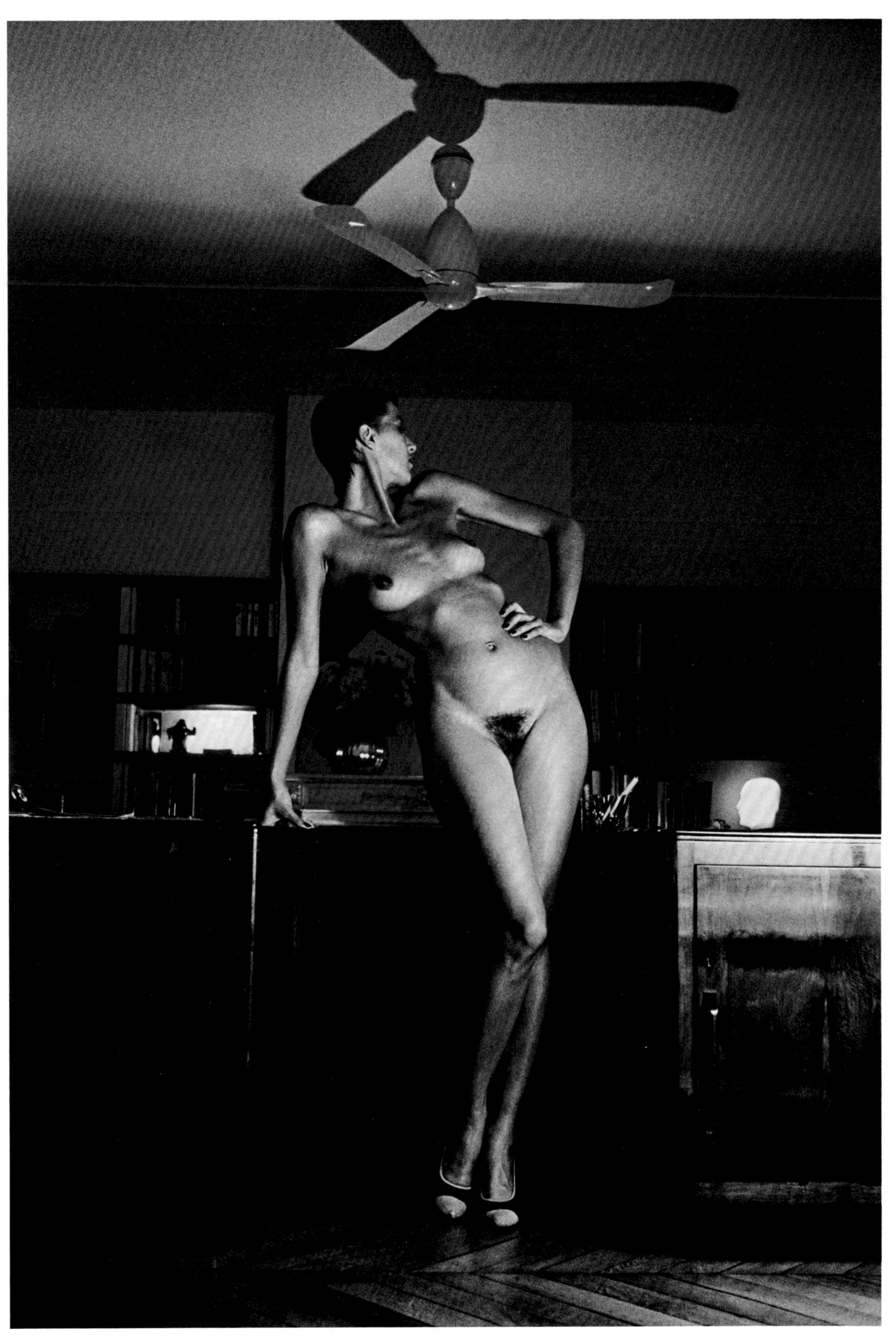

FIGURE 15: IN MY STUDIO, PARIS, 1978

BIOGRAPHIES

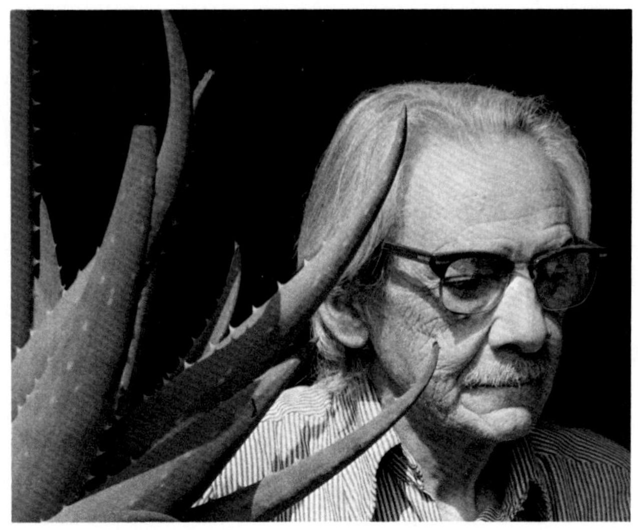

Manuel Alvarez Bravo was born in 1902 in Mexico City, Mexico. From 1908-1914 he attended Catholic Brothers' School; in 1915 he began studying accounting at night while he worked in an office during the daytime. Subsequently, he studied literature, painting and music. He bought his first camera in 1924. In 1927 he met the photographer Tina Modotti, who introduced him to Diego Rivera. In 1929-30 and 1932-33, Alvarez Bravo taught photography at the Academy of San Carlos; in 1930-31 he was a cameraman on Sergei Eisenstein's film QUE VIVA MÉXICO. In 1938 he was asked by André Breton to make a photograph for a major exhibition on surrealism appearing in Mexico City, and it was at this time that he made the famous LA BUENA FAMA DURMIENDO (GOOD REPUTATION SLEEPING). From 1943-59 he worked as a still photographer and cameraman in the Mexican film industry. In 1959 he left the film industry to become a co-founder of El Fondo Editorial de la Plástica Mexicana (Editorial Foundation of the Mexican Plastic Arts), the purpose of which is to produce books on the Mexican arts.

Recent one-man exhibitions include: Pasadena Art Museum, Pasadena, 1971; Instituto Nacional de Bellas Artes, Palacio de Bellas Artes, Mexico City, 1972; Witkin Gallery, New York, 1975; The Corcoran Gallery of Art, Washington, D.C., 1978 (major exhibition traveling to the Center for Inter-American Relations, New York; The Tucson Museum of Art, Tucson; and the Toledo Museum of Art, Toledo, Ohio). A catalogue titled M. ALVAREZ BRAVO, by Jane Livingston, was published in conjunction with this exhibition (David R. Godine, Boston, Mass. and The Corcoran Gallery of Art, 1978).

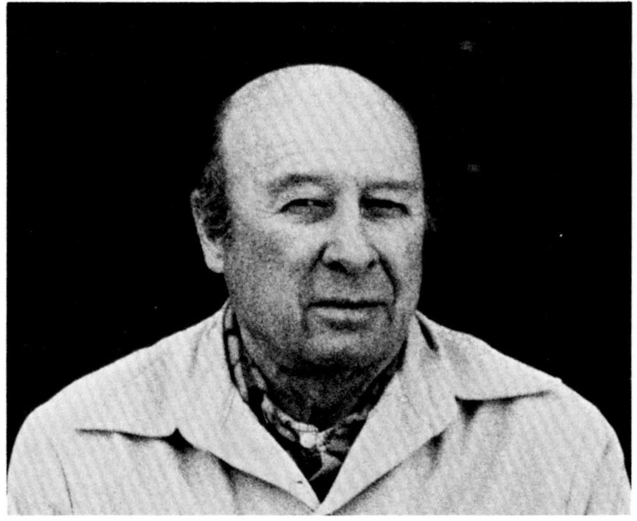

Harry Callahan was born in 1912 in Detroit, Michigan. In 1936 he married Eleanor Knapp. He became interested in photography at the age of 26 and joined the Detroit Camera Club in 1940. In 1946 he began teaching at The Institute of Design in Chicago (which later became part of The Illinois Institute of Technology); he was head of the department of photography at IIT from 1949-61. Callahan received the Graham Foundation Award for Advanced Studies in Fine Arts in 1956. He left IIT in 1961 to become head of the department of photography at The Rhode Island School of Design in Providence, R.I. He became a full professor in 1964. He received a Guggenheim Fellowship in 1971. In 1979 Callahan received an honorary doctorate in the fine arts from RISD and was elected a fellow of the American Academy of Arts and Sciences. He is now retired from teaching.

Callahan's recent major exhibitions include: The International Museum of Photography at The George Eastman House, Rochester, 1958 and 1971 (traveling exhibition); Hallmark Gallery, New York, 1964; The Witkin Gallery, New York, 1970; Light Gallery, New York, 1972, 1974, 1976-77 and 1978; The Museum of Modern Art, New York, 1976; and the 38th Venice Biennial, United States Pavilion, 1978.

Callahan's books include the following: HARRY CALLAHAN, introduction by Sherman Paul and preface by John Szarkowski (The Museum of Modern Art, New York, 1967); PHOTOGRAPHS: HARRY CALLAHAN, introduction by Hugo Weber, El Mochuelo Gallery Monograph No. 1 (Van Riper and Thompson, Santa Barbara, 1964); and CALLAHAN, edited and with an introduction by John Szarkowski (an Aperture Book in association with The Museum of Modern Art, 1976).

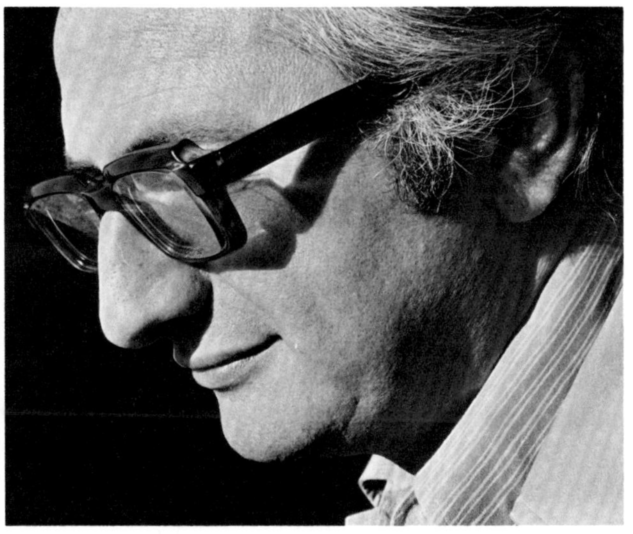

Lucien Clergue was born in 1934 in Arles, France. When he was 15 years old he began to study photography. In 1955 he made 1500 photographs of young acrobats in the ruins of Arles; in 1956 he began his work with the nude in the sea. Other series of work done during his career include photographs of the marshlands of Arles, bullfights, and dead animals. In 1957 Clergue's first book of the nudes in the sea was published: CORPS MÉMORABLES, with poetry by Paul Eluard (Seghers, Paris). He assisted in the filming of Jean Cocteau's LE TESTAMENT D'ORPHÉE in 1959. With J.M. Rouquette, he created the department of photography at the Musée Réattu in Arles in 1965. In the same year he started making films. His numerous films include: MANITAS DE PLATA (color, 52 minutes, 1968); PICASSO, DE GUERNICA AUX MOUSQUETAIRES (color, 55 minutes, 1969); LA FORÊT CALCINÉE (color, 4 minutes 30 seconds, 1970); etc. Clergue was named artistic director of the Arles Festival in 1972. He began working with the nude in the city in 1975.

His many exhibitions include: The Museum of Modern Art, New York, 1961; Moderna Museet, Stockholm, 1969; The Art Institute of Chicago, Chicago, 1970; The Witkin Gallery, New York, 1972 and 1979; The French Institute, New York, 1975; Il Diaframma, Milan, 1977; Shadaï Gallery, Tokyo, 1978, and so on.

His books include: POESIE DER PHOTOGRAPHIE (Du Mont Schauberg, Cologne, 1960); NAISSANCES D'APHRODITE (Forces Vives, Paris, 1963); TOROS MUERTOS (Forces Vives, Paris, 1963); NÉE DE LA VAGUE (Pierre Belfond, Paris, 1968); GENÈSE (Pierre Belfond, Paris, 1973); LUCIEN CLERGUE (Perceval, Paris, 1974); LA CAMARGUE EST AU BOUT DES CHEMINS (AGEP, Marseille, 1978), etc.

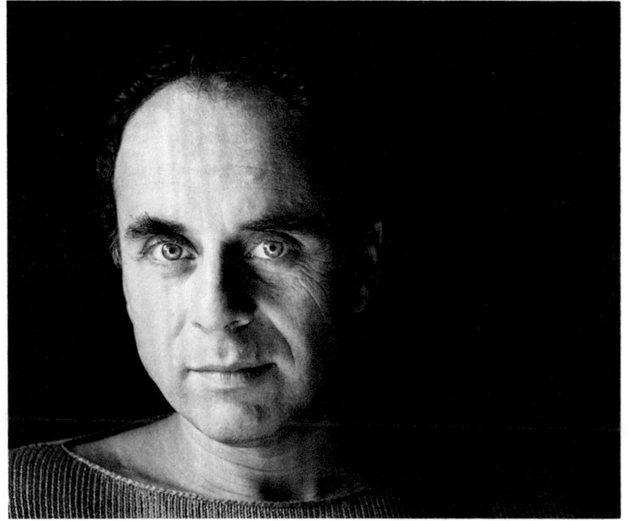

Ralph Gibson was born in 1939 in Los Angeles, California, and studed at The San Francisco Art Institute. He became an assistant to Dorothea Lange in 1962. In 1966 he moved to New York City, and, three years later, founded Lustrum Press. In 1973 and 1976 Gibson received grants from the National Endowment for the Arts. In 1978 he was awarded a CAPS grant.

Books by the photographer include: THE SOMNAMBULIST (Lustrum Press, New York, 1970); DEJA-VU (Lustrum Press, 1973); and DAYS AT SEA (Lustrum Press, 1975).

One-man exhibitions in 1976: Leo Castelli Gallery, New York; University of Guelph, Canada; Baltimore Museum of Art, Baltimore; Swedish Museum of Photography, Stockholm; Focus Gallery, San Francisco; Light Impressions, Rochester; Galerie Fiolet, Amsterdam; Texas Center for Photographic Studies, Dallas; The Columbia Gallery, Chicago; Photogenesis, Columbus; in 1977, Agathe Gaillard, Paris; Fotografiska Museet, Stockholm; CEPA Gallery, Buffalo; Silver Image, Seattle; Museum of Modern Art, Oxford, England; Side Gallery, Newcastle; Photographers' Gallery, Melbourne; in 1978, Galerie Fiolet, Amsterdam; Castelli Uptown, New York; Camera Obscura, Stockholm; Center for Creative Photography, Tucson; Robert Self Gallery, London.

Gibson is represented in 25 public collections, including: National Gallery of Canada, Ottawa; Bibliothèque Nationale, Paris; The Museum of Modern Art, New York; Pasadena Museum of Art, Pasadena; International Museum of Photography at The George Eastman House, Rochester; University of New Mexico, Albuquerque; Seattle Art Museum, Seattle; Fogg Art Museum, Cambridge; Metropolitan Museum of Art, New York; and Center for Creative Photography, University of Arizona, Tucson.

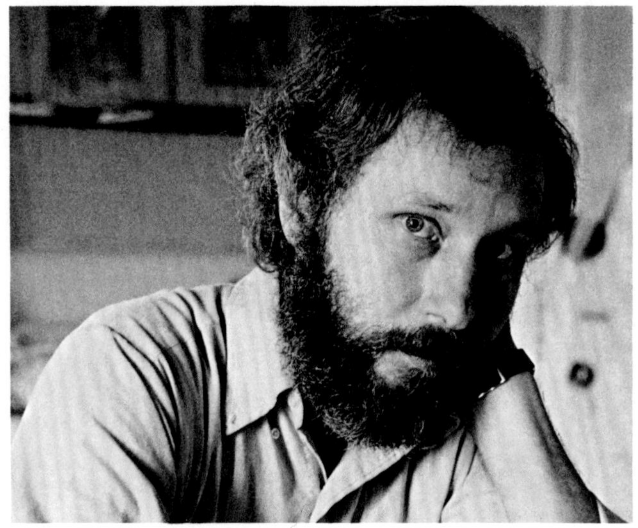

Kenneth Josephson was born in 1932 in Detroit, Michigan. He received his B.F.A. in 1957 from the Rochester Institute of Technology, and his M.S. in 1960 from the Institute of Design of the Illinois Institute of Technology. From 1957-58 he was a photographer for the Chrysler Corporation. In 1961 he began teaching at the School of The Art Institute of Chicago, where he now is a professor. He also served one-year terms as an exchange teacher at Konstfackskolan, Stockholm in 1966-67, and as an associate professor at the University of Hawaii in 1967-68. In 1972 he received the Guggenheim Fellowship; in 1975 and 1978 he received a National Endowment for the Arts award.

His work has been exhibited frequently, and his one-man exhibitions include the following: Art Institute of Chicago, Chicago, 1971; Nova Scotia College of Design, Halifax, Nova Scotia, 1973; 291 Gallery, Milan, Italy, 1974; Galerie Die Brücke, Vienna, Austria, 1976; University of Iowa Museum of Art, Iowa City, 1976; Purdue University, Lafayette, Ind., 1977; University of Southern Illinois, Carbondale, 1978; Fotoforum, Kassel, West Germany, 1978.

Josephson self-published THE BREAD BOOK in Chicago in 1973. In 1975 he made a 10-print limited edition portfolio of original prints titled KENNETH JOSEPHSON for the Center for Photographic Studies, Louisville, Ky., with an introduction by Alex Sweetman.

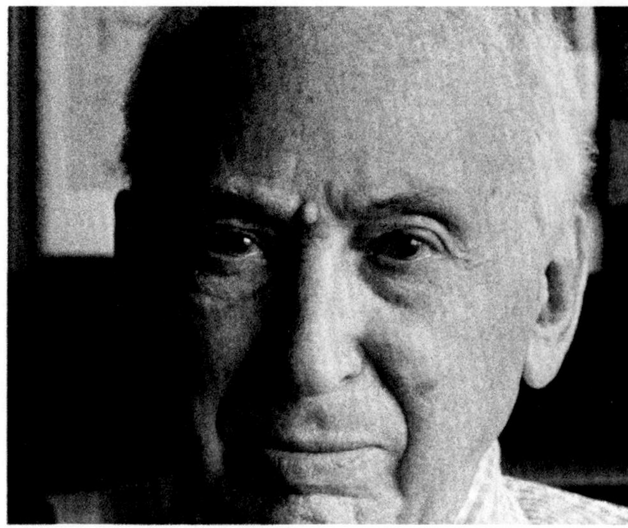

André Kertész was born in Budapest, Hungary, in 1894. After graduating from the Academy of Commerce in Budapest in 1912, he became a clerk in the Budapest Stock Exchange. He also bought his first camera. From 1914-18 he served in the Austro-Hungarian army. He moved to Paris in 1925, and for several years photographed for the leading publications of the era, including THE LONDON TIMES, BERLINER ILLUSTRIERTE, JOURNAL VU, ART ET MÈDECINE, etc. In 1936 Kertész accepted a one-year contract with Keystone News Agency in New York, and he and his wife, Elizabeth, moved to the United States for what they conceived of as a one-year sabbatical. However, they remained in New York after Kertész terminated his contract with Keystone in 1937, and, for the next 12 years the photographer free-lanced for HARPER'S BAZAAR, VOGUE, TOWN AND COUNTRY, LOOK, CORONET, etc. In 1949 Kertész signed an exclusive contract with Condé Nast Publications; he terminated this contract in 1962.

Kertész' work has appeared in numerous one-man exhibitions in museums and galleries, including the following: The Art Institute of Chicago, Chicago, 1946; the IV Mostra Biennale Internazionale della Fotografia, Venice, 1963; Bibliothèque Nationale, Paris, 1963; The Museum of Modern Art, 1964-65; Hallmark Gallery, New York, 1973; Musée National d'Art Moderne du Centre Georges-Pompidou, 1977-78.

Kertész' recent books include: ON READING, Grossman, New York, 1971; ANDRÉ KERTÉSZ: SIXTY YEARS OF PHOTOGRAPHY, 1912-1972, Grossman, New York, 1972; J'AIME PARIS: PHOTOGRAPHS SINCE THE TWENTIES, Grossman, New York, 1974; WASHINGTON SQUARE, Grossman, New York, 1975; DISTORTIONS, Alfred A. Knopf, New York, 1976.

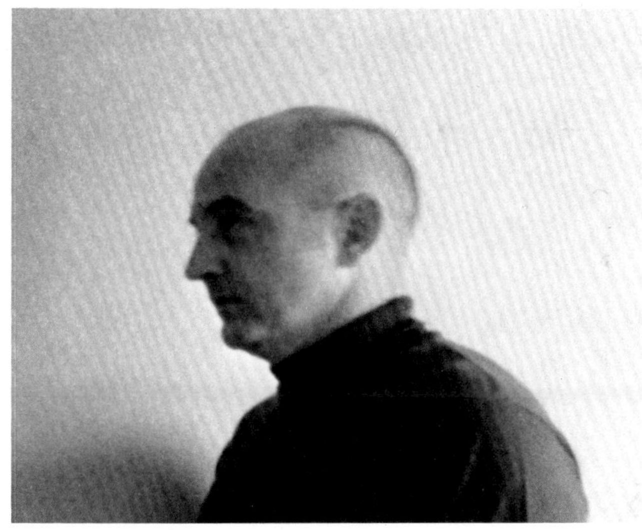

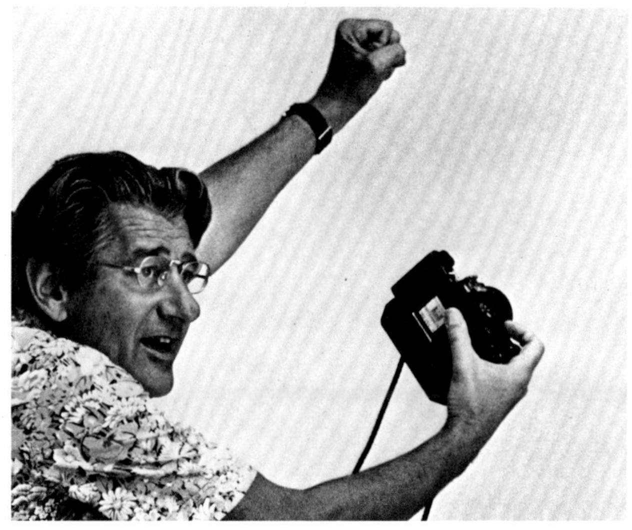

Duane Michals was born in McKeesport, Pennsylvania, in 1932. He attended the University of Denver in Denver, Colorado. In 1956 he came to New York and enrolled in the Parsons School of Design. A year later he became an assistant art director with DANCE Magazine and then began work for Time-Life as a graphic designer. He began his photography as a tourist in Russia in 1958. Since then he has pursued both commercial and personal work. His professional work has appeared in such publications as VOGUE, ESQUIRE, HARPER'S BAZAAR, and THE NEW YORK TIMES.

His personal photographs have appeared in numerous one-man shows, including: The Museum of Modern Art, New York, 1970; Delpire Gallery, Paris, 1972; Frankfurter Kunstverein, Frankfurt, 1974; Köln Kunstverein, Köln, 1975; Handschein Gallery, Basel, 1976; Sidney Janis Gallery, New York, 1976 and 1978; Camera Obscura, Stockholm, 1978; and Nouvelle Image, The Hague, 1979.

His work is represented in many private and museum collections, including: Bibliothèque Nationale, Paris; Folkwang, Essen; Stedelijk Museum, Amsterdam; and The Boston Museum of Fine Arts, Boston.

Michals has published seven books: SEQUENCES (Doubleday, New York, 1970); THE JOURNEY OF THE SPIRIT AFTER DEATH (Winterhouse, New York, 1971); THE PHOTOGRAPHIC ILLUSION (Alskog, Los Angeles, 1975) with text by Ron Bailey; TAKE ONE AND SEE MT. FUJIYAMA (Stefan Mihal, New York, 1976); REAL DREAMS (Addison House, Danbury, N.H., 1976); HOMAGE TO CAVAFY (Addison House, Danbury, N.H., 1978); and WONDERS OF EGYPT (Éditions Denoël-Filipacchi E.P.I., Paris). An eighth book, NOW AND THEN, will be published in 1979 by Éditions du Chêne, Paris.

Helmut Newton was born in 1920 in Berlin and was reared in Germany, although he is Australian by nationality. He now lives in Paris with his wife, the photographer Alice Springs. In the 1930s he was an assistant to the Berlin photographer Yva, whose specialties were fashion, the nude and portraits of dancers. In the 1960s and 70s Newton photographed for QUEEN, NOVA, VOGUE (French, Italian, English and American), JARDIN DES MODES, ELLE, STERN, PLAYBOY and MARIE CLAIRE. Today his fashion work appears frequently in French and American VOGUE. Newton is the subject of a one-hour documentary by Michael Whyte (Thames, England, 1979).

Newton's recent one-man exhibitions include the following: Nikon Gallery, Paris, 1975; Canon Gallery, Amsterdam, 1975; The Photographers' Gallery, London, 1976; Nicholas Wilder Gallery, Los Angeles, 1976; Marlborough Gallery, New York, 1978; and Canon Gallery, Geneva, 1979. He participated in the exhibition "History of Fashion Photography," which traveled to various locations in 1975 and 1976, including the Kornblee Gallery in New York, The Baltimore Museum of Art, The Museum of Contemporary Art in Chicago and The International Museum of Photography at The George Eastman House in Rochester.

Two books of Newton's photographs are available: WHITE WOMEN (Stonehill Publishing, New York, 1976) and SLEEPLESS NIGHTS (Congreve, New York, 1978).